THE
MISTRESSES

Domestic Scandals

of Nineteenth-Century Monarchs

BETTY KELEN

**BARNES
&NOBLE
BOOKS**
NEW YORK

This edition published by Barnes & Noble, Inc.,
by arrangement with Merceret Associates, Inc.
1993 Barnes & Noble Books

ISBN 1-56619-111-4

The author is grateful for permission to quote from the following:
Alexander, Grand Duke of Russia, *Once a Grand Duke* (Holt, Rinehart &
Winston, Inc. All rights reserved. Reprinted by permission).

Princess Marthe Bibesco, *Royal Portraits* (D. Appleton & Co., Copyright
1928, Copyright renewed 1958).

Egon Caesar Conte Corti, *Elizabeth, Die Seltsame Frau.*

Caroline Delacroix, Baroness de Vaughan, as told to Paul Faure, *A Commoner Married a King* (Ives, Washburn, Inc.).

Frances A. Gerard, *A King's Romance* (Dodd, Mead & Co.).

Briefe Kaiser Franz Josephs An Frau Katherina Schratt (Herold Verlag;
translation by Evabeth Miller Kienast and Robert Rie to be published in
1966 by the State University of New York).

Marie Louise, Countess Larisch von Wallersee-Wittelsbach, with Paul
Maerker Branden, *Her Majesty Elizabeth* (Copyright 1934 by Doubleday
& Co. Reprinted by permission of the publisher).

Frédéric Loliée, *Women of the Second Empire*, Alice M. Ivimy, trans.
(The Bodley Head Ltd.).

Simone André Maurois, *Miss Howard and the Emperor* (Alfred A. Knopf,
Inc.).

Count Chedomille Mijatovich, *A Royal Tragedy* (Dodd, Mead & Co.);
Memoirs of a Balkan Diplomatist (Cassell and Co., Ltd.).

Oxford Slavonic Papers, Vol. XI (Clarendon Press. By permission of the
editor).

Maurice Paléologue, *The Enigmatic Tsar* (Librairie Plon and Harper &
Row, Publishers, Inc.).

Count de Soissons, *The True Story of the Empress Eugénie* (The Bodley
Head Ltd.).

Leonid I. Strakhovsky, *Alexander I of Russia* (Copyright 1947 by W. W.
Norton & Co.).

Printed and bound in the United States of America

M 9 8 7 6 5 4 3 2 1

TO MY HUSBAND

Emery Kelen

Contents

Introduction

ROYAL MORALS
& ROYAL COMFORT

One may look at history any way one pleases. A general might see it as a series of battles, a lawyer as a list of bills. School children tend to regard it—understandably—as a heap of old bones, but one day a Durant or a Churchill might reveal to them its human shape.

Another way of looking at history is for the sheer wonder of it, as if it were an immense tattooed lady at a fair, inscribed from head to foot with remarkable patterns, some of them bold, others inscrutably intricate; but no inscription, however slight, is irrelevant to the whole, and all are guarded by immutable morphological laws.

The nineteenth-century kings form a bold design upon the skin of history. They were significant and they knew it. No one who becomes an army colonel while he is still in his nursery can ever feel like a plain man again. Their photographs show them looking perpetually proud, noble, high-minded, exalted above the earth. The very uniformity of their expressions betrays the fact that their minds had been bent to be smug, just as their backs were strapped to be straight. Quite often subdued miseries gnawed at their souls. It was their fate to cope with problems in which they had no natural interest, to marry for dynastic reasons women they could not love, and to be imposed upon from birth to death by tradition, etiquette, and protocol.

The correspondence and memoirs, particularly of female royalties, are full of complaints about the ghastly discomforts of their palaces and old castles which were unheatable in winter and unventilatable in summer, and where the great distances to the kitchens made it fairly impossible for them ever to get hot meals or to get anything at all when it was wanted. The chimneys smoked, the lighting arrangements were faulty, there were no bathrooms or running water, the corridors smelled; mice ran everywhere, and so did noxious insects and headless ghosts. No royal person could move from one apartment to another without setting off a clangorous chain reaction of soldiers presenting arms. Very young royalties, naturally, did not object to this phenomenon; they used to run up and down the grand staircases, keeping the guards in perpetual motion, very much as today's children play with the electric-eye doors of supermarkets. Crown Princess Stephanie of Austria found that she could effectively punish her small daughter, Erzsi, by prohibiting the presentation of arms as the child went by.

Many royalties suffered agonies from lack of privacy. The Infanta Eulalia of Spain wrote that she was never alone for a single instant day or night until she married, and only then, one supposes, because her husband did not care for her much. Ladies- and gentlemen-in-waiting, as well as aides-de-camp, equerries, and bodyguards followed their personages about with fanatical diligence, the more so because a nimble royalty might easily dodge away from them if he saw the chance. What is more, they really *waited*. They waited and stared while a king played tennis or croquet, storing away every inane word or action of his to write in their diaries; they waited, shuffling and scraping, in his anteroom while he tried to write a letter or read a book; they waited in the drawing-room of his mistress while he made love. Perhaps the worst thing about these leeches was that their combined opinion often had a certain obstructive effect, especially upon younger personages. When Edward VII of England was only Bertie, Prince of Wales, it was the veto of his gentlemen that prevented him from first entering the United States the way he wanted to: pushed in a wheelbarrow across Niagara Falls from Canada by the acrobat Blondin on a tight-rope.

Every small thing about royal persons seems intimately involved with history's main design. Their tutors, for example. It is dumbfounding to learn that Albert of Saxe-Coburg-Gotha, Queen Victoria's husband, whose lofty character and high moral sensibilities impressed his wife so deeply, and through her, society around the world, was tutored in adolescence by a gentleman who carried on a deliberately obscene correspondence with Lord Byron and had no patience whatsoever with the fastidious notions of his pupil. It leaves one wondering if Victorianism, at its very roots, was not the retort of a defiant young prince against this single individual.

Tsar Alexander II of Russia had for a tutor a soft-hearted, sentimental Turk—he translated Gray's "Elegy" into Russian —who used to set aside part of his salary regularly to buy the freedom of serfs, and who prompted his royal charge to devote a portion of his allowance to the same purpose. When Alexander became tsar, he lost no time in freeing every serf in Russia by imperial ukase.

History shines forth from the very uniforms the royalties wore. Every king or royal prince owned hundreds, not only the uniforms of the various ranks in every one of his home regiments, but those of every country with which he maintained diplomatic relations. Look at a picture of any monarch who habitually evaded dressing up in uniform—such as Leopold II, King of the Belgians, and Ludwig I of Bavaria—and you will be looking at a severe eccentric. Edward VII of England hated uniforms, but he wore them anyway when he had an axe to grind. His picture in naval uniform tacitly informs the world that he was in favor of pouring out millions of pounds for the rebuilding of the British fleet. A photograph of his nephew, Kaiser Wilhelm II, heroically posed in a white admiral's uniform at the prow of a battleship, reveals his determination to build a fleet of his own, including U-boats with which to sink the fleet of his Uncle Edward.

We need not trouble ourselves further about royal tutors and uniforms when we have royal mistresses, of whom, it must be admitted, this book contains a miserly selection compared to the numbers available. Our heroines have been selected more for interesting behavior than for any instruction they offer in the matter of historical patterns. Yet royal mistresses, like any-

one else, must hew close to the anatomy of their times. We see
our earliest mistress, Julie de Krüdener, walking openly by the
side of her tsar, his acknowledged favorite and courted as such
by her society, just as in the previous century Pompadour and
Du Barry had been courted. But Julie differed from the mistresses of the past in that she desired of the tsar neither
jewels nor monopolies; she was after his soul. A religious mystic,
she is symbolic of the remarkable change that came over the
post-Napoleonic world and which is expressed by a modern
student of Julie, Edward Ney: "In its various manifestations, the
rediscovery of faith was one of the most striking aspects of this
age; and thus, what might at first sight seem to be an essentially
individual problem in the life of Madame de Krüdener, turns out
to be a type-study of a wide-spread phenomenon."

The rediscovery of faith was indeed characteristic of the
first three decades of the century. It inspired some, tamed
others. For some it meant a higher regard for moral principle, for others merely a finer regard for proprieties. By mid-
century, creeping primness had pervaded middle-class life
throughout almost the whole Continent, and when Lola Montez
foolishly tried to set up an old-fashioned mistress-monarchy in
Bavaria, she was brought low by this fact alone.

Responsibility for introducing primness into royal and upper-
class circles is traditionally laid at the door of Victoria and
her Prince Consort, and this exemplary couple is certainly not
guiltless. But they were not the first respectable royalties to
reign in England. George III, a half century before, had been
a respectable man who upheld piety while denouncing immorality and profanity. When he fell in love with a Quaker
girl named Hannah Lightfoot and spirited her away from her
family to be his mistress, he did not flaunt her in the face of
the world. No one ever laid eyes on her again. Some people
believed that he kept her in a cottage around which he had
build a very high garden wall.

But even though George III had exhorted his military men to
help him set standards of public decency in England, his
notions did not find wide support in his lifetime. It was only
after the "rediscovery of faith" had made considerable headway
among great masses of people that Prince Albert could throw
his weight to the side of respectability. Even so, in the forties,

while the Byronic ideal of manhood—which loved Beauty and adored Sin—still held the upper classes in thrall, he ran the risk of being thought a great fool. Fortunately for Victorianism, the 1848 revolutions vindicated his point of view.

This period of upheaval, of unrest in England, of riots, uprisings, and outright revolts on the Continent, was the last shudder of the French Revolution, and it brought about social changes as marked as any we have seen in our own century after both World Wars. Thrones trembled and toppled as the newly industrialized middle classes rose up against archaic despotisms and incompetent kings, demanding their civil rights and a just share in the control of their destinies.

Some monarchs responded to these pressures by giving them their rights, others by removing those they had. But no matter what the kings did, no sovereign after 1848 could afford to ignore the God-fearing bourgeois frame of mind or openly flout bourgeois prejudices and predilections. While the universal belief that kings were divinely ordained still held sway and covered a multitude of royal sins, a monarch who wished to be loved, honored, and left in peace by his newly critical people nevertheless had to exhibit—in public at least—some familiarity with the Ten Commandments. The day he could walk abroad with his queen at his side and a flamboyant mistress not far behind was gone forever.

Tsar Alexander II held limitless power in Russia; yet he was obliged to build a figurative high garden wall around his beloved Princess Dolgoruky. Leopold II, King the Belgians, allowed no one to preach to him; yet when he walked in the park with the lady he called Très Belle and he stopped to chat with a cabinet minister, Très Belle was expected to step back and try to look like the sister of one of his younger aides-de-camp.

Of course there are always people who do not learn. Napoleon III was like a man who continues to dance when the band has stopped playing and the guests have gone home. Although he was politically one of the enlightened and prophetic figures of the century, when he fell in 1870, enlightened people everywhere rejoiced—*because of his terrible morals*.

We shall see also the unhappy fate of certain backwater kings in the Balkans who so misinterpreted the message of their times that they tried to transform their mistresses into queens.

The next inexorable step in the correction of royal morals was taken when the middle class, having instructed their sovereign, by means of the new free press, how they wanted him to behave, required him then to turn around and set an example for them. Some perverse Spirit of the Age had promulgated the doctrine that a sovereign had to be "the first gentleman of his country." Since, before 1848, a monarch had not been expected to do anything really well except make love, this development was in itself revolutionary. As the century progressed, handsomely bound publications appeared in great numbers, answering a huge demand of the upcoming masses for detailed knowledge of the private habits of their royalties so that they could guide themselves thereby. These were written mostly by courtiers and court ladies, and all hammer home one theme: that the male royalty under scrutiny possessed every possible masculine quality, that he could shoot, ride, waltz and play croquet better than any other royalty in Europe; that he was dazzling to the sight and had such magnetic personal appeal that beautiful women of poor self-control were apt to swoon or burble at the mere sight of him; but for all that, his private life was absolutely dignified, modest, and spotless. It was, in a word, bourgeois.

Yes, the bourgeoisie were making over their rulers in their own image, to the occasional intense annoyance of some royalties. Once, when a bishop congratulated Edward VII for having left a German theater in protest against the salacious matter being presented on the stage, the king, who had left because he was bored, stiffly replied that he had "no wish to pose as a protector of morals, especially abroad." This small rebellion does not obviate the fact that Edward was "the first gentleman" of his land, or that his people had taught him to be so in his youth by their loud outcries whenever he made a public disgrace of himself.

One further logical development occurred before the century closed, and this is best seen in the love affair of Francis Joseph of Austria and Katherina Schratt. These lovers managed to enjoy a life which, so far as the naked eye could discern, was platonic, a model of rectitude. But beneath the surface it was a model of comfort.

For the mid-century revolutions had wrought changes in two directions. Just as the bourgeois were demanding their rightful share of ruling, the rulers were demanding their rightful share of bourgeois comfort. It had been fitting and proper for royalties to live in execrable palaces in times when almost everybody else lived in execrable slums. But as the growing industries made *nouveaux riches* of industrialists, bankers, and bourgeoisie, they were moving into homes full of antimacassars, easy chairs, roaring fires, and bathrooms. Many royalties now began to regard their magnificence with distaste. When Francis Joseph built the Villa Hermes and decorated its interior—so far as one can judge by examining photographs of the rooms—by exploding liquid gold in every direction, his daughter, Archduchess Valerie, condemned it with the voice of the new age. She said that the Villa Hermes was "not *gemütlich*," by which she meant that it was not cozy or friendly.

The desire for greater coziness and friendliness in royal circles was having serious consequences. It was inducing many irresponsible young princes and royal dukes to abdicate their duties and prerogatives to settle down as bourgeois gentlemen, preferably in Paris. Some princes secretly married actresses or governesses and installed them in small obscure homes. One Austrian archduke managed a happy half measure by retiring to a Mediterranean island where he married his mistress to his valet, and by this means raised a family with proper birth certificates. Princesses also were causing anxiety by eloping with their doctors or tutors or with obscure army officers, and as the century closed, with socialists.

Such defections were of course not possible for sovereigns or princes standing in close succession to the throne. Few, to do them justice, would have seriously wished to defect, for their destiny was a sacred one, directed by a Power beyond their comprehension. Crown Prince Rudolf of Austria took the most honorable means of avoiding it—suicide. Others, like King Ferdinand of Bulgaria and Crown Prince Frederick Wilhelm of Germany, found relief in habitual maltreatment of their wives. Appalling numbers of queens and princesses, condemned by propriety to appear serene, pleased, and charmed, walked through this age bruised and heartbroken. Their fate may be compared sadly with that of the merry queens earlier in the century, who were often heartbroken but otherwise in fine fettle.

By far the best means of avoiding the rigors of an exalted destiny was adopted by the majority of respectable sovereigns: they began to build at a great rate pleasant country homes, "cottages," shooting boxes, hunting lodges, and villas on the Riviera, none of which were much larger than small *châteaux*. There they retired with their regular or irregular families to putter with their hobbies and put their feet up before fireplaces that did not smoke, while commanding all but the most necessary valets, footmen, aides, equerries, secretaries, and gentlemen to remain absent.

It was this yearning for the simple pleasures of simple people that led many royalties to appreciate the joys of traveling incognito. Ideally, personages incognito meant to go unrecognized, and no doubt some modest Scandinavian royalties succeeded in doing so. But some major royalties who loved to travel, such as Edward VII or Empress Elizabeth of Austria-Hungary, never got the hang of it. Elizabeth always traveled incognito with herds of horses, goats, and cows. Edward once sailed his yacht to Naples incognito, accompanied by eight battleships, four cruisers, four destroyers, and a dispatch vessel. For these people, the point of being incognito was not that they were unrecognized, but that they did not have to admit that they had been recognized. They could walk icily past bowing sycophants with top hats, turn their backs on social climbers, refuse to take tea with other royalties in the vicinity, avoid setting foot on red carpets that were thrust beneath their feet, put up at hotels, go on wild shopping sprees, ride ferriswheels, sleep through theatrical performances, attend gambling casinos, make assignations; in short, they could behave as they imagined private citizens did every day of their lives.

And so, toward the end of the nineteenth century and throughout *la belle époque* that glowed briefly at the beginning of the twentieth, we find many significant royalties living double lives. In Life Number One they were divine, conscientiously upholding their divinity in public behavior, becoming quite upset if anyone should dare to sneeze in their presence, or appear inappropriately dressed or ornamented, or sit down in a wrong chair. Some of them avoided the use of the first person singular as too intimate. Queen Victoria said, "*We* are not amused." Leopold II, King of the Belgians, was even more regal:

when he gave an order to his valets, he said, "Bring *him* a glass of water" or "*He* thinks *he* will wear his beard bag today."

In Life Number Two the monarch was a bourgeois gentleman. Perhaps he was a very royal, spoiled, and capricious bourgeois gentleman who required much tactful handling, but at least he was comfortable; it is not surprising to find him seated at his breakfast table with a comfortable bourgeois girl.

To be sure, some of the great mistresses of the past had been women of the middle class; but the conferring of royal favor had transformed them at once into *grandes dames*. They were loaded with hereditary titles and estates to match. They were obliged to learn the exquisite mannerisms and points of court etiquette observed by all who surrounded the monarch. They had to acquit themselves before the world.

But at the end of the nineteenth century the situation was reversed: it was the sovereign who entered his mistress' realm, and it was a private realm, touchily exclusive, secretive, discreet.

The biographer who seeks information about these love affairs is hampered by the pervasive discretion. It is quite easy to study the lives of mistresses who lived in the early part of the century. People who knew Julie de Krüdener or Lola Montez spoke of them freely, visited them, received them, and wrote down whatever they said or did.

After the forties royal romances went underground—always excepting those of Napoleon III—and it is difficult to unearth reliable information about them. One finds oneself standing about in corridors, listening to the chatter of valets and secret service agents, or having to separate vicious or sycophantic gossip from good healthy gossip. Even memoirs written by the principal characters become, after 1848, prim and evasive. One of the most famous affairs of the century was that which was thought to exist between Leopold II and the dancer Cléo de Mérode. But the autobiography of Madame de Mérode flatly denies that she was ever the king's mistress; certainly her remarks about him are so conventional that they could have been written by a perfect stranger. A much better view of this towering eccentric is offered by Caroline Delacroix, a young woman who, having gained her education on the streets of Paris, was not greatly affected by creeping propriety.

Katherina Schratt is hardly mentioned in the biographies and memoirs published during Francis Joseph's lifetime, and when she is, it is only to give the reader to understand that Francis Joseph was far too lofty-minded a monarch to have a love affair, even an elegant and delightful one.

The stupendous freak of history has such a multitude of designs that they may be picked out capriciously, for beauty, absurdity, wonder, horror, or instruction; they are changeable as one stares. In the end they dwindle to invisibility. Today a king who wants a mistress must abdicate his throne and marry her; and with presidents, the mistress pattern ends, for presidential love affairs are not permitted to exist historically at all.

· I ·

THE HOLY ALLIANCE

Some portraits of historical persons, especially those painted by Goya or Velasquez, seem so faithful to the known character of the subjects and to their actions in life that one may fancifully read their histories on their faces. This is by no means true of a certain work of Angelica Kauffmann that hangs in the Louvre, showing a curvaceous blonde playing with her child. Julie de Krüdener was a famous beauty of the Napoleonic world when she sat for the fashionable artist, a society woman who entertained her friends at parties with a stimulating shawl dance of her own invention. "She was an intoxicating dancer," wrote Sainte-Beuve. "All heads turned at the sound of her airy footfall. It might have been a vision of music herself."

The novelist Madame de Staël was so taken with Julie's shawl dance that she used it to enhance a description of one of her heroines, Delphine. It would have been impossible for any of Julie's gay friends of the First Empire to predict a day when she would be darkly described as "a female Cagliostro," still less to look forward to modern history books which occasionally compare her to Rasputin.

The society people who lived at the turn of the nineteenth century had a genius for gaiety and gossip, for elegance of fashion and good manners, and they would have died for their honor, regardless of how much they owed their tailors. But they had seen revolution topple a world and a way of life perish. They suffered from confusion of spirit, and this was reflected in their domestic lives and amorous behavior which were in a state of wild disorder. Hard cash was at the bottom of most marriages; adultery was a social obligation; marital love was vulgar unless one was very young. It was fashionable to satisfy the most infernal clamors of the flesh. Baroness de Krüdener, therefore, had the sanction of her society when she abandoned her staid husband to his duties as Russian ambassador in various damp northern capitals while she drifted westward, lovely as a cloud, exploring the amorous horizons of Paris and Geneva with handsome young officers and seeking nightly laughter in dancing and in pranks. Everywhere she went she dragged with her a weary little retinue of children, governesses, and maids.

Now and again she felt guilty. Perhaps, she thought, she should "retire to my domestic circle, instill virtue into the minds of my children, watch over the fortunes of M. de Krüdener. . . ." Occasionally she vanished altogether from the fashionable scene, and with her children she would ramble beyond the cities, slipping into country dreams and a childlike sense of unity with nature. Sometimes she would fashion a little thought into an aphorism and publish it in the *Mercure de France*. One day she wrote, "In early youth we expect everything from the outside world; we appeal for happiness to all that surrounds us, and little by little we are driven back into our own souls."

No doubt when she wrote this, Julie's looking glass was beginning to reflect fine wrinkles, but she was herself reflecting the hunger of her age: a craving for peace which, since it was not available in the outside world so long as Napoleon lived, had to be found in a private world within. It was almost as if amid the splendor of the ball and the boom of cannon, God had turned a tutelary eye upon his reckless eighteenth-century children, and this sobering glance sent thousands of them knocking upon the doors of monasteries and convents; it drove them into "pietism" and "quietism," and it set even the most frolicsome to writing long worried letters about the state of their souls.

This eye fell hard on Julie de Krüdener. It fell also upon the Tsar of Russia, Alexander I.

Any one who deals with the Romanov tsars must gird himself for strange events; only in the esoteric Orient have stranger minds held sway over so many millions of people. Other European monarchs were divine, but their divinity was conferred upon them at coronation through the mediation of priests. Compared to them the Russian tsar was something of a *bodhisattva*, a deathless incarnation of the divine spirit, and priests had nothing to do with it, since the tsar was the head of the Russian Orthodox Church.

Emperor Paul, the noseless, febrile son of Catherine the Great, summed up the situation well when he said, "The only important person in my empire is the one I happen to be speaking to, and he remains important only as long as I continue to speak to him."

Paul, who was half mad, had only one important idea in his life; he wrote in very bad French and published in the *Hamburg Gazette*: "The emperor of Russia, seeing that the powers of Europe cannot agree among themselves . . . desires to appoint a site, an enclosed place, where he would invite all other sovereigns to foregather and fight. They could bring with them as referees their military experts, war heroes and cleverest ministers . . . perhaps it won't work, but it is worth trying."

What else could his own ministers, military experts, and war heroes do with such a fool but what they did? They crashed into his private rooms at the Mikhail Palace in the dead of night, dragged him out of the chimney where he was hiding, knocked him about, stunned him with a golden snuffbox, strangled him with a silken scarf, and when he still stirred, they jumped on his stomach until his terrified soul fled.

Sixty conspirators, whose identities were never officially divulged, accomplished this deed. When it was done, one of them presented himself before Paul's son and heir, Alexander, at his apartments on another floor of the palace, and told him that his father was dead. Alexander burst into tears, and as he left the accursed palace, he fainted.

It was March 23, 1801, and Alexander was twenty-four years old, when he was hailed as Tsar of Russia. One day he would hear himself called "the Greatest of the Tsars" and even "Alexander the Blessed."

The new tsar was a towering man, smooth-faced, with eyes so warmly receptive they were erotic. His lips wore the small fat smile of his grandmother, Catherine the Great. He was thought to be the most intelligent of all the European rulers of his day except Napoleon, and he was in love with such western notions as liberty, equality, and fraternity. Genuinely kind, he seemed open to every generous scheme for the betterment of mankind. The people of St. Petersburg called him their Bright Sunshine, and they watched for him as he rode incognito in a simple uniform through the streets. Immense crowds would press around him gently, "as a great mother presses her child," never harming him, but kissing his boots, his stirrups, his reins, his horse, with tender joy. His friends were all idealistic young men, each with some unselfish axe to grind, like the liberation of Poland, the freeing of the serfs, the framing of a constitution and a proper legal code. Alexander formed a committee of all of them, and he whiled his nights away with these friends, talking frankly and familiarly about transforming his realm into another England, with parliament, schools, and justice for all.

Very little came of it. The obstacles were too many, and at the least of them Alexander tended to balk. Imperious moments caught him lost in some abstract flirtation, and the early years of his reign were marred by broken promises and betrayals of his most capable collaborators. Clearly the hidden parts of this shining character contained grave faults. We find one of them in the strange passion he entertained for his sister, the Grand Duchess Catherine. Phrases from his letters to her read as follows: "You are the most delightful mad girl that has ever existed . . . you have completely conquered me and I am mad about you . . . I adore you . . . charm of my eyes, adoration of my heart.

"It is indispensable to my happiness to be loved by you, because you are the most beautiful creature that has ever existed in this world. . . . Alas, I cannot use my former rights (it's your feet that are in question, *do you understand?*) to press most tender kisses on them in your bedroom at Tver."

At the age of sixteen Alexander, without any choice in the matter, had married a fourteen-year-old princess from Baden, who was known in Russia as Elisabeth Alexeyevna. With her finely drawn and sensitive face, her "sweet and sprightly expression," she had come to her grand duke with a touching intention to please him: "He holds the happiness of my life in his hands," she wrote, "he is certain to make me unhappy for good if ever he ceases to love me." But before long she expressed herself very differently in a letter to her mother: "At first the grand duke made me wildly happy. Now that I begin to know him, there are *trifles* about him which are not quite to my taste."

It was certainly not to her taste when, immediately upon becoming tsar, Alexander commanded his Polish friend, Prince Adam Czartoryski, to assume his marital duties towards Elisabeth Alexeyevna. The aghast young man protested; the tsar seized paper and pen and wrote out an official document formally relinquishing the person of the empress, and he forced Czartoryski to append his signature to it.

Why did he do this? Was it another perversion, or had there come to his attention some correspondence of his wife's indicating that an unpleasant situation had arisen which Alexander did not feel capable of handling himself? These are excerpts from letters written by the empress to her lady-in-waiting:

"I find no pleasure in life when I am separated from you. . . . You are always in my mind; you create a commotion there which makes me incapable of anything. . . .

"My God, I am losing my head; my wits are going completely astray. . . . If this lasts I shall go mad. . . . I love you, I adore you. . . . My heart is too full, I cannot resist it, my thoughts are killing me. . . . I have scarcely the strength to keep my tears back before other people when I see you or when I think of you. . . . My God! What a power you have over me! . . . You can conceive, I hope, how dear to me is the date of the day when I gave myself completely to you!"

Decent, flowing-hearted empress! She was taken in her teens from her "very dearest mama" and driven by a clumsy grand duke to a desperate crush. It is pleasant to record that her forced lover, Adam Czartoryski, was "one of those dangerous

men capable of falling in love as well as inspiring it," and that
Elisabeth Alexeyevna eventually forgot her lady-in-waiting and
came to think of Czartoryski as her "second self."

Alexander was rumored to be addicted to unusual erotic adventures. Even his official mistress, Madame Naryshkin, was a
little unconventional. She was very pretty, but she wore a
scornful look, and her mouth, hanging loosely and a little
askew, was not admired by every gentleman who viewed her.
She coddled the tsar and amused him, never bothered him with
questions about politics, bore him three children, and did not
ask him for one penny. She was given jewels beyond price, but
this scornful woman could walk among queens with a bunch
of forget-me-nots in her hair. Once when the neglected Elisabeth Alexeyevna courteously asked her how she was, Madame
Naryshkin replied that she felt ill and thought she must be
pregnant again.

Just as Madame Naryshkin did not disguise from the empress
that she was the tsar's mistress, so did she not disguise from
the tsar that throughout the fifteen years of their love affair
she was repeatedly unfaithful to him.

Obviously, it was not for statesmanship at home nor for his
conjugal arrangements that Alexander came to be called "the
Blessed." Opportunity was at hand, however, for him to cover
himself with glory as a military man, for at the time of his
accession Napoleon was preparing to walk across the long-
suffering earth. He would have welcomed Alexander as an ally,
in fact he wooed the tsar with promises of earthly dominion:
between them, he said, they could extend their sway to farthest
India. He might well have gained Alexander's friendship, but in
1804 he took it into his head to murder an unnecessary Bourbon
prince, the Duc d'Enghien. Alexander was outraged by Napoleon's wanton attitude toward royalty. He ordered his court to
put on mourning and barred the members of the French embassy from the court.

Napoleon's reply to this insult was stupefying. He wrote a
note expressing astonishment at such delicacy on the part of the
tsar, whose father had died under mysterious circumstances
which could not bear inquiry.

This set the field for battle. Alexander joined with Prussia,
Austria, and England to block Napoleon. But he had no taste

for war. "The idea of war weighs upon his mind and torments him," wrote Czartoryski.

Napoleon was determined to bestride the world, and with bloody footsteps he moved eastward. Alexander's baptism of fire came at Austerlitz, where, against all good advice, he insisted on commanding his armies in the field. He advanced impetuously when he should have retreated discreetly, and in Czartoryski's cruel summary: "It was precisely at the point where you were stationed that the rout was most immediate and complete." Afterwards, in the icy darkness, blubbering like a whipped boy, alone except for Czartoryski and three Cossacks, the tsar took headlong flight and slunk by night into St. Petersburg to meet his final degradation: having to turn over his command to General Bennigsen, the man some people believed was his father's murderer-in-chief.

Alexander heard Napoleon's capricious peace terms at Tilsit on a beautified raft anchored in the middle of the River Niemen. On the river bank with the rain dripping down his neck, wretched as any sacrificial lamb, waited Alexander's erstwhile ally the King of Prussia, and he was silently praying that the tsar would not acquiesce to his total ruin. But Alexander did. He also told Napoleon, "Sire, I hate the English as much as you do."

Alexander's brother, Constantine, summarized the events at Austerlitz and Tilsit: "What crimes cowardice occasions! It has made a noble, generous prince a betrayer and a robber."

Such was Alexander I of Russia.

Still, it is not always brass-knuckled heroes who draw the most exquisite designs upon the body of history. Alexander was thirty years old when he signed the Treaty of Tilsit, but even before that he had sent an ambassador to England to try to gain the favor of Prime Minister William Pitt for one of his ideas, which, he expressed thus:

"One can't hope to realize the dream of perpetual peace, but one might come close to realizing some of its benefits, if in the treaty that will put an end to the war, some clear and precise principles were laid down about the rights of man.

"Why could that treaty not state the positive right of nations to remain neutral; and the obligation of nations never to begin a war without having exhausted all means of mediation . . . ?

"Upon such principles, one might proceed to general pacification, and give birth to a League whose stipulations would form a new code of rights, which, sanctioned by most of the states of Europe, would provide a guide for all governments—especially as those who would dare to infringe it would risk drawing on their heads the combined force of the League."

This document was prepared many years before Alexander met the lady who would prod, exhort, and mystically inspire him to the deed which would make him immortal in history and win him the title of "the Blessed." He had heard of her though. In 1802 he had received notification that one of his most conscientious ambassadors, a Baron von Krüdener, had died of apoplexy, leaving a widow and children.

He graciously paid the ambassador's debts, and on the widow he settled a substantial property.

When Julie de Krüdener lost her husband, she was thirty-eight years old and still beautiful, a graceful little woman with a musical voice and a smile of pale radiance. She reproached herself bitterly upon the death of the baron who had been her elder by twenty years. She realized she should have cleaved to him more and granted him the company of his children. To make amends she settled in Lyons and wrote a novel about a young countess whose husband was twenty years older than herself, and who in the face of all temptation remained dutiful to him from the first to the last page.

It was on the publication in Paris of this novel, *Valérie*, that Madame de Krüdener made a mistake that has damned her in the eyes of many modern biographers. For, sad to say, she indulged in a bit of press-agentry. She paid for some poems to be composed and published in the newspapers, addressed to "Sidonie," a pseudonym of her own, asking with bogus pathos why she buried herself in the provinces and denied the capital the benefit of her grace and wit.

Next, as if yielding to these entreaties, she went to Paris and embarked upon a shopping expedition. In each shop she asked for Valérie gloves, Valérie lace, Valérie fichus, raising her eyebrows every time saleswomen informed her they had never heard of Valérie. By the end of the day, however, they had heard of her.

"I am ashamed on behalf of Sidonie," wrote Julie, and she

added sadly, "In Paris nothing can be gained except by charlatanism." One would imagine that Julie's remark, "You know how much one is obliged to do oneself amongst journalists in order to work up the success of a first book," would mollify anyone who makes his living by his pen, but seemingly it does not.

In her day, though, Julie's machinations worked in her favor. The critics noticed *Valérie* and they loved her. Before long, mothers of newborn sons were naming them after the book's hero, Gustave, and in the bookshops browsers were seen poring over *Valérie* and weeping silently. Julie knew the relief of a lovely woman hurdling forty who finds that brains can serve her as well as beauty. On a cloud of fame she went home to Riga to share this triumph with her mother. Aside from her lapses into rusticity and a few slight aphorisms, there is nothing in her festive existence to suggest the singular metamorphosis she would undergo there: nothing less than the complete dissolution of a fashionable lady novelist and the rebirth of a new Julie de Krüdener with powers more compelling than those of powder puff or pen.

At Riga she had as usual an admirer, and he demonstrated his devotion by walking up and down in front of her house. Once he caught her stealing a look at him through the curtains. He raised his hat and fell dead. Death in the midst of gallantry! This episode profoundly affected Julie.

Not long afterward she went to her cobbler to have some shoes fitted, and as the man bent over her foot, she looked down on his old gray head and on an impulse said to him, "My friend, are you happy?" Whereupon the man turned up to her a face of perfect peace and said, "Yes."

Julie found this reply mysterious. In those days the members of the lower classes were not supposed to be happy. That was why revolutions were being fought, and all sorts of sanguinary wars: to make the world a better place for them to live in. She therefore made further inquiries, and the cobbler explained that he was a Moravian Brother, that he believed in God, the Bible, and service to his fellow men. Madame de Krüdener desired to make the acquaintance of the Moravian community.

For twenty years Julie had chased happiness through rose gardens watered by spilled champagne; among the Moravians

she found it. With a humility astounding in a popular authoress
she settled down to prayer, Scripture study, and service among
the poor. Before long, letters were streaming far and wide
out of Riga, informing her sophisticated friends of the secret
of happiness.

This would seem like the fad of a modish and even somewhat
bird-brained lady. But time did not prove it to be so. The year
of Austerlitz, Julie left Riga and went traveling in Germany.
For a while she stayed at the court of Prussia, impoverished
now, thanks to Alexander's betrayal at Tilsit. Overcoming her
repugnance for hospital horrors, she accompanied the Prussian
Queen Louisa on endless rounds among the soldiers of the Battle
of Jena who lay wounded and festering to death. Somehow,
Julie found golden words of comfort for the queen. Louisa later
wrote to her in words of pure gratitude, "You have made me
better than I was . . . promise me always to speak to me with
the voice of truth."

Next she went to Baden, where she lived as a guest at the
house of the renowned religious writer and oculist Jung-Stilling;
and then to Ban de la Roche, where the famous Pastor Oberlin
was making barren land bloom for the benefit of local peasants.
Here again Julie must stand up before her biographers and
answer an awkward question: Why, having the friendship
of these great and useful men, did she not, like them, apply
her fortune and her efforts to the practical, immediate service
of mankind? One might just as well ask Jesus why He did not
work toward the improvement of the lepers' lot, instead of
curing a handful of them by miracle.

For Julie's true nature, which was gradually awakening in
her, was that of a mystic, and she had all the boundless egoism
that such a state of mind entails. She did not wish to do good;
she wished to be good: not to imitate Christ, as devout people
do, but to participate in His transcendental nature, as saints
do. If, by the way, she swept disgusting hovels, changed the
bandages of soldiers, and fed the poor, this was but a subsidiary
effect of her mystical nature which was, in essence, indifferent
to the "real" world around her.

Indeed, we find in Madame de Krüdener neither the strength
of intellect necessary to do good effectively nor the wisdom to
make her a memorable religious philosopher. But the mystic is

not asked, after all, to be wise, still less to establish a charitable foundation. He is asked to give all his goods to feed the poor, and beyond that to imitate birds and lilies of the field. This is precisely what Julie was to do for the rest of her life.

For the next few years, bursting to communicate her new happiness to people of her own class, she traveled around the courts of Europe, welcomed everywhere as a famous novelist, an ex-ambassadress, and a lady of charming manners. Napoleon's representative at the court of Baden described her in 1810 when she was forty-six years old: "The arrival of Madame de Krüdener added largely to the enjoyment of our little society. She had not yet taken to composing prayers and sermons, but only stories full of visions, spectres, apparitions, and ghosts, which made an immense impression upon us, especially when she told them in the evening seated amongst the ruins of the old castle of Baden. Her stories were all delightful. . . ."

One of those who shivered by moonlight was Hortense Beauharnais, Napoleon's stepdaughter, the ex-Queen of Holland. That same year in Riga, Madame de Krüdener also became acquainted with the Empress of Russia, Elisabeth Alexeyevna. A lively correspondence gradually developed between the mystic and certain young ladies-in-waiting of these queens, so that the unfolding of Julie's spiritual self became a matter of much wonder and gossip in royal courts.

At first Julie's letters were newsy, and full of conventional flattery poured like treacle over royal heads, with a digestible sprinkling of pious chitchat and religious conceits. But as the years went by they became nonstop exhortations to prayer and to confession of sin. In time, when confronted with royalties, she was apt to launch into praise of God without so much as bobbing a curtsy to the divine persons visibly present, so that some of them were obliged to flee the room choking with merriment.

Yet Julie had not gone mad. The mad are incommunicado to normal minds, and Julie was far from incommunicado. Beyond the walls of palaces, where she lived in a bare house, furnished with a Cross—for she had long since given away her property—she held prayer meetings in French and German, and as she extemporaneously prayed the treasures of her soul's journeyings came tumbling forth so that those who heard stood rooted as if they were seeing a vision, as indeed they were, the rare vision of the *exalté*, who assails the strait gate of a celestial world and whose speech describes its iridescent scenery.

In 1811 Elisabeth Alexeyevna laid before her husband, Tsar Alexander, letters that her lady-in-waiting, Mademoiselle Stourdza, had received from the mystic; because she knew that his life had become loathsome to him and that melancholy and self-hatred theatened to engulf his mind.

The years after that "masterpiece of a battle," Austerlitz, are distressful ones for admirers of Napoleon, for it was during that time that the French Emperor's ministers, minions, puppets, relatives, and allies wove a mesh of intrigue in which at last to strangle him. The Austrian Chancellor Metternich, Talleyrand, and the Tsar of Russia held most of the threads. It was a time of cold war, with its deceptions, apostasies, and gratuitious insults. With malevolence Napoleon sent to Alexander's court two ambassadors in succession whose hands were red with the blood of the Duc d'Enghien.

As Napoleon's pretended friend the tsar had become a mighty power in Europe. Handsome and kind, he played with flair his splendid public role, but Alexander was privately appalled by the duplicities in which the diplomatic life involved him. He dreamed of abdicating, retiring with Madame Naryshkin to a quiet spot on the banks of the Rhine, while the empress, properly divorced, would marry Czartoryski, to whom she had born a daughter. Tormented by these impossible dreams, he confessed to a lady, "At times I have the desire to bang my head against the wall. . . . I have no vocation whatsoever for the throne."

In the first years of his reign Alexander had named a childhood playmate of his, Prince Serge Galitzin, to the important post of Procurator of the Holy Synod of the Greek Orthodox Church—in other words, pope. Galitzin was a conscientious man, and he thought he ought to arm himself for his position by dipping into the Bible. It made a profound impression on him. He asked the tsar if he had read it, and Alexander—who in the schoolroom had defined Jesus Christ as a Jew from whom the sect of Christians took its name—said that he had not. But since he was about to undertake a tedious journey across the wastes of Finland, he borrowed a copy of the Holy Book from Elisabeth Alexeyevna, and took it with him. In the Finnish tundra he became enamored of God. After this he began to spend much time at prayer and wound up with a painful case of housemaid's knee.

His new interest did not interfere with his duplicities, or with his ceaseless oglings of court ladies, or with his rumored curious erotic adventures. God was for him, at first, another flirtation, a mere hobby. He investigated the various sects of the Greek Church, and like Julie made friends with Jung-Stilling. He condescended to receive Quakers in audience, and he established Bible Societies in Russia. Knowing his impulsiveness, his mother trembled throughout these explorations. She made him promise he would never allow the Roman Catholic pope to catch him in his fisherman's net. One wonders what she made of his odd friendship with Selivanov, the famous "Eunuch Christ," head of the sect of Skoptsys, whose members emasculated themselves in order to please Jesus better.

It is not surprising that when Elisabeth Alexeyevna called his attention to the long and ever longer letters Mademoiselle Stourdza was receiving from the mystic, Baroness de Krüdener, the tsar read them attentively.

Julie had at this time withdrawn from elegant company to live among the poor, and she was feeling deeply the pain of mankind's burdens. Her world was famine-struck, war-torn, and dominated. Whether in true prophetic vision or in passionate hope, she had become convinced that the sovereign of her native land, Alexander, was a man of blessed destiny. In her letters to Mademoiselle de Stourdza, which, couched in the language of the visionary, described her vibrant Heaven, the tsar had no difficulty in recognizing a prophetic image of himself: a hero with the brightness of sunshine, a Savior of blinding beatitude, who would come riding out of the East to crush the anti-Christ, Napoleon.

Alexander longed to meet Julie, and considering how impressed he was with her letters, it is something of a puzzle why he did not summon her to St. Petersburg. Perhaps the unrest of the times kept them apart, or the great distances across famished lands.

In 1812 the enmity between Napoleon and Alexander flared

into the open, and Napoleon thundered eastward again. Since the Crusades, there had not foregathered in Europe such an army as he led, the Grande Armée, six hundred thousand men strong, of whom few were to survive. From all parts of the dominated continent Napoleon mustered them and swept their awesome force against the heart of Russia; but the all-conquering snows of Moscow engulfed them, and they swept back again in frantic haste, leaving behind their starved, frozen dead.

On the heels of the retreating army came Alexander, and he was armed with an enchanted sword, complete faith in his destiny. It was a bloody slaughter of men. The advance might well have halted short of France, but Alexander found himself invincible in his knowledge of heavenly grace, and he insisted upon the final drive to Paris which crushed Napoleon. In his role as God's viceroy the tsar was merciful to his fallen enemy. He allowed him a little kingdom to rule on the island of Elba.

As for Alexander, he was now and forever the "Greatest of the Tsars."

The Congress of Vienna was called in September, 1814, for the purpose of repairing the broken continent. There came a fabulous gathering of royal persons, monarchs despoiled and monarchs ready to despoil again, princes and princelets without number, grand dukes, archdukes, and plain dukes, counts, boyars, and palatines, all wild with relief that the long, luxury-lacking, frightening years were over; all shouting with one voice, "Peace! Justice! Equilibrium! Indemnity!" all eager to throw etiquette to the winds and abandon themselves to the most exotic pleasures at the expense of the Emperor of Austria, Francis I.

This hospitable monarch, whose reign had seen the end of the Holy Roman Empire, placed the immense Hofburg Palace at the disposal of the royalties, provided them with three hundred magnificent equipages, established a committee to wrack its brains in the preparation of every possible form of amusement and dissipation, amateur theatricals, balls, parades, masquerades, lotteries, concerts conducted by Beethoven, *Singspielen*, hunts at Schönbrunn, and expeditions to the catacombs, where some eighty imperial Habsburgs lay buried.

There came the King of Denmark, making jolly with his repartees and Maximilian of Bavaria with his open, honest face;

Grand Duchess Catherine of Russia, whose feet her brother Alexander adored, hot in pursuit of the Prince of Württemberg; Alexander himself, keeping a jealous eye on his sister; and the King of Prussia hoping to repair the fortunes of the House of Hohenzollern.

Incognito was the rule. Grand dukes, crown princes, princes royal, and heirs apparent went habitually in civilian clothes, the better to make love without consequence. Princesses of high degree, wearing the Phrygian headdress of the *Mädchen* of Vienna, shrieked in beer-gardens, and one might have loved the night away with someone whose shirt or petticoat was embroidered with a royal crown. Throughout the city closets teemed with trapped lovers, husbands prowled with sabers drawn, duels raged in and out of bedroom doors, and corridors swarmed with happily misplaced ladies- and gentlemen-in-waiting, enraged tutors, and frantic duennas. For six gorgeous months nobody knew for sure where anybody was, except Metternich's vastly implemented network of secret police, who knew everything and wrote down in their little books material for the plots of Central European operettas good for the next hundred and fifty years.

Protocol was tossed aside. When on some formal occasion it became necessary to observe it, it was Alexander, almost the youngest of the monarchs present, who decreed that precedence should be determined by age. A democratic atmosphere ruled. A sailor, bearing a letter for Alexander, accosted him in the street and demanded, "Where can I find the Tsar of Russia?"

"I am the tsar," replied Alexander.

"If you are the tsar," said the sailor, "then I'm the Emperor of China."

"In that case, meet the King of Prussia," replied Alexander, indicating that gentleman.

"Then let's all go and have a drink," shouted the sailor, and off they went arm in arm to a tavern from which they did not tear themselves away until the sailor began to shoot up the ceiling.

Nightly the magnificent ballroom of the Hofburg, immense as it was, resounded with the music of several orchestras playing simultaneously for everyone's separate taste, waltzes, polonaises, and minuets, while throngs of ladies and gentlemen clothed in precious stuffs and enmeshed in a limitless web of light milled and danced. The balconies bore the most elegant comestibles that great chefs, brought from every part of Europe, and the Near East, could produce. Vienna was not then famous for good food, but at the Congress it began to be.

One hundred thousand people came. Rents shot sky high. Lord Castlereagh paid five hundred pounds sterling for his rooms, an unheard-of sum. Daily they rode or walked or sat or staggered about on the spacious Prater beside the chopping Danube waves, while the spreading chestnut trees sheltered a tranquil festival of elderly notables who watched the gay world throng about with its futile importunities. They saw pass by the twenty-year-old Zavadovsky, whose father, a favorite of Catherine the Great, had bequeathed him an enormous fortune; but one midnight he was awakened by two friends for a game of cards, and by dawn he had lost every penny of it. As at all international conferences there was an English eccentric buttonholing everybody in favor of a cause of absolutely no interest: in Vienna it was Admiral Sir Sidney Smith, the British hero who defended Acre, the port of Palestine, against Napoleon—and he tirelessly tried to persuade the assembled monarchs to rise in ire on behalf of white slaves in the Arab World.

Who was the veiled lady, the gossips asked each other, who walked past every day with her husband by the hand? Her tale was told behind fans: she was the Hungarian Countess Hadik who, at the age of sixteen, had been happily betrothed to her childhood sweetheart. But he had gone off to the wars, and in his absence she had caught smallpox which utterly obscured her beauty. She longed to die and began to starve herself to death.

Then one day her lover came back. He walked into her house calling, "Constance, where are you?" Unable to contain her love, she flew into his arms for a last embrace before raising her weeping face to his—and lo! In the wars he had lost both eyes. In Vienna she led him gently from concert to theater-piece, wearing a veil; he wore a black ribbon across his sightless eyes.

Alexander shone above them all. No person in Europe was more adored than he. He had left his mistress, Madame Naryshkin, at home, and instead he walked next to that "beautiful sovereign," Elisabeth Alexeyevna, who nightly enjoyed a second honeymoon with Prince Czartoryski, while the tsar chased with his erotic glance ladies whose names are too numerous to mention, but which glow in the chronicles of those times with the color of the rose.

In the midst of amusement Alexander found time daily to climb four flights of stairs to the little cell in the Hofburg that had been assigned to the empress's lady-in-waiting, Mademoiselle Stourdza. There she continued to read to him the letters she was receiving from the mystic, Baroness de Krüdener.

"Le Congrès ne marche pas, il danse," said the Prince de Ligne before he died of a cold caught from waiting about the streets for a lady-love in December at the age of eighty. While the divine royalties were dancing up a paradise, Metternich, Castlereagh, Talleyrand, Hardenburg, and, for Russia, Count Nesselrode of pie fame were struggling with the Congress's serious work—if it can be called serious work to draw boundary lines on the map of Europe. Among the monarchs in Vienna, Alexander was the only one who occupied himself with these diplomatic labors.

Meanwhile, some distance away at Karlsruhe, where Napoleon's stepdaughter Queen Hortense held her small court, her lady-in-waiting, Mademoiselle Cochelet, received a strange visitation which she later described:

"I was alone in my room when Madame de Krüdener entered. I sprang up with an exclamation of joyful surprise, and was about to throw myself into her arms when she arrested me with a solemn gesture. Her inspired mien, her prophetic accent, and her impressive pose filled me with surprise. " 'I have come to see your queen,' she said. 'I have come to declare to her what God wishes her to know. . . .' "

In answer to Mademoiselle de Cochelet's eager questioning, Madame de Krüdener continued, "Ah! You do not know what a terrible year 1815 will be! You imagine the Congress will finish its work. Undeceive yourself! The Emperor Napoleon will leave his island. He will be more powerful than ever, but those who support him will be pursued, persecuted, punished. They will not know where to lay their heads!"

The rumor of this prophecy rippled across the late-breakfast tables in Vienna, but it did not postpone a single ball. Then on

March 7 Metternich's valet got him out of bed with the information that Napoleon was not to be found on the island of Elba.
The following morning the entire Congress was in possession
of this utterly astounding fact. For five days, during which
Napoleon's whereabouts were unknown, they continued to dance,
but they did so like jeweled masqueraders in a Gothic tale
who know that one of the invited guests is Death and that he
might at any moment walk in the door. Then they heard that
Napoleon had landed on the soil of France. The panic-stricken
royalties scattered in all directions, leaving behind them countless lost decorations, crumpled *billets-doux*, royal bastards without number, and an enormous tax debt for the Austrian people.

It took a hundred days before Napoleon was finally, utterly
crushed at Waterloo. The Russians did not take part in this
definitive battle because the tsar's troops were resting and un-
ready at Heidelberg. Traveling across Germany to rejoin them,
the tsar, in great weariness, put up in a tavern at Heilbronn,
and of the magical event that took place there, he later wrote
to Mademoiselle Stourdza:

"At last I was able to breathe, and my first movement was to
take up a Book that I always carry with me, but my intellect,
darkened by heavy clouds, was unable to grasp the meaning of
what I read. My ideas were confused and my heart oppressed.
I allowed my Book to fall from my hands, while I thought what
a consolation the conversation of a pious friend would have been
to me at such a moment. . . . I remembered also what you had
told me of Madame de Krüdener and of the wish I had
expressed to you of making her acquaintance. Where can she
be at this moment, and how am I ever to meet her?

"The thought had barely flashed through my mind when
there was a knock at my door. It was Prince Volkonski to say
that he troubled me at such an hour in spite of himself, but it
was in order to get rid of a lady who absolutely insisted on seeing
me. He mentioned the name of Madame de Krüdener.
You may judge my astonishment. I seemed to be in a dream.
'Madame de Krüdener! Madame de Krüdener' I exclaimed. So
immediate a response to my desire could not be mere chance.
I received her on the spot. . . ."

Julie did not waste a moment in offering civilities to the tsar.
She pounced on him at once with reproofs for his various sins

of pride and the immorality of his life, together with her recipe for their correction, which was to throw himself with her at the foot of the Cross. The tsar listened with his head resting on his hand, shedding tears. And when Julie suddenly recollected that she was speaking to her sovereign and begged his forgiveness, he replied, "Do not be afraid. Your whole speech is justified in my heart."

They wedded like children, ecstatic in shared smiles and tears. They confessed their sins to one another, and forgave them; they prayed, and they were cleansed. They made themselves drunk with God. The tsar commanded Julie to follow him to Heidelberg. She came with her little band of disciples and took up residence in the crude anteroom of a cattle shed. "I also have my guard," she told the emperor coquettishly, pointing to a couple of cows. In this humble place the Tsar of Russia spent his nights with Julie, praying. He told her that for years he had daily read three chapters of the Bible, one from the Old Testament, one from the Gospels, and one from the Epistles, but that he had not succeeded in uprooting from his soul one solitary sin.

The news of the final defeat of Napoleon at Waterloo came to the tsar, and he set out for Paris. At Julie's behest he gave out quantities of money to the poor along the way. She followed with her party, and after a distressful journey they reached Paris and were installed at the wish of the tsar in the Hotel de Montchenu whose garden door opened on the Champs Élysées, as did that of the Élysée Palace which the tsar had preëmpted for himself.

Eleven years earlier Julie had left Paris as a successful novelist. Her return now as a prophetess and saint, with a tsar under her thumb, made a tremendous rattle. Her salon, which consisted of very few rooms, offered guests rush-bottom chairs, sermons, and prayer groups. For persons with spiritual problems, a private audience might be had with Madame de Krüdener in a small back room. Glum as it sounds, it was still the most fashionable salon in Paris. There came Chateaubriand, Benjamin Constant, Madame de Staël, Madame Récamier, and all significant dukes and duchesses to wonder at the sight of Julie, a lady with whose former pranks they were all familiar, as "clothed in white, she first prostrated herself, then gracefully rose, and with her thin hair, her inspired manner, and her high voice, seemed to enjoy the astonishment which came over the faces of the visitors."

One observer wrote: "Frankly I was not moved. This comedy seemed to be a shocking profanity."

Chateaubriand, although he liked Julie, was appalled at her behavior: "I, a man of many chimeras, hold all folly in detestation, all nebulosity in abomination, all jugglery in disdain."

Benjamin Constant, on the other hand, who was one of those suffering emotional turmoil, wrote to Madame Récamier, "She affected me in a way I never felt before."

Every alternate evening and far into the night Alexander spent with Julie, submitting his shortcomings to her prayers and correction, with such good results that she was able to write to Mademoiselle Stourdza, "His attitude has been that of the Christian hero such as, with the help of the Almighty, I had dared to predict last year."

However, Alexander's Christian heroism was not altogether beyond reproach. Julie was also to write unhappily about being obliged to suffer "the humiliation of an earthly relationship."

Julie, who was now fifty years old, retained the elegant and elastic movements of a natural dancer; her voice was "melodious, flexible, and gentle" and her conversational powers were "fluent to an alarming degree." But she was a mere wisp of the curvaceous blonde whose portrait had been painted by Angelica Kauffmann. The flesh of her face was transparent and seemed to cling to a paper skeleton, and she had the thin-boned eye sockets, the smooth, blue-veined eyelids, which artists usually attribute to saints. Those who called her "a female Cagliostro," a charlatan, could certainly not have pointed to shifty looks to prove it. Hers were the typical lineaments of the ascetic.

She has not escaped the accusation that her motives in becoming the tsar's mistress were culpable and based on her need for money. In the reign of the last tsar, the Grand Duke Nicholas Mikhailovich, a royal historian, was permitted to examine the imperial archives, and he found evidence that large bags of gold were transferred from Alexander's privy purse to Baroness de Krüdener; he also found many dressmakers' bills. Once in Julie's apartment a disagreeable incident occurred. She had among her followers a peasant girl who, in a trance, sometimes uttered words of prophecy or wisdom. The tsar was invited to witness one of her séances, and no sooner did he enter the room than the medium, presumably in a trance, began to demand money of him. Alexander was furious and flung off in a rage. Julie had some trouble in soothing him. On facts like these Julie's reputation as a religious charlatan rests.

But the question is not whether Julie extorted money from the tsar, but how did she spend it? She had given her own fortune to feed the poor, and for years she had been begging money from her rich and royal friends, from her brother who had inherited the family estates in Riga, and, after he came of age, from her son. Whatever was given to her was lavishly poured forth upon the destitute. It would therefore be incredible if in despoiled France, with the tsar as her lover, she failed to give away as much of his fortune as she could lay her hands on. The dresses also could only have gone to clothe others, for she did not resume her former fashionable ways. No one ever saw on her anything but straight gowns of plain material.

It was a matter of wonder to the cosmopolitan society that had gathered in Paris that the aging Julie held in the hollow of her hand a man of thirty-nine, the most prestigious monarch in Europe, who was a magnet for hordes of ambitious and lively women. But these ladies were up against a far different Alexander than the partygoer and ogler who had attended the Congress of Vienna. He held himself aloof from festivities. He told Julie that Paris had a bad influence on him, and he begged her to help him wrestle in prayer against the seductive forces of the city. It was soon noticed that whenever he was flattered and praised, instead of lighting up like the sunrise, his face fell and he looked grave.

Talleyrand and Metternich were perturbed by the new Alexander and baffled by the mysterious forces which, they soon noticed, were interfering with his manageability. They fought against them. Talleyrand threw a party to which he invited all the most beautiful women in Paris and the tsar; but the tsar did not go. Metternich sent posthaste to Vienna for three of the most renowned beauties of the Habsburg court. They arrived and were presented to Alexander who described the scene afterward to Madame de Krüdener: "They were dressed in the

Viennese style, not so wonderful. The whole business was a failure."

Alexander in his prime was a blond, beaming, baby-faced beauty of a tsar, kindly and winning in his expression. Yet portraits of him are not wholly pleasing. He had a remarkably small head perched atop a large body, pinched waist, and broad hips as voluptuous as those of a woman. Even "court portraits," painted to flatter, show him as an excessively girlish man, and all of them reveal his incongruous proportions: a short trunk compared to the overlong arms and legs. In fact, he has the appearance of a eunuchoid.

"It would be impossible to meet anyone more intelligent than the Emperor Alexander," Napoleon had said, "but there is a piece missing, and I have not been able to find out what it is."

A eunuchoid is not a eunuch; he may have relations with women and become the father of children. But his personality is flawed on the deepest temperamental level, and his love life is apt to be bizarre. Alexander's adoration of his sister's feet, his disposal of his attractive wife to Czartoryski, his attachment to the repellent Madame Naryshkin, his unsavory erotic adventures: all of these would be explained by an insufficiency which made him unlike other men. His ostentatious flirting led to the belief that he was a dedicated ladies' man. Yet he not only spurned beautiful courtesans, but contrary to all etiquette, he avoided the advances of such amorous queens as the exquisite Hortense Beauharnais and Queen Louisa of Prussia against whom he locked his bedroom door. Adam Czartoryski's comment upon Alexander's perpetual gallantries was that he doubted that the virtue of the ladies concerned was often in much danger.

This strange pattern of mind and his private desperation about it would certainly have been at the bottom of his attraction to the Skoptsy sect, whose leader was "the eunuch Christ"; indeed, of all his misdirected religious searchings, which brought him no peace, only housemaid's knee. It would explain his relationship to Julie de Krüdener, a passion that was both erotic and religious, like that of a Greek hero who tumbles the deceptive demons of his body and soul into the lap of his *magna mater*.

For this companionship Alexander suffered the ridicule that is the lot of a lover who must sneak in darkness through garden doors. Making his way past the moonlit patterns on the grounds of the Hotel Montchenu, he was one night set upon suddenly and pelted with a barrage of onions. His assailant turned out to be an English soldier pilfering from the vegetable garden, and the tsar asked him in for a cup of tea. When this story became known in Paris, all Europe soon set up a roar of laughter.

But when Alexander flaunted his love by daylight on the Plain de Vertus, the tsar's suite groaned for their country and the prestige of their master.

Since Waterloo, in which the Russian army had taken no part, the tsar's influence on diplomatic proceedings had been impaired. His armies had been brought up to Paris, however, and they were encamped at Champagne. In order to remind the world of Russian might Alexander commanded a spectacular military review to take place on St. Alexander's Day on the great field of Vertus, where once Attila's Huns had been turned back, to which he invited all available monarchs and generals. The day before the review Julie and all her household had been transported to Vertus. The following morning found them ensconced on an elevated place of honor near the imperial pavilion which had been constructed for the occasion.

The soldiers marched and wheeled, a hundred and eighty thousand of them with six hundred big guns, divided into geometric designs of blinding martial colors: lancers in red, Grodno hussars in green, the hussars of the guard in white and gold, and everywhere the great yellow and black imperial banners streamed against the sky while the sun ran straight stitches of light from eagle to eagle and spur to spur. There were the compact masses of the Paul Regiment with their huge miter-shaped copper hats, Mongols in long coats of mail, Finland chasseurs in their priceless arctic furs, and for the first time the people of Europe saw the swarms of Cossacks on their little ponies performing the savage swoop of an Arab fantasia. The Duke of Wellington vowed he had never seen the like, nor had he.

Seldom has God been called upon to play so prominently the second lead in military theatricals, although this role is by no means an unfamiliar one to Him. Eight altars were erected in high places for the simultaneous celebration of Mass according to the Greek ritual. The day after the military review, the huge army was again called onto the field, and the tsar stepped to the place occupied by Madame de Krüdener and led her forth. To the immense chiming of those myriads of voices in such a glorious choir as emerges only from Russian throats, he ceremoniously escorted her to each and every one of the altars, and together they prostrated themselves again and again.

"The honors paid by Louis XIV to Madame de Maintenon," wrote Sainte-Beuve, "did not surpass the veneration with which Madame de Krüdener was treated by the conqueror: it was as the ambassadress of Heaven that he received her and conducted her into the presence of his armies. Bare-headed—or at most wearing a straw hat which she flung aside at pleasure—with her still golden hair falling onto her shoulders and a few curls gathered together and fastened over her forehead; clad in a long, dark gown, confined at the waist by a simple girdle, and rendered elegant by her manner of wearing it—thus she appeared at this period, thus she arrived upon the plain at dawn, and thus, erect, at the moment of prayer, she seemed as a new Peter the Hermit in the presence of the prostrate troops."

"This day," said the tsar, "has been the most beautiful of my life. My heart was filled with love for my enemies."

Julie was devoting her whole strength to the construction of a demigod. Through him shipwrecked mankind would rise out of the deluge to a seemly life. Old things would pass away, all things would become new. She had correctly prophesied before, and now she prophesied again, with faith, that the golden age was at hand, and God's exemplary servant, Alexander, was going to bring it about. Inspired, Alexander believed this also.

Thus, while conferences lost themselves in the familiar maze of suspicion and duplicity, the bedazzled pair communed, and presently they brought forth their bright, precocious child. Julie gave it its name: The Holy Alliance.

In this renowned document Alexander revealed to the world his idea of a millennium, to begin the moment the interested statesmen had placed their signatures upon it. It prescribed that the doctrines of Christianity, that is to say charity and peace, were to be practically applied to politics; that selfish advantage would be subordinated to the common good; that the peaceful manners and honest address of private life would be extended to embrace the conduct of nations toward one another; that war would by this means become impossible.

Onions are mild compared to the ridicule that poured on the tsar when the Holy Alliance became public. Wellington and Castlereagh could scarcely contain their merriment when Alexander explained the draft to them. Castlereagh called it a piece of "sublime nonsense," and told the tsar that his master, the prince regent, could not possibly sign it without a row in Parliament such as he feared would never be resolved. Metternich called it a "loud nothing" but his emperor, Francis I, untroubled by parliaments, signed it out of politeness, as did the King of Prussia. And many a minor sovereign signed while hiding his smile behind his hands.

They were right, the Holy Alliance was absurd. It was an agreement among sovereigns, not among peoples, who were merely to be admonished to conform to it. Like the League of Nations, it had no teeth. Years later a retired French army officer made out a plan for implementing it with force, and this document went into the files of the Quai d'Orsay with the comment of an official, "What an amusing dream!"

But isn't it astounding to see this sublime nonsense, this loud nothing, this amusing dream, this modern necessity, arising from a love affair between a mystic and a eunuchoid?

It found no favor among men of practical affairs; but it buried itself in the heart of man, where the future is cocooned; and people began to talk about "Alexander the Blessed" as naturally as historians today couple his name with that of Woodrow Wilson.

We may never know why Alexander left Julie so abruptly in Paris, or why she was obliged to call upon her Savior for money to pay for her lodgings. Perhaps it was just one of what Metternich called "the periodic evolutions of the tsar's mind." Perhaps he came to realize that he was making himself look ridiculous; or perhaps he was just a jealous lover, because when anyone asked Julie who had composed the Holy Alliance, instead of saying, "Alexander the Blessed," she said, "God."

Julie now moved to Berne, where her son was the Russian ambassador. Wherever she went there were crowds, drawn by the tales of her prophecies and visions, and she preached to them, creating traffic jams. She was asked to move on, and she went to Basle, taking up residence in a hotel which soon became overrun with visitors and pressed about by crowds.

Condemnations of Madame de Krüdener and all her words soon came thundering down from the pulpits of Switzerland, and the Roman Catholics set themselves against her. Her disciple, Empaytaz, was summoned before the Mayor of Basle to answer accusations that he and Julie were deflecting the attention of teen-agers from their normal life of pleasure, implanting in them serious thoughts unsuitable for the young.

Obliged to leave the town of Basle, they buried themselves in the country, in a cottage on the banks of the Rhine in Baden. But the poor sought Julie out, and mothers came, war widows with their children, to be fed; the sick thronged to her in the belief that she could work miracles. She nursed them, begged housing for them, provided food for them or else prayer. For these masses there was no real help other than faith, and this came pouring forth from Julie. She breathed on their suffering and transformed it mysteriously into joy, a treasure to be welcomed for its own sake, engendering as it does man's unconquerable hope.

Of herself she said in those days, "I seek nobody. . . . It is the people who come to me. Can I drive away the starving poor, the destitute orphan, the distraught and sin-laden soul? I say to myself: what would our Lord have done under similar circumstances? The answer is clear. . . ."

Once a wretched woman came to her with most of her face destroyed by disease. Julie held out her arms in welcome and kissed her. But only the Quakers praised Julie at this time.

As the landscape around the cottage was now a vast encampment, the police decided their services were needed. Two gendarmes were stationed at the door of the cottage with orders to prevent the assembly of crowds. Soon Julie had them walking behind her, carrying her bundles. The authorities dishonorably discharged them and sent a new guard, a man noted for his brutal conduct and violent temper. Julie's household nervously awaited trouble, and it came: immediately upon his arrival the man began to belabor with his saber some beggars lying in the road. Julie went out to him, touched him gently on the shoulder and said, "Whatever are you doing? Don't you know that this is the place where all the gendarmes get converted?"

She then spoke to him severely about his sins and how fortunate he was to have committed them, since Jesus would view his repentance with especial joy. Within short order the man was crying like a child and begging to be prayed for. From that time forth he took much hard work off Julie's shoulders.

In the famished winter of 1817 she opened bread and soup kitchens for people in dire need of bread and soup. They came in ever increasing numbers, sleeping in ditches, huddling in scanty lean-tos in the woods, climbing the frost-brittle trees round about, whenever she stopped to preach. The Basle and Baden authorities now decided on concerted action. They performed the usual antics of authorities: spun cordons, thrust back crowds, threw up ropes, buffeted the young, barked at the old; they carted the sick away. The newspapers meanwhile printed scurrilous denunciations of Julie, accusing her of preaching free love and prophesying to servant girls that they would one day walk in silk while their masters peeled vegetables. To make matters worse, Julie published a document addressed "To the Poor," the sentiments of which were found to be nothing short of revolutionary. This was not to be borne. She was expelled from the territory, her lares and penates smashed behind her, and she was driven to wander from place to place through northern Switzerland and Germany, backward and forward across frontiers, followed by throngs of starvelings, and risking everywhere riots and stonings. She was not permitted to rest more than a few hours at a time, or, as the anger of the police mounted, even to pause for a meal, but was compelled always to move from one temporary halt to another.

But while this persecution—it was nothing less—raged against her, in certain quarters, the very last you would expect, sympathy was growing in her favor: among the ranks of Protestant ministers and Catholic priests. As in her wake more and more people were turning to their churches and the confession boxes were full, and even adamantine Jews came, asking to be baptized, these ministers, once bitterly opposed to her, joined hands to help and protect her. She denied sectarianism for herself. She said she was an Early Christian.

Little has been quoted here of what survives of Julie's preachings. Her prophetic pretensions, her emotionalism and egoism are difficult to endure. And yet, when she lived, people who had no lack of common sense were tremendously moved by her. One of these, a Professor Krug of Leipzig, went to see her to clear up a matter of some scholarly interest: the precise authorship of the Holy Alliance. After assuring him that it was the immediate work of God, she went on to say that the first conception of the Alliance had sprung up in the mind of the noble and pious Emperor Alexander, and that he had brought her a rough copy which she had corrected.

Julie then continued, "I have no need of anything. I require nothing from the world. I already experience celestial joys. I am so indescribably happy. I ardently long to see all mankind participating in my joy."

Even after this barrelful of "I's" Professor Krug regretted that he was not possessed of more warmth of temperament, because he confessed he was tempted to prostrate himself before her and venerate her as a saint.

We must assume that there is a compelling ingredient in the living presence of the mystic that has the power to reach the rare depths of mind and heart. The Hindus comprehend this in their word, *darshan.* They travel for miles, simply to experience *darshan,* the consciousness of the living presence of the holy one, who does not necessarily speak to them at all.

Baroness de Krüdener is certainly one of the most remarkable characters to have wandered through the century of our great-grandfathers. One of her pleasing qualities was the affection she inspired among her intimates. Her husband, who had every reason to execrate her, was tenderly devoted to her. She was adored not only by her children, but by such unlikely people as a stepdaughter and her in-laws; unlikelier still, she kept the friendship of rival female novelists like Madame de Staël. People who had robbed her of money followed her forever, and her disciples were her disciples for life.

She was probably a good woman. She does not deserve to be remembered in history as a harpy with her talons in a tsar. We will therefore show her in a pleasant moment when she was old and lived on her family estates at Riga, where she attended to the spiritual welfare of the local peasants. The incident was seen by a gentleman who did not know at the time who she was:

"It was a fine summer's evening when, as I was walking along the banks of the river, an open carriage drove by, in which an old lady dressed in gray silk was seated beside a young man. Without knowing it was Madame de Krüdener, I experienced a singular impression at the sight of this person.

"A moment later the carriage stopped and the old lady got down. . . . I soon realised the cause: there was a group of girls close by on the banks of the river, busily washing clothes, and Madame de Krüdener, perceiving them, could not resist the temptation of getting down and preaching them a little sermon. She accordingly made her way to the laughing country girls who opened their great eyes with wonder, and getting up on a bench, she addressed a homily:

" 'What are you doing here?' she cried out in the dialect of the country people with a loud voice. The girls looked at one another laughingly and replied that they were washing linen.

" 'Very good,' answered Madame de Krüdener, 'you are washing your body linen, but do you think of the stains that lie on your consciences, of the spots on your celestial clothing, that will drive you one day to confusion and despair if you appear before God without having washed them? You open your big eyes and you appear to ask me with surprise how I can know that there are any stains on your celestial vestments. Believe me that I know it most indubitably. . . . The souls of all of us are similarly circumstanced.'

"And thus the discourse was prolonged in a style at once familiar and yet mystical, but always borrowing its metaphors from circumstances of daily life and within reach of the simplest minds. The effect was prodigious . . . these girls passed from a state of stupid astonishment to gathering up fragments, and then following every sentence, and as they did so their former boisterousness changed into an aspect of modest decency. Gradually they left their work, went up to the old lady, and falling on their knees, they wept, whilst she, elevated above them, smiled with the smile of love and stretched forth her hand to bless them."

Alexander had left Julie abruptly in Paris, but it cannot be certain that he cast her out of his life as discourteously as he seems to have done. One cannot safely plumb the confluence of minds between a hero and his pythoness. She may have used her fluent conversational powers to persuade him to take a vow of celibacy, because at this time he dismissed his mistress, Madame Naryshkin. Julie, in the meantime, was expending great sums of money on soup kitchens, the source of which is hard to explain. She said that it came from God.

In 1821 she visited St. Petersburg, and the tsar appears to have avoided her company and even to have snubbed her. Still it is singular to find her residing at the palace of the tsar's confidential friend, Prince Galitzin.

Alexander had returned to Russia with the halo of the Holy Alliance around his head, determined to fashion his country into the Christian big brother of nations he had envisaged. But the task was too much for him and it fell from his hands. He lost himself in piety, and his knees grew lumpy. He fell under the influence of a sinister nobleman named Arakcheyev. Once, this man, observing that a young girl who was one of his serfs was not sweeping his garden walks properly, commanded that she be knouted to death, while her friends stood in a circle around her, chanting the Office For the Dead.

The liberal, humane Alexander appointed this malignant person his viceroy, and Arakcheyev ruled Russia the way he kept his garden walks clean. It was under his government, the "Hour of Arakcheyev," that there sprang into being secret revolutionary societies that were not suppressed until they turned into the Russian Revolution.

On Christmas morning, 1824, Julie de Krüdener died in the Crimea. In the following months Alexander planned an extraordinary excursion: a second honeymoon with his wife, Elisabeth Alexeyevna.

The empress had suffered greatly because of her repudiation by the tsar, and yet the estrangement between them had never been complete. Alexander had paid her faithful social visits once a week. He had borrowed his first Bible from her. She knew him well enough to place before him in a time of desolation the letters of Madame de Krüdener. Recently she had nursed him through an illness, and when she herself fell ill, the tsar announced that he would take her to Taganrog on the Sea of Azov for her health.

To her dearest mama, Elisabeth Alexeyevna wrote with joy about this new companionship.

But what an inconsiderate choice of site! It was a wintry town with a climate imposed by the inhospitable steppes and a putrid sea. There was no suitable accommodation for the imperial pair, only a damp fort.

On September 13 Alexander left St. Petersburg, not neglecting to visit the monastery of his patron saint, Alexander Nevsky, where a *Te Deum* was sung for his safe journey. It is said that on this visit he ordered a mass to be sung for the dead, while he prayed over an open coffin. Then, on leaving the city, he ordered his coachman to stop at an elevated spot. Standing up in the open carriage, he gazed upon his city for a long time before giving the command to proceed to Taganrog.

Some days later the ailing empress left the city and arrived in Taganrog to find that Alexander had been busy hanging curtains, laying carpets, and placing other amenities in the bleak fortress that was to be their home.

But her satisfaction at this domesticity was short-lived. In the last days of October, Alexander was seized with restlessness. He organized excursions in the vicinity of Taganrog; then farther, to spend five days with the Don Cossacks; finally he went on an expedition to the Crimea, where he visited various religious establishments, churches, monasteries, and shrines. One of them was the Armenian Church of Karasu Basar, where the body of Julie de Krüdener was lying; the tsar prayed long next to her coffin.

The tsar returned to Taganrog ill of a fever. On November 28 he was better. Yet the same evening Elisabeth Alexeyevna sadly wrote to her mother: "When one thinks that one has arranged everything for the best and is free to enjoy it, there always arrives some unexpected trial. . . ." On the same day her diary comes to a full stop.

On December 1, 1825, the tsar was pronounced dead of an infection. Some delay took place before the coffin was returned to St. Petersburg, and it was therefore impossible to expose the body in public procession, as was the custom. Only the members of the imperial family ritually identified it, and Alexander's mother, Maria Feodorovna, looked down upon the dead, seized the hand, and said, "Yes, that is my beloved son."

The coffin of Alexander the Blessed was then placed in the Fortress Church of Saints Peter and Paul whose tall golden needlespire captures the long, level flames of a distant sun.

Eleven years later a tall man riding a magnificent horse rode into a small town in Siberia without his proper papers. Like all vagrants in that immense concentration camp, he was given twenty lashes with a knout and set to work in a factory.

Certain peculiarities were noted about him: he was extremely kind and very pious; he was cleaner in his person than need be; he owned a valuable ikon bearing the letter *A* with the imperial crown; and not long after his arrival, a Romanov, the Grand Duke Michael, came in his wake and wanted to slay the official who had condemned the stranger to twenty knouts.

Clearly Feodor Kuzmich was an exceptional person. He was released from his factory work and allowed to take up residence in a small cottage, where he lived as a hermit.

In the years that followed legends multiplied around this saintly old man: that a soldier, on sight of him, had fallen on his knees to the ground; that rich carriages occasionally stopped by the cottage where he lived; that he had housemaid's knee. When people questioned him, he pointed to a little bag he wore around his neck and said, "This contains my secret."

Historians assiduously attack our favorite tales: Marie Antoinette knew the difference between bread and cake; George Washington told lies; little Louis XVII and Anastasia died their deaths. But the severest historian does not dare to deny positively that Alexander I, the Greatest of the Tsars, ended his days as a holy man, Feodor Kuzmich, in Siberia. In his time and long after, those in a position to know the truth were silent; those who might have guessed were noncommital.

As the years passed and the legends persisted some were curious enough to investigate the mystery. Old letters, recollections, wisps of gossip have come to light. To this day evidence accumulates that in 1825, with the probable complicity of his wife, Elisabeth Alexeyevna, and perhaps of his mother, various friends, and at least one of the doctors who attended him, Alexander escaped his unendurable half-life by a masquerade of death, and that the body of some other man was placed in his coffin and buried next to Romanovs in the Fortress Church of Saints Peter and Paul.

It is believed that in mid-century Alexander II went to the Church of Saints Peter and Paul with trusted friends and workers sworn to secrecy, had the coffin opened, and the remains of a man removed and reburied elsewhere. In the latter part of the century Alexander III is said to have again opened the coffin and found it empty. The Soviets also were troubled by the legend, and when they opened the coffin, it was empty.

To the present day new surprises accumulate as living persons continue to give up their forefathers' secrets. Alexander's recent biographer, Leonid Strakhovsky, has revealed a most staggering aspect of the affair: the little bag that hung around Feodor Kuzmich's neck was sent to St. Petersburg with the rest of his papers, and it was found to contain a note in code. The code was quite recently deciphered. It proved to be a note written by the murdered Emperor Paul to his mistress, and it read as follows:

"Anna Vasilievna: We have discovered a terrible flaw in our son. Count Pahlen informs me of Alexander's participation in the conspiracy. We must hide, tonight, wherever it is possible. Paul."

It was dated March 23, 1801. That was the day Paul's son— who would one day be called "The Blessed"—ascended the throne of Russia.

· I I ·

THE LADY WITH
THE WHIP

One of the young princes who was seen to be enjoying the rococo facilities offered to him at the Congress of Vienna was Ludwig, heir to the throne of Bavaria. He was twenty-nine at the time, and already famous as a lover of poetry and the arts, and we may imagine him wearing in Vienna that attractive costume affected by admirers of Lord Byron, a velvet jacket with a puffy bow and tapered trousers.

It is not known whether Ludwig put much stock in Julie de Krüdener's prophetic utterances, but he appreciated her other qualities: he procured a portrait of her to hang in his private collection, the *Schönheits-Galerie*, which consisted of paintings of the most beautiful women Ludwig had ever seen. He used this gallery the way other people used their chapels, for silent meditation. Here royal protocol was outlawed; here Ludwig's powerful sister Sophie, an Archduchess of Austria, had to hang on the same wall with the picture of Ludwig's butcher's daughter; here any milkmaid could take precedence over an ambassador's wife.

One day Ludwig was to hang one portrait too many in his *Schönheits-Galerie*, that of a woman whose beauty surpassed them all, and she was the one who would destroy him.

•   •   •

Bavaria was one of the few lands of Europe to come safely out of the Napoleonic scourge. This was due to the astute behavior of Ludwig's father, Maximilian, who had supported Napoleon all the way up to the top of the emperor's fortune, and then, at exactly the right moment, switched sides and helped to finish him off. When Maximilian died, Ludwig found himself absolute ruler of a fat piece of pan-Germany, unravaged, prosperous, and loyal to the last potbellied, beery burgher; and with a soldiery so staunch that a whole regiment of them cut off their beards and mustaches in order to stuff a fine mattress as a present for Ludwig.

For almost a thousand years his ancestors, the Wittelsbach princes, had ruled by divine right the land of fairy tales, and they were closely related to all royalties round about. Their women, many of whom were beauties, constituted a major marriage reservoir for the extremely fastidious Habsburg archdukes; they frequently exchanged spouses with their lunatic neighbors of the House of Hesse; an occasional wild Hohenzollern was brought down from the north; and spare family members of the Dukes *of* Bavaria could always be married off to their close relatives, the Dukes *in* Bavaria. By the nineteenth century the family tree of the Wittelsbachs had acquired a curiously ingrown appearance: sisters show up as aunts, uncles slip down to the position of brothers-in-law; mothers and fathers are kissing cousins, and there is a general telescoping of grandparents. These facts did not greatly devalue Wittelsbachs on the marriage mart because they suggested that distilled royal blood flowed in their veins; still, had they been horses instead of princes Charming, you would not have wished to bet on any of them. They came to be called "the mad Wittelsbachs," and indeed, many of them were either amiably or hopelessly mad.

Ludwig I was amiably mad. Deafened in childhood by French guns, he had grown up with a loathing for uniforms, spurs, flashing sabers, and other expensive trappings of his métier. He had a passion, on the other hand, for classic ruins, Italian gardens, and Roman villas. He loved his fairy-tale land of Bavaria, with its diamond coronet of mountains and its deep-lying luminous mists, but he saw at once what it lacked: Greek temples. Everything he looked at seemed to have been designed by the

Brothers Grimm. Ludwig resolved to remedy this defect in his lifetime.

He dispatched archaeologists to dig up statues, and in his capital at Munich he built the Glyptothek to house them. All the wonderful paintings military Wittelsbachs had stolen in times gone by were brought together and placed in a building of equal magnificence, the Pinakothek. At Ratisbon he raised a massive fake Parthenon, which he called the Valhalla, and placed in it busts and statues of all the famous men of Germany except Luther. As Ludwig grew old quaint Bavaria began to shimmer under the moon with plinths, pediments, pillars and porticoes, and a statue of Ludwig in a toga.

The lion's share of the money for these stupendous works came out of his subjects' pockets, but he did not ask sacrifices of them that he was not willing to make himself. Ludwig's home life was parsimonious. He had a wife called Thérèse, one of those exemplary queens whose smile was pinned on her at birth and not removed until death. She smiled when she went to the theater in an old dress and also when she saw her seven baby Wittelsbachs eating black bread. She probably informed them that it made teeth grow like marble columns, but the truth was quite the contrary.

In spite of what he cost them, the people of Bavaria found their king an endearing sight—with his high, fine nose (inbreeding is good for noses) and his eyes squinting against the sun—as he leapt around in the mud of building sites, shouting directions, dodging columns in flight, urging his workmen to hurry, because time was not enough. Covered with the dust of fine marble, he would plod home to the Residenz like any common workman, and little it mattered that traffic had to be stopped and streetfuls of people had to stand about, hats off, while this weary toiler went by. Sometimes as he walked through the streets he would see a lady in a veil, and this had a curious effect on him. He would stride up to her, raise the veil, and peer underneath. Once he was heard to say, "Madam, you are right!" as he let it fall again. These veil-lifting activities were, of course, only research for his *Schönheits-Galerie*.

Like his idol, Lord Byron, Ludwig loved Beauty and believed in Sin. He also wrote poetry and he had the advantage over

Byron in that he possessed the means to keep down his competitors, for example, Heinrich Heine, whom he banished from Bavaria. Thus, though the king's verse (which was written in German with imitation Greek and Latin scansion) was in the opinion of Heine and other critics terrible, it may be stated that very little better came out of Bavaria in his lifetime. Sin was taken care of by a series of mistresses culled not for beauty alone, but for thrift and a willingness to prize interesting old potsherds above expensive jewelry.

When Prince Metternich, the mighty Austrian chancellor, saw what Ludwig was up to in Bavaria, he thought it proper to remind him that he was a Catholic prince, and he therefore sent him a black pack of political Jesuits to run his country for him while he was occupied with his work. Pleased, Ludwig ran them up a few magnificent churches.

The minions of St. Ignatius of Loyola are the villains of nineteenth-century politics as they were the heroes of previous centuries when they governed on behalf of illiterate or disinterested princes. Now as the middle classes were wanting to try their hand at power, looking with hindsight, we see the unbudging Jesuits standing like black shadows against progress; but it must have seemed to them that they stood for order against chaos and revolution. They were at bay almost everywhere in Western Europe in mid-century, but not for the present in Bavaria. There they kept God in his Heaven with the consent of the king, abetted by his feudal lords, his loyal burghers, his soldiers, and all who rested comfortably upon the toil of peasantry, which in turn found its main prop and support in God. It can be seen that there was a solid sphericity to life in Bavaria, and this is the hardest of shapes to kick to pieces, to stamp on, or to break between the teeth. If you want to destroy it, you must penetrate to its quiescent heart and blow it up.

Thus matters stood in 1846 when the king was sixty years old. One day he was sitting at his desk with his aide-de-camp, attending to business, when there came bounding into his office a young woman with hair like the wine-dark sea and eyes flaring blue like a pair of St. Elmo's lights. Her dress was torn at the bosom, possibly from the efforts of a guard to restrain her. She seized a knife or some scissors and slit it well down the front, so that the astounded king could more easily investigate what his eyes were fixed upon with consuming curiosity. After a moment the aide-de-camp was told to leave the room.

"*Lola has come!*" These were to be the catchwords of Lola Montez; indeed for a long time they were a household expression for any swift, dangerous arrival.

But where she had come from to begin with was a thing that engaged the liveliest imaginations in Europe for nearly twenty years.

Lola Montez was the daughter of Spain's most glorious toreador, Montes; or else she was one of the legendary by-blows of Queen Maria Christina. Since she wore a white collar and loved sin, she might well have been the daughter of Lord Byron and a Scottish washerwoman; or perhaps she was a babe of noble blood stolen by Seville gypsies and taught to dance—if only she could keep time to music. Lola's speech offered no clue to the mystery of her origin because she spoke nine languages including Hindustani, all with a foreign accent.

What everybody knew about Lola was that she was the most beautiful woman that ever had struck the earth; that her capacity for love was livelier than all the houris in paradise; that a man had only to look at her to burst into flame; that she accepted as lovers only men who were princes, kings, or of outstanding genius; and that her best friend was a whip.

Students of Lola discovered that she possessed all but one of the twenty-seven points laid down by an Arab voluptuary as necessary for lovely womanhood: three white: skin, teeth, hands; three black: eyes, eyelashes, eyebrows; three red: lips, cheeks, nails; three long: body, hair, hands; three short: ears, teeth, chin; three wide: breast, forehead, space between eyes; three narrow: waist, hands, feet; three thin: fingers, ankles, nostrils; three plump: lips, arms, hips. Lola's one glorious failure was in her eyes, which were a special blue, said to combine the different shades of sixteen varieties of forget-me-not.

The common ideograph for beauty in the nineteenth century called for a perfectly oval face, eyes like those of a stricken doe, and lips like pomegranates ripe for plucking. Thus was Lola described and thus was she depicted by countless artists who squeezed the various parts of her into a hackneyed scheme with embellishments of their own, so that each portrait seems to represent somebody else, and all flatly contradict her photographs. These show a lady made of altogether sterner stuff. In them her jaw appears square and shaped rather like a snow shovel. The cheekbones are those of a Tartar chieftain. The eyes are pushed apart by a heavy, downward jut of bone. Her teeth seem built to eat bear steak. Yet all of these hefty masculine features are slanted and tilted together into a pattern of tender delicacy. It is as if Botticelli had turned up in his garden a collection of primitive bones and set himself to fashion them into a Venus, hollowing down the cheeks, lifting the brow sensitively, shaping with love the lips of a mocking child, and punctuating the whole with an exquisite Gothic nose.

All the violent contrasts of her being were brought to an essence in her remarkable eyes, which had an expression both commanding and supplicating, like the eyes of an imprisoned panther. Many who knew her placed themselves willingly under her command; those who opposed her were likely to be slashed by a whip. She had, in fact, a striking array of those dangerous personality traits modern psychologists associate with the paranoiac: megalomania, delusions of persecution, an absolute need to be considered innocent and right. She was a play-actor, a liar, a reckless gambler, a secret mystic, and murderous.

But now that she is dead, her biographers tend to respond to the supplication of those eyes, and they forgive her all of it.

For several years, while Ludwig of Bavaria puttered with his marble slabs, Lola had been living the uninsured life of an adventuress. The Earl of Malmesbury seems to have been the first to notice her, when she was about twenty-one. She made him believe that she was the orphaned daughter of a Spanish officer shot for his political sympathies. Of course he took her under his protective wing. This arrangement must have ended badly, because soon afterward we find Lola—according to her autobiography—singing in the streets of Brussels for her livelihood. She was rescued by a kindly German who took her to Warsaw and secured for her a dancing engagement in the state theater. At this point she made her first bid to set the world on its ears. Her account of the episode is written in the third person:

"It was in Warsaw that her name first became involved in politics. The Paskevitch, Viceroy of Poland, an old man, fell most furiously and disgracefully in love with her. Old men are

never very wise when in love, but the vice-king was especially
foolish. Now the director of the theatre was also Colonel of the
Gens d'Armes—a disgraceful position of itself, and rendered
peculiarly so by him, from his having been a spy for the Russian
Government. Of course the Poles hated him.

"While Lola Montez was on a visit to Madame Steinkiller, the
wife of the principal banker of Poland, the old viceroy sent to
ask her presence at the palace one morning at eleven o'clock. She
was assured that it would be neither politic nor safe to refuse to
go; so she went in Madame Steinkiller's carriage, and heard
from the viceroy a most extraordinary proposition. He offered
her the gift of a splendid country estate, and would load her
with diamonds besides. The poor old man was a comic sight to
look upon—unusually short in stature, and every time he spoke
he threw his head back and opened his mouth so wide as to expose the artificial gold roof of his palate. A death's-head making
love to a lady could not have been a more horrible or disgusting sight. *These generous gifts were most respectfully and
very decidedly declined.* But her refusal to make a bigger fool
of one who was already fool enough was not well received.

"The next day the Colonel director of the theatre called at
her hotel to urge the suit of his master. He began by being per-
suasive and argumentative; and when that availed nothing, he
insinuated threats, when a grand row broke out, and the madcap
ordered him out of her room.

"Now when Lola Montez appeared that night at the theatre,
she was hissed by two or three parties who had evidently been
instructed to do so by the director himself. The same thing occurred the next night, and when it came again on the third night,
Lola Montez, in a rage, rushed down to the footlights and declared that those hisses had been set at her by the director, because she had refused certain gifts from the old prince, his
master. Then came a tremendous shower of applause from the
audience; and the old princess, who was present, both nodded
her head and clapped her hands to the enraged and fiery little
Lola.

"Here, then, was a pretty muss. An immense crowd of Poles,
who hated both the prince and the director, escorted her to her
lodgings. She found herself a heroine without expecting it, and,
indeed, without intending it. In a moment of rage she had told

the whole truth, without stopping to count the cost, and she had unintentionally set the whole of Warsaw by the ears.

"The hatred which the Poles intensely felt towards the Government and its agents found a convenient opportunity of demonstrating itself, and in less than twenty-four hours Warsaw was bubbling and raging with the signs of an incipient revolution. When Lola Montez was apprised of the fact that her arrest was ordered, she barricaded her door; and when the police arrived, she sat behind it with a pistol in her hand, declaring that she would certainly shoot the first man dead who should break in. The police were frightened, or at least they could not agree among themselves who should be the martyr, and they went off to inform their masters what a tigress they had to confront.

"In the meantime the French consul came forward and gallantly claimed Lola Montez as a French subject, which saved her from immediate arrest. But the order was peremptory that she must quit Warsaw."

This rigmarole can hardly be true, but like the Black Mass it is the truth spelled backwards. Herein lies everything Lola insists that we believe about her unless we wish to be cross-buttocked with a whip: she is an immaculate lady who sips tea with ladies of position; though pure, she inflames wicked men; she is on the side of the oppressed, as they are on hers; people who are cruel to her are intolerable, aesthetically and politically, and quite often they belong to sinister secret societies.

Small nuggets of fact glow in the blackness: that Lola was roundly applauded in Warsaw for her beauty; that she was hissed for her inability to lift up her feet in time to music; that one of the chronic uprisings against tsarist rule occurred while she was in Warsaw; that she was clever enough to leap onto the crest of trouble and make herself the heroine of it. One other thing seems certain: that Lola, far from fastidious and fresh from beggary in Brussels, would hardly have declined a heap of diamonds and a viceroy's love had these advantages been offered to her. Not long afterward she was to confess to an ungallant writer of memoirs that her ambition was "to hook a prince."

We find her faithfully pursuing this aim at a military review held by Frederick William IV of Prussia in honor of his guest, Tsar Nicholas I. Suddenly there is commotion among the onlookers: the horse of a certain ballerina, excited by the noise and glitter or else by a fierce jab from a pair of spurs, breaks out of the crowd and prances forth, straight toward the royal bloc. The ballerina might easily have fallen into the arms of a king had a guard not dashed forward and caught her reins; whereupon the ungrateful young lady raised her whip and brought it furiously across the man's face.

But throughout Europe millions of people who depended on royal embarrassment to make their conversation glow began to remember the name of Lola Montez.

So on, through the dreary hinterlands of Germany. Then at Dresden she trapped her first genius: Franz Liszt. Here is a love affair to capture the mind: the loveliest woman of all time and a man whose saturnine looks reduce the glamour of Phoebus Apollo. For a while Liszt immersed himself in this new passion; they traveled everywhere together, and he wrote a sonata in her honor. If only Lola were not forever bounding into the spotlight! He made the mistake of taking her along with him to Bonn, where, in the presence of many royalties, including Queen Victoria and Prince Albert, he ceremoniously unveiled a statue to Beethoven. In honor of this occasion the dignitaries of the town held a banquet of state. Lola crashed the banquet hall, leaped onto the long table, and danced among the dishes.

Before long Liszt perceived that if he did not get Lola off his hands, he would become immortal for the wrong reasons. One day, after a fierce quarrel and a tender reconciliation, while Lola was asleep, he quietly absconded from their apartment, locking the door behind him. "I understand women," he told his coachman as he bowled off to freedom. He meant that he had already paid the landlord for the furniture Lola was going to break when she woke up.

The liaison with Liszt lifted the lovely girl out of obscurity. She obtained a dancing engagement in Paris where gossip centered around her whip. "Let's see if her foot is as light as her hand!" came the cry from the audience. They soon realized that it was not, but at first hiss Lola astounded them with a trick that was to stand bad dancers in good stead for a full century: she advanced to the footlights, lifted up her leg, tore off her garter, and flung it into the pit. Théophile Gautier attended this performance as a critic, and the author of *Mademoiselle de*

Maupin grasped at once her essential masculinity: "We imagine that Mlle. Lola would do better on horseback than on the stage," he wrote.

But the gossip columnists began to make much of Lola. She pleased them by inventing for herself a characteristic costume in black lace and silk, with red, red roses; and by the announcement, "I am subject to my whims and sensations alone!" Exquisite and notorious and possessed of a fine foul mouth, she gained entrée into the salon of George Sand, along with Victor Hugo, Honoré de Balzac, Eugène Sue, Théophile Gautier, and the poet and political philosopher Alphonse de Lamartine. From these "liberals" Lola must have learned much about hypocrisy in high places, the machinations of Jesuits, and the plight of oppressed masses. She must have read and wrangled over the startling stream of propaganda emanating from the fortress of Ham where the Bonapartist pretender, Louis Napoleon, was imprisoned together with his paper, pen, and ink. Perhaps excited by all this, she began to have fantasies of political power, because her autobiography of this period describes quite unconvincingly a secret mission to Russia where she assisted Tsar Nicholas I with some knotty problem of state, hiding in a closet of the Winter Palace when unexpected visitors arrived. Of her further adventures in Russia she wrote, ". . . a great magnate conquers her in Petersburg; Grand Dukes perform their tricks; and Circassian Princes die for her. But soon she has had enough of caviar and vodka. What, she wonders, is the good of becoming fuddled with drunkards and wasting valuable time on half-civilized Asiatics?"

If only Lola had not felt compelled to tell fabulous lies, what true tales she might have told of the giants of France who were her friends and lovers during these years! They were not so remiss about her. "Lola Montez was a charmer," wrote Gustave Claudin. "There was something—I do not know quite what —about her appearance that was provocative and voluptuous, and which attracted one." Dumas *père* took her home with him, but he is said to have remarked of her, "She has the evil eye and will bring bad luck to whoever links his destiny with hers."

Most curious was the reaction of Richard Wagner: he took one look at her and fled. "A painted woman with insolent eyes!" he cried. It is a relief to know that people of evil brilliance recognize each other instantly and sheer away, but strange to reflect that Lola was destined to obsess the mind of Ludwig I of Bavaria, and Wagner that of Ludwig II; that one day the great musician would face a mob at Munich and hear himself cursed with her name: "*Lolus! Lolus!*"

When she first arrived in Paris, Lola had acquired a lover named Leigh for whom she ran up some bills before trying to shoot him. Eventually she came to rest with one, Dujarier, a journalist and part owner of *La Presse*, and he seems to have been deeply attached to her. Dujarier fought a duel with a rival newspaperman named de Beauvallon and was killed. In the sensational murder trial that developed from the affair Lola appeared in court swathed in black for mourning and ruffles for witchery. With the eyes of France on her she mounted the witness box and lifted her veil, while ". . . a murmer of admiration ran through the gathering." Racked with sobs, weeping inconsolably and for once with no enemies in the audience, she played the role of womanhood bereft—except in one magnificent sentence when the true Lola came striding forth, dashing and outré: "I myself could handle a pistol more accurately than poor Dujarier, and if he had wanted satisfaction, I should have been quite willing to have gone out with Monsieur de Beauvallon myself!"

When the transitory wonder of de Beauvallon's trial faded, Lola was about twenty-seven years old. She had little money and the smallest talent, and she had not yet hooked her prince. She therefore resumed her dancing career in the princely states of Germany, and lo! she hooked one. The ruler of Reuss, a tiny bit of land in Thuringia, became infatuated with the lovely dancer, notwithstanding the feelings of his subjects, who called her the Fair Impure.

But if Henry, Prince of Reuss, had a fault, it was that he liked people to be better than they should be. Once, wishing to reward in grandiose fashion his fire department for having put out a fire, he offered to shake the hand of the oldest of them, *provided that the man could produce a proper birth certificate.*

Inevitably Lola developed flaws in his sight. One day it was pointed out to him that whenever his mistress crossed the palace grounds, she walked right over his flowerbeds. His disenchantment was swift and final. "You must be a she-devil!" he roared at her, and he cut her out of his heart and realm.

On to Homburg, Carlsbad, Stuttgart—friendless and with dwindling cash. These must have been tormenting times for Lola. She was not, of course, altogether unacceptable as a dancer; her form was "the most intoxicating and womanly imaginable" and the mere sight of her set the house on fire. But there were always those who, having put down money to see the odd, pedantic dances of Spain, resented an imprecise performance, and they hissed. Lola, who did not like to admit shortcoming, darkly suspected that hissers were really members of the Russian secret police, planted by her old enemy, Viceroy Paskevitch of Poland.

Thus, when upon her arrival in the Athens of Germany, Munich, she was told by the manager of the state theater that she would not be permitted to dance there because she was not good enough, she was desperate enough to march straight to the Residenz, fight past the guards, take off her clothes, and transfix Ludwig I of Bavaria with her one matchless sword, her beauty.

Within hours he was making excuses to his ministers: "I know not how—I am bewitched."

He looked at his beloved temples and his poems with jaundiced eyes: they were but misplaced stones and word puzzles without a *hetaira* to bestow on them nobility or grace. Now Lola had come, and the spellbound king discovered that her wisdom was as unique as her beauty, that she doted on Greek columns and classic verse, that her powers of conversation were heady with Parisian polish, that she knew all about government, and that she considered him the most enlightened monarch in Europe.

Five days after her arrival in Munich the king summoned his ministers, his Jesuits, and his court, and produced Lola with these words, "I have the honor to present to you my best friend. See to it that you accord her every possible respect." Perhaps then, catching their guarded smirks, Lola realized that she had not only hooked her prince, but found her soul's necessity: persecutors. Henceforward to the end of her life, when she was reviled there would be the ruthless, remorseless members of the Society of Jesus at the bottom of it.

For the present Lola's dancing career reached an apotheosis when Ludwig ordered a command performance and packed the house with claques. After this triumph Lola refused to dance again. She had no need of vulgar applause when Ludwig's poems, written to her praise, were served at breakfast every morning.

> "By thee my life becomes ennobled,
> Which without thee was solitary and empty;
> Thy love is the nutriment of my heart;
> If it had it not, it would die!"

wrote Ludwig. But we need not rely on the baroqueries of the infatuated monarch to realize Lola's magnetic beauty at this time. We have the memory of a lady who was a small girl in Lola's day:

"As I was walking in the Briennerstrasse . . . I saw a veiled lady, wearing a black gown and carrying a fan, coming towards me. Something flashed across my vision, and I suddenly stood still, completely dazzled by the eyes into which I stared, and which shone from a pale countenance that lit up with a laughing expression at my bewilderment. Then she swept past me; and I, forgetting what my governess had said about looking round, stared after her until she disappeared. . . . 'That,' said my father when I reached home, 'must have been Lola Montez.' "

Occasionally the opinion is advanced that the friendship between Lola and Ludwig was platonic. This would make nonsense of some of Ludwig's purple poems, and also of Lola's public statement that the king's twilight passion was like that of a man of twenty. True, there existed a puritanical Lola, but she inhabited Lola's lies, not Lola's reality; Ludwig was described by one of his sisters as having *"toujours le feu aux flancs."* No, these two were lovers, but the king loved Lola for more than her beauty and fire. Elderly, lonely as the deaf are lonely, and a little queer, he had that arty disposition that borrows fortitude from a masculine woman. Humane and liberal, perhaps he had long felt Jesuit-ridden, perhaps yearned to enrich Bavaria with some more urgent need than still another museum.

As for Lola, she was a woman from nowhere, the secret of her life had yet to be revealed, and when it was, it proved to be searing cold. Surely in Munich's sham Mediterranean warmth, enshrined at last in the love of a king, she must have felt blessed. She must have translated her hunger for power into a hunger for the public welfare. Some modern writers have a high regard for her reforming zeal, because her political ideals, however unstable, were those we treasure today. William Bolitho sees her quite worshipfully as "Lola with her little whip standing across the path of parties, Empires, the Church itself. . . ."

She commenced her labors the moment she set foot in Bavaria and observed that matters there did not accord well with the principles of government favored by Parisian liberals. "I talked to the king," she said, "as I do to everyone, openly, frankly, and without concealment." She showed him "the cloven hoof" of Jesuitism where he had not noticed it before: on the press, in the schools and the university. She ". . . told him of the errors and abuses in his government . . . of the perfidy of his ministers . . . exposed to him especially the art, duplicity, and villainy of his Prime Minister, Baron Abel, a Jesuit who had wormed himself into his confidence."

This Abel had served the king for years; Lola was after his head within days. Having ignored the new favorite at first, as he had ignored many others, Abel must have felt like a man stunned by the falling branch of a tree where no trees were visible. Sensibly, he fought the big lie with others. The Jesuit press began to scream that Lola was an emissary of Satan, or worse, of Disraeli; that she was in the pay of Freemasons bent on the destruction of Mother Church; that she was the Apocalyptic Whore. Expostulatory letters arrived for Ludwig from his sister, Empress Caroline Augusta of Austria, which he ignored. He bore up also under the news that the Bishop of Augsburg wept daily tears over his moral condition. Lola insisted in her writings that she had a confrontation with Metternich himself who offered her an immense fortune and the title of princess if she would consent to leave Bavaria, but that she indignantly rejected this insulting transaction.

"She is king, then!" shouted Abel at his king, and Ludwig replied, "Yes, she is king."

Abel's ministry now addressed a private remonstrance to Ludwig, imploring him to look to his dignity and his country. Ludwig refused it and asked for resignations. A new cabinet was formed, which, after some raking and weeding, became known as the *Lolaministerium*. It was under Lola's thumb, and she spent her time directing its governmental labors. She had routed her enemies within eight weeks of her arrival in Bavaria.

Since Lola Montez was now a European power (and she would remain so for almost two years) it was evident that she needed trappings: honors, jewels, a palace, and other such things. Jewels were plentiful: the Wittelsbachs had been collecting them for a thousand years, and Queen Thérèse wore hardly any. For honors, Lola was created Countess of Landsfeld, Baroness Rosenthal, and she was given a substantial income to maintain these ranks. Ludwig further commanded the queen to adorn his mistress with the Order of a Canoness of St. Theresa, and the queen graciously did so. This good old queen was indeed the only person in Bavaria who kept her head throughout the Lola fiasco.

Now for the palace: Bavarians were thunderstruck to see their king, for the first time in his life—and not without some groaning—deflecting marble, workmen, and money away from his public buildings to build for his favorite an Italian palace, crammed with gold, velvet, paintings plundered from the Pinakothek, and such conceits as a glass staircase and a perfumed fountain. Two sentries were detailed to march up and down in front of it, and next to it stood a gold-trimmed coach lined with ermine with two mounted soldiers to follow it about.

"What Lola wants, Lola gets," people said. But when she asked for a private chapel and a confessor, embellishments proper to a Pompadour, she had to do without them. The Count Archbishop informed Ludwig that his clerics in a body had refused the post of Lola's confessor, "fearing for their virtue."

But what a strange request! Was it romantic foolishness or the cry *de profundis* of a woman who was beginning to be frightened of herself. For Lola's position of honor and responsibility had failed to calm for a moment her disorderly ways. She had thrown a priceless vase at her interior decorator in a squabble over a bill. She had boxed the ears of the chief of police. A young soldier sitting next to her at a banquet records, "on the floor between us was an ice pail with a bottle of champagne. A sudden quarrel occurred with her neighbor . . . applying her foot to the bucket, she sent it flying across the room."

An American student wrote, "I am the only friend she ever

had at whom she never threw a plate or a book or attacked with
a dagger, poker, broom, or other deadly weapon."

An English journalist who resided in Munich wrote: "Everyone whom she does not like, her prejudice transforms into a
Jesuit. Jesuits stare at her in the streets and peep out from the
corners of her rooms. All the world adverse to herself are puppets
moved to mock and annoy her by these dark and invisible
agents."

She bought a bulldog and taught it to snarl at Jesuits, bite
them if need be; but her true protector was the whip she needed
to control the dog. Once, this dog attacked a tradesman deliver-
ing beer, and the man defended himself with his whip. Lola
pulled him down from his cart and slashed him savagely across
the face. Ludwig's reaction to these events was:

> "But the heart's goodness shows itself;
> Thou hast a highly elevated mind. . . ."

The people of Bavaria watched the *Lolaministerium* rise over
their land like the fickle dawn of a thunderous day. There were
some who supported her; many Protestants supported her on
principle, and like all the countries of Western Europe at that
time, Bavaria had its share of Republicans of all creeds. For
a while such people shouted "Lola and Liberty!" and the name
of Lola Montez began to show up in the writings of the great.
Mr. Disraeli watched her activities with cynical interest. Her
former lover, Liszt, thought that Lola was the very spirit of the
nineteenth century. The *Times* of London approved the *Lolaministerium*.

The bust of Luther went into Valhalla; the Code Napoléon
went into effect; the press was unmuzzled. But as time passed
Bavarians, regardless of creed or political complexion, found
themselves bitterly humiliated to receive these favors not from
the hands of their king, but from those of the king's strumpet.
Soon, even in the Protestant north, when Lola visited there, people shook their fists, and she had to face a crowd with a pistol.
Lampoons, cartoons, satires, obscene jingles multiplied in Lola's
free press, which Ludwig collected and had richly bound:
". . . this mountain of mud as witness to Bavaria's shame," he
said. He wrote poems also, advising all ungrateful worms to
creep back into their darkness.

Most ominous was Lola's failure to win over the youth of the country. She was young and well-intentioned, she breathed the wind of change; yet the university students, the noisy young sprigs who might have brought health to her purposes rejected her. Only about twenty students rallied around her, forming a "Lola Guard." They called themselves the Alemannia and they promptly became outcasts among their fellows.

We do not have certain knowledge whether the salacious tales of Lola's doings with these youths are true or not; of orgies in her palace to which they had easy access since they had rented a house at the bottom of her garden. Such tales were credited by Professor Johann Döllinger, a famous Catholic divine, who wrote to a friend, "For Lola Montez they formed a sort of male harem, and the particulars which have transpired, and with which, of course, I must not pollute your ears, leave no doubt that she is a second Messalina." Ladies, when they passed the Countess of Landsfeld, began to draw their skirts aside; when she attended the theater, boxes near hers suddenly became empty. All of this added to her impelling sense of outrage.

One day while walking, Lola encountered a Professor von Lassaulx, teacher of philosophy at the university, and she set her bulldog on him. The offended divine then called a meeting of university professors to denounce the *Lolaministerium*. Ludwig replied as he replied to all Lola's critics: he dismissed them. The students now rallied to the defense of their masters; they gathered in a mass in front of Lola's palace, joined by rabble with sticks and stones which very soon came smashing through the windows. Lola graced the occasion by appearing on a balcony with a bottle of champagne in one hand and a glass in the other. With raffish gestures she drank the health of her tormentors and threw them chocolates, and she also threw her dog. While this carousal was in full swing, a carriage drew up and the king alighted. A shamed silence fell on the crowd. Ludwig entered Lola's house and remained there for some time, but when he reappeared the mob still hung about, and shouts were heard. Not often has a Wittelsbach driven through the streets of Munich to the sound of insults.

The student riots continued. Iron grillwork had to be put on Lola's windows. The military found themselves drawing sabers on their own youth. Lola threatened to close down the university,

which was Jesuit-controlled. She received every sympathy from
Ludwig:

> "Thou has lost thy cheerfulness,
> Persecution has robbed thee of it;
> It has deprived thee of thy health;
> The happiness of thy life is already departed."

As the year 1847 passed, the nexus of the trouble shifted from
constitutional reform to the right of the students to be educated
by their proper masters. The tables were turning against the
Lolaministerium. Never one to avoid a row, and with only the
Alemannia to support her, Lola faced mobs again and again,
haranguing them on behalf of democracy and bringing her whip
down around her. Once the boys had to form a phalanx and escort
her to safety at the Residenz. Still, to the entreaties of friends,
advisers, and royal relatives, Ludwig turned his deaf ear, and he
commanded a remonstrating bishop, "You stick to your stola,
I'll stick to my Lola."

As this hullabaloo was boiling up, the Prussian ambassador
in Munich, Count Bernstorff, received a secret communication
from King Frederick William IV of Prussia, written in the king's
own hand at Sans Souci.

"I am charging you, my dear Count, with a commission the
performance of which demands a certain degree of . . . delicacy.
The commission is somewhat beyond the accepted limits of what
is purely diplomatic in character. It is a matter of handing a
certain trinket to a certain lady.

"The trinket is of little value, but, from causes you will be
able to appreciate, the lady's favor is of very high value to myself.
All depends on the manner in which the gift is presented. This
should be sufficiently flattering to increase the value of the offering and to cause its unworthiness to be overlooked. My acquaintance with the lady and my respect for her should be adroitly
described. . . .

"You will, of course, immediately perceive that I am alluding
to Donna Maria de Dolores de los Montez, Countess of Landsfeld."

One imagines the count sitting slack-jawed as he takes in the
horrible implications of this letter: his master in the clutches

of the Apocalyptic Whore, the House of Hohenzollern brought to dust, the German confederation torn asunder, his own career like chaff in the wind. But it was only Frederick William having his little joke: the next few lines revealed that the lady in question was really Countess Bernstorff, and that the trinket was a memento of a recent occasion when the king had been his ambassador's guest.

On February 8, 1848, the king gave the order to close the university. Now the students ran mischievous in the streets, joined by burghers and all whose livelihoods depended upon them. For three days they rioted, hindered not at all by the military who were tired of drawing blood on their younger brothers. The Alemannia skirmished valiantly for Lola, but they were twenty among hundreds. Once, when they were beleaguered by police and fellow students in the café, Lola sped with preposterous bravery down the hostile streets to rescue them singlehanded. She was recognized, people swirled around her and welded into a bloodthirsty mob, shaking sticks and throwing stones. She ran to the shelter of the Austrian Embassy, but the Swiss Guards shut the doors in her face. She might have died in the streets that day, except that one ironical door opened when she flung herself against it: that of the Theatiner Church.

After that she remained in her palace, still calm and fearless and certain of the king's support.

But from the windows of the Residenz, Ludwig was looking down into the streets, watching the ominous furniture of revolution appearing everywhere: barricades made of carts and beer barrels. Now Lola's enemies, perhaps even her friends, had his ear with the most telling argument: his beloved's life was in danger. An order was placed before him, banishing Lola. On February 11 he signed it with a staggering pen.

Lola received this document in stunned disbelief. He had written to her:

"The ties of love will tie us so much closer
If the world attempt to tear thee from me."

Now she was thrown over, betrayed; what was worse, she was left at the mercy of the rabble. The guardsmen detailed to the protection of her person were removed, and the crowd was at her gate. According to her own account women of title, a countess and a baroness, were in the forefront—"I cannot call them *ladies*," wrote Lola. There was nothing to do but depend upon courage and luck. She packed up her jewels and fled her house with the help of her faithful Alemannia. Gaining the shelter of her coach, she broke down the streets, but she was seen and pistol shots were fired, while mobs followed, shrieking. Thus was Lola Montez driven from her kingdom.

In front of her pretty palace, meanwhile, a rabble was breaking down her door. An elderly and disheveled man tried to shoulder his way to the front of the crowd, shouting "Fools! Fools! The house is empty!" When they saw their king, trembling and weeping in their midst, the people stopped aghast. A silence fell. The soldiers presented arms, someone shouted *"Heil Unsern König!"* and the fond old cry was taken up as the king was led away.

What a pity Ludwig spoiled it all with a line straight out of comic opera: "They would have wanted Lola," he said, "had her name been Loyola!"

Lola did not give up without a struggle. Disguised as a peasant, she returned to implore the king to rescind her banishment; with grief he ordered her to be escorted to the Swiss border. Soon she was back, disguised as a man. Again and again it was rumored in the town that she had been seen, and Lola-hunts became a popular drunken sport among the inhabitants of Munich.

Ludwig made a desperate effort to save the situation. He sent a message to Lola, directing her to go to the house of a noted exorcist, and to this learned gentlemen he sent a command: "Drive the devil out of her!" The exorcist was annoyed by having to involve himself in this ticklish love affair, but he did his best. He locked Lola in a turret and fed her raspberry juice. After a while he wrote, "Lola has grown astonishingly thin. My son, Theobald, has mesmerized her, and I let her drink some asses' milk."

After a while, to his joy, Lola escaped.

In the end, Ludwig told her peremptorily that she must go away and not come back. He said that he loved her and would write some poems for her.

. . .

Royal mistresses of yore, having accepted their *congé*, generally entered a convent, or they sank into pathos and eventual oblivion. This could not happen to such as Lola Montez, whose life was still to unwind to its cruel climax. On the contrary, it was King Ludwig who sank from sight. In the disorders following the overthrow of the *Lolaministerium* he was obliged to abdicate his throne in favor of his son—who maintained many of the reforms of Lola's government. The people of Bavaria, with a feeling of relief, watched their most distinguished private citizen bury himself once more amid his building blocks.

The Countess of Landsfeld, whose every movement was followed by a cortège of young bloods, rakes, and newspapermen, wandered on the Continent for a while. Her name was scandalously linked with the son of Sir Robert Peel and even with Louis-Napoleon who, having escaped from imprisonment at Ham, was about to become President of France.

Next she went to live in England, where she met and married a cornet of the Life Guards, a Mr. George Heald.

For almost two years Lola had lived in the thronelight without anyone of consequence knowing who she really was. Rumors had flown thick as flies, which she had blandly embellished with lies. Shortly after her marriage to Heald the world was to stand agape as something was torn from her many-veiled secret. Her husband was twenty years old and very rich. Moreover he was heir to the fortunes of numerous elderly unmarried relatives. No sooner did these see their cornet stricken by a fascinating adventuress than they rallied to his aid like a herd of elephants around a wounded young bull. They made expensive research into Lola's past, and before long the Countess of Landsfeld found herself charged with bigamy and sitting not on the dock exactly, but on a chair in front of it, as was her privilege as a noblewoman. Beside her sat Mr. Heald, squeezing her hand.

Lola now confessed that she had been previously married to a certain Captain James, that he had taken her to India as an innocent bride, and there had basely betrayed her with another woman. However, said Lola, she had been divorced from James by a special Act of Parliament. This statement came as a huge surprise to both Houses. Released on bail, Lola and George Heald quietly left the country. Little more came out of it, and legend closed in on Lola once again.

Shortly afterward she was seen in Spain wearing a marvelous wine-red gown and gambling away large quantities of Mr. Heald's fortune. Standing with her eyes riveted on the tables, she was observed to put her hand repeatedly over her shoulder for money, like a hunter for ammunition. When her faithful bearer confessed that he had run out of it, she hit him over the head with a clenched fist and said, "Learn that he who has the honor to accompany Lola must always have money at his command!"

Other matters ruffled the domestic serenity of the countess and the cornet. Lola was receiving letters and love poems from Ludwig; also a ring. As a matter of fact the cornet was unpleasantly aware when he walked out with his wife, that he was escorting also a spectacular collection of the Bavarian crown jewels. He grew pale and wan. One day he showed up at the office of the British consul in Barcelona with a parcel containing a bloodstained shirt. He said that Lola had been after him with a carving knife, and he wondered what the consul thought he should do.

What he eventually did is not precisely known. Some say he drank himself silly in Lisbon and drowned there in a stupor; others that he lived for years and finally died in England.

Throughout her struggles for social justice in Bavaria, no people on earth had followed Lola's adventures more sympathetically than the Americans. She realized that a huge fortune was awaiting her across the sea among democrats who were dying to lay eyes on a genuine countess. She embarked therefore for the New World on the same ship as the great Hungarian revolutionist Lajos Kossuth, who ignored her throughout the voyage; but on their arrival in New York Harbor they were greeted by cheers from a double crowd of Americans which both accepted as their full due.

She is beautiful! She is irresistible! She is the embodiment of female grace! Such were the accolades that greeted Lola in America. Since she had been working hard at her dancing, she was applauded even for that. If, she told the press modestly, she were the woman she was credited or discredited with being, ". . . my admirers, I think, would be still more plentiful than they are." Americans at first seemed good-naturedly willing to admire Lola without discrediting her, and to accept her in her idealized version of herself.

But violence now had her firmly in grip. At the slightest criticism she would seek out newspapermen in their pubs and editorial cubbyholes and lay her whip across their backs. An unfavorable audience would bring her to the footlights, making faces and demanding that all Jesuits should stand up and be counted.

We see her crossing the Isthmus, "in the full zenith of her evil fame, bound for California . . . a good-looking bold woman with fine bad eyes and a determined bearing; dressed ostentatiously in perfect male attire, with shirt collar turned down over a lapelled coat, richly worked shirt front, black hat, French unmentionables, and natty polished boots with spurs. She carried in her hand a riding-whip. . . . An impertinent American . . . laid hold jestingly of the tails of her long coat; and, as a lesson, received a cut across his face that must have marked him for some days."

Lola's life in America has a mystic shimmer, like that of a soul in a poem, suspended between Heaven and Hell. She wished to be immaculate, invulnerable to odious vulgarity; she enforced this position with a whip. She wanted to be taken for the valuable minister of a king; but she put a tasteless travesty of this episode on the boards, entitled *Lola Montez in Bavaria*, and made box office out of it. She pretended to be a sublime dancer; but when dancing failed, she let people shake her hand for a dollar a shake.

In California she married a person named Hull. The Gold Rush was on, and with her husband Lola settled in Grass Valley close to the mines, in a home of sufficient modesty to seduce many a biographer into believing that she yearned for peace and rustic simplicity. But for furnishings she sent to Ludwig in Bavaria and made him pack up the contents of her palace; for a lap dog she tamed a grizzly bear and walked out with it, carrying a whip.

She danced the Spider Dance. She was a sensation among miners, who left gold on the ground to come and see this skirmish between Lola in tights and rubber spiders hidden in the folds of her short skirts which, with many a shudder and wriggle, she shook out of their hiding places and squashed beneath triumphant feet. "Look up a-ways, Lola!" they shouted, "there's another one further up!" This lascivious horror brought her the sort of criticism she abhorred but also courted.

No, Lola's cottage in Grass Valley was not a hideaway; it was more like an eagle's nest, a Berchtesgaden, where a polluted and tormented soul cleaves to the clean savagery of the wild, miles above persecutors, but not so far away that thunder and lightning may still not come crashing down from it.

Tawdry scandals multiplied. One day while on tour, she packed up Hull's effects and threw them out of the hotel window. Living alone in Grass Valley, a German gold-hunter, Baron Adler, was her lover for a while. One day he walked into the mountains, never to be heard from again. There is no reason to suppose that Lola had anything to do with his disappearance; but mindful of her behavior toward other lovers, there is no reason to suppose she had not.

Yet, to the present time, the people of California do not remember Lola Montez unkindly. They keep her house in Grass Valley and point it out to passing motorists. What do they remember? A daring girl who would ride miles into the hills, carrying necessities to miners? A lonely woman who would sit up all night with the sick children of pioneer wives? A creature of loveliest romance, appearing in the wilderness like a snow queen in her furs, driving her sled with dash? Her star shone black, and still she was incandescent.

The Wittelsbachs have a legend that when one of them is to die, an ancestor steps out of a picture and accosts that person. In 1854 this visitation came to Queen Thérèse. Shortly afterwards she died.

About this time Lola gathered together a theatrical troup and went on her last major dancing tour in Australia. This is an unnerving tale of fiery speeches from the footlights, of moonlight flits from creditors, of cross-buttocked critics. At the mining town of Ballarat, Lola was just about to lash down on a disobliging newspaperman, when she was interrupted by the man's wife, who seized the whip and beat Lola unconscious.

After that the company took ship for home. One quiet night a scream was heard from an upper deck, and Lola was found there in an apparent swoon. She said she had been talking to her manager (who was also her lover), but he was nowhere to be found. He had fallen, or thrown himself, or perhaps he was pushed, overboard.

Lola's life was now drawing toward an event that evaded the attention of her biographers until recent years, when it was brought to light by Helen Holdredge: nothing less than her marriage to the widowed ex-King Ludwig of Bavaria. The private papers of the Wittelsbach family contain a record of this marriage in 1857 when the king was seventy-one years old and Lola thirty-seven.

Ludwig was idyllically happy to have bound his "Woman of Spain" to him in a union which no mob could put asunder. But Lola was miserable. The Wittelsbach family seem to have been the chief culprits. They could not endure the presence of this adventuress in their midst, and they amused themselves by taunting and shaming her. They did so in the presence of Ludwig, who was by now very deaf, and so noticed nothing and did not defend his wife.

Throughout her life Lola had sustained her social position with romantic fictions about her origin. Now that she was confronted by the contempt of royal Wittelsbachs, she had no defense. She bore with it for several months and then left Ludwig.

She had marriage lines in her pocket that could have made her a fortune in America, for surely that entire country would have queued up to shake hands with a genuine queen. But she said nothing about them. For she carried with her Ludwig's last gift, syphilis, and when she returned to the United States, she had begun to die of it.

For a while, her beauty remained, and she tried to make her living by public lectures. Those who flocked to them to see the "Demosthenes in dimity" and learn such sultry practices as the *Art of Beauty* and *Gallantry* were disappointed. The famous enchantress seemed oddly puritanical. She had no patience with artifice. "There can be no *dew* on a painted lip," she admonished her audience; and "the bosom . . . is often transformed into a shape and transplanted to a place which deprives it of its original beauty." One reporter summed up Lola's beauty secret: ". . . jolly long walks in thick boots and snug wrappers for the benefit of the complexion."

Whips and pistols were no more in evidence. Perhaps, when

she became aware of her illness, it was through fear and defense-
lessness that she began to study the Bible. No wonder that she
attempted to use it at first as an aggressive weapon, waylaying
innocent mothers in parks, reading to them and warning them
against sin and the wages of it.

But there can be no doubt about the true conversion that took
place in Lola Montez toward the end of her life, or the depth of
her sincerity. What Bible story set a noose on her? Mary
Magdalene? Or Jesus, beside Himself with a whip?

She went to the miserable places where wayward girls and
fallen women were kept, made friends with them, talked to
them, helped them no doubt with money so long as her money
lasted. Yet those who had seen clearly her drabness when she
wore the costume of a queen were no more pleased with her
than before. They pointed gladly to her fall and did not know
that this fall was to be much further than any eye can gladly
follow.

Of course, there were always people who knew who Lola
Montez was, but the truth did not show up well against the
romantic glow of Lola's lies. Once, in Bavaria, in the days when
she spoke to everyone "openly, frankly, and without concealment," the Countess of Landsfeld had addressed a majestic letter
to the *Times* of London: "I was born at Seville in the year 1823;
my father was a Spanish officer in the service of Don Carlos; my
mother, a lady of Irish extraction, born at the Havannah, and
married to an Irish gentleman, which, I suppose, is the case of
my being called sometimes Irish, sometimes English, and Betty
Watson, and Mrs. James, etc.

"I beg leave to say that my name is Maria Dolores Porres
Montez, and I have never changed that name."

Two years before her death she was called to court in London
as witness in a case of debt. When asked her name, she was
heard to say, "Eliza Gilbert." Sensation in court! The newsmen
leapt to their duty. Before long, the world was in full possession
of a pitiful story.

She was Irish, of course; dull Irish at that. Her father was a
minor officer in the British East Indian Army; her mother had
been a Dublin milliner who, to lend herself style, claimed noble

Spanish blood. Lola, born two months after a hasty marriage, had been christened Maria Dolores Eliza Roseanna Gilbert.

Lieutenant Gilbert died in India. The mother then made an advantageous match with a man who became adjutant general of the forces in Bengal. Like other Anglo-Indian children, Lola was sent home to England to be educated as a young lady of honorable position. When she was in her teens, her mother came to take her back and the two of them went wild with shopping, so wild in fact that Lola became suspicious. She asked questions of a certain young Lieutenant James who had traveled from India with her mother. She learned that she had been promised in marriage to a very rich man of sixty, and that she was shopping for her trousseau. Lola then eloped with the lieutenant, and her mother returned furious to India, followed shortly after by the guilty young couple.

The marriage did not prosper. It cannot matter much whether Lieutenant James was as false a husband as she made him out to be—Lola was fond of playing the role of innocence betrayed. Her real betrayal was to come from an intolerable quarter; because when Lola left her husband and returned to England to try to make her living on the stage, her mother put on mourning dress; she had black-bordered cards printed which she sent to all her friends; she pronounced her daughter dead.

Lola cannot have been the only wild girl of the nineteenth century to be thrust out by a respectable family, but few could have been so cruelly cut off, deprived of identity, swatted, obliterated; none could have had Lola's furious *daimon*. Miss Gilbert was dead. But Lola Montez saw to it that the whole world knew she was alive, and perhaps she was playing all the while to a distant audience of one.

Once, the great Countess of Landsfeld might have longed to encounter the general's wife. But on the day that Lola was informed by her doctor that her mother was on her way to America to see her, she was destitute and friendless; she was fouled with a loathsome disease; paralysis had set in, and her face was twisted to one side. It was thus she had to endure the scrutiny of her mother.

She had not to endure it long. The lady, it seems, had come only to claim whatever property her daughter had to leave.

When she found there was none, she took the next ship to England, leaving ten dollars toward Lola's welfare.

Not long after, in a filthy room that had not even a bed but just a pile of rags in a corner and with a harridan to care for her, Lola Montez said to the Episcopal minister who had come to see her, "Tell me more, tell me more about my dear Savior." And then she died.

· III ·

THE GAUDY EMPIRE

Albert of Saxe-Coburg-Gotha, the obscure prince who had been found to marry Victoria of England, was a man of stern principles, and one of the sternest of them was that the morals of almost everyone he knew were obnoxious. He set himself, therefore, through remonstrance and personal example, to correct them. By his efforts royal family life in England achieved such a degree of dullness that it came to be regarded as a national asset, a status symbol that reflected well upon the morals of the entire nation. Competing royalties throughout Europe were obliged to respond to it by keeping their mistresses repressed and out of sight.

Of course, you cannot expect the French to imitate the English. For two decades there was time left in France for a vivid mistress to glow on the left arm of a sovereign, and the Second Empire flourished in the heart of the century like a game preserve for such exotic, near-extinct creatures.

Two women in particular, one good and one evil, made their bids for enormous power in the affections of Napoleon III.

1.

Miss Howard

❦
❦ ❦

The first Napoleon had a sense of family duty, and this extended to his in-laws. When he saw a vacant throne, he put a relative on it. When he saw a relative, he made a throne vacant. He got rid of two relatives with one throne by marrying his brother Louis to his step-daughter, Hortense, and setting them both up as monarchs of Holland. The pair cared nothing for each other and for Holland even less. When Napoleon fell, they separated, and Hortense took her younger son, Prince Louis-Napoleon, to live in exile in Germany.

Louis-Napoleon was probably not his father's son, but one does not know whom to blame him on: a Dutch general? a French count? or that historic progenitor of kings, the Unknown Equerry? The boy grew up with a shadowy father image at his luminous mother's little court-in-exile, where he must often have had his curls smoothed and his cheeks pinched by the mystic, Julie de Krüdener; perhaps he had listened aghast to her ghost stories. His mother called her son "gentle and obstinate." His tutor pronounced him backward. In fact, he was not stupid, but he had a slow-flowing, abstracted mind, and as soon as he was old enough he grew a mustache which he could twist when somebody asked him a sudden question. Even before this mustache had reached its man's estate, he joined the Carbonari, an Italian secret society dedicated to the harassment of the pope and the Austrians, who between them owned the best parts of Italy, and in the following years he proved himself to be a first-class harasser and intrigant; and in his spare time, a *charmeur* of women.

In 1832 death overtook *l'Aiglon*, Napoleon's son, and since other members of the Bonaparte clan were old or aimless, Prince

Louis-Napoleon found himself principal Bonapartist pretender to the throne of France against the incumbent, King Louis-Philippe of Orléans. He took up his chancy profession with complete faith that God was on his side and would lead him eventually to the Tuileries.

The French people, even to the present day, entertain an "ism" endemic and totemic to themselves: Bonapartism. It is the notion that a man in uniform can solve problems that a man in civilian clothes cannot solve: feed the poor, maintain the franc, balance the power, silence the priests, mend the streets, free the trade, and do it moreover in the face of ridicule and scurrilous argument. The leader must be honorable, benevolent, pious (within limits), and above all he must look glorious, preferably on horseback. He is a nation state in human form.

King Louis-Philippe reigned over a France that rattled with the impassioned voices of priests and pretenders, bankers and bourgeois, royalists, constitutionalists, autocrats, free thinkers, people who tilled and people who milled, those who liked Germany and those who did not. Subversive elements were the Red Republicans (if you can conceive of such a thing), and at the bottom of the barrel the humblest heart had found a voice which asked everyone please to move a little so that it could have air, and also light.

The king, well-meaning but incompetent, pursued a policy of "Nothing, nothing, and again nothing." Probably Napoleon the Great would not have understood what all these voices were saying. But in 1840, as a concession to popular sentiment, Louis-Philippe had caused the remains of the hero to be brought from St. Helena to the banks of the Seine, where they were entombed, and in the mass mind Bonaparte was deified. He was the Spirit of France which understands everything.

Now the young pretender was coming into the public eye, wearing the magical name and losing no time in making himself famous on horseback. In 1836 he had persuaded a colonel of the French garrison at Strasbourg to turn over his men to him, and he marched them up and down the streets to the tune of a military band and the rhythmic shouts of *"Vive l'empereur!"* Louis-Napoleon hoped that they would follow him all the way to Paris, but they did not. Instead, he was arrested. Louis-

Philippe treated him mercifully and released him into exile; acquiescently he traveled for a while in the United States before returning to England to plot another foray against the king.

In 1840 he organized an invasion of France with an army consisting of fifty-six Frenchmen and Poles, few of whom were told what they were doing. With them he proposed to land at Boulogne, take command of a French garrison, jump on a horse, and march grandly on Paris. The English Channel foiled this scheme as it has foiled others in the opposite direction. The members of the expeditionary force became violently seasick and were easily rounded up by the French coast guard. The best that came out of it was the story that on this adventure Louis-Napoleon had taken with him a tame eagle which was kept flapping around his head by a piece of bacon hidden in his hatband.

This time Louis-Philippe took strong measures against the pretender. He sentenced him to "perpetual imprisonment" in the fortress of Ham in marshy Picardy. But lest Louis-Napoleon become a martyr, "an eagle chained to a rock" like his sainted uncle, he was allowed every comfort: friends with whom to conspire, writing materials with which to bombard the press with propaganda, and a lovely laundress to wash his linen and make his bed and lie in it.

From imprisonment he wrote to a friend: "I shall leave Ham to go to the Tuileries or to the cemetery."

When he had been a prisoner for six years, the king sent some workmen to Ham to repair the leaks in the roof. From one of them Louis-Napoleon stole a suit of rough clothes, and having chopped off some of his mustache, he strolled away from Ham disguised as a workman with a plank on his shoulder. Two days later he was walking down Jermyn Street in London, to the alarm of passers-by who thought they were seeing his astral body.

After his *attentats* at Strasbourg and Boulogne the skeptical French had laughed at Louis-Napoleon, refusing to see in him a reincarnation of their hero. But after his escape from Ham there were many who did not laugh, because in prison he had written several books, one of which was *The Extinction of Pauperism*.

Louis-Napoleon had every reason to sympathize with paupers. He had by this time used up his own fortune on his pretensions

as well as on women, and he had run through that of several of
his friends and supporters. Had it not been for the perverse hospitality shown by the English to the nephew of their former
bitter enemy, he might have wondered where his next meal was
coming from. As it was, he was able to dine out on his reputation
as an arch-adventurer and on his subsidiary fame as an arch-
seducer. Smart Londoners were even willing to grant him royal
precedence into the dining room, if afterwards he would regale
them with tales of one fantastic sort or another. Louis-Napoleon
was not a good talker; he was by nature a silent man. One evening at Lady Blessington's, while he was being made to talk
for his supper, he fixed his eyes for stimulation on the most
beautiful girl in the room, a Miss Howard, and by the time he
had finished his story she had fallen madly in love with him.

Miss Howard was born Elizabeth Ann Haryett in 1823, the
granddaughter of the owner of the Castle Hotel in Brighton.
Her elder family members, having earned through hard work
enough money to retire respectably, did so, only to be defeated
by the younger generation which has little respect for respectability. In her mid-teens Elizabeth Ann, a splendid horsewoman,
made the acquaintance of a well-known jockey, Jem Mason,
and she soon ran off with him to London where she lived as his
mistress. Probably in order to spare her family embarrassment
she renamed herself Harriet Howard. It is suggestive of Miss
Howard's strong and obstinate character that even after Jem
Mason had ruined her and tired of her, he did not put her out
onto the streets but continued to support her. Of course, he must
have known that he would not have her on his charge for long,
for she was strikingly handsome with that chiseled style of
beauty greatly admired in England, especially by the horsy set.
In her case the stern features were softened slightly, and like
most girls who will one day be very fat, she was delightfully
delicate at waist, wrist, and ankle.

When she was eighteen, her protector was able to pass her
on to a certain Major Martyn who set her up splendidly in a
great house surrounded by servants and also horses. He placed
a large fortune at her disposal, cautiously giving the principal
into the hands of a man of business named Nathaniel Strode.
No fallen woman, enjoying the wages of sin, was ever so well
sheltered as Miss Howard.

And yet this daughter of an estimable family must have carried a secret weight of shame. She bore a son to Major Martyn, and rather than declare the baby a bastard, she presented it at church for baptism as the child of her own mother, and herself as its elder sister. Major Martyn, on the other hand, treated the arrival of a son with unalloyed delight and endowed the child richly, while showering even greater wealth upon his darling Harriet.

When her boy was four years old, Miss Howard attended a party at Lady Blessington's and found her eyes joined by those of Louis-Napoleon, a man to whom women hardly ever said no. Without apparent hesitation she abdicated her position as a leading "professional beauty," erased from her life her generous lover (whose feelings in the matter are not recorded by history), and taking his boy with her, moved into a modest establishment on Berkeley Street which she pretended was a lodging house—but which had one permanent, nonpaying guest, Louis-Napoleon. She also kept open house for his fellow conspirators who were constantly traveling to France on secret missions, bribing and subverting army officers and campaigning among the poor in an effort to impress them with Louis-Napoleon's opposition to poverty. Lack of money had slowed these efforts for a while, but now they were rolling in it. The pretender's "fair landlady" had placed her large fortune at his command.

Miss Howard was twenty-three when she fell in love with Louis-Napoleon and he was thirty-nine. She gave him the whole love of her heart. Nevertheless, she cannot be altogether absolved of ambitious pride and self-interest. After becoming the pretender's mistress, she allowed her small son to grow up in the snobbish belief that he was the son of a Bonaparte prince rather than of his own excellent father. For herself, she longed for respectability, so lightly thrown away. She was riding on a star which she hoped would bear her above the sneers of petty people to royal heights, and if that star was slow in rising, then she would pay for it to rise more quickly.

She was intelligent and energetic, dignified and discreet, the perfect companion for a politically ambitious man. In order to fit herself further for her future eminence she spent her mornings at studies she had neglected in her teens in favor of horsemanship. For history, she engaged as tutor the well-known author of *Eothen*, Alexander Kinglake. So well did her education progress that Louis-Napoleon decided to confer on her an honor: the laundress of Ham had borne him two sons, and he imported these boys from France and entrusted their upbringing to Miss Howard.. "Now I have three sons!" she cried in jubilation. "Thank you, dear," said Louis-Napoleon. "Say rather that *we* have three sons."

But even while this superb confidence man was misappropriating his mistress' fortune and her affections, the seeds of his destruction were being sown before his eyes. For Harriet's history teacher, Kinglake, fell in love with her and wished to seduce her. Upon her refusal the historian conceived such a jealous hatred for his rival that it festered in him for years. When, at the height of Louis-Napoleon's glory, Kinglake published his *History of the Invasion of the Crimea*, he depicted the pretender and his supporters—whom he must have met at Berkeley Street —as a parcel of brigands, who had cynically contrived the Crimean War in order to deflect attention from their misdeeds. This devastating viewpoint not only became the credo of Red Republicans in France, but it shook public opinion in England, preventing an *Entente Cordiale* between the two countries. For lack of England's support, the Second Empire was to face a bitter day and lose it; but that day might never have dared to dawn had it not been for the influential Kinglake's enmity. Miss Howard is inconspicuous in history, but she bent it in more ways than one.

Had Louis-Napoleon any love for his mistress? It was said of him that he loved all women too well to be faithful to one. Even while he lived with Miss Howard he was wooing a Miss Rowles, whose address was Camden Place, Chislehurst. It is possible also that during those slow years while he waited for his luck to change, he had spoken of it optimistically to Eugénie de Montijo, a young Spanish beauty, who had come husband-hunting in London and was the rage of the season. A letter exists which purports to have been written by Eugénie to the pretender before 1848: "You long for the possession of power, to become consul, president, possibly dictator. If, as you wish, you become emperor, the place for an empress must be kept vacant."

It is believed that Eugénie de Montijo, one of the few ladies known to have successfully staved off the amorous assaults of Louis-Napoleon, was assisted in writing this and other tantalizing letters by her mother's great friend Prosper Mérimée. The novelist had attached himself to the Montijo family while traveling in Spain in search of literary material; in fact it was Eugénie's mother who had told him the story of the Andalusian gypsy Carmen. Such an interest did he take in the social success of young Eugénie, so well did he direct her behavior and instruct her in the arts of coquetry, that quite a lot of the history of the Second Empire developed into a human tragicomedy constructed by Mérimée for his own entertainment. Certainly, it lacked only a Bizet to set it to music.

In 1848, the same year that saw Lola Montez driven from Bavaria, the various discontents of the European peoples gathered into widespread riots and revolutions. One of them toppled the throne of Louis-Philippe and obliged him to flee the Tuileries in a hackney cab. With astonishing speed a strong Bonapartist party formed in France, and Louis-Napoleon found himself elected by the people of Paris to represent them in the National Assembly. By the end of the year, against the ferocious opposition of motley partisan Frenchmen, he had become President of France. He took up his residence in the Élysée Palace, where Alexander I of Russia had once let himself out by a garden door to visit Madame de Krüdener. The prince-president also had a garden door giving onto the rue du Cirque, where Miss Howard was installed with their three boys and the prince-president's dog, which she had agreed to bring up also. There, as in London, she contrived discreet little dinner parties with important people for Louis-Napoleon, and presided over the smoke-filled rooms where his friends, supporters, campaigners, and conspirators gathered to map out his political strategy—which they did all the more comfortably, knowing that their hostess' checkbook was in the *secrétaire*.

The French people, seeing Miss Howard riding in the Bois with her three boys, viewed her on the whole with approval. "Who says our prince-president is a fool?" they asked. "He has brought back from England the best horses and the most beautiful woman!"

Harriet was behaving herself so far with superb good manners, keeping herself discreetly in the background. Yet her position was an uneasy one: while she received at the rue du Cirque the most influential people in France, the "best people" did not even recognize her existence. The Princess Mathilde, Louis-Napoleon's socially all-powerful cousin who was his official hostess, refused to have anything to do with the mistress. "She isn't even married!" said the princess, who suspected, probably rightly, that if Harriet had so far refused to establish her social position by a marriage of convenience, it was because she wished to be free to assume one day a supreme position as the official mistress of an emperor; nor did the Princess Mathilde put it beyond Miss Howard's ambition to bob up under the diadem of an empress.

For that was the great game on which all of the conspirators had staked their hopes and Harriet's fortune: the restoration of the Empire. As a prince-president, Louis-Napoleon was obliged to listen to parliamentary arguments, but not for a moment did he forget that a Bonapartist may rise above frail manmade constitutions. He therefore spent much of his presidential term campaigning heavily in the provinces, with Harriet still unobtrusive, but sticking close. Sometimes she followed him about in a cart dressed as a peasant. Once, on such a tour, apartments were requisitioned for her in a house which belonged to a gentleman of a puritanical turn of mind, and he was provoked to write a letter, inquiring nastily, "Have we returned to that epoch when the king's mistresses proclaimed the scandal of their lives throughout the cities of France . . . ?"

Indeed we had, but it was not well for this gentleman and others to become aware of it yet. The prince-president wrote a meek letter in reply: "I own that I am guilty in seeking in illegal bonds the affection which my heart requires. As, however, my position has hitherto prevented me from marrying, and as . . . in my native country, from which I was so long absent, I possess neither intimate friends nor ties of childhood, nor relatives to give me the joys of family life, I may well be forgiven, I think, for an affection which harms nobody, and which I do not seek to make conspicuous."

Now here was a truth that Harriet was beginning to perceive: he did not seek to make her conspicuous. In growing panic she abandoned her public pose as the prince-president's domestic pet and began to make demands. She insisted that apartments should be provided for her at Louis-Napoleon's residence at the Château of Saint-Cloud. She compelled *chefs de protocole* to break their heads in contriving for her a position of dignity at official functions; she devised a crest for her carriage, the head of a horse; she appeared in the prince-president's theater box drenched in diamonds. Louis-Napoleon was too honorable to reproach her: his term as president was drawing to a close, and any day now he might have to ask Harriet for her diamonds.

She had already made over to him by a false sale her rich Italian properties, on which he was able to raise mortgages. It is believed that in the year 1852 she placed at his disposal all of her liquid assets, including her jewels. Was it Harriet's money that paid for the drums in all the regiments in France to be slashed so that no call to arms could be sounded on the Second of December? That was the day when, by a *coup d'état*, Louis-Napoleon overthrew the Republican government. After a speech in which he gave to the country his golden promise, *"L'empire, c'est la paix!"* he was confirmed by plebiscite Napoleon III, Emperor of the French. The following day he was in the Tuileries, Miss Howard by his side, gloating over it, room by room.

For the next seventeen years he would not permit parliamentarians to be heard in France: this is the major offense for which history has condemned him. There was another offense, however, with which even his admirers have found reason to reproach him, and this lay in his secretive, inaccessible personality.

Portraits of Napoleon III show a little man with stumpy legs and a head too big for him. While his barrel chest provides ample space for a martial display of jewels and ribbons, these fail to lead the eye away from his short legs and ignoble paunch. With his spiked mustache and oiled hair he looks like a barber dressed up as a lion tamer. His eyes are disquieting: under the heavy lids they seem remote and passive. His contemporaries said that they were like dead water, and they called him "the imperial sphinx." A courtier wrote of him: "His suave and deep smile, his vague and veiled look, indicate a man who would rather talk with himself than with those around him. He remains days without speaking . . . his soul, like his face, is of marble."

This is too harsh, for Napoleon was a gentle, courteous man who never maliciously hurt anyone, but he was a born conspirator, and deception was so built into his being that one might even call him honestly deceptive. No sooner had he become emperor, and even while his "dear and faithful Harriet" was no doubt mourning over her account books at the rue du Cirque, Napoleon planned against her a monstrous deception. He sent a delegate to the Countess de Montijo, offering the position of official imperial mistress to her daughter Eugénie. The countess declined the offer.

Eugénie had extended her husband-hunt to Paris, traveling with an expeditionary force which, besides her exceedingly shrewd mother, consisted of Prosper Mérimée, and a relative-by-marriage who was a brother of the great Spanish Duke of Alba. Despite the presence of this nobleman, the Montijo ladies were regarded in the most elegant French society as little better than adventuresses. Eugénie's grandfather had been only a Scotch wine merchant, and her mother was rumored to have personally served wine in the back room of his shop before capturing, probably in his cups, the Count de Montijo, a grandee of Spain, and marrying him.

Eugénie was exquisite, with her Spaniard's antique profile and her Scotchwoman's blue eyes and red-gold hair. She had spent her teens dashing about the streets of Madrid on half-wild Andalusian mares, and the figure she cut riding in the woods at Compiègne, Napoleon's country seat, was such as to make the emperor's dead-water eyes light up like magic lanterns. Her resistance to his tender siege was the first defeat he had sustained since becoming emperor. He could hardly believe such bad luck. His passions were kept carefully on the boil by Eugénie's accomplished coquetry, directed from the wings by Prosper Mérimée, her mother, and the Duke of Alba's brother.

"What is the road to your heart?" the harrowed monarch entreated Eugénie, and she replied, "Through the chapel, Sire."

But it was desirable for the Emperor of the French to lead through the chapel a royal princess who would win for his dynasty the recognition of other royal courts. Unhappily, just as it is hard to get recognition without a princess, it is hard to get a princess without recognition. At the very idea of marrying the upstart emperor, Carola Wasa of Sweden burst into tears. His preposterous appeal for a Hohenzollern princess was not even communicated to the princess in question. A niece of Queen Victoria turned him down. He was denied even by ladies a certain deputy described as "scrofulous German princesses with feet as big as my own."

The humiliating rejections multiplied. Unexpectedly, the emperor told his ambassadors to break off all negotiations. It had occurred to him, with sudden delight, that if his dynasty was to get quickly under way, what he needed was not a princess but an empress; and that he could make an empress out of anyone he chose.

He wooed Mademoiselle de Montijo on damp mornings in the woods. He gave her a horse, which she hated. He gave her a jewel of emeralds shaped like a leaf with diamond dewdrops, which she loved. One day he made a chain of flowers and put it on her head, saying, ". . . while waiting for the crown."

The news of these enchanting incidents charmed almost no one in Europe. They aroused chagrin and animosity among hostesses who had closed their doors to the Montijo ladies; among crowned heads who, having refused Napoleon their own sisters, were now faced with having to address this random Spaniard as *ma soeur;* and among the regiments of Napoleon's feminine admirers, one of whom wailed, "Had I resisted Bonaparte, I had been Empress of France!" Princess Mathilde is said to have begged him on her knees, with tears, to desist from his wooing of Eugénie. Most serious of all were the mutterings from the multitudes of France who, having elected a *parvenu* emperor to the throne, were furious that he now proposed to give them a *parvenue* empress.

Among the letters that went like jumping mice from Paris carrying the news of the imperial courtship across the Continent, there was one that sounded a dubious note: ". . . His repugnance to marriage up to now has been only too well proved, and certain old English chains, which are still very near, and which are the terror of those who love him, may restrain him."

Yes, all the outrage, the envy, the devastated hopes in Europe would have taken small room against those which now crowded into the heart of the lady they called Miss Howard. Napoleon had not of course deprived himself of Harriet's love for Eugénie's sake, any more than he had deprived himself of any other love for Harriet's. He was too honest a deceiver for that. He had not even reproved Harriet, when in her anxiety and panic she had crashed a ball at the Tuileries to which she had not been invited.

He had spent tender nights with her, had soothed her fears and kissed her tears away; but now she was beginning to bore him with her accusations of false faith and broken promises. She wrote to a friend: "His Majesty was here last night offering to pay me off; yes, an earldom in my own right, a castle, and a decent French husband into the bargain. . . . Oh! the pity of it all! I could put up with a dose of laudanum. . . . The Lord Almighty spent two hours arguing with me. . . . Later he fell asleep on the crimson sofa and snored, while I wept."

Harriet had been prepared to accept equably her lover's marriage to a royal bride, especially if it left her own position as his Egeria intact; but to be thrust aside, cheated of a crown by a woman whose grandfather was as plebeian as her own was intolerable. Furious at the waste of her life, she lost her head and began to make a scandal. She had secrets locked away in her bosom and documents to match them in her *secrétaire*. A detective records: "It was necessary to give her 150,000 francs to keep her quiet." This sum may actually have been not hush money, but an installment of Napoleon's huge debt to his mistress, the existence of which was not known to everybody; especially as the emperor, in order to explain away money payments to Harriet, used to refer to her as a dear relation of his, "much impoverished."

Napoleon was not niggardly, especially to women he had loved, and he was to recompense Miss Howard, not only with the return of her real estate, but with hard cash equivalent to four million dollars. There was one loss in her life, though, that he could not fulfill, and he was aware of the danger she presented. In January, 1853, he paid her a visit. Gently and persuasively he explained to her that a difficulty had arisen. He was being blackmailed by scoundrels in England, and the honor of the Second Empire was in jeopardy. Only his dear and faithful Harriet was sufficiently in his confidence to be entrusted with the handling of this delicate matter. Would she therefore undertake on his behalf a secret mission to England?

Overjoyed that she was not to be cast out of his life and that he needed her still, Harriet said that she would. She set out by coach for Le Havre, where she intended to cross the channel by the Southampton packet.

But as we know the English Channel was an enemy of Napoleon III. For a second time rough weather upset his well-laid schemes. The packet did not sail, and Miss Howard, after spending the night at an inn at Le Havre, opened her newspaper on the morning of January 23 to read: "His Majesty the Emperor yesterday announced to a state gathering in the throne room at midday his engagement to Mademoiselle de Montijo y Kirkpatrick. . . ." In a sick rage Harriet sprang into her traveling carriage and sped back to Paris. Arriving at the rue du Cirque, she found her house in a shambles, the servants fled, her *secrétaire* rifled, her cabinets burst open, her dresses, books, music, strewn upon the floor. No valuables were missing, but every shred of paper from which could have been gleaned the history of her liaison with Napoleon, his love promises, his political secrets, his paid bills, had vanished.

And so, on that January day when Eugénie put on a string of wondrous pearls and went off to be married at Notre Dame, Miss Howard was huddled in the rue du Cirque, perhaps too heartbroken to reflect that pearls at weddings stand for future tears.

Thanks to the ministrations of her man of business, Nathaniel Strode, and to Napoleon's financial honesty, her fortune was built up again. She became the owner of the Château de Beauregard, near Paris, and she was permitted by the emperor to use the title of Countess of Beauregard. For a while she even had the happiness of receiving her lover back into her arms, especially on those occasions when Eugénie locked him out of her bedroom. The emperor used to start out for Beauregard in his coach, dressed in martial splendor; but on the way he would take off his star-studded coat and don a civilian jacket over his imperial trousers, so that by the time he greeted Harriet, at least the upper half of him was a plain prince-president, just as in the heyday of their love.

In the course of time these visits ceased, and Harriet was left to her own devices. The beauty of her face endured, but she became very fat. She married an Englishman of good family who, while spending her money on his stables, despised her and refused to support her social position. She was cruelly deprived of her two adopted sons whom she had raised and loved as her own, because their mother, the laundress of Ham, had followed Napoleon's advice and married a decent Frenchman, and she desired to complete their upbringing herself. Harriet's own son, Martin, whom throughout his life she had deceived about his parentage, shamed her horribly when on his twenty-first birthday before the assembled guests he spoke up: "Now that I'm grown, Mother, won't you tell me who my father was?" The poor lady slapped his face.

Her faults were those of snobbish pride, her foolishness no worse than that of other women who have loved adventurers. Apart from these, she was good-hearted, generous, and charitable. She never regained respectability but when she died, large numbers of the poor followed her funeral.

Her will provided a large sum of money to found a refuge in England for young girls who had been seduced away from their homes.

2.

The Gaudy Ladies

Now Eugénie sat at the top of her times, crowned with Josephine's diamond-and-sapphire coronet, and the Sacred Talisman of Charlemagne was on her breast. The French people were stunned when she refused a valuable jewel voted her by the City of Paris as a wedding gift on the grounds that the money was needed by the poor; they looked again at "the Spanish woman." They saw a lady of exquisite posture with the curved mouth of a coquette and the eyes of a *pietà* downswept in dolorous sensitivity; yet the boldly modeled brow gave her a look of vigor. Soon the disaffected ladies who had vowed they would never come to the Tuileries, never bend the knee to Eugénie, drifted back to court if only to see what she was wearing.

The royalties of Europe were not so easily beguiled. Queen Victoria and Prince Albert behaved like anyone who acquires

questionable neighbors: they ignored them. Tsar Nicholas of
Russia, obliged to address Napoleon, chose to call him *Monsieur
et bon ami* instead of *Monsieur mon frère*, the prescribed
usage among sovereigns. It was only when the valorous deeds
of French soldiers in the Crimean War had made the Second
Empire the foremost military power in Europe that Victoria
reluctantly invited Napoleon and Eugénie on a state visit.

Eugénie was in a tizzy about this event. A minister was sent
to England in advance, ostensibly to talk about politics, but in
reality to spy out whether all points of etiquette and protocol
were going to be observed. The imperial couple would have
dined badly at Windsor off silver plate when all the world
knew that gold plate was put before really important guests.
Satisfied as well as may be, the emperor dressed up like the
aurora borealis in a general's uniform, and Eugénie put on a
fright of a dress made out of yards of Scotch tartan, a stuff
much fancied by the Queen of England who used to cover her
furniture with it; they crossed the Channel, landing at Dover.

To their relief, Prince Albert met them at the pier. The towns
on the road to Windsor were decorated with bunting. Crowds
had gathered, cheers were heard. At Windsor town the shops
were closed for the day. Inside the ancient walls, royal Victoria
was waiting, and this was the moment, or never, that Eugénie
would learn whether she was a *parvenue* or an empress.

The Queen of England was captured at once by Eugénie's air
of deferential dignity. These two became bosom friends for life.
What is even more dumbfounding, Albert the Good took a liking
to Napoleon the Imperfect. They used to sing duets together.
Albert's confidant, Baron Stockmar, summed up the impression
Napoleon had made in the true spirit of English Victorianism:
"Whatever his sins against morality have been till now, the
reception he has met with will for his whole life prevent him
from sinning against England."

In 1857 Eugénie gave birth to the prince imperial, and the
star of empire rose in glory to remain overhead with hardly a
wobble for years. Napoleon's immense mustache and goatee,
which resembled an imperial eagle affixed to the front of his
face, was widely copied by men of taste, including Buffalo Bill.
He pronounced himself for "material order," and grasping that
exuberant spending was the next best thing to it, he instructed

Eugénie to be extravagant. She threw herself into this sweet travail with such style and flair that there was no feminine eye in the world that did not smile or frown on her. Everything she did to herself was imitated. To this day we wear her famous hairdo. She fell in love with crinolines, and across the face of the earth this fashion spread like spotted fever. At first the crinolines were made of horsehair, which prickled and wilted; cane was tried next, but it proved to be bumpy. Wire hoops netted with steel coils were introduced, and women fainted and labored with their weight. Whalebone might have saved the situation, but it kept snapping, and as for rubber tubes inflated with air, a strong wind could blow the whole contraption, lady and all, away. It is hard to see why, but once Eugénie said to Napoleon, "I don't know what I ever did without my cage."

Neither did the silk factories of Lyons know what they ever had done without Eugénie's cage. As it was, they buzzed, and so did factories which made immense pieces of furniture for ladies to sit on or gargantuan trunks for ladies who traveled. There was a building boom as houses were raised with rooms big enough for more than three ladies to congregate.

Money flowed into the chests of provincial lacemakers and embroiderers; jewelers and hairdressers became great men; Eugénie's parfumeur, Guerlain, and her dress designer, Worth, established their own dynasties; and all the genius of the French people for inventing peerless superfluities flourished as it had not done since the day Marie Antoinette's head fell off. The stock market boomed, huge fortunes were scattered to the winds and made again. It was the fashion.

Napoleon poured his phantom gold into the very stones of Paris, made the city a lacework of *étoiles* whose rays were bowered boulevards so wide that they are still almost wide enough. A small boy, Lord Frederic Hamilton, stood and watched the magnificent equipage of the emperor and empress go by, and he stared with schoolboy awe at the endless perspective of gaslit arcades on the rue de Rivoli; and he reflected how strange it was that his mother remembered this city as a place of mud.

It was a gaudy empire, the harridan grandmother of *la belle époque*. Music played without cease, carriages rolled day and night carrying gem-laden guests from matinée to fête to theater.

Fantastic masquerades were popular as they offered a chance to ladies to take off their corsets and crinolines and clothe themselves sensibly. At a famous ball in 1860 one lady was the Goddess of Fire in her resplendent rubies. Another was the diamond-studded Sky. On one costume, "Huge emeralds fastened ostrich-feathers to a flame-colored mantle with a deep gold border. Its wearer's headdress was a double diadem consisting of a gold rim, from each curve of which hung a pear-shaped diamond, and a superimposed Greek diadem, studded with gems. She had a necklace composed of stones as large as hazel nuts and a second one of emeralds from which was suspended a diamond the size of a pigeon's egg. Her slippers were embroidered with precious stones, and in her hand she carried a gold scepter at the extremity of which shone the magic carbuncle of the Good Fairy."

Complaints have been raised that all this splendor failed to call forth splendid talents, and this is true. Victor Hugo, Napoleon's enemy, lived in exile on the Island of Guernsey, weaving his opposition into angry verse. Fortunately, lesser Frenchmen are good enough. Flaubert, Dumas *père* and *fils*, Théophile Gautier, Alfred de Musset, and the brothers Goncourt attended the salon of the intelligent Princess Mathilde; and perhaps in times of affluence and social change, these lighter spirits speak most eloquently to great masses. Because the court honored men of letters, an intellectual aristocracy was formed in France under the Gaudy Empire such as Voltaire never knew.

Now that the imperial pair had received the Windsor stamp of approval, all of royal Europe converged on Paris. Everybody came who owned a pair of dancing slippers; even sober citizens were attracted by the Great Exhibitions of science and art. The daughters of joy, whose saint was Napoleon, came from everywhere and nowhere to embellish the boulevards and sweep the streets. As they rose in the world, they became by curious geometry *les horizontales*, and it was the fashion for men-about-town to squander huge fortunes on them. These mistresses "drove their horses more gently than their lovers." They owned equipages that matched those of the empress. Their jewels in a theater box outshone the glare of the stage, and they lived in palaces and became collectors of exquisite objects of art. Baron Rothschild, calling on one of them, said, "My dear, I feel as if I have come from a garret."

Many of the *horizontales* were actresses, and the stage was a place of exhibition for their wit as well as for their bodies. Offenbach wrote his enchanting music for them, Dumas *fils* and Ludovic Halévy wrote the books. But no script was so sacred that a girl of devastating charm and wit might not turn to the audience and deliver her own lines on life and love. So we shall never see these operettas as Offenbach saw them, and perhaps that is why we rarely see them.

Each of the *horizontales* had her *cachet* that identified her for all Christendom and Araby. Hortense Schneider lived on the avenue de l'Impératrice, which was called *le passage des princes* because it was; and also because Madame Schneider had earned for herself the same soubriquet. One of her ardent admirers was the Khedive of Egypt, Ismail. Once, pining in Vichy for her company, he despatched a secretary to summon her at once. This woolly-headed individual delivered the message instead to a person with whom the Khedive did heavy business in France: Schneider, the famous gunmaker.

Mr. Schneider made haste to Vichy and presented himself at the Khedive's palace. He was flattered to be shown to rooms of silken luxury, crammed with flowers, swimming in rich perfume. In the pearly bathroom he found that a warm bath was waiting to refresh him after his dusty journey, and he was blissfully immersed in delicious waters when the door opened to admit the head of the Khedive wearing a graceful smile—that is, until he laid eyes on his cannon-founder.

Thérèse Lachmann played with francs like a child playing with sand. Once an impecunious admirer pursued her for months, passionately. At length she instructed him to bring her ten thousand francs in small notes. "We'll waste them together," she promised him. He somehow acquired the necessary investment and arrived at Thérèse's boudoir to find her gracefully arranged upon a couch beside which a marble table had been placed. On this altar she piled the crumpled notes and set a match to them. "I promise that your flame shall be allowed to burn as long as the notes," she told him. In very short order, money and passion were consumed, and she looked ironically at her lover. To her astonishment his face wore the same expression. "They were counterfeit," he said.

Anna Deslions played the slut in old slippers and drank wine out of a common bottle. But in her gambling salon there was an enormous Chinese basin which she kept filled with gold and banknotes for the convenience of her guests.

The sisters Drake had an apartment designed in a maze tricked out like a fairy grotto, and here several visitors could be entertained at once and never meet.

Léonide Leblanc bestowed most of her attention on Louis-Philippe's heir, the Duc d'Aumale, who had stepped into Napoleon's old shoes as chief pretender to the throne. She had a wax figure of her lover made, which she placed at a desk in a quiet room, poring over a volume by lamplight. On receiving other guests, she would tiptoe to this door with her finger to her lips and open it stealthily, just enough to afford her guest a glimpse of the great man wrapt in an aura of destiny. Then, as silently, she would close the door, and bear him off to the jollier quarters of her palace.

The staircases of these *horizontales* rang with the footsteps of every great man of affairs of the empire, including those of Napoleon himself. "All women have equal worth in love," he proclaimed, "no matter what their social position. A garden which no one is allowed to enter may contain delicious fruit which only the proprietor may taste; but why should not a garden open to all also contain such delicious fruit?"

Men of letters made a great fuss over the girls and developed a fad for lamenting their ambiguous lot. Blanche d'Antigny was the model for Zola's *Nana*. Esther Guimond, an extremely intelligent and witty woman, insisted that she, and not Marie Duplessis, was the original *Dame aux Camélias*. Ill of cancer, from which she died, she came out of an agony to find Dumas *fils* sitting by her bedside. He said, "Good! Now I have my fifth act!"

Alas, it is doleful to look at the photographs of these glittering ladies of the Second Empire and to realize that they were admired less for fairness of feature than for opulence of form.

At first there was no communication whatsoever between the

demimondaines and ladies of rank. But as Eugénie's reign of
fashion took hold urgent messages sped between the two classes
of women, carried by their common dressmakers. Soon the girls
took to riding in the Bois. Then Esther Guimond took a seat on
the grandstand at the races, saying, "If I do not belong to the
social set of the ladies present, I do to that of the men."

In turn the *grandes dames* invaded the haunts of the *horizontales*. Princess Metternich, Eugénie's daring friend, was the
first lady of comparative virtue to enter a public restaurant
and dine there. Now the great chefs grew proud. Not only did
their art enhance Paris, but as they were lured abroad by
fabulous salaries mealtimes improved all over Europe.

The times were leveling the classes, but still quaint lines were
drawn. No lady would have permitted a gentleman to pay for her
meal in a café. Not one of them, no matter how long her list of
lovers, would have flaunted presents from them of more than
trifling worth.

It was not fair to say, as old-fashioned royalists did, that
Napoleon and Eugénie kept no etiquette at their court. Like
parvenus everywhere, they were punctilious in such matters.
Eugénie is said to have engaged the great *tragédienne* Rachel
to teach her how to bow; and Prosper Mérimée proved to be as
excellent a director for an empress as he had been for an adventuress.

Still, manners at court were not so stately that there was no
leeway for a duchess to throw up her skirts and perform the
cancan, or for a gentleman to make breadballs at lunchtime
and throw them into the open mouth of the little prince imperial,
or for the entire court to engage in acrobatic games which involved turning the ladies upside down. No doubt Napoleon's
personal peculiarities contributed to the relaxed atmosphere.
It was noted that however stagnant his eyes were on ordinary
occasions, such as when he listened to the good advice of
ministers, at the sight of a pretty woman "he trembled and his
eyes lit with an immediate flame." Women delighted to provoke
this miracle. "It is very amusing," wrote the Marquise de Taisey-
Chatenoy, "to watch the evolutions of the great coquettes. One
evening, Mesdames de Neuvied and de Saint-Brieux changed
their places more than ten times . . . crossing the drawing

room's length and width *en biais*, in order to pass before the emperor and receive a compliment from him."

Napoleon said: "Usually it is the man who attacks. As for me, I defend myself, and I often capitulate."

Once he attacked. He was just taking a seat on the sofa in a dimly lighted room when his hand fell on a lacy frock covering a shapely silken leg, and he pinched it. But it was the Bishop of Nancy, who rose up in a howling rage.

An observant gentleman of those times said that there were but two ladies at court to whom the emperor had not capitulated, and he wasn't quite sure about those. The Marquise de Taisey-Chatenoy has kindly left for our instruction a record of the amorous methods of this monarch, whose quest for "the affection which my heart requires" was advanced by so many. She relates in the first person an adventure of an extremely close friend, whom she calls Paulette. It took place shortly after the emperor had acquired for the enjoyment of his court at his country seat at Compiègne, "the famous *manège* of flying wooden horses," in other words, a merry-go-round.

"I got off at the first stop, terribly dizzy, and was directing my steps toward a bench . . . when I felt an arm seize me and support me: it was the emperor. 'Walk a little . . . it will do you good,' he said. I rose and took a few steps. Suddenly he put his arm around my waist, bent his head, and kissed my hair and my neck, and I heard him whispering into my ear: 'This evening.'

"He then offered me his hand and made me mount the famous sorrel horse with green velvet housings on which was embroidered the letter N. with the imperial crown.

"When I found myself in my room, I was happy. . . . The door suddenly opened, and my husband entered like the wind. I began to tremble, but I learned that he had just received the emperor's orders to leave at once in order to be present at a sitting of a Commission. He had hardly disappeared behind the door when my maid came to tell me that in the absence of my husband, I was to occupy a more comfortable room situated at the extreme end of the corridor: the blue room!

"The evening was long. The emperor did not speak to me at all. This neglect contrasted so strongly with the attentions he had displayed toward me a few hours before that I was terribly disappointed. Just before midnight, when he was about to retire, I felt he was looking at me. . . . I raised my eyes and found that I was not mistaken. He turned and went slowly out, his head inclined, and twisting his mustache.

"A few minutes later, I also left and went to my new room and inspected it. I wished, before the expected attack to re-connoitre its weak points, and to find those places through which the enemy might enter.

"I then undressed without looking at the horrible door, and shivering slightly dived into bed and disappeared under the coverlet. My maid put my things to order, blew out the lamp and covered the fire with ashes.

"A night light was placed on the mantelpiece. What was going to happen? Foolish question! I knew! Perhaps at the bottom of my heart, there was a slight feeling of satisfaction at the thought of the coming defeat. The weathercock turning on the Castle Tower broke in upon the profound quiet.

"I waited, but not for long. A slight noise came to my ears, and the door—that terrible door, opened softly. Silhouetted against the corridor lamp stood the emperor; but not the emperor with whom I was familiar. He had neither sceptre, nor crown, nor the mantle lined with ermine and embroidered with golden bees. He wore neither his general's uniform covered with orders, his sword and riding boots, nor his ceremonial costume with the great red ribband, knee breeches, silk stockings and buckled shoes.

"No, the emperor whom I beheld was stripped of all human pomp. He appeared as a simple—very simple—mortal.

"The clothes which hid the august form consisted of a mauve silk pyjama suit. On the left side there was a handkerchief in a pocket, and on the collar shone a bee embroidered in gold.

"Had his long mustache not been waxed, I could not have recognized him. He advanced with uneven steps because of the darkness. With one foot he pushed aside the armchair. I saw his shadow approaching my bed; it bent. I closed my eyes. My destiny was accomplished.

"The situation lasted but a short time. The emperor recovered his calm and majesty promptly. I looked at him from the corner of my eyes. His eyes were closed, and the ends of his mustache, now unwaxed, were hanging down limply. He was breathing heavily.

"The night light suddenly went out. 'Oh!' I exclaimed, vexed a little. 'Ah!' sighed the emperor. A moment later His Majesty rose and crossed the room, guiding his steps by means of the furniture. The door opened and closed and I found myself alone.

"My clock struck two. It had struck half past one a few moments after the door had opened for the first time. . . . half an hour was sufficient to make me an empress!"

To the humiliation of Paulette, her effects were removed from the blue room the next morning, and when the wooden horses turned again, the emperor helped someone else to mount the sorrel. Vengefully Paulette stole out at dead of night and—so she said—unloosed some screws, so that the next time that horse raced around it toppled and the lucky lady fell heavily to the ground, her crinoline over her head.

3.

The Countess Castiglione

Napoleon once told his cousin Mathilde that he had been faithful to Eugénie for six months after their marriage. In the years that followed, the empress' jealous tears fell heavier than imperial pearls. She did everything possible to correct him. She locked her bedroom door against him; she took bitter leaves of absence in Scotland and Biarritz; she railed at him. Her expostulations pierced the cracks in the walls of the old Tuileries, sped between lines of interested courtiers and into the history books. Oddly enough, dignified people of her time had no patience with Eugénie's lapses in self-control, which they attributed to her faulty pedigree. Napoleon, on the other hand, was much praised for his wise handling of domestic crises: he simply bowed his head and weathered the storm, murmuring now and then in his German accent, " 'Ugenie! . . . you know my affection! . . . 'Ugenie!"

In view of Eugénie's renowned virtue and her expressed dislike of the act of love, many people believed and still believe that the empress was sexually frigid and therefore partly to blame for her husband's libertinism. If so, the emperor did not complain of it: it was always sweet to come back to the empress, he told his cousin Mathilde.

Eugénie was certainly fastidious, perhaps sexually dormant, and her religious feelings prevented her from listening to would-be lovers. But she was an abundantly vigorous woman, and it is not surprising that she tried to find her life's meaning in affairs of state, in the grasping of political power. As one of Napoleon's chief advisers, she suffered the same exasperation as her colleagues on the Council of State. For the enigmatic emperor seemed to have no backbone, only obstinacy; no intentions, only plots; no plans, only impractical schemes. He went for long walks with his ministers, never addressing a word to them. He held significant interviews, stopwatch in hand. When in doubt, he was apt to consult not his ministers but fortune-tellers and mediums. Worst of all, when he had finally arrived, with Eugénie or some other adviser, at a sober decision of state, he was apt to reverse it after consultation with a companion of the night.

When Eugénie was old, she was to confess to a friend in veiled language her dread of these mortifying "influences by night."

In 1855 there came to the emperor from Italy the most dangerous influence of all in the person of Virginia Oldoïni, Countess de Castiglione, and she was sent to him as a present by the King of Sardinia's chief minister, Count Camillo Cavour.

Cavour! The name glows in the affairs of the Second Empire like a muffled lantern at a spot where devilish men meet. Yet he was but a plump little person who in Italy was engaged in the same task that occupied Bismarck in the north: he was trying to make some sort of logical unit out of his country, which was full of headless states preyed upon by brigands. Since his master, King Victor Emmanuel of Sardinia, was powerless, he was obliged to work with whatever unscrupulous means came to his hands.

In the eyes of Cavour and Victor Emmanuel the biggest brigand in Europe was Emperor Francis Joseph of Austria who owned Italy's rich northern provinces. To combat him military force was needed. Napoleon had it. The Countess Castiglione could get it.

The countess was a dreadful woman who wrings the heart. She was the daughter of a diplomat, who was probably not her father and had no interest in her, and of a sickly mother. She grew up friendless in a vast palazzo in Florence which belonged to her grandfather, the famous jurist, Lamporecchi. Once a young client of her grandfather had seized her affectionately in his arms and called her "the most ravishing little girl in the world." He was the Bonapartist pretender, Louis-Napoleon.

When she was five years old, a high chair was placed in the family box at the theater so that she could be made to sit there night after night, absorbing culture; but she slumped and dozed. When she was twelve and her great beauty was becoming famous, her mother put her on the marriage market. Suitors in number appeared at the palace gates. A young widower named Count Castiglione, visiting in London, confided to Napoleon's ambassador, Count Waleski, that he was looking for an English bride. Waleski said to him, "Go back to Florence, present yourself to the Marchese Oldoïni, using the name of your eminent friend, Cavour. Meet her daughter, marry her, and you will have the most beautiful wife in Europe."

At fourteen, Virginia was a bride. And since her husband was equerry and procurer for Victor Emmanuel, she was very soon a mistress. Count Cavour, who was Virginia's cousin and one of the few persons for whom she had the slightest admiration, also became her lover, and he quickly convinced himself that the beautiful girl's talents could be used in the highest service of her country. And so, for some years he instructed her in the game of political intrigue, and then, providing her with a wondrous wardrobe, he sent her to Paris, a feathered and be-jeweled arrow aimed at France. "Succeed, my cousin, by whatsoever means seem good to you, but succeed," he briefed her. To a colleague he wrote, "A beautiful countess has just been enrolled in the Italian diplomatic corps. I have invited her to flirt with the emperor, and I promised her that if she succeeds, I will get her brother the position of secretary to the embassy in St. Petersburg."

She was about twenty years old.

She began her role discreetly enough by paying calls on Princess Mathilde and Countess Waleska. As a noble Florentine she moved onto a ready road in Parisian society. Perhaps some advance press-agentry had been provided to announce her as "the most beautiful woman in Europe," but this was the title she insisted on; in fact she shortly promoted herself to "the most beautiful woman of the century."

Those portraits of Virginia that emphasize her long, slanted eyes and delicately classic features support the opinion of Count de Vieil-Castel that "it is impossible to behold a more seductive creature, more perfectly beautiful." But her photographs are curiously revealing of her flaws: a small mouth twisted with sulks and a stony glance. The women of the court were quick to sense her adamantine soul. "A myth cut out of pink marble," said Princess Metternich. Eugénie's secretary, Madame Carette, wrote, "Her beautiful face recalled to mind those divinities whom the ancients sought to appease by sacrifices. You can form some idea of this extraordinary person by imagining a most beautiful statue come to life."

In November, 1855, a ball was held at the Tuileries to which the countess came late. Such had been the general curiosity about her that upon her entrance the orchestra stopped playing and the dancing ceased. In all the excitement of silence she advanced and made her reverence to the imperial couple; then she retired to a prominent seat. Eugénie took a kindly step toward her, but she was intercepted by her husband who, with a rare piece of swift thinking, told a handy duke to dance with the empress, while he speedily advanced upon the Countess Castiglione and offered her his arm. It was noted that he executed the steps of the quadrille with more nimbleness than his short legs usually permitted him.

Every Monday when the various ministries held balls, it was the same story. One evening at Compiègne, while the artists of the Comédie Française were giving a command performance, Countess Castiglione excused herself on the plea of a headache. It was immediately evident that the stuffing had gone out of the emperor's evening: he looked distrait and kept pulling at his mustache. For almost one act he endured his bereavement, then in plain sight of everyone, he left the empress' side and disappeared for the rest of the evening. The next morning it was widely known that he had personally gone to relieve his anxiety concerning the beautiful Florentine's health.

The empress was alarmed. His ministers looked at him with eyes full of mute enquiry. Napoleon let down his heavy lids and played the imperial sphinx. All questions were answered very shortly when a costume ball was held at the foreign ministry and the countess attended, dressed arrogantly as the Queen of Hearts in a gown whose transparency was somewhat modified by decorative hearts, strategically placed. Nevertheless it was Eugénie who made that costume immortal with her famous quip: she fixed her eyes on one of the decorations and said, "You wear your heart rather low down, don't you?"

Bitter times were in store for the empress and for her court ladies as the new mistress consolidated her gains. Countess Castiglione was a woman utterly attached to her own image; she was possessed of a natural hatred for other women, and she wore on her face always her deep desire that they should die of jealousy when she passed by. When it became plain that she enjoyed the emperor's difficult confidence and her portrait was raised on the walls of his private apartments, Eugénie could not dismiss her from the court, but her ladies could and did refuse to serve her tea and cakes. The countess haughtily requested another lady who had been served to pass over her own.

The countess wrote, "My mother was stupid in chaining me to Castiglione. Had she brought me to France, no Spanish woman would have reigned there."

It became apparent, nevertheless, that she considered herself to have stepped into the empress' shoes. She devised for herself a magnificent headdress made out of feathers in the form of a crown. In defiance of Eugénie's prescription of the crinoline as correct court attire, she caused consternation by appearing on a grand occasion in a tight dress. It was observed that she never wore corsets; indeed, this proud, friendless, cold woman appeared gay only at masked balls and *tableaux vivants*, those favorite entertainments of the period at which actresses appeared quite naked and even ladies could participate very sparely attired. "She would be a model to Phidias and pose only in her beauty," wrote a somewhat disenchanted lord of Vieil-Castel. "She veils it only as much as is necessary to be admitted into a drawing room."

The fame of her beauty had by this time spread so far that wherever she went, people climbed on trees and carriages to catch sight of her. In England ladies and gentlemen of quality actually clambered onto the furniture the better to see her passing through a salon. She bore this attention with complete self-possession, stone cold. When artists besieged her, as they frequently did, she would throw back her laces, asking, "Do you wish to see my arm? My foot? My leg?" When Napoleon asked her how she could remain unmoved by such adulation, she coolly told him that if he had been accustomed from babyhood to being called God's most exquisite creation, he too would remain unmoved.

Her crowning triumph over Eugénie was the rape of the hairdo. In those days a woman's hair, which was her most glorious ornament, was never cut but was arranged in monumental shapes, and the competition was lively. On the occasion of a grand ball Eugénie announced to her ladies that she had instructed Monsieur LeRoy, her personal hairdresser, to create for her a coiffure such as had never been seen before in France.

Countess Castiglione summoned LeRoy and informed him that she wanted the same coiffure. The hairdresser protested painfully, but in the end he had no chance against the demand of the favorite. Besides, she assured him that she would not dream of wearing it on the same evening as Eugénie, but that afterwards she desired to be the first to flatter the empress by imitation. He therefore delivered to her house the model, brilliant, light, superb.

On the night of the ball, Eugénie radiantly introduced her secret fashion to the world; only to be blasted by the sight of the younger, lovelier Madame de Castiglione wearing on her head exactly the same escalade of hair, feathers, and jewels. Of course, the expressions on the faces of the two ladies were absolutely different.

LeRoy was dismissed. He went into a state of depression over the affair, and he is said to have died of it. But perhaps the most touching victim of these years was another Countess Castiglione, a Swiss. "Tell them," she would say to the lackey announcing her name at the Tuileries, "that it is the ugly one."

"No one could possibly confuse her with me," hissed Countess Number One, "but her toilettes on the rue de la Paix are charged to my account."

With all of her mischief the countess by no means neglected her duties as the agent of Cavour. She had established contacts with all the foreign ministries, and by day she was to be seen driving from one to another carrying a portfolio bursting with documents. She was in correspondence with many of the leading princes and governing bodies in Europe. And since she was not a woman to play only the middle when two ends could be played against it, she was secretly intriguing with the Duc d'Aumale, the Orléanist pretender, and also with the arch-Republican, Napoleon's sworn enemy Thiers. Little she cared how closely Napoleon's police followed her about by day, so long as she had complete influence over their master by night.

As for Napoleon, he was in Paradise, having found means to indulge in that form of politics dearest to his heart: intrigue. A line of secret communication was established between France and Italy which dodged the tiresome advice of ministers and chattering ambassadors. Straight from Napoleon's pillow the countess would drive to the border, and there in the darkness meet her husband, coming from Cavour. Whispered secrets were then exchanged, promises made, plots put on to boil. Well might Napoleon tell the Prussian ambassador, "Pay no attention to the words of my ministers. I, and I alone, know the policy of France."

His ministers sought to fight fire with fire. They secured the services of an excellent *horizontale* named Marguerite Berranger, a woman of low habits who had once been a circus rider. They divined that Napoleon would not be able to resist a woman who could turn somersaults on a horse; indeed, she is said to have made an excellent first impression by entering his presence walking on her hands. Now the complete emperor was satisfied: he had one mistress who was political, and another who was horsy. The countess nibbled her little lips and told everyone that Eugénie had visited the circus rider in person and offered to buy her husband back.

In 1858, with none of his ministers having an inkling of what he was about, Napoleon met Cavour in secret at Plombières. Here he placed his resources at the Italian's disposal. The man who had said, *"l'empire, c'est la paix,"* was committed to a war with Austria that was none of his business.

When the Countess Castiglione informed him that Emperor Francis Joseph of Austria had sent his troops across the border, the emperor marched his men into Italy. After a brilliant series of victories and with the war half won, he stopped in his tracks, quickly signed a peace with Francis Joseph, and marched them back to France.

Historians may tussle over the various reasons why Napoleon failed to carry this war through to the end. We are concerned only with the designs upon history's skin, and it is enchanting to observe that while it was Countess Castiglione who had ordered him into Italy, it was Eugénie who ordered him to come back. The empress had been left in Paris as regent, and she had become alarmed at Bismarck's mustering of Prussian troops on her unprotected eastern border. Therefore she had called Napoleon home, and courteous as always, he had come. This uxorious behavior won him the everlasting animosity of Victor Emmanuel, the "First King of Italy," who, upon watching his savior depart, shouted after him, "Good riddance!"

The countess fulminated. She had chased Napoleon up the *massif* of fortune and he had failed to plant his flag upon the summit. She was only twenty-two, and yet this was the climactic failure of her life which she was never able to repair and from which she never recovered. "I would have made him a conqueror," she wrote, "in word, in deed, in private and in public . . . but my Napoleon did not dare, and I abandoned him and his concerns."

She did not precisely abandon him. The truth was she was beginning to get on Napoleon's nerves. He had recently complained to Princess Mathilde: "I am persecuted by three women. I have the blonde on the ground floor of whom I am trying my best to get rid (this was Madame de la Bédoyère). Then I have the lady on the first floor (Countess Castiglione), who is very beautiful but bores me to death, and there still remains the blonde on the second floor (Countess Waleska), who follows me everywhere."

His police were forever warning him of the countess' habit of worshiping two-faced gods; strange characters with false-looking whiskers were continually seen going up and down her staircase. One night, shortly after the Italian campaign, Napoleon, paid what might have been his last amorous call upon the countess, taking with him as usual his aide, General Fleury, and a secret policeman. As they entered her establishment, the policeman whispered to the emperor, "Don't forget we are in the house of an Italian." Softly they ascended the stairs. A door opened, and Napoleon and Fleury were admitted into the countess' drawing room by a maidservant. She did not see the policeman who had secreted himself on the landing.

The maidservant returned to the landing, leaned over the banister and clapped her hands three times. A man appeared, running lightly up the stairs. He approached the drawing-room door, but before he could turn the handle, he fell dead. The policeman had knifed him from behind.

The maidservant screamed, Fleury came dashing out, seized her and shut her in a cupboard, while the policeman searched the dead man, finding on him a revolver and a poisoned stiletto. Then they dragged the body out of sight. General Fleury had the delicate task of interrupting Napoleon's private communion with the countess and bearing him safely home.

Under grave suspicion of having been party to an attempt upon the emperor's life, the countess was now banished from France, and Eugénie was able to seize a hatchet and cut down her odious portrait from her husband's walls. In justice it must be said that the adventure, with its concealed body and vanished witness, might easily have been a police conspiracy designed to rid themselves of the tiresome countess. If so, their trouble went for nothing. A woman in possession of documents of state need not be banished if she does not please. Like Miss Howard, the countess had documents, and unlike Miss Howard she knew where to hide them.

However, for a little time Countess Castiglione chose to remain absent from Paris. She treated herself to a holiday, taking a house on a lonely hilltop near Turin where she lived a life of studied isolation, receiving few visitors, and when she did, stifling their conversational attempts by cold silence or by muffled monosyllables. With her lived her small son who, unaccountably, is credited to her husband, Count Castiglione.

A French diplomat, Henri d'Ideville, drawn by idle curiosity, sought and was granted an interview with the countess. He found her in the company of her child and servant, and she was exactly as gossip had led him to expect: a haughty, self-absorbed woman, with the appearance of a goddess, but one from whom the divine spark was absent. Her great beauty evoked in him no flicker of desire. Still, he was drawn to visit her again, and then again.

One day he found her alone. Her heart opened, she began to talk, to confide, even to entertain. She revealed herself, according to d'Ideville, as a warm, generous person, far superior intellectually to the majority of her sex, possessing originality and also nobility of mind.

Very likely they became lovers. D'Ideville found in her exclusiveness and deliberate hauteur, a riddle that engrossed him, and he begged her for an explanation. She replied out of the glooms of her failure to hold Napoleon: "I scarcely began my life, when my role was ended."

On another occasion she exposed the deep layers of her narcissism. She said that the Eternal Father Himself had not known the thing he had created when He brought her into the world. He had molded and fashioned her until, when she was complete, He lost His head before His own marvelous work, and He left her in a corner, instead of putting her in her true place.

There may be still another answer to the countess' riddle. In the course of her intrigues with the Duc d'Aumale she made the acquaintance of one of his secretaries, a young man named Estancelin, and she fell in love with him. But Estancelin astutely assessed her driving, dominant nature, and he steeled himself against her. Though he became her lover—and in fact for forty-five years he was to be her only loyal, faithful friend—with regard to his own career and aims, which were modest and honorable, he did not for a moment allow her to become an "influence by night." She wrote to him, "The woman who could influence you has yet to be born."

Much of what we know about the Countess Castiglione is gleaned from the incessant letters with which she bombarded

Estancelin until her life ended. One of them, written in old age, reads: "What I wanted was a serious, deep, lasting bond, to be handed down by us to our descendants, to be hidden under no iron mask, without fear, shame, or scruples: no half-love, no carefully concealed affection; a connection accepted by the world, admitted by society, received at court, recognized by our families, sanctified by time. . . ."

So wrote a woman who spent her whole life conspiring in the dark. Perhaps Estancelin's own comment about her is the wisest: "With a woman, and a political woman especially, can one ever find out the truth?"

The countess returned to Paris and was soon steeped in intrigue and in sin. According to a story told by Prince Napoleon, the brother of Princess Mathilde, an English millionaire, Lord Hertford, gave her a million francs—more than a quarter of a million dollars—to spend one night with him. The Englishman was eccentric enough: he owned 250 clocks and drove himself wild trying to make them keep time together. But in his transaction with the Countess Castiglione he kept a level enough head, for he exacted such good value for his money that she had to remain in bed for several days.

Assiduously she continued to tend the cult of her beauty. She staged extravagant *tableaux vivants* and stunning receptions. Once she received her guests in a room draped entirely in black, while she was dressed in white. When she fell ill of a fever and called her doctor, she kept him waiting for hours while she made her toilette. Finally, she received him in a state of complete collapse, but marvellously coiffed and dressed in feathers, furs, and jewels.

She had herself painted in the nude in the pose of Goya's "Naked Maja," but, the gossips said, she was jealous of the surpassing beauty of the portrait and slashed it to ribbons.

As her son sprouted she became afraid that he would betray her passing years. She dressed him in the uniform of a groom and made him sit outside her door with the valets, and ride on the back rail of her coach.

In 1867 she mourned the loss of her husband. Count Castiglione died on the Duke of Aosta's wedding day after a fall from a horse. From the countess Estancelin received a detailed report of the events leading up to the tragedy.

The Duke of Aosta was the brother of King Victor Emmanuel, and all the silk and gold lace in Italy was bunched together in the courtyard of the palace in Turin waiting for the wedding procession to start for the church. But there was a delay. The first maid of honor could not be found. A search was made, and she was discovered hanged in a closet, holding in her cramped fingers the bridal wreath. The horrified bride refused to wear the wreath, but it was decided to hush up the tragic affair. The procession formed again.

It was then discovered that the colonel who was supposed to lead the procession was not among those present. A new search was made, and he was discovered three hundred yards from the palace, having fallen from his horse, a victim of sunstroke. The procession formed again without the colonel and prepared to leave the palace grounds.

But it could not. The guard who was to have opened the gate had forgotten to do so, and he was not to be seen anywhere. By the time they found him, he was bathed in blood, having become so terrorized by his error that he had attempted suicide. At about that time the high functionary of state who had written out the marital agreement fell inert against the cushions of his carriage, his face blue. He was dead of apoplexy.

Suddenly a shot was heard. It was the first witness to the marriage, committing suicide. The bridal cortège was still at the gates.

The young couple were now thoroughly panic-stricken. The idea of going to the church was abandoned entirely. A decision was made to go by train to Stupenigi and be married there, and since the gates were now open, all the magnificent equipages fled the damned place and clattered down the avenue lined with merry crowds and with music playing everywhere. They arrived at the railway station to the stupefaction of the station-master, who had not expected such an elegant event.

Edward VII once said of Victor Emmanuel that beneath his crass manners lurked noble qualities, and the countess' story unveils one of them now: the ability to get a wedding party on a train. He crammed them all aboard, crinolines and uniforms, feathers and cockades, ladies' trains and dangling swords. Then he gave a shout and the train began to move. At that moment the excited stationmaster took a notion to run across the tracks. The train ran over him.

Now Victor Emmanuel lost his head and ran about, beseeching the gods like a defeated general in the field, "Truce! Truce! Cease fire! Enough of death!"

He then told everyone to get back into the carriages. "We will drive to Stupenigi," he said.

The procession formed. Beside the carriage of the royal couple rode Count Castiglione, tightly dressed in the red uniform of a Maltese Knight. Suddenly someone noticed that he was losing his balance, that he was down, that he was under the wheels of the wedding coach. Everyone stopped, the bride swooned, Crown Prince Humbert rushed to the fallen count and raised him; but the carriage wheels had crushed his chest. Deep in the wound glowered the Maltese Cross, a decoration which had been presented to him in honor of the occasion. In a few minutes he was dead.

"He is dead!" wrote the Countess Castiglione, "and I still preserve his gala sword, his decorations and the Grand Collar of the Knights of Malta, and I keep the three francs and forty centimes that he had in his pocket. And here I am, a widow at seventeen, with a child to raise in a foreign land without a penny, probably to see him die in the same uniform."

She was wrong, first of all about her age, a point on which she was especially furtive; about her son, who died young of smallpox; about her wealth, for her jewels were more splendid than those of Empress Eugénie; and in all likelihood about the wedding, which is not thus described in any other memoir, and in fact is not remembered at all except that the accident to Count Castiglione actually occurred. We may assume that the ghastly report was invented from beginning to end by the countess as a baroque literary shrine to her husband's memory.

Yes, her mind was going astray. The closed cabinet of her soul was becoming rank, and sickness had crept in. Her diplomatic employers were beginning to notice this and to lose confidence in her. She continued for some years to conspire with Thiers for the overthrow of the empire. She appears to have been instrumental in bringing about a reconciliation between the pope and King Victor Emmanuel; the pope gave her a valuable tiara and bracelet in appreciation of her efforts. And after the Franco-Prussian War she assisted Republican France to work out armistice terms with Prussia, before turning against the republic to conspire again with the Duc d'Aumale.

In Christmas Eve, 1875, she moved into a house on the Place Vendôme, timing her arrival for midnight, so as to compete with God's other perfect creation, the Infant Jesus. She made this house inpenetrable with a system of locked doors, and received no one except Estancelin, who had to stand outside and whistle before he was admitted; and then he had to pass through three locked doors, the last of which was a secret revolving door. Her rooms were draped in black with purple fringes, the ceiling moldings were painted black, and black shutters blocked out the light. There were no mirrors to show what she looked like, aging, fattening, losing her teeth.

Her companions were two abominable little dogs whose filth reeked, and the dust was thick. Although her coachman had to be ready to leave at a moment's notice, she never left her rooms except at midnight to walk her dogs. "The more I see of men, the more I love dogs," she wrote.

The fruit of an invalid mother and an indifferent father, she had been even in her best years remote and secretive; now secretiveness had become sickly seclusion, and she was suffering also the fate of spies whose usefulness has waned and who are discarded. She filled her time writing letters to Estancelin, full of self-aggrandizement—"I created Italy, I saved the pope!"—and complaining of the ingratitude of principalities and powers. "The steps of a throne," she wrote, "whether ascended or descended, are inaccessible to love, duty, gratitude, friendship, privacy, remembrance, sometimes even to courage, honesty, truth, and invariably to frankness, uprightness, loyalty. Never any generosity and no trust. Such are princes. . . ."

In the end her letters became quite incoherent, and when she came to the bottom of her page, she would turn it sidewise and write crisscross over what she had written before.

Her last will renounced all relatives and connections except Estancelin, ". . . in remembrance of twenty-five years of whistling." It provided that her two dogs, which had been stuffed, should be adorned with their most splendid jeweled collars, and made to sit vigil at her bier. Upon the closing of the coffin they were to be placed at her feet where they might serve as cushions. Her person was to be adorned with her fabulous nine-row necklace of black and white pearls and two bracelets. Her body was to be clothed in the batiste and lace chemise she had worn that evening at Compiègne, when she had won Napoleon.

Alfred de Musset, invited to an imperial ball, walked down the grand staircase and surveyed the sea of splendor. "I would not give you a penny to witness the last act," he said to his companion. "I would sooner pay not to be compelled to do so."

Bismarck, the Prussian chancellor, wrote the last act. For years he had watched for a chance to contest his military power against France, and in 1870 an opportunity presented itself to bait Napoleon. It was not the emperor but Eugénie who went wild. Provoked to reckless anger, she insisted that war be declared against Prussia, and the French nation joined her in the delirious cry, "À Berlin!" Napoleon, although he had been for some time ailing with a singularly painful disease of the kidneys, mounted his steed and led his men to war.

Misfortune went along as his aide-de-camp. He lost the little war in whose mighty backwash France, Germany, and all of us are still rocking.

In this tale of Napoleon's moral shortcomings, not enough has been said about his qualities which won him the loyalty of brilliant men and the adoration of many. He was humane and generous. None of his preferred women ever died in want, and all of their children were cared for regardless of whether they were his. The sons of his laundress at Ham grew up to be two contented counts. Their foster brother, Harriet Howard's son by Major Martin, was given equal title, position, and preferment.

The emperor was courageous and in his public behavior always loyal to his image as the embodiment of an honorable nation state. He bore himself nobly in the disastrous war when, faint with atrocious pain, his eyelids swollen so that they sealed his eyes, purple-skinned and shivering, so ill that it was a relief for him to bang his head against a tree, he still did not forsake his troops, but giving over his command to others, followed them through the battle of Sedan, the Calvary of his empire. He was taken prisoner by the Prussians.

In prison the Prussians twice sent him emissaries to offer him back his throne at terms dishonorable to France. Napoleon refused them in spite of the beauty of the emissaries. Both had been his mistresses, and one of them was Countess Castiglione.

Eugénie had been obliged to disguise herself and flee for her life from the infuriated mobs of Paris. With the gallant aid of Napoleon's American dentist, a Dr. Evans, she escaped to England, and there she moved into a house called Camden Place, Chislehurst. Once it had been occupied by Miss Rowles, a former sweetheart of Napoleon. Now it belonged to Nathaniel Strode, Miss Howard's man of business.

Released by the Prussians, Napoleon joined her there. Two years later, he died of kidney stones, a faulty husband and statesman, even a faulty conspirator, but not a faulty dreamer. He had dreamed of an industrialized nation where all voices would be heard and everyone would have enough to eat; of a free, responsible press; of a canal cut through Central America which would unite the Atlantic and Pacific Oceans; of tunnels under the Alps uniting France and Italy; of a common market in Europe; of a universal monetary union. Such was his passion for impossible dreams that he even adopted other people's: he supported Henri Dunant's *outré* notion of an International Red Cross.

To the last he was at war on poverty, and at the time of his death, he was trying to invent a cheap stove to warm the homes of the poor.

The culprit, Eugénie, lived until 1920, as if damned to meditate on her sins for half a century and finally see what human sacrifice follows the recklessness of rulers. One day in 1918, it is said, when she was old, hieratic, transparent, she took her stick and walked down to Napoleon's tomb, where she gravely read aloud over his catafalque the Allies' armistice terms to Germany.

She had been beautiful when he had closed his eyes on her. They had lived those years at Camden Place on terms so warm, so amicable and devoted, one might almost swear that they had been in love.

·IV·

ROMANCE

&

COUNTER-ROMANCE

The walls of the Élysée Palace have looked down on a number of the characters in this book, and if walls could talk, they would be bitterly complaining now that they are reduced to looking down on pious *présidents de la République*. Throughout the Second Empire the Élysée was used as a residence for distinguished visitors of state, and among those who attended the Great Exhibition of 1867 there was none who evoked more public curiosity than Tsar Alexander II, a Romanov, semi-Oriental, the absolute ruler of lands that stretched across unintelligible areas of the earth. No doubt some people recalled that a few years before, when his father, the autocratic Nicholas I, had visited Victoria and Albert at Windsor Castle, where sumptuous apartments had been appointed for him, he had sent down to the stables for a pile of straw to lie on. Visitors to the Exhibition, therefore, even though they were aware that Alexander II was a liberal, "Western-oriented" tsar, watched him carefully in the hope that he would do something strange.

He did not disappoint them. He entered a public restaurant with a dozen or so gentlemen-in-waiting, and in his liberal Western-oriented way, ordered them all a meal, and ate with them. But the gentlemen-in-waiting ate standing up.

One day when the tsar was driving back with Napoleon III from an eye-shattering display of royal, imperial, and military splendor on the field of Longchamps, a Polish anarchist shot at him and almost killed him. Napoleon and Eugénie, so sensitive on points of etiquette, were in an agony of embarrassment over this hitch on one of the supreme days of their reign. The tsar, however, remained calm. A statesman of quality, industry, and idealism, he was accustomed to the attentions of assassins. The same evening, unperturbed and chill, he endured a glittering reception at the Tuileries, with Eugénie on his arm. But we can have no doubt that through it all his mind was fixed upon the girl, young enough to have been the youngest of his daughters, who had rushed to his apartments at the Élysée Palace after the assassination attempt, to fling herself into his arms, to kiss him and touch him and assure herself that he was alive and whole.

In the excitement, she had passed without much notice. She was living unobtrusively in Paris with her former governess, and she was destined to spend her life shrinking from public sight. To this day, very little is known about her love affair.

But one thing is known for certain, that no mistress and no wife was ever so dearly loved as Princess Katherine Dolgoruky.

Alexander had mounted the immense pyramid of tsardom upon the death of his father, Nicholas, in 1855. Nicholas had been a soldierly tsar who whipped an argument between Greek Orthodox and Roman Catholic priests into the Crimean War, and having done so, insisted upon reviewing his troops while suffering from a high fever; thus he had died of mindless heroism just a few months after the men of Her Majesty's Light Cavalry Brigade had perished of the same complaint.

Almost the first thing Alexander did upon stepping into his father's shoes was to wind up his father's war.

The new tsar was widely acclaimed as the handsomest man of his time—and he was, for a tsar. He was tall, as a Romanov was apt to be, and as elegant as a fair-growing Ajax. An imperial crop of whiskers grew willingly on his face, and around them were grouped a snub nose, puffy cheeks, and full, well-formed lips. He had an honest, soulful expression and his glance was like velvet seen through frosty blue glass. It is a surprise to find a junior member of the diplomatic corps, Lord Frederic Hamilton, complaining that there was something in his voice and look reminiscent of the Great Mogul addressing an earthworm. But of course he knew Alexander in his old age after the tsar had acquired the habits of remoteness and of fear.

At the age of twenty, while on an educational tour of Europe, he chanced to pass through the tiny principality of Hesse, where he laid eyes on a dark beauty, Princess Wilhelmina, fifteen years old, and he gave his father no peace until a marriage took place. The young couple must have been blissfully happy: a spate of little grand dukes and duchesses emerged from their suite at the Winter Palace and ceased only when Wilhelmina—who was known in Russia as Maria Alexandrovna—became tubercular. During the many years she lay sick, gradually becoming more querulous and pious and eventually falling entirely under the influence of her confessor who disapproved of her husband's politics, Alexander and his wife drew apart.

Alexander might normally have taken mistresses without provoking more than spicy gossip at court; but it was whispered that some of them were of rather tender years. Turgenev, the great satirist, dared to write, though in vaguest terms, of such an affair in his novel *Smoke*, whose young heroine at her first ball was seen and preëmpted by a certain highly placed personage. Turgenev went further: he hinted of a young girl, seduced by the same high personage, who became pregnant and committed suicide. If such a tragedy occurred, it must have grieved Alexander, because he was a kind and gallant man. But it must be admitted that while in other areas of his life he was characterized by dignity and moral grandeur, in matters of love, he had little self-control.

That peremptory heart of his, seeking sanctuary, found it finally in a child of ten. When Alexander was thirty-eight, he traveled to Volhynia in order to witness military maneuvers which were taking place there. Arrangements were made for him to put up at Tieplovka Castle, which belonged to Prince Mikhail Dolgoruky.

The Dolgorukys were among the oldest of Russia's aristocratic families. In fact, those who think of noble blood as if it were a kegful of fine brandy would say that Dolgorukys were nobler than Romanovs, since they traced their descent from Rurik, the Scandinavian chieftain who had founded the Russian monarchy. Once, a Princess Dolgoruky had married a Romanov tsar on his deathbed, and she had even jumped into bed with him though he was dying of smallpox. Unfortunately, he died there and then, so that the marriage was annulled, and a peasant prophet was promptly found to say that swift death awaited any Romanov who married a Dolgoruky.

By the nineteenth century the family had splintered and scattered; some were great, others obscure, some rich, some downright poor. Portraits of Dolgorukys show a fascinating family trait: great, humorously mocking eyes, from which sadness is by no means absent.

Prince Mikhail Dolgoruky was an obscure country landowner, and on the occasion of the tsar's visit his family had squeezed themselves discreetly into one wing of their castle in order to make room for the sovereign's suite. Shortly after his arrival Alexander chanced to see a little girl with a long dark-gold mane of hair streaming behind her riding her horse hard into a river, but the animal balked and floundered about in a confusion of splashes. The tsar approached with some well-meant advice, whereupon the child told him everything she thought about horses, rivers, and interfering military gentlemen. Banging away at her steed, she succeeded in getting it across the deep water and emerged soaking wet to confront the tall stranger.

"Who are you?" asked Alexander. She told him she was Prince Mikhail's daughter Katherine.

The governess who shortly came seeking Katherine was electrified to find her sitting on the monarch's knee while he caressed her and stroked her shining hair. Katherine soon was dining, scampering, and riding with the tsar. Alexander was enchanted with the child and made her his companion. Throughout his stay at Tieplovka, Katherine was seen to be leading majesty about by the nose.

In the year that followed, by a coincidence such as is usually relegated to Victorian novels, Katherine became Alexander's ward. Prince Mikhail had become involved in unwise speculations which impoverished him. In order to prevent creditors from taking possession of the Dolgoruky estates, the tsar placed them under imperial trusteeship and assumed the guardianship of the children—Katherine and her several brothers and a sister.

In this way Alexander gently bound himself to his beloved child; but at the same time two other Russian children were

being bound to him by threads beyond his sight. One was a boy
named Andrei Zhelyabov, and he was a serf. Once he had seen
his young aunt raped by her master and his uncle flogged. The
other was a girl, an aristocrat, the daughter of the Governor-
General of St. Petersburg. Could the tsar, on some official visit to
her father, have met Sophie Perovsky? Is it conceivable that he
could ever have bent his great whiskers over little Sophie, and in
his playful way have pinched the fat cheeks of his mortal enemy?

The tsardom was designed by Peter the Great like a vast
step-pyramid on which theoretically any Russian might climb
from one rank to the next, as soldiers do. After reaching a certain level, he became a "noble," with the right to own land
and the serfs bound to it. At a still higher level he became a
"hereditary noble," and so on. All strove upwards, and the
system enabled a nobody like the young Dostoyevsky to regard
himself as a noble. But from the time of Nicholas I, Dostoyevsky and many others were beginning to look downward and
perceive that one third of the population was stationary: some
twenty-five million serfs, known in Russia by the soulless word
"souls," who possessed no personal rights, who could be knouted
to death at the whim of their masters, mated like cattle, sold
away from their wives and children, or lost over a game of
whist. In fact, they were slaves.
Yet their condition was not founded on the bedrock of history
like that of the medieval serfs of Western Europe. They were
wild Tartars, really, whom Peter the Great had bound to the
land in the hope that they would settle down and build Russia.
After two centuries they still lived abysmally, in total ignorance:
they believed that all men outside Russia were deaf and dumb.
Nor were they models of the noble savage. Quite often they
turned on their masters and beat or slew them, or they set fire
to the granaries that held the results of their forced labor. Far
from remembering Peter the Great as the father of their country, they remembered him from the folklore of their ancestors as
Antichrist.
By Alexander's time channels out of this trap had opened
for some. With the permission of their masters, or even at their
command, serfs were moving off the land into the cities, where
new industries were springing to life. From the money they

earned they had to pay *obruk*, a percentage, to their owners. Still, some serfs by individual enterprise were becoming free, rich, and even distinguished. Dostoyevsky's friend and benefactor Suvorin, editor of the *New Times*, Russia's most influential newspaper, was born a serf.

At the very apex of the pyramid was enthroned the tsar. "If you wish to comprehend the social secret of this empire," wrote a French diplomat, "turn your back to the door through which the sovereign enters and look at his entrance by reflection . . . on the faces of those present. The whole vital force of these men and women is concentrated in their eyes, which seek those of the master. We have never contemplated this spectacle without having been reminded of the first appearance of the rays of the sun on the crests of the mountains at the instant when it rises. You have no need to look behind you to know that the sun has risen: you are informed of it by this quivering light on opposite summits. In the same way, you have only to look at the faces of the courtiers to be able to see that the emperor is about to come, that the emperor is coming, or that the emperor has come."

Remote as a heavenly body and insulated by courtiers from his people, yet the tsar's autocratic will was the sole government of the country. In theory not a stone in all the Russias could be shifted from one side of the road to the other except by the will of the tsar, not a hole dug or a house built. Such actions had to be recorded by a member of the civil service on a piece of paper, which, accompanied by bribes, would eventually wend its way to St. Petersburg to be scrutinized by the appropriate official who was but an extension of the tsar's will. Lest the smallest action threaten the autocracy, all had to be kept under surveillance by the secret police. Russia was really ruled by a vast body of semiliterate bureaucrats and semiefficient police, with each individual preoccupied in moving up the pyramid by means of bribery, character assassination, imagination, personal charm, or intrigue. Their deep-grained Byzantine corruption went hand in hand with the Byzantine beauty of Russian palaces, their spangled art and gorgeous music, the Oriental mysteries of their religious sects. To alter the smallest portion of the system was to tear the lavish costumery of the land.

How could a tsar, who was after all not a heavenly body

but a plain man look down so far and see his people's need? Yet ever since Catherine the Romanovs had recognized the urgent need for reform, most of all for the emancipation of the serfs. In a land where people measured their wealth by the number of "souls" they owned, it was a task from which Catherine herself had shied away, as had her eccentric son Paul. It intimidated the idealistic Alexander I; and his brother, Nicholas I, the autocrat *par excellence*, easily persuaded himself to let well enough alone.

But Alexander II had been educated by his tutor Zhukovsky to put away his pocket money to buy the freedom of serfs. From early boyhood he had serfs on his conscience. As a young prince he had worked on a commission studying the brutality of the "flogging gentry." As tsar he had no sooner wound up his father's quarrels at home and abroad than he handed the serf question to a committee with an autocratic command to act without delay, ". . . not making all sorts of excuses to postpone a plan of legislation until the Day of Judgment. . . . I hope that after all the palaver, you are actually going to make a move to do something. . . ."

And so, at last it was done. Alexander II's manifesto freeing the serfs was signed. On the very day—March 4, 1861—that Abraham Lincoln took his oath as President of the United States it was read to the people, and human chattelage ceased forthwith in Russia. It is surely an unexampled event in history that without civil war, on a single day, by the good will of a single man, twenty-five million people went down on their knees as slaves and got up again free.

Alexander was aware that if human rights were not bestowed from above, they would be seized from below. In that sense he was faithful in his fashion to his sacred autocracy. But considering the opposition he faced up and down the pyramid, beginning with his own family and including every grumbling Russian who had to face up to a new balance in society, Alexander may also be seen in the light of a revolutionary quite as daring as any who were going to attack him by gun, dagger, mine, or bomb. He believed strongly that an ideal Russia could be constructed on its past history. His enemies believed strongly that Russia could grow only if the past were utterly razed. In sum, they all believed strongly in something beside their own comfort, and thus in the manner of classic tragedy their tales are entwined.

The year of emancipation brought the first attempt on the tsar's life when, as he returned from a holiday in the Crimea, a student leapt onto the steps of his carriage and fired inside. The tsar was unhurt.

A fortuneteller predicted that he would survive seven such direct attempts upon his life.

The serf Zhelyabov was free now, a tall strong lad of excellent intellect for whom schoolmasters predicted a scholarship at the university.

Sophie Perovsky was seven years old, and she was not a happy child. Her father was a domestic autocrat.

The tsar inevitably placed his ward, Katherine, to be educated at the Smolny Institute in St. Petersburg, an establishment founded by Catherine the Great for young ladies of noble birth. The mighty empress had deigned to teach Smolny girls; succeeding Romanovs continued to confer imperial patronage on the school, visiting it regularly, sending treats for Christmas, and keeping a sharp eye on the young ladies who, upon graduation with all modern accomplishments, found their paths brilliantly lit with positions at court and marriages of great advantage.

But never was a Smolny girl watched by a monarch as closely as Princess Dolgoruky was watched by Alexander II. He was not a pretending man: his favoritism was a scandal among the student body. He used to pay Katherine private visits at the school and whisk her off for wild rides in his sleigh along the lonely shores of the Gulf of Finland. Once, it is said, huddled with the tsar under the fur covers, Katherine slipped a pair of scissors out of her muff and cut a little piece out of his coat which she afterwards wore as a talisman around her neck. Perhaps even the tsar felt embarrassed at having to face the headmistress with pretexts to see Katherine. He sometimes brought himself to sneak onto the chaste grounds of Smolny at twilight, hide behind a tree, and by whistles draw his child to the window.

His growing passion to make her his mistress is evident. He arranged that she should be graduated from Smolny a year earlier than was usual so that after her presentation at court she could participate in his social life. To this end he prepared a nest for Katherine: he advanced her elder brother, Mikhail, in the army and provided him with the means to marry a beautiful Neapolitan lady. When their home was established on the road to Peterhof at a convenient distance from the Winter Palace, Katherine went to live with her brother, and day after day the tsar called upon the Dolgorukys, to the flattery at first of the Neapolitan lady who believed herself—as did all St. Petersburg—to be the magnetic pole of the tsar's desire. But since she was deeply in love with her husband, even such a glamorous shadow was an embarrassment. Princess Mikhail Dolgoruky took to falling ill of migraine headaches when the tsar arrived. Instead of being dismayed by his hostess' affliction, the tsar seemed to thrive on it. Prince Mikhail would come home to find his sovereign lord romping on the Dolgoruky floor, up and down the Dolgoruky staircase, amid a pile of Dolgoruky dogs and Katherine.

Katherine was an exquisite person. She had the sort of face that used to decorate the most expensive boxes of chocolates at the century's turn: a smoothly carved cameo face, grave around the mouth, with the hint of a smile to make the expression sweet, and impudent Dolgoruky eyes. Though her features were aristocratically fragile, the cheekbones were broadly Russian and strong, softened by baby fat; and crowning all her enchantments was the dark-gold hair, piled up.

One spring day as she walked, followed by her maid, through the summer gardens of St. Petersburg, still lightly covered with snow, the tsar passed by with his aides-de-camp. Abruptly leaving his gentlemen, he approached Katherine and drew her into a secluded place, caring not a jot for the attentive eyes that watched him. He leaned toward her, whispering urgently, but something he said must have confused her because she pulled away from him.

After this meeting, the pair seem to have avoided Katherine's home. They met instead in parks, seated on benches like other loving couples, shrouded by the blossoms of summer, the leaves of fall, and then by rain and snow. Katherine was not captured at once, but how could she fail to be captured in the end? She was a girl in her teens, and like every girl of her age she took it for granted that her lover would blaze above other men. At her presentation at court she would have seen the tsar with eyes even more dazzled than those of Théophile Gautier, who turned giddy looking at Alexander II through a canyon of light, "a flood of radiance and the reflection of candles, mirrors, gold, diamonds, and precious stones . . . the scintillation of an anthill," his tall figure elegant in a tight white tunic edged with flounces of Siberian blue fox and trousers of sky-blue, his expression of majestic firmness, his light eyes "having a particular effect" against the brown of his complexion. Katherine must have seen those arctic eyes melting to kindness as he looked at her and singled her out from all the wondrous women.

In summertime Alexander's court removed to Peterhof, a summer residence Peter the Great had raised to put Versailles to shame, surrounded by immense gardens stretching to the Bay of Finland. There, in July of 1865, Alexander took Katherine walking. They came to a small, columned pavilion named Babygone, a sort of belvedere built on an elevated spot surrounded by undulating lawns set with flowers and massed trees beyond which the Finnish waters glittered with muted northern lights. Here Katherine became the mistress of Alexander. And before he let her leave him, he showered her with kisses and he is traditionally supposed to have sworn to her then, "Today, alas, I am not free. But on the first occasion, I will marry you, because I consider you my wife before God. *Au revoir.* I bless you. . . ."

Katherine had an old friend, her former governess, Mademoiselle Schebeco, to whom she confided her new state, and she said, "How was I able to resist him for a full year? How was it possible I didn't love him earlier."

She was seventeen, the tsar was forty-five.

During these years Alexander continued with his reforms. In 1864 he established *zemstvos*, provincial elected governments; immediately afterwards fourteen thousand schools opened. Recognizing that these schools could not flourish without teachers, he threw open the universities to everyone, rich and poor, and these blazed day and night as throngs of people, not caring if their feet froze off, stood for hours outside the packed lecture rooms, listening through the windows. Before this, in Russia, the liberal arts had been tantamount to black arts, forbidden knowledge. Now they were suddenly made available, and rich students commonly took up subscriptions so that poor ones could be educated. In Alexander's reign the giants of Russia flourished: Dostoyevsky, Tolstoy, Turgenev.

Alexander reorganized the judiciary and established the right to trial by jury. He outlawed the barbaric custom of flogging as a punishment; relaxed the censorship of the press; and it was his aim to break the power of the Third Section, the secret police. His prestige in the eyes of orderly liberals in Russia cannot be exaggerated—Dostoyevsky called him "our angel tsar"—and abroad he was hailed as "the Liberator," especially in the United States, which sent a delegation to pay him compliments.

But in his own country murderous passions had been unleashed. On April 14, 1865, Abraham Lincoln was assassinated. The same day of the following year was deliberately selected to put an end to the life of Alexander II. On that day, as he took his morning walk in the Letny Gardens and stopped beside the carriage door to put on his cloak, a revolutionary who had been standing nearby raised his pistol to fire. A passer-by hit his arm upward so that he missed his aim. He was arrested and put on trial, and at this trial the presence of large numbers of Nihilists was revealed in the land.

In the early years of their love Alexander and Katherine met in a room of the Winter Palace which had once been the office of Nicholas I. Katherine entered it by a side door giving onto the street to which she had a key. The tsar came through various corridors, isolated staircases, and unused anterooms by which the office was separated from the main part of the palace. Its decoration was what you might expect of a soldier who slept on straw. There were a few murky portraits, some books of military strategy, a scratched-up desk, and in the corner a couch covered with rough blue cloth. In this room their love flowered and became firm. By and by news of it filtered through the court and came to the ears of the empress, whose illness took a turn for the worse.

The Dolgoruky family found themselves in an unbearable position. Princess Mikhail Dolgoruky, a lady of impeccable breeding, was even suspected of having sold Katherine for her husband's advantage; nor could Katherine's other brothers now accept any promotion unaccompanied by sneers. Princess Mikhail therefore took her young sister-in-law off to Naples to the home of her own family, and there she arranged every sort of entertainment for Katherine, balls and parties, picnics and excursions to places of ancient legend in the hope of somehow mending the girl's life and providing her with a suitable husband. But couriers came daily to Katherine from the tsar, bearing letters and Oriental sweets, all no doubt romantic mementos of her clandestine life as the chosen one of the tsar.

When the tsar went to Paris to attend the Great Exhibition of 1867, Katherine left Naples and joined the tsar in Paris. After the assassination attempt, when she rushed to his apartments to make certain of his safety, he clasped her in his arms and swore that he would never allow himself to be separated from her again.

In 1871, to Katherine's joy and the tsar's despair, Katherine became pregnant. Alexander's view of the matter was entirely selfish. He could not bear the thought that Katherine might die in childbirth, and he dreaded the public revelation of his dishonor.

Katherine hid her condition successfully beneath her heavy winter costume. On May 11, 1872, her pains commenced, and as she had agreed with the tsar, she went by public coach, without a maid, to the office of Nicholas I at the Winter Palace. The emperor, who had received her message, joined her at once. Comforted by his presence, her pains grew less, and experienced father as he was, Alexander advised that it was probably a false alarm. He left her alone to rest on the blue couch; an old soldier was stationed outside to call him if need be.

At three o'clock the following morning this veteran woke the tsar from his bed, and he came to Katherine to find her in intense pain. A manservant was sent to fetch the doctor and a midwife, but through some misunderstanding neither of them arrived. For hours Katherine labored on the blue couch, with the tsar kneeling beside her, clinging to her hand. After hours of profound anguish, the doctor came—somehow the midwife never did arrive—and during the difficult delivery the Tsar of Russia helped the doctor to bring forth Katherine's son, while he never ceased to plead, "Sacrifice the child, but save her at any price!"

The baby was named Yury—after Katherine's ancestor Yury Long-Arm who in 1147 had founded Moscow. His friends knew him as Gogo, but he had few friends and for a while no name really, or even a home. He was spirited away by the Chief of the Imperial Bodyguard, General Ryleyev, and brought to live in that official's house on the Moika Canal, next to the long walls of the Imperial stables.

The first to hear about this birth was the German ambassador, who had a good spy service. The imperial family was outraged. The empress was said to have received the news in silence and never to have spoken of it. Shortly after, she received from her husband a cruel command: to appoint Katherine a lady-in-waiting. This meant that the tsar's mistress would be permitted to move into an apartment in the Winter Palace with her son.

Katherine was installed in an apartment directly above that of Alexander which matched his, room for room, window for window, door for door. The empress' rooms were directly adjacent to those of the tsar. The two women used many of the same palace domestics, valets, messengers, and cooks. Only once in her life did Maria Alexandrovna indicate the excruciating presence of Princess Dolgoruky, by pointing upwards in the direction of her apartment and saying, "I can forgive the offenses done to the empress, but never the torments inflicted on the wife."

It is not easy to excuse the callousness of Alexander to Maria Alexandrovna, who was the wife of his own choice. It is explainable only on the grounds that like other nineteenth-century monarchs, Alexander was brought up in the belief, as superstitious as any peasant's, that his actions were divinely inspired. He was a representative of God on earth, and whatever he did, since God could do no wrong, had to be accepted by others.

Throughout these early years of Alexander's love for Katherine, Zhelyabov had been attending the University of Odessa on a scholarship, but he was expelled for firebrand activities. He was a splendid man with a face both rugged and thoughtful, brilliant of mind, and possessed of a magnetic personality which gave him no trouble at all with the girls. He spent the ensuing years familiarizing himself with revolutionary literature smuggled in from abroad. He later held secret classes for workingmen more ignorant than himself. He also developed a hobby: fishing with dynamite. He was observed to take a special excitement in the suspense before the crash, and the way dynamite could send impressive fountains of matter into the air.

Sophie Perovsky had come to detest her autocratic father, and when she was seventeen, she left his house. For a while she supported herself by copying. Later she took a medical course and learned midwifery. Her object was not to make a living; like many thousands of young people throughout Russia, she was irresistibly inspired by the idea of "going to the people," teaching them, tending them, and helping them to a point where they could help themselves.

It was the sheer impossibility of this task, that of raising millions of people from the lowest condition to one of positive value that turned such people as Sophie Perovsky and Zhelyabov into Nihilists. Looking back on them, knowing the futility of their actions of hatred, whose results plague us to this day, we must still grant them their selflessness, which was the only virtue they had time to learn before they died.

In the early seventies the tsar built his love strongly around Katherine, and she had need of a fortress. Her presence in the palace was a national scandal. She was the posted sign of adultery, loathsome to the sight, a person whom others instructed their children to turn their backs upon. It was taken for granted that she prayed daily for the death of Maria Alexandrovna. Her own family petitioned to deprive her of the right to use their name.

Two years after Gogo a daughter was born to Katherine. The tsar now tackled the matter of the civil standing of these children. He was obliged to deny them his own name, Romanov, lest other Romanovs refuse to recognize it, and for similar reasons the name Dolgoruky was not expedient. A new surname for Katherine was therefore devised, again derived from her historic ancestry: Yuryevsky.

The tsar then issued a secret ukase which read: "We accord to the minors, Georgy Alexandrovich Yuryevsky and Olga Alexandrovna Yuryevsky, the rights belonging to the nobility and we raise them to the dignity of prince with the title of Highness. Alexander."

By bestowing upon the children the patronymics Alexandrovich or Alexandrovna, he recognized them as his own, and when another daughter joined the family, she received the same patronymic and titles. The tsar with his own hands tore up the children's baptismal certificates. The secret ukase was left in the safekeeping of General Ryleyev.

The children lived with Katherine in her apartment above that of the tsar. An elevator was installed between the two, and Alexander used it every spare moment of the night and day. He took his state papers to his mistress's rooms and worked on them there. From this, probably, arose the notion that Katherine was behind his liberal policies, and the group around the empress, which included her grown children and the tsarevitch, then hated them the more. The oxygen-filled bedchamber of the exalted invalid became the nucleus of a new political philosophy directed against Alexander's reforms. It was called Pan-Slavism, and not only did it complicate Eastern European politics for decades to come, but in a transmogrified version, it still does.

So private was the life in Katherine's apartment that one can only guess the source of the steadfast love between the aging monarch and the young woman. In the nineteen thirties a novel, *Katia*, was published by Princess Marthe Bibesco, in which various episodes are presented as being derived from family anecdote, especially from a cousin of Katherine's. According to these, Katherine might have held the tsar by sheer playfulness. Alexander had indeed a streak of childishness in his nature, the selfishness of a child as well as the charming appeal. His life as an autocrat was beset by sycophants, and his path as a reformer grew thickets of enemies. He therefore doted on this distracting companion whose teasing and perverse nature seems reflected in her serious and mocking face. They romped like children in that secret apartment, with Gogo and a pack of dogs, played hide-and-seek among the massive gilded furniture; and it was a day of high triumph for Katherine when she baffled the tsar utterly by climbing onto the immense mantelpiece and hiding behind a statue of Nicholas I that adorned it.

This view of the domestic life that prevailed in the irregular family is strikingly confirmed in nine letters, recently published, which passed between Alexander and Katherine when Gogo was about six years old. Also evident is the parents' anxiety for their children's standing in the eyes of the world and of

Heaven; as well as the tedium of the lovers' sleeping arrangements whenever they found themselves separated.

Excerpts from six letters written by Alexander to Katherine in French and Russian, in a small, neat, beautiful hand: "Oh! how I love the happy times spent with you and our dear children. . . . Gogo's game of pretending that I was giving him his bath pleased me a lot, for it shows once more how much he thinks of his papa, and that he feels himself loved. . . . May God keep them and not refuse us his blessing."

"Good morning my soul's angel! I slept well, though sighing not to have you next to me. . . ."

"We have just arrived here through a frightful blizzard. Before I go to dine . . . I want to tell you, dear, that I love you and my whole life is lived in you. Oh, how I enjoyed the company of our dear children. Dear Gogo has never been so adorable, and he was so happy to be left alone with me. Olga, too, was sweet. God guard these dear beings, and may he give us his blessing one day. I hope you will sleep better than last night, though we won't sleep together—and we'll both miss that."

"I'll go to bed sighing not to do so with you. . . . I confess that your dream made me desire you. . . ."

Excerpts from three letters written by Katherine to Alexander in misspelled French and Russian in a huge, round, wild, hand which almost rolls off the side of her page: "Yes, it's true that our happy moments form our life, and that we are always impatient to be together; only then do we feel really alive. It is so good to be so madly in love, to belong to the adored one alone and to have nothing to blame oneself for—I know that comforts and rejoices you. . . . As for Mimushka, he wouldn't spoil the ottoman, he's too well brought-up a dog, and so gentle that he deserves to be spoiled. . . . I am afraid you might catch cold. I love you, you are my life, my everything."

"Oh what boredom! I don't know what to call it, I only know it exists. I slept badly because I want you, yes, yes, yes! . . . Alas, I hoped in vain the cold would bring you back. Instead, here I am like a soul in pain. . . . I'm so worried you'll catch cold. . . . I love you so terribly, my life, my happiness, my all, you are the breath of my life . . . and our love is our treasure, and I know that you never could deceive me. . . . May God bless you and help us!"

"Good morning, dear angel. I love you and it overwhelms me

terribly. I slept well, and felt myself filled with our *lingerles*,*
but it didn't thrill me as I like, because I am sad about your
cough. . . ."

Apart from her love, Katherine's life must have been wretched.
When on official occasions, as lady-in-waiting to the empress,
she appeared in the royal suite, she was seen to keep her eyes
down, not daring to smile at anyone and find her smile un-
returned. Alexander protected her as far as he could. A lady
who at dinner had criticized Katherine was awakened from her
sleep the same night by the police and banished from Russia.
Alexander's powerful chief minister, Shuvalov, was heard to say,
"I'll break that brat's neck! (*Je la briserai, cette gamine!*)"
The following day the tsar said to him, "I congratulate you. I
have just named you ambassador to London."

Wherever Alexander went in peace or war Katherine went
with him, for he was jealous of every moment spent apart from
from her and his little family. She was even seen, dressed in the
habit of a nurse, on the Turkish Front. Around the magic center
of his life terror pressed him closely, for plots against his life
were continually being uncovered. His personal courage was
never in question, but on a visit to England it was noticed
that his eyes bulged so that the white showed around the iris, and
this could have been a sign of the tension under which he lived.

Alexander's foreign policy in Europe had a peaceful bent. In
1875 he faced down Bismarck, who, having battered France in
the Franco-Prussian War, wished to finish her off in a new war.
Alexander averted this with the words, "Now understand this: in
case of a new war I should not be neutral."

But he expanded eastward in Asia and allowed himself to be
prodded by his Pan-Slavs into a war with Turkey, thus arousing
the ire of the English under Disraeli who were on their way to
empire in the East. A popular song was incessantly heard in
London music halls:

> "We don't want to fight
> But by jingo! If we do,
> We've got the arms, we've got the men,
> We've got the money, too. . . ."

---

*French and Russian translators at the United Nations are not familiar
with Katherine's word *lingerles*.

from which the words "jingoist" and "jingoism" came into our
language.

The point was made that "The Rooshians shall not 'ave
Constantinople," and indeed they did not. By means of an un-
beatable combination of Bismarck, Disraeli, and a popular song,
they were despoiled of the fruits of their victories against the
Turks at the Congress of Berlin. And because of this Alexander's
enemies at home increased their bitterness.

In April, 1879, he went out for his morning walk, a habit
he refused to give up in spite of the danger to which he exposed
himself. A revolutionist, Solovyev, ran up and opened fire on him.
The tsar dodged and "proceeded in a zigzag manner, moving
now to the right and now to the left." He escaped with a hole
through his clothing. At his trial the assassin refused to betray
the smallest information against his accomplices. "If I were to
confess, they would kill me here in prison where I am," he said.
It was evident that the terrorists had achieved a Mafia-like
organization.

This was the fourth attempt against the tsar's life, not
counting the numerous plots foiled in time by the police, or mines
which for one reason or another failed to go off. A young nephew
of Alexander's remembered that during this time the Winter
Palace was like a besieged fortress, and one couldn't tell if the
butler who served one's coffee were not the bearer of an infernal
machine. The tsar developed a phobia against girls who wore
glasses. He said they were all anarchists.

The police were beginning to look nervously upon the habit,
prevalent among young intellectuals, of "going to the people."
Sophie Perovsky was arrested, and she was tried with other
persons of her age in a process known as the Trial of the 193
in St. Petersburg. One of her fellow defendants was Zhelyabov.
Ninety-four of the accused were acquitted, including these two.
The humanity with which the young revolutionaries were treated
by Alexander's new courts is in itself revolutionary, considering
that his father, Nicholas I, had sent Dostoyevsky to hell in
Siberia for chattering about politics, and had hanged a posse of
aristocrats for asking him an intelligent political question.

In 1879 revolutionaries from all parts of Russia came together
with a view to co-ordinating their activities. They met at

Lipetsk, a place of mineral springs and gardens which Peter the Great had established as a pleasure resort, and they pretended to be trippers who had come to play games and enjoy the sunshine. But at this meeting revolutionary activity became organized terrorism with its mood of relentless animosity to the tsardom. Liberalism, as represented by the tsar, was repudiated as being impotent, weak, and slow. Only terrorism, which aimed at the utter destruction of all existing institutions, without regard for human life, was deemed effective in preparing the ground for the building of a new Russia.

Not all of the revolutionaries believed in this extreme philosophy. But at Lipetsk the sheep, as it were, were separated from the goats. Groups were formed of people of like mind, and duties in various fields, both peaceful and violent, appointed. On the first day of the meeting, Zhelyabov found himself appointed a leader of the Nihilists, and his work as a member of the *Narodnaya Volya*, the "Will of the People" group, was to take place in St. Petersburg. This group, whose number varied around a couple of dozen more or less (for members were constantly being arrested), later held a meeting in a forest at which Alexander II was formally condemned to death.

Zhelyabov, wrote a friend of his, ". . . just by his appearance stood out from the rest of us. He was a man who compelled attention at the first glance. I first met him at Perovskaya's."

On his first meeting with Sophie after the Trial of the 193, Zhelyabov had attempted a flirtation, but she had repulsed him rudely because she hated all men. He exclaimed in anger, "You can't do anything with a woman like that!" and perhaps his chagrin was multiplied because not only was she beautiful, but she had been born an aristocrat, and he a serf.

And yet when Sophie cast in her lot with the violent *Narodnaya Volya* group, she recognized that she was falling in love with Zhelyabov. It could not have accorded her much joy. Love affirms one's right to be alive, and Sophie had marked out for herself only the right to kill and then die. One cannot imagine the contacts between these two, who could never have planned their lives or expressed a single rapturous hope or made a promise to each other; we don't know if they ever went walking with insolent gaiety past a policeman, or if they ever boated on the Neva, leaning dizzily together to watch its mesmerizing rush.

It is impossible to conceive of their love words mixed with talk of dynamite.

But we know that in some rickety flat, under false names, with the executioner's face still hidden from their imagination, these two became lovers and that Sophie loved Zhelyabov.

In the fall of 1879 Alexander took Katherine and the children to Livadia in the Crimea, where the imperial palace perches lightly atop a slope above the Black Sea and a marvelous wide sweep of steps leads to the nearest licking wave. Here they lived their immune hours, far from court cabals, Nihilists, and all hatreds; here Alexander drew pictures of Katherine in the nude which reveal the tsar to have possessed the talent for draftsmanship that occasionally turned up in the Romanov family. The drawings touchingly disclose his tenderness for her: they trace every darling curve with feather strokes, and they show his joy in the splendid billows of her long hair. Surely he worshiped her, because he drew her always in some goddess pose, Venus reclining, or else rising lightly aloft with some heroic object of the bedchamber, such as a looking-glass, in her hand.

They believed themselves free of watchful eyes, especially since the empress had been sent by her physicians to the south of France for her health. But they were watched. The terrorists were watching them.

On November 17, the tsar left Simferopol by train for the long journey back to St. Petersburg, leaving Katherine behind for a few extra days of sunshine. A telegram was sent by the watchers to the small market town of Alexandrov: PRICE OF FLOUR TWO RUBLES, OUR PRICE FOUR. This meant that the tsar was traveling in the fourth coach of the second of the imperial trains.

For some weeks Zhelyabov had been busy at Alexandrov on the railway line where the tsar's train would go by. He had passed himself off with his considerable charm to the townspeople and the authorities as a small businessman who wished to open a factory. He leased a house which he occupied with several conspirators, and by night they buried under the railway two brass cylinders, each containing forty pounds of dynamite, which they connected by leads to a portable battery. It was a rainy season, and soon the rain would turn to snow which would betray their tracks, and so they had worked hastily and sleeplessly, slipping and floundering in the slough, and throwing themselves into muddy ditches when the patrols guarding the tracks went by. Zhelyabov caught a feverish cold, but he did not stop work; in fact he insisted on doing most of it himself.

On the morning of November 18 in a veil of rain he crouched over his battery, dizzy with fever, but with his eyes fixed passionately on the point where the tsar's trains should come thundering out of the mist. The first train came into view, passed, and roared away. The second appeared. With every nerve at a pitch of exact action, the conspirators counted coaches, and as the fourth coach passed over the cylinders, Zhelyabov pressed the switch. Nothing happened. Something had gone wrong, and they never found out what it was. The train vanished into the fog, and the exhausted terrorists wound up their wires and sought their obscure beds, hoping that when the train reached Moscow, Sophie would have better luck.

At Moscow, Sophie had played a role similar to Zhelyabov's. Dressed as a worker's wife, she had gone to that city some weeks before with another member of the *Narodnaya Volya* who pretended to be her husband. They had rented a shack about fifty yards from the railway tracks, furnished it with the necessities of a Russian household—a table with chairs, a samovar, and an ikon in the corner. For a time Sophie occupied herself with marketing, housework, and allaying the suspicions of nosy neighbors.

Meanwhile, other conspirators of the *Narodnaya Volya* were lying low in obscure lodgings in the city. But before daybreak they would gather in the cellar of Sophie's house and, working eighteen hours a day, they dug a long, crooked tunnel through to the railway tracks: it was crooked because none of them had a notion how to build it straight.

It was hardly more than an animal's burrow, three and a half feet high and two and a half feet across, and so poorly was this lethal tunnel built—close to the surface and cursed with every kind of mischance, cave-ins, floodings, and misdirections —that it is a wonder their nerves survived its building. One digger who lived his days worming through it carried poison with him in case he should find himself buried alive. All were prepared for sudden death. A bottle of nitroglycerin stood innocently on the floor of the shack. Sophie was to explode it with a pistol shot if the police discovered their hole.

But the police did not discover it, even when the conspirators were obliged to mortgage the shack in order to buy a drill with which to pierce the rocky railway embankment and officials came on an inspection tour.

Looking back on such incredible luck of the terrorists, one cannot help wondering if the police and the bureaucracy were not riddled with people who would gladly have seen the tsar killed, whether their politics were on the right or the left. Gandhi said, "It is the reformer who is anxious for reform and not society, from which he should expect nothing better than opposition, abhorrence, and even mortal persecution."

On November 17 the group received the telegram about the price of flour. On November 18 they waited restlessly, hoping that Zhelyabov's attempt at Alexandrov would have done their job for them. But when they learned that the tsar had arrived safely at Kharkov, they knew that it had failed and that the rest was left to them. Sophie was given the task of watching by the window and of counting trains and coaches. The actual blast would be set off by the man who had laid the charge.

At 10:30 on the night of November 19, the first of the tsar's trains passed. Half an hour later, the second. The count was made to the fourth coach. Sophie gave the signal, the cap of hell shot off, a black tongue thrust into the dark, driving fountainwise great shafts of iron, steel, and wood, and the screams of wrenched metals tore the air. Surely the conspirators must have embraced each other, kissed and wept before they fled into the night. They left behind them a samovar on the boil and the candles under the durable picture of the Mother of God still lit.

The tsar learned of the explosion in the Kremlin, where he was spending the night. Ordinarily a baggage train preceeded his own as a precaution against just such attempts. But at Kharkov, owing to difficulties with the locomotive of the baggage train, he had impatiently ordered his own to change places with it.

"What do these miserable people have against me?" he cried in despair. "Why do they hunt me like a wild beast?"

• • •

Now all the important persons in the life of Alexander II came to Petersburg: the two women who loved him, the invalid empress and Katherine, to huddle in their respective shells at the Winter Palace; Zhelyabov and Sophie Perovsky to the apartment which they occupied under the guise of brother and sister; and the members of the *Narodnaya Volya* from whom shortly afterward a proclamation went out asserting once more "Alexander II to be the personification of arbitrary, cowardly, and ever more violent despotism; he has merited the death penalty by the pain he has caused and the blood he has shed."

Alexander was indeed causing pain and shedding blood, though not by his own wish. The police, whose power in Russia he had wished to curtail, were now busier than ever. The prisons were filling, as the names of the Nihilists were gradually extorted. Some had been hanged as a result of assassinations of public officials. Torture and flogging were resumed illegally, and in the Fortress of Saints Peter and Paul the revolutionaries were frequently locked in cages which hung over the latrines. Few retained consciousness after eight hours.

Repairs were made at this time in the cellars of the Winter Palace. Carpenters were going in and out, each one searched by the police. One of the carpenters was a revolutionary named Khalturin, and he had a plan, which he brought to Zhelyabov, to blow up the Winter Palace.

This pondorously ornate mass of stucco, built by Catherine the Great's architect Rastrelli, and painted in dreary shades of raspberry red, was a city in itself, as populous as many a thriving town in Europe at the time. It had its splendors. The ceilings of its great ballrooms were so high that they could hardly be seen. The winter gardens, broad balconies filled with every kind of exotic tropical plant which bloomed through arctic Russian winters in a perpetual haze of steam, were one of the wonders of the century. But the housekeeping of this huge place left something to be desired. Once, in a general reorganization, a number of cows were discovered in the attic, kept by servants who liked their cream to be fresh. Also there were several back doors that could be used by thieves, as well as by mistresses or even by murderers. Khalturin knew of these.

Day after day, as he worked in the cellars of the palace, Khalturin brought in bits of explosive and kept them under the pillows of his cot. When he realized that he was being slowly poisoned by the fumes, he transferred his store to a box where he kept his clothing. It might have been searched at any moment, but this was a risk he had to take. By the middle of January, 1880, he had brought a hundred pounds of dynamite into the Winter Palace. His box, which in fact became the mine, was kept in a room directly below a guardroom, which was in turn just underneath the tsar's dining room.

And now a little mercy seems to have crept into the councils of the *Narodnaya Volya*—or else impatience. It was Khalturin's ambition to blow up the entire palace gloriously, imperial persons, chamberlains, mistresses, ministers, servants, cows, and all. But Zhelyabov talked him down. It was better, he said, to blow up the tsar in his dining room, together with a few unlucky bystanders.

It was ascertained that the tsar dined at half past five, or at latest six. At five in the afternoon of February 5, Khalturin broke the lamp in the cellar room so that no one would see the curious arrangements he had made, and then he had tea in the dark with other workmen. At five-fifteen he was seen in the room alone, fiddling with something in a corner. A little after six he joined Zhelyabov outside the Winter Palace, and the two stood together in a corner of Admiralty Square, watching.

On that evening the tsar was expecting the visit of his wife's nephew, Prince Alexander of Battenberg. As is usual with in-laws, the prince was late to begin with and when he arrived, he had far too much to say. They talked in Alexander's private office, and it was not until twenty minutes past six that the tsar and the prince at last got under way to dinner. Just as they were descending the stairs, the tsar's dining room blew up; ten soldiers and one civilian were killed and fifty-six persons were wounded.

Alexander wasted no time in apologies to his guest. He bounded up the stairs, from which all lights had disappeared, toward Katherine, and he met her with her children on their swift way to him. They clung together on the landing. The empress was forgotten, and indeed she heard nothing, though she was quite nearby, because she was in a coma. It was Alexander's sixth bare escape.

For the members of the *Narodnaya Volya*, it was a catastrophe. Khalturin left the party in disgust, and the group was further depleted by wholesale arrests.

Zhelyabov and Sophie Perovsky were now the sole remaining authorities in the group. Though the habit of doom had grown on them, their hearts at this time were not entirely in their work. Rumors were alive throughout the nation, carrying to many a message of astounding hope, that Alexander had made the Armenian liberal, Loris-Melikov, his chief confidant and adviser. Loris-Melikov was committed to offering a constitution to the people of Russia.

This constitution was based on Alexander's elected *zemstvos*, which were now to be drawn together into a national deliberative and advisory body: not a parliament in the Western sense, but an inevitable step toward one, and a huge pound of flesh taken from the breast of tsardom.

It was believed that Katherine was behind this constitution and that Loris-Melikov was her creature, or she his. As a matter of history, we do not know that to Katherine the word "constitution" had much more meaning than it did to a certain Russian soldier who believed that it was a title accorded to the wife of the Grand Duke Constantine.

Shortly after the Winter Palace attempt the empress died.

Many years before, in the belvedere called Babygone, in the gardens of Peterhof, Alexander had made a promise to Katherine: "Today I am not free. But on the first occasion, I will marry you. . . ."

He said nothing of this now, and neither did she. On the day that the light coffin of Maria Alexandrovna was borne on the shoulders of her tall sons and the tsar to the sepulchre of Saints Peter and Paul, one of her ladies-in-waiting, Princess Yuryevsky, was absent from the funeral procession.

Then, exactly four weeks after the Empress died, Alexander told Katherine that on the Sunday when the fast of St. Peter would end, he would marry her.

Very few people were informed of this decision. Even the officiating archpriest was advised only at the last minute. One of Alexander's confidants, Adlerberg, voiced opposition and begged the tsar to wait a decent interval. "I have waited fourteen years," replied the tsar, and he added, "Remember, I am master in my house, and I am the only one who can judge what I have to do."

The tsar's sudden, almost sacrilegious marriage can be understood only in the light of his anxiety to establish the social status of his small children and of his perpetual fear of death.

The marriage took place at Tsarskoe-Selo, the imperial country seat. The emperor wore a blue uniform of the Hussars of the Guard and Katherine wore a plain beige dress. He met her before the ceremony, kissed her on the forehead, and said, "Let's go."

They walked together through a long passage to a bare room where the archpriest, his assistant, and a psalmist awaited them. Before a little portable altar, such as the army uses, and with the barest of utensils—a crucifix, a Bible, some candles, and the nuptial crowns—the tsar married the woman he had loved since she was ten. Following instructions, the archpriest repeated the marriage formula three times with the full title of the groom: "His Majesty the Emperor Alexander Nikolayevich, the very devoted servant of God, marries Ekaterina Mikhailovna, servant of God."

In recognition of their many kisses the archpriest gave them no command to kiss each other. After the ceremony they walked back to a private room, and there Alexander kissed Katherine and in the most ordinary voice invited her to come for a drive. Silently the husband and wife joined Mademoiselle Schebeco and the children, and silently they drove in the park.

Then to his family Alexander spoke: "I have waited long for this day—fourteen years of suffering. I could not go on any longer. I have always had the sensation that a weight would smash my heart." His face broke. "I am afraid for my happiness," he cried. "Ach! May God not take it away from me too soon!"

Many years later the tsar's nephew was to recall in his autobiography that grim day when the members of the imperial family were formally commanded to pay their respects to the tsar's new wife. The Grand Duke Alexander Mikhailovich was only a boy at the time. Just a few hours before he met Katherine he had learned the awful meaning of the word "mistress," and the secret of the lady he had been forbidden to approach who lived in an out-of-bounds apartment in the Winter Palace:

"Even the impassive Grand Master of Ceremonies was visibly

embarrassed next Sunday night when the members of the imperial family gathered around the dinner table at the Winter Palace ready to pass their pitiless judgment on 'that awful woman.' His voice expressed grave misgivings as he announced, tapping the floor three times with his ivory handled staff:

" 'His Majesty the Emperor and Princess Yourievskaya.'

"My mother turned her head away in plain disgust. My future mother-in-law, then the wife of the heir apparent, Grand Duke Alexander Alexandrovitch, lowered her eyes. She would not have minded it so much for herself but—she was thinking of her sister Alexandra, married to the Prince of Wales. What would old Queen Victoria say when she heard of this disgrace?

"The Emperor walked in briskly with a strikingly attractive woman on his arm. He gave a gay wink to my father and then sized up the massive figure of the heir apparent. He counted on the loyalty of the former, but he had no illusions as to the attitude of the latter. Princess Yourievskaya gracefully acknowledged the formal bows of the grand duchesses and sat down in Empress Maria Alexandrovna's chair! Prompted by curiosity, I never took my eyes off her. I liked the sad expression of her beautiful face and the radiance of her rich blonde hair. Her nervousness was obvious. Frequently she turned to the Emperor, and he patted her hand gently. She would have succeeded in conquering the men had they not been watched by the women. Her efforts to join the general conversation were met by polite silence. I felt sorry for her and could not comprehend why she should be ostracized for loving a handsome, kind and cheerful man who happened to be the Emperor of Russia.

"A long association did not dampen their mutual adoration in the least. At sixty-four Alexander II acted like a boy of eighteen. He whispered words of encouragement into her small ear; he wanted to know whether she liked the wine; he agreed with everything she said; he looked at his relatives with a friendly smile, inviting them to enjoy his idyllic happiness, and joked with me and my brothers, extremely satisfied that at least we youngsters had taken a fancy to the poor princess."

This observant imperial urchin saw Katherine at other such gatherings and was indelibly impressed by the spectacle of her mortification before the court. But even then she knew that within a few months she would be covered with those garments of reckless splendor that were reserved for Romanov empresses, and crowned. The tsar wished it, and the coronation was to take place in the Kremlin in Moscow.

The news, which shortly became certainty, that Loris-Melikov had laid the draft of his constitution before the tsar and that Alexander intended to sign it, might have given pause to the terrorists but for the large numbers of their comrades imprisoned in the fortress. Zhelyabov, whose name was now known to the police as that of the tsar's most dangerous foe, was tiring of his role. He was thirty-one. It is not unlikely that he had looked at himself and Sophie, so gifted with beauty, intellect, and strength, and wondered how they had become mixed up in a death machine. But his comrades had run their risks and lost; he could not refuse to organize another attempt against the charmed life of the tsar.

The tsar was accustomed to attend a weekly military review in the riding school of the Mikhail Palace. Afterward, he usually called on his cousin, the Grand Duchess Catherine. Ordinarily he went from the Winter Palace by way of the Catherine Canal, and returned by the street called Malaya Sadova. It was on the Malaya Sadova that the conspirators rented a small shop and set up as cheese merchants. What providential luck prompted them to open a cheese shop? No sooner had they begun to burrow their tunnel from the cellar to a point under the middle of the road than they hit a sewer, and the stench that rushed into the cellar, up the stairs, into the shop, and out to the street could have been explained only by cheese. Even so, the number of young people going in and out of the shop provoked suspicion and the police came to look them over. They poked around the hole in the cellar wall which was camouflaged by removable boards covered by wall paper; and they noted the large barrels of dirt which had been removed from the tunnel. But they seem to have suspected nothing.

Zhelyabov worked in a frenzy through the detestable filth under the Malaya Sadova. Lately he had wondered if nitroglycerine done up in small bombs would not be a more convenient weapon against the tsar. The others were not enamored of this idea. The bombs had to be held above the head and thrown almost vertically, blowing both victim and assassin to bits. A compromise was reached. The tunnel under the Malaya Sadova would be burrowed by Sunday, March 1, 1881. A bombing squad would stand ready to go into action if the mine failed. And if all else failed, Zhelyabov volunteered to move in on the tsar with a dagger. By this time the members of the *Narodnaya Volya* had worked themselves into a fanatical determination to kill the tsar by one means or another.

Then, on February 27, in a general roundup by the police, Zhelyabov was arrested. The arresting officers had no idea what a prize they had netted until they brought him into their head-quarters. There a policeman recognized him and exclaimed, "Why, you're Zhelyabov!" The terrorist replied with laughter, "Your humble servant! But it won't help you!"

That night and the next day when Zhelyabov did not come home, his accomplices were almost decided that the attempt would have to be postponed, but they had reckoned without Sophie. She had permitted herself a petrified love. Now she was hard as stone. It was Zhelyabov's due that the attack he had planned should be attempted. She ordered, and she had the authority to order, that they must go through with it.

On Saturday morning February 28, the tsar took Holy Communion in the chapel of the Winter Palace. As was his privilege, he took the wine from the hand of the priest and held it to the lips of his children.

Around midday Loris-Melikov told him that Zhelyabov, the man whose name echoed in his nightmares, had been arrested. But the minister recommended that the tsar should nevertheless not attend the military exercises at the Mikhail Palace on the following day. "Why not?" asked the tsar. "With Zhelyabov arrested, why not?"

Loris-Melikov had no answer to this question. He did not conjecture the existence of a woman who loved Zhelyabov utterly. So he dropped the subject. The tsar went at once to Katherine's rooms to tell her about Zhelyabov's arrest.

That evening, a framed picture of the tsar that Katherine kept on a table fell down. The tsar picked it up and dropped it again. "No luck," he said.

Soon after Mademoiselle Schebeco joined them for a game of cards, and she was told of Zhelyabov's arrest. She nevertheless supplicated the tsar not to go to the military review on the following day, and the princess also begged him to stay indoors. He replied, "Why shouldn't I go? I can't live like a prisoner." Autocratically, he dealt out the cards. But before he went to bed he had yielded to the worried women, and it was settled that he would stay at home all day on Sunday.

The next morning he attended mass with the princess, and later received Loris-Melikov, who had decided that without delay the tsar must be induced to approve his draft for a constitution and sign it. Afterward the minister came rattling down the stairs and in his excitement almost knocked over Mademoiselle Schebeco who was ascending them. "It's a great day in the history of Russia!" he rejoiced, and he opened his dossier to show her the imperial signature on the constitution, and she saw more: the document had been signed not only by the tsar, but by the heir apparent and by the grand admiral, the Grand Duke Constantine. Loris-Melikov said, "I'm taking it to the printing office, and it will be published in the papers on Monday morning."

Meanwhile the tsar had rejoined Katherine. "It is done," he told her, "I have signed it!" and she replied, "Thank God! I am so happy." They kissed each other.

The tsar then said, "I am so happy that it almost gives me a feeling of fear."

Later that morning he received a visit from his sister-in-law, the Grand Duke Constantine's wife, and this lady was dismayed to hear that he would not be attending the military review. She said that her young son would be attending it for the first time, and if the tsar were not there, it would blight his memory forever. "Then I'll go!" said the tsar with alacrity, and he gave the lady his word.

This review, weekly though it was, was one of the grandest sights in old Russia when the tsar's tall Chevalier Guards paraded in gorgeous racing patterns in the huge riding academy of the Mikhail Palace. Only military men received invitations to view it, and members of the foreign diplomatic corps used to wrangle themselves temporary military rank just to witness it once. Of course the tsar could not have deprived his young kinsman of the added sparkle of his presence.

Before he left Katherine begged him to state a time to the

minute when he would return. The tsar had a new baby daughter on his knee, and he jiggled her as he gave the program of the day. He would leave the Winter Palace in one half hour, preside over the parade, call on his cousin who would be hurt if he did not, and not later than three o'clock he would return to the Winter Palace.

"And then what shall we do?" he said.

"What do you want to do?" said Katherine.

They agreed that they would go walking in the summer gardens. The tsar exacted a promise from Katherine, who was not a punctual woman, that she would have the whole family ready and with hats on to go walking at three o'clock. Then he embraced her and said good-bye. She said, "Promise me that you will not go on the Malaya Sadova. Promise me that you will go both ways by the Catherine Canal."

The princess had learned from Loris-Melikov that the Malaya Sadova was under suspicion, but the broad quay with a canal on one side and a park on the other seemed safe enough. So the tsar promised that he would go both ways by the Catherine Canal, and he said good-bye. He rode in a carriage flanked by six Cossacks, and after them came two sleighs containing police officers.

He presided over the military review and called upon the Grand Duchess Catherine. He left her and got into his carriage, giving the order to proceed down a street which avoided the Malaya Sadova and turned onto the Catherine Canal. As this unaccustomed direction became plain, a young woman standing on the corner of the Nevsky Prospekt took out a snow-white handkerchief and blew her nose with it. It was a signal to the conspirators that all their work in the sewer had gone for nothing and that the bomb throwers were now to take their stations on the quay. The young woman then scuttled swiftly along the Prospekt over the lumps of dirty snow to a bridge where she crossed the canal and stood to watch. Sophie had chosen to wear the costume of a herring-woman on that day when she planned to see an autocrat die. She was in ill health; for weeks she had lived on cheese. She had not slept since Zhelyabov was arrested because she had been helping to make four bombs; she had just come out of a coffee shop, where she had breakfasted with one of the bomb throwers. We may imagine her with a pallid harassed face, to which a feverish flush was drawn, hurrying over the bridge.

The tsar's carriage turned to the right on the Catherine Canal, slowing a little. The first bomb thrower should have been there, but he had lost his courage and had slunk away.

The quay was almost deserted. There were a few passers-by, a little boy pulling a bundle along the ice, a young man strolling along carrying a parcel, and another one leaning with his arms folded against the railing of the quay.

Now the tsar's coachman, under orders from Katherine, suddenly picked up speed. He put on such a spurt that the mounted Cossacks were taken unawares, and they swept after him at a gallop. The strolling young man was surprised too. He turned as the carriage flew past and threw his parcel frantically under the back wheels. There was a great fracas of breaking wood and glass, the screams of horses, and a cloud of snow and smoke. When it cleared, dead horses and men lay upon the ground.

The carriage staggered and stopped. The tsar got out, unhurt. He had survived the seventh attempt upon his life.

He walked back to where the bomb had exploded. He bent over a fallen Cossack, and then straightened to look at his assassin, who had been seized and was being held in the middle of a growing crowd of people. The tsar's brother, the Grand Duke Mikhail, came running from the next street, twisting through the crowd, and as he approached he heard someone shouting, "Where is the emperor?" The tsar then called out loudly, "I am all right, thank God!" But he raised his stiff finger and pointed to the small boy screaming in red agony on the pale dirt of winter.

Then the assassin lifted his head and spoke: "Do not thank God yet!" The tsar turned away from him and walked toward the damaged carriage.

A man stepped away from the railings of the quay and came quickly forward to confront the tsar. He held his hands vertically above his head and brought them down swiftly with a thundering crash like elemental hands, and the last conscious sight he saw were the puzzled, staring, great kind eyes of his sovereign, Alexander II.

When the smoke cleared the bodies of twenty persons lay in

the snow with the murderer and Alexander. The tsar's face was torn and he was trying to lean up on his hands. His clothes were ripped away and his legs were naked and destroyed; blood streamed around him. The crowd was in a screaming panic, to such a degree that their mass hysteria contaminated the fourth bomb thrower. Tucking his bomb under his arm, he instinctively raced forward to help the tsar.

The Grand Duke Mikhail lifted his brother and with others carried him towards the police sleigh. The tsar said, "Very cold." And he said, "Take me to the palace."

That was where Katherine was waiting to go walking in the gardens where he had wooed her once. They took him there and laid him on a couch. One by one, family by family, the imperial clan gathered around it, staring and sobbing and sickened at the sight. Then Katherine came. Of course she was not ready and dressed, she never was. She was half naked in a pink and white negligee. She fell over the body of the tsar crying, "Sasha! Sasha!"; kissing his hands and trying to stem the dreadful flow with the beautiful stuff of her dress. He opened his one eye and looked at her. The doctors worked around him. They worked for half an hour, and then Katherine fell to the floor like a cut plant, for they said that he was dead. Her pink and white negligee was soaking wet with blood.

Throughout his life Alexander had taken a child's pleasure in the ornate uniforms of his regiments, but by his own instructions he went to his sepulchre in the plainest of drab suits. "I don't want to appear before the throne of God looking like a circus monkey," he had said. One shining thing went into his coffin: it was Katherine's hair. After the imperial family had finished viewing the body and before the coffin was closed, she entered the Fortress Church heavily veiled through a back door and placed that marvelous decoration beneath his hand.

In the few days that remained to Sophie Perovsky before her arrest, she lost her senses. She rambled in the streets and incessantly concocted wild plans to rescue Zhelyabov from the fortress. She saw him again at their trial.

"Have you been following the trials?" wrote Karl Marx in London to his daughter Jennie, ". . . they are sterling people through and through, *sans pose melodramatique*, simple, businesslike, heroic . . . they try to teach Europe that their *modus operandi* is specifically Russian and historically inevitable . . . about which there is no more reason to moralize than there is about the earthquakes in Chios."

The day after Marx wrote this Sophie, Zhelyabov, and three other members of the *Narodnaya Volya* were publicly hanged.

Hangings were infrequent in Russia. Most criminals were sent to Siberia or else they were shot. There was only one hangman, Frolov, and part of his wages was a large quantity of vodka which he consumed immediately before he performed his task. No trap door was built into the scaffold. The condemned, enswathed in a white shroud, was made to stand on a stool, a rope was placed around his neck and tightened, the stool was pulled away, and then the drunken Frolov labored with the rope until death came to the rescue.

Sophie was third in line for this sickening transference, Zhelyabov fourth. Zhelyabov kissed Sophie tenderly before they clothed her in her white shroud.

The tsarevich succeeded to the throne as Alexander III, a great stone monolith of an autocrat who could tie silver table-forks into knots and who hated all Western notions. He tore up Loris-Melikov's constitution through his father's signature and through his own. He undid his father's works. He hunted down the revolutionaries vindictively, and in his hatred of the West suppressed every healthy thought of reform in Russia. In this way he was able to hand over the autocracy intact and unimpaired to his son Nicholas II, the last of the Romanovs, who was slain in a cellar in Ekaterinberg.

Katherine retired to the south of France with her children and lived until 1922, long enough to see her husband's dynasty come to its end.

Once she said, "If only God had left him to me, even a cripple and without his legs, he would still have been alive, he would still have been himself. Like that he would have belonged to me more than ever, because then he would have been bound to abdicate."

We cannot speculate what road history would have taken had Alexander lived and had Russia become a constitutional monarchy. It is only certain that one bomb laid waste four lives.

· V ·

TRÈS BELLE &
TRÈS VIEUX

Napoleon III dreamed of creating a Paris where everyone would want to spend his holidays, and no one has blamed him for that dream: certainly not the bearded gentleman who, as the century piled up its years, became an ever more familiar sight on the long riverside quays, "wrapped in a long, dark ulster, wearing a pair of galoshes over his enormous boots, and a black bowler on his head, carrying in his hand an umbrella that had seen better days." Occasionally this venerable person would stop at a book stall and haggle with the vendor for a yellow-backed book. Or he would enter a knickknack shop and poke among the offensive objects assembled there, all of whose prices he found ruinous. If he bought anything, he counted out his money twice.

One day he dropped into a restaurant for luncheon and ordered a plate of vegetables. As it happened a customer at a nearby table had just been given the same dish, and after picking it over and hating it, he had angrily called the waiter to take it away. The waiter put it on a sideboard, then, after a discreet interval, placed it before the old gentleman. And he, oddly enough, although he had seen the shabby transaction, made no protest at all, but ate his plate of vegetables—because after all he was a king, Leopold II, King of the Belgians. He might wear old clothes and haggle over second-hand books; neglect his wife, consort with loose women, subvert his sister's fortune, and enrich himself with "red rubber" from the Congo. But he would never publicly reprove a waiter, for he was a royal Coburg, and as he said of himself, "At least the old chap has breed, don't y'know?"

Leopold II shone with majesty: a man of grand height, with intent, far-thrusting eyes like the stare of a big-game hunter's gun. His nose and brow were copied from those of Olympian Zeus, but his beard was his own invention. There was nothing ornamental about it, like the beards of those nineteenth-century gentlemen who went about curled and oiled like Babylonian bulls; nor was it a silky pet like the beard of Santa Claus, nor a long companionable beard such as a philosopher might grow for midnight stroking. It was a monstrous, uncordial thatch, cut straight across the bottom at its thickest growth in a perfect rectangle: the beard of an arrogant, calculating, secretive man who wishes to terrify and at the same time hide.

Still it was not the only beard of its kind. There was another gentleman in Paris, a certain Monsieur Mabille, who was said to be the image of the King of the Belgians, and he cultivated a twin beard. Sometimes, as Leopold wandered in the city streets, he would pause beside a kiosk to regard superciliously the abundant caricatures on display of himself enwreathed in the frothy petticoats and supple legs of dancing girls. Then *le roi des Belges et des belles* might permit himself to remark with cold humor to one of his gentlemen: "There! They're teasing that unfortunate M. Mabille again! And how like me he is! Lord, how he looks like me."

Leopold was the most loathed man of his century, and therefore the most caricatured. The French *agent de Sûreté* who had charge of his happiness and well-being when he visited Paris did his best to steer him clear of kiosks. But Leopold was not easily steered away from his chosen path, and confronted with *lèse-majesté*, he viewed the insolent drawings with apparent equanimity. If he showed emotion at all, it was only the exasperation of an utterly superior person for the misguided multitude. For Leopold was not only wicked, he was intelligent, one of the most intelligent men ever to occupy a throne. Everything he did was either scandalous or brilliant. It was only natural that when in his sixty-fifth year he fell in love, it should have been the sort of love that would infuriate zealous gossips, since it could not be mentioned before delicately reared ladies or anywhere that children would be likely to overhear; a baroque, inexcusable, indecent affair that had to be ignored by respectable ministers to the Belgian crown, even while the king capered with his love before their very noses.

But the caricaturists never ignored anything Leopold did. They made hay of him and his love right through the day of his funeral.

Napoleon the Great complained that no matter what enemy he fought, somewhere in their midst there was a Coburg. When Napoleon III first set eyes on Countess Castiglione and looked around for a handy duke to engage the attention of his wife, it was a Coburg duke who was handy. Wherever in Europe there was a spare princess to be married off or a crown going begging, an idle Coburg could always be found to assume the burden. When in 1830 the Belgian people broke with the Dutch House of Orange and made of themselves an independent nation with a constitution which required but a king to lend it importance in the eyes of other kings, they naturally looked around for a Coburg prince to whom to offer this post. They found one, and he became known as Leopold I, King of the Belgians.

A lesser man than Leopold I would have chafed to be a mere constitutional king, condemned to reign and never to rule; to array himself in crimson velvet and ermine robes which were attached by invisible wires to shabby shopkeepers. But Leopold of Coburg had a cold, clear, self-serving intellect. He saw what was hidden from the sight of others, that in the coming tussle between kings and constitutions it would be the constitutions that would survive, together with those kings who nimbly learned to balance on them. He therefore devoted his life to becoming the perfect model of a constitutional monarch, and with original statecraft he conceived the role of such a monarch in the body politic for his own time and for ours.

As for worldly domination, it was by no means beyond the grasp of this brilliant man. By shrewd manipulation of Coburg weddings Leopold I achieved by marriage bed what Napoleon had failed to achieve by cannon: a mighty invasion of his relatives into the ruling families of Europe. And as the troubled, revolutionary tides beat against thrones and toppled them, all of these Coburgs and their in-laws came to look upon clever Uncle Leopold as an oracle, the Nestor of Kings.

His great coup in this direction was the pairing off of his niece, Queen Victoria (for whose very existence he was responsible, having engineered the marriage of her parents), with his Coburg nephew, Albert. Gently and persuasively, but nonetheless coldly, these two intelligent gentlemen, Leopold and Albert, went about changing the nature of sovereignty in the person of the little queen. They tamed her wilfulness, cried shame on her weaknesses, plucked away her silly Georgian feathers, rattled her until she did not know whether she was a Whig or a Tory, and set her beaky nose toward a future world, where as a sovereign she would not merely conform to a constitution, but be it; be also her people, every one, of all parties, creeds, colors, and cultures of men; be as powerless and as mystically necessary as a Queen Bee.

Constitutional monarchy, as we understand it today, was an efflorescence of Coburg genius. The quality of genius, so rare among royalties, would, with the death of Prince Albert, leave the ruling house of England, and never again would that nation be troubled by a ruler lavishly endowed with brains.

This was not to be the case in Belgium. Leopold had a son and heir, an uncommunicative, obedient, respectful youth, and he grew up almost unnoticed in his father's giant shadow. He was to succeed to the throne as Leopold II, and in a curious repetition of history's design he was to raise himself as craftily as his father had done to power far beyond that of old-fashioned kings and newfangled constitutions.

In 1865, when he acceded, few people in Belgium knew what manner of man the second Leopold was. Perhaps his tutors had wondered at a boy who could hand in his figures with never an erasure. His sister Charlotte might have guessed. On the occasion of her wedding to the Archduke Maximilian of Habsburg —a marriage that would make of her the wretched, mad Empress of Mexico—Brother Leopold wrote an anonymous newspaper article, expressing opposition to large dowries for royal princesses who were going to carry off the money to foreign lands. "It is superfluous to work for the profit of unborn archdukes," was his opinion. But among the comfortable Belgian merchants and small manufacturers with their medieval languages and shiny suits, none could have imagined that Leopold II was a financial wizard who would gather them up in his destiny and compel them to follow him as helplessly as the tail of a comet follows its thrusting matrix across the blackest skies.

Like other Coburgs, Leopold had been used advantageously in his father's marriage game. At the age of eighteen—it was the same year that Napoleon married Eugénie—he had been married by proxy to Marie-Henriette of Habsburg, the sixteen-year-old daughter of the Palatine of Hungary. She turned out to be plump and frivolous. Before Leopold had done with her she was thin and miserable. In public he treated her with cold contempt. In private he forbade her to open her mouth in his presence unless specifically addressed. Nor did he hide from her or from anyone his vast preference for those plentiful *parisiennes* who danced in the back rows of the chorus.

By some form of *noblesse oblige*, children were born of this marriage: a boy and two girls. The boy, the heir to the throne, died at the age of nine. In cold blood, after years of contemptuous neglect, Leopold began to overwhelm his wife with amorous attentions, to which the Habsburg princess could only submit. She became pregnant and another child was born. But it was only a third princess, Clementine. After that, the king had nothing more to do with his wife. He banished her to the royal villa at Spa and denied her all but the most parsimonious allowance. When the queen died, she died alone, though her husband was nearby, enjoying a holiday with his mistress.

The two elder princesses, Louise and Stephanie, grew up conscious of their father's hatred, knowing themselves to be in his eyes reminders of the vile insult death had dealt him in seizing his son and heir, and sparing these girls for whom dowries would have to be provided.

Louise was disposed of young to Prince Philip of Coburg. She went to this marriage so shockingly ill-instructed that Prince Philip was obliged to train her by means of alcohol and pornographic literature. She endured him for twenty years. Then she ran away and to compensate herself for having been born began to throw her money away in morbid extravagance. Her father contrived to have her shut up in a madhouse, and of course this enabled him to sequester her inheritance from her mother. She eventually escaped from her asylum, but she moved through life in a swirl of howling creditors.

The second daughter, Stephanie, was brilliantly wed to Crown Prince Rudolf, heir to the immense Austrian Empire. But he, that hero of *grande romance*, shot himself one night at Mayerling with his mistress, Baroness Vetsera. Stephanie, who was disliked by her husband's family and detested by her own, was left to spend her life as a floating royal nuisance. At length she begged her father's permission to marry a Hungarian count. Leopold refused. When Stephanie married her count in spite of him, he was able to seize Stephanie's fortune also.

His third daughter, Clementine, was Leopold's only legitimate child for whom he manifested affection, the more so because the queen disliked this daughter who was the symbol of her ruined life. Clementine was a handy hostess for his table, and in his old age a handy walking stick for his limbs, which were afflicted with rheumatism. When she fell in love with Prince Victor Napoleon and asked her father's permission to marry, Leopold found reasons to refuse—why waste a dowry on Clementine?

As for his sister, Empress Carlota of Mexico, who can say whether, in his avarice, he found comfort when upon losing her empire, she lost her reason? She became his ward, and he allowed her to live out her weird days in his Château de Bouchout. Of course he assumed the management of her financial affairs.

The shabby deeds accumulated, evoking the contempt of every proper Victorian. The caricaturists depicted the King of the Belgians clutching a half-dressed damsel who whispers into his beard: "Do you recognize my drawers, Majesty? I got them when you auctioned off your wife's things." They showed him walking down an icy street past a black-clad beggarwoman and musing, "Strange! I could have sworn that was one of my daughters!" Nevertheless, it was not merely for his shortcomings as a *paterfamilias* that Leopold II was loathed.

Those who knew him might well have found sufficient reason to detest him for his habitual condescension. Once a staunch Republican said to him, "I do not hold with monarchies and kings. Nevertheless, I recognize your great superiority and I confess that you would make an admirable president of a Republic."

"Really?" replied Leopold. "D'you know, I must remember to pass the compliment along to my doctor. I'll say, 'Thiriar, you're an excellent doctor, and I think you'd make a good vet.'"

He was aloof, isolated, intimidating. His ministers, those guardians of the constitution, who should have held the whip, trembled in fear of his caustic reprimand. "My ministers are mostly idiots," said he. "They can afford the luxury. They have only to do as I tell them."

He could not help being clever, and moreover, right. Once, working with his ministers, a breeze blew a stack of papers off the desk. The ministers sprang to pick them up, but Leopold stayed them and pointed to his nephew, Albert, the heir apparent to the throne. "You pick them up," he said.

The ministers were aghast to see their future king scrabbling at their feet for papers, but Leopold explained, "Leave him alone. A constitutional king must learn to stoop."

Had the king no cordiality for anything? Well, there were his gardens, his hothouses full of rare and famous blooms, dragged from their habitats to his own to be pampered and adored; and his acres of orchards, espaliered, spreadeagled, so that the branches grew as he wished, not as they wished. It was his pleasure to walk endlessly among his beloved, tormented trees, counting his fruit and when as a child Princess Louise had dared to pick a peach, he missed it and punished her severely.

Still, no one would have labelled him Nero or Pizarro for callousness to his ministers or his fruit trees.

Queen Victoria—with her predilection for odd, brilliant men—rather liked her Cousin Leopold. This surprised her equerry, Ponsonby, because, as he said, "his morals were notorious."

Yes, they were. So much so that once his Belgians prevailed upon a respected priest who had known the king from youth to remind him of the fact. The priest did so. He detailed at length some adventures of which his sovereign had recently been the hero. When he had done, the king favored him with a glance that would have congealed a polar bear. "How very odd!" he said. "Only yesterday, someone was telling me the same about you. And d'you know, I didn't believe it!"

All the same, Leopold loved the uncountable fruity girls that grew on the espaliers of Paris. They, at least, had no reason to complain of his parsimony: he lavished jewels on them, enjoyed them, then sent them packing with a smack. He was the symbol in his time of the *vieux marcheur*, the old womanizer. When he grew old, manufacturers of tonic pills employed his portrait to advertize their product.

The most famous of his women was a singularly beautiful dancer at the Opéra named Cléo de Mérode. It would have been like Leopold to have sought this *artiste's* acquaintance for the sole purpose of teasing the great and stately Belgian family of the same name. Cléo herself insisted that she had a full right to it, that she came from a collateral and impoverished branch of the Mérodes, so that although born a marquise she was obliged to earn her living as a dancer.

The king launched his assault on Cléo in the manner of a man who anticipates no contradiction. Walking past her house one day, he cleverly managed to give his gentlemen-in-waiting the slip. He hid behind the concièrge's loge until his hounds lost scent, then slipped in the door, skimmed up the stairs, and rang the bell of her apartment. She was in her negligée and was speechless to see the King of the Belgians standing at her door. Not the man to give any girl the chance of saying no, Leopold skipped inside, closed the door, and using the familiar *tu* in speaking to her, informed her of his pleasure: she was to receive him in the foyer of the Opéra the following night.

The foyer of the Opéra had been for some time past a convenient common ground where gentlemen about town might make the acquaintance of the ballerinas, and there was always much gaiety and animation there in the hour or two before the ballet began. Only members of the Jockey Club—that is, the rich and wellborn—were admitted, and the French anecdotist Loliée tells us that among the dancers themselves strict protocol was observed.

"The first to arrive are the seven or eight charming members of the front row, the most applauded and courted. They proceed to shake hands with five or six of the important personages with whom they are on familiar terms and who condescend to extend to them their all-powerful protection. They then form into little groups of twos, retiring to discreet corners with the titular lover or the favored one of the hour.

"The little choristers and beginners come in a little later, closely pursued by the younger subscribers and teased by the older ones. They take possession of the divans at the four corners of the room, laughing and joking, and nibbling at the sweets or admiring the trinkets that have been given to them by the generous clubmen."

Such exalted persons as kings did not join this carnival. They used instead the dark corridor that led from the foyer to the wings which was jealously guarded against intruders by an elderly dragon of the dressing room. It was her privilege to lead royal persons through the darkness by the hand.

But the eccentric King of the Belgians proposed no such hole-in-corner arrangement to Cléo de Mérode, though at that time she danced in the back rows of the ballet. He commanded her to stand out in the full glare of the foyer with the prima ballerinas, the gay blades of the Jockey Club, the raconteurs and famous journalists, and to introduce him round about. She was in a state of considerable trepidation; this required consultation with her mother. Madame la Marquise had known in her own life the agonies of obscurity for a beautiful woman, and she said, "Do it."

There was to be no obscurity for Cléo. She became a prima ballerina commanding huge sums in every capital of Europe, and for ten years she walked magnificently clad in showers of silks and gems as Leopold's official mistress. Great artists painted her sultry beauty and sculpted her form of supple strength and delicacy. Whatever she wore became the rage, including the pretty silk ribbon she placed straight across her brow, and which in various forms lasted women as a fashion throughout *la belle époque.*

It is said that the Shah of Persia once paid Cléo de Mérode ten thousand francs—two thousand dollars—just to converse with him for one hour. She made the most out of such easy-gotten riches—after all, she had a financial wizard at her disposal to handle her investments. His name was Cléopold.

Cléopold! How this nickname stuck in the proud Coburg's craw! He could look with indifference at the comic portraits of himself with Cléo's arms entwined about him like rubbery vines while he adorned her with jewels, explaining, "These are only part of what I stole from my daughters, *chérie!*" Or at cartoons of the princesses standing drably at the door of a magnificent salon where the king reclined, closely involved with Cléo, saying, "But father, couldn't you just give us some of Cléo's old clothes?" He was icily unconcerned by the most vicious one of all which showed him returning from his queen's funeral to Cléo, chortling, "Cléo! How happy I am! I feel young again! Hooray for being a widower!"

But Cléopold! The king was so aggravated that he went to the extreme length of declaring publicly that far from enjoying the favors of Madame de Mérode for the last ten years, he had never set eyes on her in his life. He even staged a little act one night at the Opéra when he asked an important official to present the lady to him, saying that he had never met her, though he "had often heard of her." The important official promptly adopted the view that the king was uncommonly deep.

"And yet it was perfectly true," recalled his *agent de Sûreté*. "He had never set eyes on her in his life. The fact was proved by the candour of the words which he addressed to the charming dancer when she was brought up to be presented. 'Allow me to express all my regrets if the good fortune which people attribute to me has offended you at all. Alas, we no longer live in the days when a king's favor was not looked upon as compromising. Besides, I am only a little king!' "

Surely this performance would persuade us all if we did not have Cléo's word in her autobiography as to the manner of Leopold's invasion of her apartment and the favor he conferred on her in allowing her to receive him at the Opéra. And yet Madame de Mérode has denied steadfastly that in all the scandalous years that followed, she was ever the mistress of Leopold II.

We gladly accept the word of all concerned, especially as it does not matter. It was certainly not for his reputed affair with the lovely Cléo, or with all the *gamines* and *bambines* in Paris, that Leopold II was the most abhorred man of his time, and the loneliest.

Leopold was abhorred because of the ghastly outcome of his financial wizardry. For this was the great gift he was born with —an instinctive understanding of the peculiar habits of money. As a young man he had traveled widely around the world. He had not troubled much to absorb the culture proper to a royal prince; instead he had noted populations, industries, commerce, and economic conditions. He was able to look at a crowd of

Chinese and grasp at once how much work they might do per man hour and per year, if properly persuaded; how much money could be wisely invested in them and how much could be expected to take wing for home. All his life he had been busy multiplying his private fortune, as well as those he appropriated from his female relatives, and he was becoming very rich.

His Belgians were not at all aware of what he was up to. They were sitting back in their shabby shops reflecting how grand it was to have a king who was related to all the royal families in Europe. It would have alarmed them to know that once, on a visit to the Acropolis, their king had picked up an ancient stone and on it inscribed these words: BELGIUM MUST HAVE COLONIES.

He was certainly not the only person in the world who was dreaming about money and colonies. At the end of the nineteenth century people were interesting themselves in these items as avidly as at the beginning of it they had interested themselves in God. But it is intriguing that one of those who were born into the money age fully armed to take advantage of it should have been a king; and it is bizarre to imagine Leopold, looking like an Olympian, sitting at his dinner table spread with silver and solid gold, Belgian linen and Brussels lace, deep in conversation with a man of the new age, ugly and lumpy with thorny hands, whipped eyes, and scared mouth.

This browbeaten specimen had been conceived by a Welsh servant girl under a bush, and his mother hated the unwelcome fruit of her day off! She gave him to the workhouse—she didn't want him! Forever after, two mighty nations, England and America, would carry on a subdued journalistic wrangling as to which of them deserved the greater credit for his being. However, it was the Welsh girl who was responsible for his being, and when in Africa he discovered the place where the great Congo River spreads into a lake before throwing itself in passionate cataracts upon the sea, he named this wonder of waters, as a Welshman would: Stanley Pool.

Leopold was wining and dining Stanley because he was determined to wheedle out of him the Congo, that treasure chest of rubber, ivory, and rare raw materials for the Belgian factories. He had been watching this funny-looking empire builder for years, long before anyone else recognized that the man was building an empire for some lucky nation. He had watched him trying to give his treasure chest to the English, and he had smiled when they turned it down. Now he was listening sympathetically while the messianic little man explained to him about his Congolese, his beloved cannibals, who lived in a state of nature and were preyed upon by Arab slave traders. Give them a little Christianity and a few more clothes, teach them the virtue of honest labor, and they would promptly stop eating one another and become jolly chaps! Leopold heartily agreed. Missionaries and educators must be sent to the Congo, and troops to fight the Arabs, and long bolts of cotton to make everybody decent. In his infinite generosity, out of his own pocket Leopold would finance Stanley in the building of trade stations, roads, and other appurtenances of civilization. Stanley might safely leave the rest to him.

Of course, as he was fond of saying, he was only a little king. But he had the prestige to call all the explorers and geographers in Europe together into a study of the Congo and establish before the eyes of the whole world how direly the Congolese stood in need of succor. He was able to get the nations to join in a philanthropic organization under his own presidency dedicated to freeing Congolese from slavers. And when they became bored with this, he could finagle it into an investment company and attract investors. And when the investors found things going slow, he could get control of all the shares.

He could, and did, in fact, create the Congo Free State, and by wiles and guiles, he induced all major powers to recognize it with himself, Leopold, as a sort of benevolent caretaker. What they failed to notice was that it was no longer an international investment company of philanthropical interest, and that it was by no means free. Leopold owned it.

He did this incredible thing invisibly. For a long time the financiers of Europe and the interested nations and governments were unaware that Leopold had put the Congo under his beard and was working it for profit. By the time they realized the true state of affairs the Congo had been legally annexed to Leopold. Now, he was the richest of kings, surely one of the richest men in the world, raised far in power above his rank, his constitution, or his parliament. He had met the imperialists and the money-men on their own ground, and he had duped them.

For seventeen years the cartoonists drew Leopold flying high on golden wings, holding in his royal hands the only orb worth holding, a bag of money.

And then he was shot down! Rolled in mud and blood by a finicky British consul!

This villain's name was Roger Casement, and in 1901 he was Her Majesty's Consul in Boma, or more accurately, a British spy against the Boers. His duties took him up the Congo, where he made voluminous notes. There began to flow into the foreign office reports in horrid detail of appalling events there: of black men driven for days into the jungle under killing tropical storms to collect rubber, pressed into chain gangs, made to labor under the lash, shot dead if they did not bring their quota of rubber back; of men emasculated; of women raped; of burdensome babies thrown to the crocodiles; of useless old people tied to stakes and burned alive. And everywhere there were men, women, and children wearing stumps of arms, their hands cut off because somehow they had failed to please.

Up and down the mighty river, wrote Casement, tribes hitherto friendly ran away in panic at the approach of white men. According to his estimate, during the seventeen years of the existence of the Congo Free State, the population had been cut in half. Ten million black people had been murdered, for "red rubber."

Casement's revelations broke cataclysmically over the world. The Americans, who had been the first of the powers to recognize the Congo Free State, rose up in wrath, and all their anger was syphoned by Mark Twain into his bitter, gorge-raising *King Leopold's Soliloquy*. The British, who had been kicking themselves for having refused the Congo when Stanley offered it to them, added horror to their mortification. The members of the Aborigines Protection Society sent up a cry of anguish. But there was nothing anyone could do, because the Congo was a private estate which belonged to Leopold.

How did the king reply? He said that the British ought not to pose as humanitarians. He said that he had driven the slave traders out of the Congo and now he had the right to be repaid for his labors. He said that Casement had exaggerated. He appointed a commission to study conditions in the Congo. By various delaying tactics he was able to work the Congo for five more profitable years.

But the King of the Belgians was now the most loathed monarch since Nero. Even his own Belgians hated him, and when he rode through the streets of Brussels, they watched him pass in bitter silence.

What could his thoughts have been during those years? Perhaps he had not the emotional capacity to feel shame. None of the nineteenth-century money moguls—possibly excepting Diamond Jim Brady—was noted for human sympathy. It was said of Leopold that he had not a heart of stone but of a gold harder than stone, that he was a man devoid of sentiment and of sentimentality, impulse, and generosity, and that in his nature the softer feelings had no place.

Therefore it was indeed a freak adventure that one day when the king was sixty-five years old, love came flying, and like a pigeon of the streets that rests its comic beauty on the grimy statue of an Olympian god, it alighted on Leopold II.

It all began at the Champs Elysées Palace Hotel, a flamboyant hostelry which devoted itself to the comfort of very rich notables visiting Paris, and in whose corridors a sharp-sighted king might easily harpoon a provocative *horizontale*.

Caroline Delacroix was sixteen years old, the youngest of thirteen children of a poverty-stricken railway mechanic. Her mother had put her to toil in a laundry; another honorable career was open to her as assistant to one of her older sisters who had a handbarrow at Les Halles from which she sold vegetables. However, Caroline had still another sister who was a successful *horizontale*, and it was to this profession that she was apprenticing herself—until her sister grew jealous and threatened to cut off Caroline's fortune in golden hair. Caroline then placed herself under the protection of a cocky little gambler named Durieux who could not pay their rent. He was working hard at the race track one day when Caroline's doorbell rang and a woman she had never seen before entered to tell her that she had been observed at the Champs Elysées Palace Hotel by a Very Important Personage; and that she would find it to her advantage to appear at a certain address on the following day. Caroline clearly recognized fate's operations because her clock which had just struck noon struck by mistake thirteen times.

She presented herself punctually at the agreed address, and was conducted by a parlormaid into a smallish room lighted with floor lamps. "Just as I was entering, two extraordinary words rooted me where I stood. A gentleman of military bearing, standing, was saying as he bent before a personage with a long white square beard sitting in an armchair in the center of the room, 'Yes, Sire! Yes, Sire!' Was I dreaming?"

In front of the bearded personage was a chair under a lamp. The military gentleman and the woman who had summoned her the day before stood on either side. Caroline was now told to sit down on the chair under the light.

There ensued a long inquisition in which the military man and the woman asked alternate questions, forcing her to turn her head from side to side. The beard remained still, but Caroline could feel two thrusting eyes boring into her, and she began to falter and tremble. The woman then brought her a pile of jades and crystals, inviting her to admire them. She realized that it was now her hands that were undergoing scrutiny. Suddenly from the satyr's Santa Claus there came an abrupt explosion, "*Bien!*" The other two vanished from the room "as if sucked off by a giant vacuum cleaner."

"*Très Belle*," said the King of the Belgians in a tone whose sweetness won her instantly, "Do you know who I am?"

"Yes!" replied Caroline. "You are Oscar, King of Sweden."

Leopold laughed. He bent forward to take her hands, saying softly, "Hands mean a lot. And yours, thank God, are not those of a courtesan. Courtesan's hands are always small and pudgy."

Later, he said to her, "Now what shall you call me? You are Très Belle. I am *très vieux*. Très Vieux! Yes, call me Très Vieux! That pleases me very much."

Within a day, Très Belle found herself magnificently installed in the Champs Elysées Palace Hotel (of which the king held much of the stock), with new luggage for traveling in the wake of the king, and a great stack of francs to squander on dressmakers. It remained to write Durieux a note explaining that she had gone on a sudden trip to South America.

The first time her sovereign summoned her to Brussels, an adventure in the style of Dumas *père* awaited her. She had put up at the Hotel Bellevue. At nine o'clock in the evening a carriage driven by a coachman who was a mute called for her. She was driven across the square and down an avenue, and presently the coach stopped in the shadows beside a wall. She dismounted and noticed nearby a small wooden door. As she stood hesitating before it, the door suddenly opened and there loomed Leopold. "Madame! You here? What a surprise!" he exclaimed, and he drew her into his enchanted garden.

For a while they wandered in the most romantic mood down silvery paths through a silent leafy realm. Then the king stopped before a low door which looked as if it might have been the door of a crypt or vault. He unlocked it and led her inside. To her astonishment she was in a pretty marble hallway leading to an apartment. One of the rooms, Leopold told her, had been created especially for her by the world-famous decorator, Jansen. He showed it to her. It was full of books! It was a library! The walls were totally banked with rows of cedar shelves bearing leather-bound books in serried, tedious ranks.

But now the king was busying himself with levers and buttons, and remarkable transformations were taking place in that room. Pale satin draperies unfolded to hide the books from view. A wall slid away and a bed came rolling out of it, a gilded, lace-and-satin-covered jewel of a bed. A piece of furniture that had been a sober desk broke up to reveal a washbasin and all that a lady could possibly need for her toilette. Shining over all was an exquisite chandelier garlanded with crystal.

Such was the fairy chamber into which Très Vieux introduced Très Belle. But even stranger was the domain that had opened to her in that metal heart of his.

The first to notice that the old king was in love with a *fille de joie* was Charles I of Roumania—Très Belle called him Charles of Rheumatism. Of course he babbled. Courts and cabinets buzzed and snickered. Now the cartoonists discovered that the Congo had an empress.

Très Belle was very pretty, a big girl, with roguish eyes, and all robust charms. No image of a goddess was she, but a bibelot of the kind Leopold liked best, picked up in the market place and brought home ill-wrapped. But he was accustomed to enshrine such bibelots in palaces of richest splendor. Humbly and unpretentiously Très Belle entered into the kingly world, full of gratitude for favors. "To start from nothing," she wrote many years later, "to have no ambition . . . then suddenly the miracle! To be able to draw the attention of one of the most powerful men of the time, to please him. . . ."

She wrote of herself as if she were a figure of folk dreams, a goose girl who finds unrolling before her a plush carpet leading to a treasure cave with modern plumbing. But this was not a dream! Gifts beyond the imagination of an *horizontale* were showered by Très Vieux upon Très Belle: villas and gardens, carriages and cars, the queen's ornaments, furs especially chosen for her by Russian noblemen, flunkeys in silk breeches, a retinue of cooks, maids, and chamberlains to accompany her everywhere, and the Castle of Balincourt for her very own which it was the king's delight to rebuild, refurbish, and embellish with every costly fantasy, such as a silver bathtub set in porphyry, a swimming pool of gold mosaic, and an English point lace bedspread worth twenty thousand dollars.

Now in the caricatures of Leopold there was a change of detail. They were no less scurrilous, but whereas for years thousands of drawings had shown the king in situations suggestive of the utmost frivolity, never had he been drawn with a smile: always the pouncing eyes, the massive nose and inhospitable beard, something of a barracuda swallowing a shaving brush. But now, as he was depicted dancing with Caroline, in bed with her and caressing her, the artists bent their pens to produce on the face of the king the semblance of a senile grin.

We can do much worse than accept the intuition of caricaturists to understand the secret of Très Belle's complete conquest of the king, especially as she bore them out with the following reflection: "Men are funny," she wrote, "and kings are the funniest of men. Maybe it is because they live apart, as if behind a Chinese wall, and so often only diluted truth reaches them. Besides, people don't laugh enough with them, don't joke enough. They do not see themselves as they really are. When I pointed out to Leopold one of his extraordinary manias, he was astounded."

She was only sixteen when she met Leopold: how could she know that the manias of kings may be ominous? She thought it was hilarious that his papers had to be ironed out every morning, since he could not bear to touch them with the slightest crease; that daily four buckets of salt water had to be brought from the sea to bathe him; that he refused to wear gloves because they prevented his skin from breathing; that he was mad for motor cars and was a speed demon; that he had a passion for secret doors, secret rooms, and underground passages and would buy any property that smacked of Edgar Allan Poe; that he had a horror of microbes and was terrified of sneezes, so that any equerry of his who wanted a day off had only to simulate a sneeze.

One dampish day the king had a rendezvous with Très Belle in the woods, and she was much amused to see him wearing great rubber boots that came up around his hips and an enormous fisherman's jacket and hat, and with his beard carefully encased in a waterproof bag of his own design which was attached to his hat by cords. He was wounded to see his mistress ready to fall on the wet grass with mirth. "This bag prevents my beard from getting wet," he explained. "By protecting my beard from the rain, I am trying to avoid catching cold."

Some say that when the king first brought Caroline home, she had no manners and poor speech. This did not prevent her from finding plenty of fault with Leopold's undiscriminating habits, especially with his shabby clothes, his old, nondescript uniform, and the famous general's cap with torn and tarnished braid. On the day she destroyed that foul symbol of Belgian majesty, his old straw hat, and replaced it with a new one, he turned on her in rage. "Do you think I'm made of money?" he furiously roared. She soothed him by assuring him that the new hat had been bought from a street stand, marked-down, cut-rate, mauled goods.

As love's first benediction wore away, they quarreled and fumed at one another; at least the king fumed, while Très Belle lit a big black cigar and blew the smoke around. When they went traveling, such scenes made their keyholes among the most rewarding in Europe. Once, after an outbreak of hostilities at Trouville, Leopold banged off to spend the night in the Villa des Mouettes, a fashionable brothel, and he returned to tell the tale.

Yet they held together, finely balanced by mutual need: his for her friendship, hers for protection. He lived in terror that she would forsake him; she that he would let her go.

Then came the acid test. For Très Belle had the unbelievable folly to resume her acquaintance with her former lover, Durieux the gambler, and she could not help inviting him to admire her present affluence. She received him at the Villa Vanderborght, next to the royal castle grounds at Laeken, which the king had commanded Girault, architect of the Petit Palais in Paris, to restore for her. It had been decorated by the imaginative Jansen. Slack-jawed, the young man stared at the wonders it contained, especially at Très Belle's bedroom, where numerous mirrors adroitly reflected the bed. He asked if he could come again.

Sunday after Sunday—which was Très Belle's day off—Durieux came to Vanderborght. Of course it was bound to happen. They were in the billiard room and Durieux was poised over a difficult shot when Leopold walked in. Durieux staggered and looked as if he was going to faint. The glance of Très Vieux was aimed at him like an elephant gun about to go off. Très Belle began to shake with fright, but with her whole life at stake, she was the first to pull herself together. "Sire," she said, "allow me to present to you my brother, Étienne."

At once, "like an ice-cake that melts in the rays of the sun," the old "chap of breed" was all urbanity. He shook hands with Durieux, welcomed him warmly, sat down beside him. He put Durieux through a grueling inquisition. It seemed he was minutely familiar with the affairs of Étienne, his health, his hopes, his projects: also those of the other members of the Delacroix family. Interminably, he posed questions which were "like bandarillos and darts planted in the miserable Durieux." Très Belle recorded this scene as the worst remembrance of her life in Brussels. When her lover was reduced to the consistency of minced jellyfish, the king ceased. He turned his back on his mistress. He went out, and he did not come back.

For two weeks there was not one word from him, not a message. Complete silence. During this time Très Belle had opportunity to learn how huge a royal villa is, and how solitary it can seem to an abandoned *horizontale*. The newspapers had gotten hold of the story, and the scandal broke world-wide. Articles appeared in the Socialist papers, and the titillating, humble story of her origins was spread abroad. Every eye that had ever glued itself to Caroline's keyhole was found to add detail to the salacious gossip.

Two weeks, and the king was as dead. Then one night when she was alone in her room, sick at heart, and resigned to be thrown out onto the rubbish heap, the door opened and Leopold appeared. He had a newspaper in his hand.

"Très Belle," he said. "I don't believe a word of all these horrors, and I'll never mention them again."

She sank to her knees on the floor before him. She seized his hands and covered them with kisses.

One of the things Caroline had found funniest about Leopold at the beginning of their affair was his faith in the childishly simple strategems he devised for keeping their encounters hidden from the public eye. She traveled with him everywhere, took the same train, alighted at the same destination, stayed at the same hotel, ate in the same dining room; for that matter she shared the same keyhole. Yet she was forbidden to speak to him in public, greet him, or acknowledge his presence in any way. A cheerful girl, she contented herself with making faces and waving at his gentlemen-in-waiting.

Every morning she was under instructions to walk in the park with her maid, where Leopold would meet her, and with an air of amazement bid her a loud good morning. The maid would then fall back with the king's aide-de-camp, while Leopold walked next to Très Belle. On rainy days this same performance took place between carriages.

But when in 1902 the queen went her lonely way to death, and after the Durieux crisis had been surmounted, Leopold looked into his heart and found Très Belle established there as a fixture. He no longer played games. He was a king, after all, and though his nature was full of guile, hypocrisy was beneath his dignity. If his Belgians did not approve of his mistress, they could shake their fists.

That is exactly what they did. The people of Belgium could not endure the sight of the disreputable favorite, flaunted in their faces at the very time that the Congo scandals broke world-wide; when magazines were filled with photographs of Negroes without hands; when kiosks displayed caricatures of Leopold, the Cannibal Coburg, feasting upon the bodies of black men and of decent people holding their noses in the presence of the Belgian crown.

Whenever Caroline went shopping in Brussels, the people crowded around her with insults. One day, as she rode in her carriage, some housewives gathered, and skipping excitedly in the roadway, they picked up some stones and threw them at her. After this incident the king did an astounding thing. He called the Minister of the Interior to him and informed him that if

Caroline was obliged to leave Belgium on account of such hostility, he, Leopold of Coburg, their king, would leave also. He would abdicate.

But Caroline had deadlier enemies by far than the mob, and more persistent ones: the Princesses Louise, Stephanie, and Clementine. More was at stake for these ladies than the prestige of the Coburgs or of the Belgian crown: there were those millions, billions of francs comprising the private fortune of their aged father. Their campaign was statesmanlike and began with a frontal attack: they delegated Clementine, who lived with their father as his official hostess, and who was the only one of them Leopold could tolerate, to expostulate with him.

His reaction was terrible. Clementine was consigned to her room and commanded to eat all her meals alone. He then had her removed to a villa which stood halfway between the Castle Laeken and the Villa Vanderborght. In this way she could see her father daily visiting Très Belle from her front window.

Now on informal occasions Caroline performed as Leopold's hostess when he summoned to his table the most exciting and significant people in Europe. To think of the eminent Victorians she must have met, including Stanley! A further triumph was in store for her when, shortly after the rout of Clementine, she accompanied Leopold on a Mediterranean cruise during which he was officially received everywhere. The king carefully refrained from introducing Caroline, so that everyone might politely assume that she was Princess Clementine.

On this journey Très Belle became pregnant. The king brought her back to France, and their son was born after a long and painful labor during which Leopold did not leave her side for an instant. He rewarded her with an honorary title: Baroness de Vaughan.

The princesses were now in a panic and ready to strike again: Très Belle had to be seduced away from the king. A succession of handsome and gallant young courtiers were introduced to her company, all eager to carry out their patriotic mission.

Fortunately for the baroness, her servants were excellent friends with Princess Clementine's servants, so she had a spy service all her own; besides, she was intelligent and outspoken, and when she saw a man behaving like a jackass, she did not hold back from telling him so.

But she was almost taken in by His Majesty's second chamberlain, one Devermont. He laid his plans with cunning, displaying at first mere friendliness, next respectful admiration; at last he judged it time to reveal an ardent heart. One morning, when she was staying at a Paris hotel, he showed up at the door of her rooms. Très Belle admitted him. He then told her bluntly that he was madly in love with her and that his life was unbearable on that account. She replied innocently.

" 'Look here,' I said, 'you are not serious. Life is not unbearable because one is in love. At twenty those things are understandable, but not at your age.'

" 'Not at my age? What do you know about that?' and a flow of tears drowned his cry. As his sobs threatened to continue indefinitely, . . . I told him there was no hope:

" 'Even if I were free, even if the king died, you could never be anything else to me than a friend.'

"Next the scene changed, as in a few minutes it was going to change several times. Devermont took a revolver out of his pocket and held it to his temple.

" 'If you persist in denying me, I shall kill myself.'

"His tears and the revolver frightened me. But beneath my fear I remembered a warning the king had given me often: Be wary of men who cry and threaten to kill themselves; they are generally plain blackmailers.

"I did not move when Devermont pressed the trigger. The revolver made a funny noise; the chamber was empty.

"My fear disappeared. I was disgusted. 'So that was your revolver! You are only a shadow of a man and a poor miserable charlatan!'

"Furious, he picked up his weapon.

" 'So, you believe that this was all arranged. You think that I knew this revolver was empty. I did not know it! My friends, who know my passion for you, must have taken the cartridges out! But what does it matter? The window remains. If I throw myself into the street, will you still believe that I am acting? Will you still persist in not believing I am mad for you?'

" 'Yes,' I said, bursting out laughing, 'if you do that, I'll believe you!'

"He opened the window. I did not make the slightest effort to keep him back, yet my apartment was on the fourth floor facing the street.

" 'You are sending me to my death!' he shouted. 'It is murder, because you must have guessed a long time ago that I am in love with you. . . . You want my death. All right, your wish will be fulfilled immediately.'

"He assumed a pose, to give me time to think. However, I don't know why, he only made me laugh.

" 'Well,' I said to him, 'what are you waiting for? Go on, please jump!'

"To my horror, he jumped!

"I cried out. I was on the verge of fainting, and yet I had enough courage to go to the window and look out. To my great surprise, life was going on as usual in the street. . . . There was no shapeless body on the pavement. . . . I was wondering if I were not going insane when I noticed that beneath my window was a wide balcony and that from the room opening on it came some whispering.

"Devermont had been bluffing, and he had bluffed in a masterly fashion. . . . He had executed his scheme so well that I could not help admiring him."

No, she was no fool, this random mistress the king had picked up on the streets of Paris, nor was she a dull enemy. "Give back his sword to a scoundrel," she said, "and he will run it through your body. But forgiving is permitted to noble natures."

One of the pleasant things about Caroline is that while she violently resented being looked down upon, and dreaded chance meetings with Princess Clementine who invariably examined her as if she were made of purest crystal, she could—at least thirty-five years later—express sympathy for the princesses' point of view.

Eleven months after the birth of her first child Très Belle became pregnant again, and the attacks against her increased in virulence. Her enemies now determined that the king must be persuaded to believe the new child was not his own.

In order to remove Très Belle to a friendlier climate the king rented for her the Château de Lormois near Paris, and he visited her faithfully three times a week. Peace was present in the gentle countryside and in the friends around her. But twice a day peace was blasted by the arrival of mail containing all manner of poisonous letters which she could not bear to open nor yet to throw aside. All repeated the same hideous threat: the child about to be born is not the king's; and he will know it.

Perhaps she might have become inured to the letters, if Leopold's demeanor on his visits had not aroused alarm. Usually so gay when he was with her, he now seemed haunted, and ice seemed to beset his heart. How, after all, could he ignore the suggestions that were continually being made to him by courtiers, by reasonable ministers of government, by articles in the Socialist newspapers, which every morning, like the constitutional ruler he was, he dutifully read. Surely someone had made certain that a joke of the cafés would come to his attention. It was a conversation between two Belgians: "*Enfin, tout de même, elle lui a donné un fils avec l'aide de Dieu.*"

The other replies: "*Je croyais que c'était avec l'aide-de-camp.*"

Leopold knew, of course, everything that was to be known about vilification. When he walked lonely and bemused between his espaliers, he might have recalled how the cartoonists drew them, hung with countless severed Negro hands. But when all had been turned over in the turmoil of his mind, the facts remained: his mistress was *très belle*, and he was *très vieux*.

Caroline was terrified. She entreated her doctor for the latest medical miracle, scientific means to prove to the king that the child was his own. "Suppose it looks exactly like the king?" she besought him.

"No good," replied the doctor. "It has long been known that a child can easily look like the person who is in its mother's thoughts throughout pregnancy."

One day the doctor went to Brussels and dined with the king. In their conversation, they brought the nightmare into the open, and the king definitely expressed his conviction that the child was not his own. For some reason the doctor felt it necessary to tell Caroline of this, so that she went into her labor crushed, knowing that every enemy of hers and every scandalmonger in Europe was waiting for her imminent disgrace. She felt done for.

But when that second son was born, all slanderous tongues were silent. Courtiers, ministers, and servants found their cackles sticking in their throats. Far and wide from Belgium the news spread into every tavern and café, every newspaper office, and

every drawing room, where gossips gathered to review the sins
of kings, and for once they were short of breath. For the child
had come into the world on Leopold's Saint's Day, and Almighty
God had written on it the signature of its father: it was born
without a hand.

Leopold listened behind the door while the doctor broke the
news to Caroline. Then he came in, shaking with sobs, and
gathered her into his arms.

As Leopold became old and lame his brain remained as lucid
and incisive as ever it was. He devoted his last years to securing
his vast fortune against the depredations of the princesses. By
every craft and guile, including large-scale embezzlement, he
piled up money and then hid it in foundations, false-fronted com-
panies, and investments in far corners of the globe. He constructed a nest of legal disputes between the Belgian Government
and the princesses in which they might wrangle for years. In the
end—if he knew governments—the money would remain with
his true heir, Belgium. Already he had arranged for the transfer
of his beautifully tended estates and great parklands to the
people on his death. One year before he died he turned over the
Congo Free State to the Belgian Government, and as the Belgian
Congo it was neither worse off nor better off than the colony of
any other nation.

He continued to quarrel with, terrify, suspect, and love Très
Belle. He delighted in his sons. He would go to the public
markets, fill his pockets with sweets, load himself down with
toys, and return to them, treasure-laden. They called him, obviously, St. Nicholas—Colas for short—and they pulled his beard.
They were even permitted to play with his saber and bedraggled
old general's cap while the king looked on "trembling to see
them handling such precious objects." He appointed a lawyer to
find a way that they could be legally recognized and entitled
princes of Coburg.

A supreme skeptic all his life, he became in these last years
reconciled with his religion. One Easter, while they were staying
at Nice, the king took Caroline for a motor ride, refusing all
company. He was observed to be very nervous, and she to be
greatly excited. It was inferred, indeed it became almost a certainty among gossips, that the King of the Belgians had married

Baroness de Vaughan at San Remo over the Italian border. Years later the baroness herself divulged the truth: that he had merely arranged, secretly and with difficulty, to take Holy Communion together with his sons' mother. But from the time of that drive Caroline's life became easier: she was treated with greater respect.

Then, suddenly, the princesses shot another bolt. They appealed to Cardinal Mercier, Primate of Belgium, to separate their father from the obnoxious woman. This was a vicious stroke to test the king's new need for decent Catholicity against his need for Caroline.

The cardinal agreed to carry the matter to the Pope. He went to Rome and spent two weeks there. He returned. Caroline, whose spy service among domestic servants had informed her of what was in the wind, followed his movements avidly in the newspapers, but she did not dare to query Leopold and tried by covert glances to read her future in his face.

They were staying at her Château of Balincourt when the cardinal requested the king to come to Brussels for a conference. The king went and remained a week. He returned to Balincourt, kissed her and said not a word. Queasy with apprehension, Caroline presided over a dinner party, and when the guests had gone, the king kissed her again and said, "Très Belle, tomorrow we'll have to have a serious talk." That kiss felt to her mightily like the kiss of doom.

The following morning Leopold entered her room and spoke in ominous tones. He explained what she already knew, that the cardinal had gone to Rome on the insistence of the princesses to speak about her with the Holy Father. Très Belle pretended astonishment.

"Do you know what the Holy Father said to His Eminence?" Très Belle did not know.

"The Sovereign Pontiff decided that I would either have to send you away or marry you. I assured the cardinal that I would obey the Holy Father and marry you."

She almost swooned with relief.

By marrying Caroline, not only would Leopold make his peace with God, but he would make certain that all of the properties he had given her, and all of his visible fortune, every centime, every stone and flower, every knickknack and secret passage, every blade of grass that did not fall to Belgium or was not tied up in foundations, would belong to Très Belle and her sons forever.

He returned to Brussels to arrange everything. About a week went by. Très Belle received a telegram: COME AT ONCE. She went, and joined Leopold at Laeken where they supped together, the king in an exceptionally scintillating mood.

But afterwards, he took her hands and said, "You are going to be very brave, Très Belle. You have to be. For I am going to die."

He had an intestinal complaint, and the doctors had been in conference for the past week. He was to be operated on within the next two days. He was seventy-four years old. His chances of surviving had been given to him as one in ten. He told Caroline: "I am convinced of my death for my own reasons. First, I am a sick man. Secondly I am a well-known man. There will be too many doctors around me. One doctor is a good doctor. Two doctors are half a doctor. Three doctors are worse than no doctor at all. You'll see; they'll do so much for me, they'll kill me."

If it weren't for having to shave off his beard to disguise himself, he declared, he would gladly go to the public free dispensary where only one doctor would be found to bother with him.

Thus, out of respect for his beard, the king laid himself upon his deathbed. At nine o'clock the next morning Très Belle made confession and took Communion. Then she joined the king, who was wearing a white flannel dressing gown, while she wore her black traveling dress. The Canon of Laeken Castle was there. He married them. The king then called one of his trusted ministers and said, "I present to you my widow. I place her under your protection."

The marriage papers were reposed with the Church.

The following morning, at dawn, six Congolese trunks were delivered to Caroline. They contained papers and bonds symbolizing the fortune the king had willed to her. She would have to find a way to smuggle them out of the country.

Meanwhile the king was brought to the Pavillon des Palmiers, a small nest in the center of his great hothouses and gardens, commanding a wide view of them. It was in this exotic ambience, where he had collected all of earth's exquisite masterpieces, that he wished to die.

The doctors operated on him successfully. They told him that

if he survived three days, he would survive. Delighted to be
wrong for once, the king called for his newspapers to be read
to him. Of course he would survive! And he would take Très
Belle and the boys for a holiday to his splendid Riviera estates.
A cot was brought for her and placed beside his bed. Since in
her confusion she had brought no nightclothes, the king commanded that a nightshirt of his be given her, and he laughed
to see her staggering about in this ridiculous garment. He was
gathering strength by the hour.

The next day a great joy was in store for him. For years,
with incredible foresight, Leopold had been badgering his Belgians to arm themselves against aggressive neighbors "to stop
anybody from passing through us." He had vastly extended
and modernized the fortifications at Antwerp; and for the last
five years he had brought all the weight of his personality and
sarcasm to persuading them to pass a bill for obligatory military
conscription.

Now with their king dying, this desire was to be granted him.
The Senate hurried through the vote. Monsieur Schollaert, the
Prime Minister, came to the Pavillon des Palmiers with the news,
and with shaking hand the king signed, "Leopold," on the decree
which would in 1914 enable Belgians to hold a narrow bridge
of war, and perhaps spare Western Europe from the treat of
being ruled by the Kaiser.

When he had signed, he said some words strange to his lips:
"The king is content." Monsieur Schollaert left the sickroom
trying to restrain his weeping.

Why did he weep? And what were all those people doing in
the park, pressing about the Pavillon des Palmiers? They hated
their king, didn't they? For years when he went through the
streets they had turned away and not vouchsafed him a spon-
taneous cheer. Why honor with anxious presence the end of a
shameful era?

Could they have begun to realize already that unlike the deaths
of most kings, Leopold's would not mark the end of an era, but
a beginning? Were they instinctively aware, without yet assess-
ing it, of all he had done for them? He had drawn to their shores
fabulous wealth; he had flung out their commerce and spread
their land with works of usefulness and grandeur; out of his
own genius he had manufactured for his people a mystique, a

destiny as a modern nation, and he had compelled them to become involved with it. For decades, Belgium would move ahead, impelled by Leopold.

Remote, proud ruler, you are sick, and you cannot roar at us if we inquire of you: Did you kill all those black men? Did you cut off their hands? Did you exist in life as you existed in the awful imagination of Mark Twain, poring by night over the Congo reports: "On our way the soldiers saw a little child, and when they went to kill it the child laughed, so that the soldier took the butt of his gun and struck the child with it and then cut off its head." Did you cry in despair, "I wish it hadn't laughed!" and then go on to kill more children?

Or is it possible that the Casement Report was a stupendous lie, paid for by the Germans or by jealous English businessmen; or likelier still, developed from far slenderer crimes by Casement himself, to draw attention and rescue him from rotting in a jungle as Her Majesty's Consul at Boma?

Roger Casement was an Irishman, a patriot, and during World War I he acted as an *agent provocateur* and saboteur against the British. He was arrested in 1916, tried for treason, and hanged. He shines in the annals of Eire with the light of an archangel, a man who gave his life for his country's freedom.

For all that, at Casement's trial it became clear that at the bottom of his nature lay the shiftiness of the born spy, the agitator, the paid troublemaker. He was a neurasthenic, a megalomaniac, a mythomaniac, a perverted man of lurid imagination and lurid doings. In the words of the counsel who defended him, a patriotic Irishman, "Casement ought to have been a 'con man.' . . . He would tell you the most appalling falsehoods and not only believe them himself, but make you believe them too."

That cruel deeds occurred in the darkness of Congo jungles, there can be no doubt. They were occurring all over the world where moneymen with guns were teaching the virtue of work to primitive peoples, and collected from colonial governments a percentage on their results. But that such deeds were perpetrated by a chain of command, known, tolerated, and indeed directed by Leopold is believed by many historians today to be unlikely. Roger Casement provided sufficient evidence for only one case to be investigated, and this turned out to be lies. The investigating commission found many abuses, but it did not find ghastly horror. It has never been properly explained why responsible residents of the Congo had not noticed these famous atrocities. Anthropologists had yet to invade Africa and other areas of the earth where Arab slave traders preyed upon the population and note the black man's trick of cutting off the hands of his beloved wife and children to make them less attractive as merchandise.

Très Vieux, we have dared to speak on your behalf. Once you said, "They say that I do not like the truth. It is false! But I do not like that in telling it to me, they forget that I am the king."

Now the truthteller is on his way to you. He is winding slowly past your orchards, your night-blooming flowers, your silent tame deer, and his hand is stretched toward the Pavillon des Palmiers. Let us see if he will pay you the respect you deserve. You awaken Très Belle with a sneeze. A sneeze? No wonder you were always terrified of them: thanks to beard bags, you never sneezed. The doctors crowd around. "I sneezed!" you snap at them. "Go back to bed, all of you." You lie back, you doze. Then you sit up, you clutch your throat and cry, "Très Belle, I am choking, choking. Oh! I am choking!" You shake off her hands, scatter the nuns, get to your feet and stand up to your royal height, and now! Great king, he has touched you with his enmarbling hand.

Très Belle, evicted from the king's deathchamber so that the royal family might enter without suffering an embarrassing encounter, returned to her Villa Vanderborght. She found it sealed by order of Princess Louise. What a trick to play on one's stepmother!

The Church came forward with the marriage papers, and the State came to unseal her property. A few days later Très Belle huddled in a shadowy place to watch from a distance Très Vieux traveling by. In the streets hawkers were selling caricatures of the king and photographs of herself.

One dark night the Baroness de Vaughan slunk out of Belgium incognito, and a very good riddance to her. With her went six Congolese trunks. What is inside them? the customs guard wanted to know. He ordered her to open one. He gazed down upon the bonds. "What are they?" he asked. And she, whose quick mind had so outraged and delighted the King of the Belgians replied, "Music paper. My father is a composer."

"Pass!" said the customs guard.

She sold her Castle of Balincourt to Sir Basil Zaharoff, the recluse and munitions maker. Later she married, thus giving her Coburg sons a name. Unfortunately it was that of Durieux, the popular sporting gentleman, and he quickly divested her of fifteen million dollars.

·VI·

THE SERBIAN NIGHTMARE

When finding extenuating circumstances for the misdeeds of nineteenth-century kings, one must be careful not to question the authority of the Divine Spirit with which they were insufflated. On principles that were both religious and superstitious the dread and fear of kings rested. To nineteenth-century conformists Habsburgs were holy and Roman; Bourbons were hallowed by brave work in the Crusades; the roots of Wittelsbachs, Coburgs, and Hanoverians lay side by side with Snow White and the Seven Dwarfs; Romanovs had remote compacts with Oriental djinns; and even the Napoleons made a sublime show with their glitter and their cannon.

But what about kings who were poor and powerless, and whose ancestors *within living memory* had fed their own swine? These were Cinderella-kings, and a miraculous glass slipper was needed to lift them into the highest royal realms.

Monarchs like this, however, had a certain advantage from the point of view of designing, ambitious, or even loving women. Entirely unsupported and unprotected as they were by awesome majesty, it was not beyond the dreams of a royal mistress to become a wife: not a mere subwife, such as Louis XIV, *le Roi Soleil*, had once made of his children's governess, Madame de Maintenon; or a guilty-conscience wife, such as Tsar Alexander II made of Princess Yuryevsky; or a legal-swindle wife, such as Leopold II, King of the Belgians, had made of Baroness de Vaughan; but a queen with a crown who might stand in the thronelight and receive the homage of multitudes.

Of course, there was a condition—there always is. Such women had to be prepared to deal with unruly, unstable, turbulent races of people, like those who inhabited the Balkans.

The history of Serbia is a tightly braided account of wars, insurrections, and revolutions, all due to the fact that this insignificant collection of mountain farmsteads, full of sturdy men and pigs, lay at the junction of three mighty empires with conflicting ambitions and religions: Austria, Russia, and Turkey. It lay like a bone, surrounded by three monstrous dogs.

For five hundred years the Turks had managed to keep an uneasy hold on Serbia. Periodically the Serbs would rise against them and with the aid of either Austria or Russia, give the Turks a thrashing. Then either Russia or Austria would make a peace treaty with the Turks, handing Serbia back to them as part of the bargain. Sometimes the Serbs would have to turn around and beat back the encroaching Austrians or Russians, this time perhaps with the assistance of the Turks. At one time they even fought Turks with Turks, for Serbian politics tend to have more layers than a slice of *baklava*.

Thus the Serbs emerged at the beginning of the nineteenth century—an illiterate tribe of pig raisers with no hereditary nobility or class of learned men, acknowledging as leaders only those of their number who had the enterprise to abandon their pigs and hide themselves in mountain fastnesses, where they lived the romantic life of *haidukes*, brigands, robber barons, preying upon Turks, Austrians, Russians, and eccentric English travelers. That is why to the present day, if you wish to dress up as a brigand for Halloween, you must procure something resembling the Serbian national costume.

Illiterate as they were, Serbs were not precisely uneducated. They had *guslars*, or bards, who traveled from mountain hideaway to farmstead, carrying with them their *gusle*, a one-stringed instrument. In magnificent, long-lined poetry they chanted the deeds of their heroes to the people, perpetuating more or less accurately their gory history, and as with other poetically gifted people, like the Irish, the Norse, and the Hindus, this epic poetry was a fountain of proverbial wisdom and knowledge to the Serbs.

In sum, the Serb presented a particular public image to the eyes of other Europeans: he was a brigand with ferocious whiskers and—because of a complicated wedding of Turkish, Tartar, and Slavic eyefolds—a crisscross glance like a snapping pair of scissors. He was valorous, proud, egalitarian, fiercely independent, fiercely poetic, touchy, and ardent-hearted.

Two terrible men dominated the century. One was Kara George—Black George—the last of the Serbian "culture heroes," indeed, perhaps the last in the world. Once he had been a peaceful pig tycoon, but he had been obliged to flee with his household before the Turks into Austria. When his old father, the patriarch, had faltered, Kara George had shot him dead. However, no man becomes a culture hero for brutality, but for weakness: an Achilles must have his heel, a Samson his hair. Kara George's weakness was impulsiveness, and he knew it. After he had returned to Serbia to embrace the life of a brigand, the Serbs implored him to lead them in a new uprising against the Turks and to become their ruler afterwards. He did his best to dissuade them. He said, ". . . he did not understand how to govern, his impetuosity rendered him unfit for office, that he could not wait to consult, but would be inclined to kill at once."

These modest protestations were waved aside. Kara George became the commander of the Serbs and after many a brave battle, duly glorified in verse, he shattered the power of the Turks in Serbia in 1804.

Now he was faced with the responsibility of providing some form of orderly self-government for his people. Irritated that he could not sign his name and furious that so few of his ministers could sign it for him, one of his first acts was to build schools, including the High School in Belgrade. Imagine a culture hero founding a high school! It is even odder to reflect, in passing, that this school almost immediately produced a genius —Vuk Karagdich, a peasant who defined and grammaticized the Serbian language, devising a particular alphabet by means of which Serbs could write down their traditional poetry and preserve it forever.

In 1813 the Turks rolled back again, and Kara George behaved with his usual impulsiveness: he turned tail and fled into Austria.

At this time a second terrible man stepped up to assume the leadership of Serbia. His name was Milosh Obren, and like Kara George he had been a pig farmer and subsequently a brigand. But he was a far more level-headed man than his predecessor. Instead of fighting the Turks, he soothed them. In return for Serbia's autonomy he agreed to pay an annual tribute to the sultan. Of course, Milosh Obren used the respite to smuggle arms into the country and hide them. At the right moment he struck, and again the Turks were thrashed. After this defeat they became merely nominal suzerains, and the only signs of their existence in Serbia were the crescent flag flying over the fortress in Belgrade and a few fly-covered Turks smoking cigarettes underneath it.

Milosh Obren now claimed a reward for his virtues: he declared himself and his descendants hereditary princes of Serbia.

The friends of Kara George sizzled with rage at this action whereby the crown was snatched from the deserving brow of their absconded hero. Kara George himself steamed back from exile to claim the throne. Not long after he set foot in Serbia the prince, Milosh Obren, received a gift in a basket. He opened it. It contained the head of Kara George. No one knows for certain whether Milosh Obren had ordered this gift to be brought to him, but he received it cost on delivery all the same. Because during his life, and long after he died, for almost a century, his country was to be torn asunder, its progress undermined, its people demoralized by fierce factional conflict, a vendetta between rival royal families—the Karageorgevich and the Obrenovich and their followers—in which the crown was snatched by one dynasty or the other, and every patriotic Serb was condemned to be born and live and die with murder on his mind.

One thing, though, can be said for patriotic Serbs: they assassinated not only their good kings but their bad ones.

Perhaps because Serbs lived close to the elemental source of violence and poetry, in which source magic also dwells, occult forces seemed to occupy themselves to an extraordinary degree with Serbian affairs. Every one of the central events to be related about the successive Obrenovich monarchs, Milan and his son, Alexander, was prophesied by seers and mediums, or was accompanied by dreams and omens, or else was speeded on its dreadful course by witchcraft and spells. All the prophecies were famous in their time. Some of them even seem to be supported by evidence.

The first prophecy pertinent to the story occurred in 1865 in Odessa, where some ladies holding a tea-party invited a gypsy to entertain them by telling fortunes. The gypsy did so; then, taking the hand of a six-year-old daughter of a visitor, she exclaimed, "Glory to God! I see her wearing a crown!" The ladies laughed at the notion of this colonel's daughter becoming a queen, but the little girl, whose high-flying brows like the wings of a soaring black gull would have suited an empress, stored this prophecy in her heart, and she remembered also the gypsy's concluding words: "I do not clearly see how, but she will also lose the crown. Some tree, or some timber will be the cause."

1.

The Accursed One

In the eighteen sixties an Obrenovich prince, Michael, ruled in Serbia, an able and beneficient monarch, whose death was nevertheless ardently desired by the Karageorgevich faction. Prince Michael had no direct heir, and wishing to preserve the Obrenovich line, he remembered that he had a young relative, who was a grandnephew of Milosh Obren. The father of this child had died of drink, and his mother, Marie Catargi, had no morals. She was whiling away her widowhood as the mistress of a Roumanian nobleman in whose castle she engaged in the wildest possible carousals, leaving her little son to grow up in the courtyard in a state of total neglect—illiterate, ill-fed, and covered with filth, with stablemen for tutors and gypsies for playmates. The only sign the boy, Milan, showed of having royal blood was that one day while playing a game of kings with a gypsy chum, he accidentally hanged him.

Milan was scrubbed, deloused, hastily clad in clean clothes, taken to Belgrade, and thrust slouching before the Prince of Serbia, who was appalled; but his heart was nevertheless touched. He appointed tutors to teach the boy to read and write and to instill in him princely qualities. Some of this effort was rewarded. Everything Milan was taught to do he did well. Soon he was sent to Paris, where he creditably attended the Lycée Louis-le-Grand and was privately instructed in the household of a kindly, liberal-minded scholar, Professor Huet, whose wife found Milan friendly and charming and bestowed on him the only maternal affection he ever knew.

Once his mother—who had gladly received from Prince Michael a remuneration for being deprived of her child—came to see him. "The effect produced on the young prince was as if a viper had suddenly crossed his path. It was with the utmost difficulty he was prevailed on to go to his mother . . . he remained stock still. She became hysterical and cried, 'My son, you do not know your mother?'

" 'No madam,' replied Milan quietly and coldly.

" 'I am your mother,' cried Marie vehemently.

"Milan took two steps forward, took her hand and kissed it.

" 'You no longer love your mother,' she said in a tragic tone.

"The prince gazed at her. Her eyes sank before that look of silent reproach. Marie laughed.

" 'It is quite indifferent to me,' she said, 'whether you like me or not. We can get on without one another. Good-bye.'

" 'Good-bye,' answered the young prince . . . but when his mother had gone and before Huet had time to reprove him for his undutiful conduct, he burst out crying and wept for more than an hour."

The personal charm and intellectual gifts which won Milan the regard of Prince Michael and his tutors were to remain with him all his life and gain him the affection and loyalty of a newly arising class of educated Serbs. But he had been shaped in his tenderest years by debauches and gypsies, and no one could put into him a royal heart.

On May 29, 1868, a queer old peasant named Matha came racing down the streets of the market town Ujitsa in Serbia, shouting at the top of his voice, "Oh, brethren! Help! Help! They are murdering our prince! Oh, see the blood! Help him!" He was immediately arrested. But four hours later an official telegram arrived from Belgrade, announcing Prince Michael's death by assassination. He had been out for his evening walk in the deer park at Topchider, not far from Belgrade, with three female relatives and two attendants. He had exchanged courteous greetings with three citizens who passed him by. A moment later the citizens had shot the prince in the back, not forgetting the ladies, one of whom died on the spot, while the rest of the company fled, badly wounded and screaming.

The assassins, devotees of the Karageorgevich, had laid well their plan. They would slay Prince Michael, then race off to Belgrade and declare their pretender Prince of Serbia. But as good Serbs, they had a duty to epic poetry, and they therefore dallied over the prince's body, plunging their daggers into it again and again—forty-five dagger cuts were counted afterwards. While thus engaged they were seen from afar by a park keeper who raised an alarm. The assassins were arrested and the body of Prince Michael was placed upright in a carriage and driven as if alive through the streets of Belgrade. With the time gained the Skupshtina, the National Assembly, met and proclaimed the boy, Milan, as their ruling prince.

Meanwhile the peasant, Matha, was being questioned by the Ujitsa police. They found it impossible to believe that this simple man was part of a complicated conspiracy; furthermore his neighbors came forward to testify that he was clairvoyant and frequently had visions of events happening far off or in the future. Naturally the police urged Matha to have more visions. What would be the fate of their turbulent country, they asked him? The seer replied at length. It is said that he predicted in astounding detail the history of Serbia for decades to come. The mayor himself listened and his secretary took notes. Matha's predictions were then rolled up into two bundles and placed in the archives of the Court of Justice of Ujitsa, where very few people read them, but almost everybody knew someone's brother-in-law who had done so.

When fourteen-year-old Prince Milan came from Paris to take up his inheritance, he found the flags of Serbia flying, and most of the splendiferously embroidered cloaks of Serbia spread for him to put his feet upon. The rest were kept firmly on the shoulders of the disgruntled partisans of the Karageorgevich. In the main, out of love for Prince Michael, the Serbs took his foundling heir to their hearts, and for a long time they did not regret it. Milan shot up to his majority looking in court dress every inch a robber baron, strong and manly with the promise of hearty fat. The expression on his face was open, kind, and sentimental.

A flaw was found in him in his eighteenth year, when he was sent on a grand tour of the major capitals of Europe and on his return presented a bill of expenses that seemed somewhat fat for a country with a lean purse. Well, generosity can be forgiven in a hearty young prince. For the present his privy purse was ample, for Prince Michael had been a frugal man. Indeed, Milan felt rich enough—though mistakenly—to begin rebuilding Belgrade to look more like Paris. His capital in those days was an ill-smelling place full of old wooden houses; it had one main street. Down with the wood, up with the marble! commanded the prince. Before long there were palaces and villas set along stately boulevards and the officers of Milan's army were encouraged to wax their whiskers, get their uniforms fitted properly, and strut along the boulevards, as the saying went, "tidy as English officers." This elegance set the ladies to beautifying themselves. Students, returned from foreign universities, brought with them polished manners. The lovely village dancing girls came crowding in to share the glamor, and places were established where roistering might take place. Civilization was coming to Belgrade, and Milan was proving to be a Serbian Prometheus. Now he could squander his inheritance not only on buildings but on dancing girls and gaming tables.

In those days the most glamorous gaming table in Central Europe was that which belonged to the Magnates' Club in Budapest, where Hungarian noblemen nightly pushed their fabulous wealth about. While his reforms were in progress, Milan spent much of his time with them. The magnates, who were proud of the numerous quarterings on their family shields did not wish at first to admit this offal from a Roumanian courtyard, but after they had been admonished by their master, Emperor Francis Joseph in Vienna, they permitted Milan to enter their club and deposit his money there. Farther afield, in Vienna and Paris, casinos and racetracks learned to welcome the Prince of Serbia; because it was becoming more and more evident that the fates that had bestowed so many fine qualities upon Milan had withheld from him that one gift without which any man is born to waste his life: luck.

It was becoming urgently necessary to find Milan a wife, not only for the dynasty's sake, but for the dowry's. Representations were sent to all the royal families of Europe, great and small. Polite excuses wended their mournful way back to Belgrade. Like Napoleon III, Milan learned that divine monarchs will call an upstart "brother" much sooner than they will call him "brother-in-law."

Eventually there was laid before Milan the portrait of a young Roumanian lady of sixteen. She was not royal, but she was well-connected. Her father, a colonel in the Russian army, was a Moldavian landowner of great wealth; the young lady had the best hourglass shape in Europe. When Milan, with bulging eyes, gazed upon her portrait, he exclaimed, "That's the one!" and he took himself expeditiously off to Paris, where Natalie Keshko was finishing her education, and proposed to the girl who—according to her report—had been expecting a royal suitor for ten years.

Milan prepared for the wedding with lavish hand. It was held in Vienna, where the Emperor Francis Joseph generously placed the imperial horses with their emblazoned coaches at the disposal of the cortège. There was a sumptuous reception at the Golden Lamb Hotel, which had been decorated for the occasion like a sultan's seraglio with Milan's Turkish treasures, tapestries, fabulous carpets, and potted exotic trees. Then, after a short honeymoon, during which the royal couple became enraptured with each other, they went home to Belgrade to present themselves to the Serbian people.

The Serbs had been displeased by Milan's failure to provide them with a princess of the blood royal, and they were not awaiting Natalie in the best of spirits. And yet, no sooner did they set eyes on the young princess than their mood changed. If ever an entire nation fell madly in love at first sight, the Serbs fell in love with Natalie. They detached the horses from the royal carriage and harnessed themselves to it, while men and

women by the thousands ran in rivers down Milan's new boulevards in a delirium of joy.

A second religious ceremony was held at the Cathedral of
Belgrade; and when afterwards they beheld Natalie standing at
the top of the cathedral steps in a waterfall of white lace and
diamonds, with her high-winging black brows and eyes like
moonlit seas, how could this nation of antique poets resist her?
Slowly, carrying her remarkable arabesque curves lightly, she
moved down the steps on the arm of her stalwart prince, a delight to every snapping Serbian eye, and mounted the wedding
coach. Then suddenly, the enchanting scene became a shambles.
Black clouds were gathering above and the rumble of thunder
was heard in the distance. The coachman smartly cracked his
whip, but the white horses did not move. Again, the whip
cracked, and the horses reared, but they would not go forward.
The sky darkened and the crowds swayed uneasily as they
stretched their necks to heaven. Some guards came to steady
the horses and urge them ahead, but they would not budge.
For fully ten minutes they heaved and churned with their white
legs flying, while numerous agitated Serbs jumped about,
prodding and shouting, making all efforts to get them started
short of picking them up and carrying them. All of this time the
pair in their marriage clothes were clinging to the sides of the carriage as to a dinghy in a squall, in momentary danger of being
cast out onto the road.

The crowds were silent now. They knew that they were in
the presence of a calamitous omen. When the coach at length
proceeded, it wended soberly through a glum throng.

The old ones said that it was the blackest day in Serbia within
their memories. And yet, the sky could have poured down stink-
ing pitch and still it would have been fair in comparison to the
conspiracies that were now being woven in the foreign offices
of Vienna and St. Petersburg to engulf the marriage of this pair,
so Orientally handsome, so gifted and in love.

Anyone who embroils himself deeply in the political history
of Serbia runs a slim chance of ever seeing the light again. Essentially the Serbs were a tribal people who, like other Balkan
tribes, were trying at that time to work themselves into a modern
state. Complicating their policies was a racial hope: they called

it the "Slavonic Cause." It was a poetic yearning that one of these days all of the South Slavs, the Jugoslavs, would be united into one nation—of course with the Serbs as leaders. In addition they entertained the "Serbian Dream"—a passionate desire that all of the Serbian people, now dispersed in various places on the Balkan peninsula, should be brought together into a national unit. Such notions had sustained them through centuries of servvitude to the Turks.

Toward the end of the century these ideas were kindled by a master scheme emanating from the heart of Russia called Pan-Slavism—a philosophy which prized people of Slavic blood above all others, especially when they belonged to the Orthodox Church. Really it was a backlash against the Western-style reforms of Tsar Alexander II: at any cost the tsar's mind had to be turned away from his constitutional mania and bent toward the problems of brother-Slavs in the Balkans, who were not only smarting under the lash of the Turk and laboring under the errors of Islam and Roman Catholicism, but were menaced by the nibbling creep of the Habsburg Empire.

Austrian interests in the Balkans were no less benevolent. Here were all these unstable tribes trying to push themselves into a modern way of life but hampered by the fallacies of the Greek faith and those of the Prophet. Ought they not rather to be incorporated into the vast confederation of Habsburg states, set to producing attars for the perfumes of Viennese ladies, tobacco for enormous Tyrolean pipes, and pigs for a *Székely* goulash?

If, therefore, you were born a Serb at the end of the nineteenth century, you had a number of decisions to make: whether you favored the Karageorgevich or the Obrenovich family as rulers of your country; whether you were a Russophile and Austrophobe, or vice versa; whether you favored Pan-Slavism wholly or only the "Slavonic Cause"; and where you stood with regard to the "Serbian Dream."

Over and above these you must make up your mind of what political persuasion you might *pretend* to be for reasons of self-interest, as well as to which of them you were willing to be subverted by bribery or threats. Finally, no matter what you were or pretended to be, as a Serb you were addicted as to a drug to membership in some secret plotting and election-rigging society.

Prince Milan knew, of course, that he had a duty to the "Slavonic Cause." When, in 1876, the Turks launched upon one of their periodic persecutions of Christian minorities in Bulgaria, and in Serbia the Karageorgevich faction set up a loud mutter about the military heroism of their young pretender, Peter, there was nothing Milan could do for his honor's sake but declare war on Turkey—a case of bone biting dog.

The Serb forces were soon in difficulties, thus kindling the sympathies of Pan-Slavs in Russia. Tsar Alexander II had then no other course but to yield to their badgering, push the Serbs out of the way, take over the war against Turkey, and win it. The tsar, as we know, was cheated of the fruits of his victory at the Congress of Berlin by Disraeli and Bismarck who, though uncertain where to find anything on the map of the Balkans, were yet certain of one thing: they did not wish to find any Russians on it.

For Serbia, though, the outcome of this war brought about a day worthy of celebration in epic poetry: for the first time in five hundred years tribute did not have to be paid to the Sublime Porte. The crescent flag could be drawn down from the war-harrowed old fortress of Belgrade and the fly-blown Turkish soldiers kicked awake and advised to go home.

It was truly an unlucky Cinderella-prince who could not manage to fashion out of this event a permanent guarantee of his royalty and divinity. But Milan, alas, had no luck; and he was already hard at work placing his chips on the wrong color. Certain incidents in the peace negotiations had queered his faith in the good intentions of Mother Russia and her Pan-Slavs. It seemed to him that while the Russians wished the Balkan Slavs to be united, *they did not wish the Serbs to be the leaders*. Instead they were promoting the Bulgarians as the dominant South Slav race, a plain reversal of the natural order because, as everyone knew, if you left a Bulgarian and a Serb alone on a desert island, the Bulgarian would soon make the land bloom like a rose, but it would be the Serb who would order him to do it.

The young prince therefore deemed it necessary to loosen his country's ties with Russia. In 1877 he signed a secret treaty with Austria-Hungary, throwing Serbia under the economic domination of the Habsburgs.

This act was directly against the temper and the poetic preference of his people, who would cheerfully have murdered him with multiple dagger wounds had they known anything about it. Even history, which does know about it, tends to the viewpoint that he stabbed his Mother Russia in the back and sold his country to the Habsburgs in return for the payment of his current building and gambling debts. Rarely has it been granted to Milan that he might have shared the convictions of many Western-minded Serbs, who perceived the reactionary dangers of Pan-Slavism and wished to shape their country along Western lines rather than borrow the complex miseries of tsardom.

By means of the secret treaty with Milan, Emperor Francis Joseph of Austria was joined in direct diplomatic battle with the tsars for the domination of the Balkans. That was why the day was black when Milan of Serbia married Natalie Keshko. For even before she had donned her wedding dress, the Russian ambassador to Vienna had sent a dispatch to St. Petersburg, couched in terms something like these: "When Natalie Keshko, a good Russian, enters Belgrade as princess, Russia will put her foot on Serbia."

For two decades, Europe was to watch aghast as the giant empires contended in the persons of Milan and Natalie.

Natalie entered her kingdom with the same determination that any energetic bride brings to her dream house: to run things the way they ought to be run. An intelligent girl, brought up in the Russian aristocratic tradition with a dash of Paris added, she was the superior in sophistication of most of the women of Belgrade. Her chic style in clothes and conversation, no less than her French chef, brought immediate prestige to the throne. The Russian diplomats were not stupid in supposing that such a woman, given an hourglass shape, would lose no time in getting her young husband and his country firmly under thumb. They must have stroked their whiskers in gladness on that day when Natalie expressed a liking for lilies of the valley, to watch how swiftly Milan leapt to command a whole field of these flowers planted for her pleasure.

What they left out of account—besides Milan's secret treaty —was that both the prince and the princess had rousing tempers.

Hostilities opened over the dowry. It is possible that Milan was gypsy enough to imagine that a rich girl like Natalie carried her money around with her in bags. He was dumfounded to learn, when he commanded it to be brought before him, that his wife's fortune was tied up in profitable land investments and could not be touched without her consent. Well, his privy purse was empty and his gambling debts were pressing: Natalie must sell something. But Natalie would not sell anything. The meanest princess in Europe would have been likely to sell her last button before permitting her husband's name to be cursed by gamblers, but Natalie was not a princess. She was just a strong-minded girl who was being advised from the beginning by relatives and diplomats that the best way to keep a man like Milan at heel was to hold her pursestrings tight.

This conflict was dissolved in their common happiness and the nation-wide rejoicing that attended the birth of an heir. Their son was born in 1876 during the Turkish War, which was temporarily halted while the soldiers beat drums, composed poems, and threw garlands of flowers around each other's necks. Tsar Alexander II himself stood godfather, bestowing on the child not only his name but his nickname, Sasha; and, as one day would be remarked, his bloodstained destiny.

Now those members of the court who were secretly devoted to the interests of the pretender, Peter Karageorgevich, had to redouble their efforts to cover the Obrenovich with ignominy and confusion. Certainly they had not left the teen-age bride in ignorance of the extraordinary number of girls in Belgrade and elsewhere who had enjoyed the admiration of Milan before his marriage. One such lady could not have gone unnoticed, because she had created quite a commotion at the wedding by romping forward brandishing a loaded revolver and shrieking insults at the prince on behalf of her unborn child. People of good breeding said at the time that Natalie ought not to have allowed incidents like this to get on her nerves. They suspected, and rightly, that she was a prude. But Milan's political enemies soon found that her proud temper could be used as a handy weapon to belabor Milan. Prompted, she began to torment him with jealous rages. The slightest roll of the prince's eyes in mixed company—and Milan had naturally rolling eyes—would bring the storm signals into her own, and before long the news came out of Serbia that its ruler was spending long, love-curdling hours of the night beating tearfully at his wife's bedroom door, which was usually adamantly closed to him.

One day, Milan showed an enchanting portrait of his wife to a friend. "Please look at this photo intently," he implored, "and you will see that she has the face of a tigress. She was born cruel."

To the uninflamed eye Natalie does not seem to resemble a tigress, but her lips, when not wearing a smile, compressed tautly downwards at the corners. One can imagine this unkind expression on public display on the occasion of a state banquet when, seeing her husband deep in conversation with a minister, she inquired the subject of their discussion. On being told that they were speaking about education, she said loudly to the minister, "Then I am sorry for you. For you have been talking about education with a man who has none."

One day Milan, smoking a heavy Balkan cigar, entered his wife's boudoir and found it newly laid with a rich white velvet carpet. He spat on it.

In exacerbating the royal marriage, the Karageorgevich faction was not at first working in harmony with St. Petersburg. The Russian diplomats had begun by desiring greater agreement between Milan and their tool, Natalie. But as the years passed it was becoming gradually clearer to them that the Prince of Serbia would not dare to thwart their policies as consistently as he was doing unless he had some mysterious, hidden strength—for example a secret agreement with Austria-Hungary.

When it dawned on them that Milan was not wholeheartedly for the Pan-Slavic cause, they closed in unmercifully on the young wife. She had failed them as an instrument to control her husband, but she could still be useful in demoralizing and destroying him. They now joined with the adherents of Karageorge to envenom the mind of Natalie, while holding out to her the hope that one day her dog of a husband would be tied up, and she herself would reign in Serbia as regent for her son.

But behind her back, in the smoke-filled rooms of Byzantine palaces, it had already been decided that a new tool must be looked for with which to rule Milan.

When, in 1881, the liberal Tsar Alexander II was assassinated and was succeeded by Alexander III, a perfect bear of a Pan-Slav, these diplomatic plots increased in malevolence. The following year Prince Milan enraged the new tsar by taking himself to the ancient monastery of Zhitcha, where the medieval Serbian kings had been crowned, and there causing the annointing oil to be poured over his head and breast. He declared himself a king. Now Natalie was a queen, as the gypsy had predicted. But never was a queen more hated by her spouse, for Milan had by that time identified his wife as his chief enemy.

"The castle is in utter confusion," wrote an officer of the guard in Belgrade. "One scandalous scene succeeds the other. The king looks ill as if he never slept. Poor fellow, he flies for refuge to us in the guardhouse and plays cards with the officers. Card-playing is his worst enemy; it will work his total ruin. He loves it passionately and plays excitedly for high points . . . he loses constantly, while the others win. When he plays with us, and consequently for small stakes, he is equally unlucky and never wins sixpence."

One advantage was coming out of the quarrels in Serbia: the gamblers and the gossip sheets got their hero back again. King Milan made no secret of his preference for fields of love and laughter far away from home, and as before his marriage, he was frequently finding high matters of state to discuss in Budapest, where the magic tables of the Magnate's Club could make his money disappear faster than anywhere else in Europe.

In Budapest there were two beautiful sisters, actresses who were greatly sought after by the members of the Magnate's Club, and who indeed could not have afforded their joyous establishment on an exclusive park without the hearty support of the fattest in their land. Milan, while in Budapest, was a daily visitor at their villa, and he arrived so punctually that the urchins of the neighborhood would gather in crowds to watch the King of Serbia alight. When he appeared they would cry lustily, "*Éljen! Éljen!*" which is Hungarian for "*Geronimo!*"

Eventually the king remarked that the portraits of these two sisters were being shown in the shopwindows of Belgrade. He bade an equerry inquire at a stationery store why this was so. The equerry was told by the store owner, "Why shouldn't we sympathize with them? They are our beloved relatives!"

In Vienna, Milan became affectionately attached to a singer

whom he notified of his admiration by sending her a picture of himself. The picture was quite an ordinary one; she might have bought it at any newsstand. It was the frame that Milan pinned his hopes on. For one of the king's talents was an artistic flair, and he had designed this frame himself in beautiful traceries of wrought gold, with his own initials and those of the singer entwined in diamonds around a diamond-studded musical symbol.

Two days later he received a note of thanks from the singer. The diamonds, she wrote, were such excellent imitations that anyone would have thought they were real.

Mortified and puzzled, Milan sent an aide to request the return of the frame which he then sent to a jeweler who verified that the diamonds were indeed false ones. The king dug into his wretched privy purse to compensate the singer with a jewel of uncontested value, and he spent the next two years wondering what had become of his diamonds. One day, passing by a jeweler's shop, he saw a frame of the same design in the window. He entered and inquired of the jeweler, "Is that your work?" The jeweler replied that it was. "But the design," persisted the king. "Did you design it yourself?"

"Well, no," admitted the jeweler. "I copied it from a frame brought in here by a lady a couple of years ago. She wanted the diamonds to be removed and replaced by false ones."

The reports of such ludicrous episodes spread far and wide and became inseparable from the crown of Serbia. Milan excused himself adroitly to his ministers, some of whom he knew would have preferred to serve Peter Karageorgevich. "I know I am a source of embarrassment, but you must bear with me as a necessary evil for which you are yourselves responsible. By assassinating my uncle, you arrested my being educated by a French philosopher and democrat. You took me into your hands, and whatever I am today, remember that I am the product of the education which you gave me."

He did not, however, succeed in excusing himself to Natalie, who reacted violently with public insults to every public scandal. Clutching her son to her bosom, she would shower kisses upon his head, while shouting abuse at his father above it. It is said that the small Sasha had occasionally to skip nimbly aside when Milan, breathing fire, sprang at his mother to strike her down.

Both Milan and Natalie loved their son, but they were far

too enmeshed in their own difficulties to note which way they were bending him. In common with most people of their generation, they underrated the inconsequent minds of children, who may be terrified at one moment and the next quickly comforted by sweets. Sasha was twelve before Natalie thought of begging Milan to moderate his temper toward her, because the boy was "beginning to understand." In the meantime Sasha was observed by the courtiers about him to have a winning and affectionate nature, but for all that to be rather a nasty little boy who enjoyed playing practical jokes upon his elders. Once, while journeying down the river, he asked why all the people on the bank were cheering him. "Because they love you," he was told.

"If you love me," he shouted to the multitude, "show it by throwing your hats into the river!" And he laughed to see those countless peasant hats floating downstream to the sea. Almost all the uncharming anecdotes about the childhood of Alexander of Serbia seem to be anagrams of a question: How much could he get away with before somebody murdered him?

The Austrian emperor, Francis Joseph, viewed with dismay the gradual demoralization of his tool, Milan, and his reasons were not wholly political, for although the emperor contained more of the divine spirit than any other monarch in Europe, he was no common snob: he liked the King of Serbia. He used to call him *der Dicke*, the fat one, and when Milan dined with him, he always instructed his cook to prepare foods that were slenderizing. Upon hearing rumors that Milan had become a wife beater, he sent his son, Crown Prince Rudolf, and Rudolf's wife, Stephanie, on a visit to Belgrade to instruct Milan and Natalie on the proper behavior of a royal couple. It is not known if their remonstrances had a moderating affect on the Serbian domestic strife, but it is a fact that shortly after this visit Rudolf took to beating Stephanie.

In 1885, Milan's Austrian masters made him fight a war against Bulgaria. He went reluctantly to the front, accompanied by bevies of dancing girls, packs of playing cards, and great cases of champagne, and he amused himself with them while the Bulgarians cut his men to pieces. He returned to Belgrade to find his wild-eyed citizens gathering in tight knots, and wanting to tear him limb from limb. From this time forth Karageorgevich plots against Milan's life increased in number and in imaginative power.

Of course, from his early youth when he had come from Paris to be Prince of Serbia, Milan had lived around the corner from death. Even as a boy he had been warned by his regents never to give audiences without a revolver in his pocket; and the danger had not abated in the course of his reign as the anti-dynastic movement had grown to embrace almost every patriotic Serb. Naturally one cannot speak of Serbian assassins in the same breath as Russian Nihilists. No burrowing through gloomy sewers for them! Serbs are poets: they shoot off firearms more for the splendid rattle they make than in hope of hitting a target, and they lay their plans with fine, careless rapture. Once, for example, when a group of assassins had planned to murder Milan in a hotel room, they confided their intentions to the entire hotel staff. Forewarned, the royal guard arrested the assassins, who afterwards escaped and made their way to Russia. One of them was Nikola Pashich who at the Versailles Conference succeeded in fashioning his brother-Slavs at last into a nation and became known as the "Father of Jugoslavia."

The conspirators quite often left out of consideration that their discreditable prince was very well liked by his personal servants. Once some of his ministers and advisers planned to dispose of him during a meeting of state. A certain General Blazich was delegated to put poison in Milan's wineglass while the prince was called from the room. But this was done in full sight of a footman who slipped out and warned his master. Milan returned to the table and, indeed, noticed a white powder in his glass.

"I invite my friend Blazich to empty this glass to my health," he announced. There was a stunned silence around the table. Milan, who was very strong, arose and took hold of the general's arm so that his bones were heard to crack. "You dog!" he hissed in the culprit's ear, "Empty that glass, or I'll strangle you!" Blazich picked up the glass. "Long live the prince!" he cried; he drank, and died.

Milan's Serbs shot at him and missed. They pulled rails from under trains in which he rode. They built a triumphal arch all carved and bowered with roses in his honor which had been fixed to crash while he stood under it; but it did not crash at the right moment. They sawed the planks of a dock on which he was scheduled to stand and christen a riverboat so that he would fall into the water and drown. Apparently they did not foresee that a number of partisans of the Obrenovich would be standing by, ready to pull him out.

But though they failed to kill Milan, they were slowly doing away with him. He said to his ministers, "For me [the throne] is a rack on which I have been for no fault of mine daily tortured. You call me intelligent. But what use can I make of my intelligence? I wish to serve my country, and I have my own ideas how best to serve it, but how can I work them out when I am told that my first duty is to watch the enemies of the dynasty, to defeat their conspiracies, and be prepared to meet, day or night, the bomb, revolver, or knife of an assassin."

Only the bitterest critics of Queen Natalie suggest that she was actively involved in attempts against the life of her husband. Those who knew her intimately considered that she was too religious a woman to stain her conscience with murder. But that she desired his ruin is certain. Once she stood in a hotel room in Vienna looking down into the public street and vowed to the Russian ambassador standing at her side, "He will walk here, while I rule in Belgrade."

The Serbs would have liked nothing better than to be ruled by Natalie, for they had not ceased to adore her. Nevertheless she too went in fear of her life as she recalled the gypsy's gloomy forecast that she would lose her crown by some reason involving trees or timber. In 1886, when she was twenty-seven years old, she related the prophecy to a friend, saying, "Now, as the first part of the prophecy, against all probabilities, was realized, I am afraid the second part may also be fulfilled. The critical years are coming. Whenever I drive in the Deer Park and enter the wood, I find myself calling to the driver, 'Take care of the horses!' That is because I think the horses might grow restive, rush through the forest wildly, and perhaps a low branch of a tree might catch and kill me."

That Deer Park, where Prince Michael was killed, was indeed a fatal place for the Obrenovich dynasty. It is said that one day when Queen Natalie went riding there, watchful as always for the treachery of trees, she passed by a sylvan grove and saw her husband there, embracing the wife of his private secretary. This lady's name was Madame Artemesia Christich, and she was the daughter of a timber merchant.

Madame Christich is certainly one of the most enigmatic royal mistresses ever to change the course of her country's history. It was generally agreed by those who wrote down their impressions of her at the time that "she was not exactly beautiful; she had a muddy complexion and a bad figure, heavy and large-waisted. . . ." Also, she was several years older than the king. But she had magnificent black hair and beautiful, soft, expressive eyes; and though she lived in a country where such eyes are not uncommon, the glance of Artemesia was held to have a magnetic quality that other eyes did not.

Her father had been a successful businessman of Constantinople and builder to the sultan, and she had grown up in the seraglios of the Sublime Porte. Except that she spoke Greek, Turkish, and French, she had no particular accomplishments, and she was much Natalie's inferior in personal charm. And yet she had managed to make many friends in Belgrade; there was something mysteriously attractive about her, as even Milan's disapproving ministers had to admit. We can imagine that she had certain harem qualities, quite different in allure from Natalie's Parisian airs and perhaps more compatible with the Serbian culture of the time. Her busy salon, instead of containing spidery furniture that could not be sat upon and faddish carpets that were spoiled by spitting, would have been equipped with all of those hedonistic conveniences which Turkish bashaws and bumbashaws have passed along to our European world: sofas, divans, davenports, and ottomans. Thick, luminous rugs, centuries old, would have been piled on one another amid mountain ranges of silken poufs and cushions, and around Artemesia there would have been the calm digestive noises of hubble-bubbles, a narcotic cloud of incense, glowing braziers, and pots of coffee thicker and more heartening than Natalie's *potage St. Germain.* In such a nest she wooed King Milan, and during the most dramatic and fatal years of his reign captured him to the exclusion of all others.

She carried on her intrigue with the king under the very nose of her husband, the king's private secretary, Milan Christich, and apparently with his approval. Daily the people of Belgrade lined up along the streets of the city to watch their king ride by to visit the house of his favorite, and beside him the seat of his open carriage was piled high with gifts of unimaginable splendor. It soon became known that in addition to these, hundreds of thousands of the silver dinars King Milan had recently minted, each bearing his own portrait, were being syphoned from the privy purse, from the budget for building national railways, from his share of the Danube fisheries, and poured at the feet of this beloved frump.

Many people, at the time and since, have believed that both Monsieur and Madame Christich were drawing additional income from the Russian Foreign Office; that Artemesia Christich was, in fact, the new weapon that the Russian diplomats had found to replace the useless Natalie as a means of influencing Milan.

But how was it possible that an ugly woman could subjugate a king who had spent his life ranging far afield to seek out the prettiest faces and the most supple bodies in Europe?

We, with our instant psychology, might recollect Milan's deprived youth and his neglectful mother, and we would wonder if Milan had not been captured by the maternal qualities of the elderly Madame Christich, who had a soft bosom supported by a nice fat waist. The nineteenth-century Serbs, however, drew their knowledge of affairs from far deeper wells than this. For them it seemed clear that Artemesia Christich, besides her personal charm, had charms of a very different nature at her disposal; that their king was in fact in the toils of a witch.

We need not trouble ourselves with country superstitions. Instead we have the opinion of His Excellency Mr. Chedo Mijatovich, architect of much of Milan's foreign policy, a Western-educated man, a historian and ethnographer, and as ambassador to the Court of St. James the respected friend of as many eminent Victorians as Sigmund Freud himself. Certainly he was not a man one may lightly accuse of crass superstition. And yet in matters of witchcraft he is not to be gainsaid. His own mother, as a child of six, had been kidnaped by a witch who obliged her to play the part of the unsullied virgin without whose services Slavic sorcerers are unable to produce their spells; it was years before the girl's family found her and kidnaped her back again. Nothing this Serbian minister had learned at his mother's knee caused him to doubt that occult mischief was behind his sovereign's love affair: "Whenever he spoke to me of her, I derived the impression that he was on the road to madness. He insisted that she was born to be a queen, that she was a woman possessing a heart and brains of such quality that no other woman in the world could be compared with her, that we—his cabinet ministers—were not worthy to lace her boots, and, finally, that she was the greatest statesman in Europe, far greater than Bismarck."

He said also, "Poor King Milan was not only fascinated, but completely hynotized by her. . . . He almost mechanically executed . . . her wishes."

Thus the king's new happiness in his mistress did not strengthen him, it weakened him; it strengthened instead the rumor of an old prophecy that the Obrenovich kings would be destroyed by means of women. For Artemesia's mission was, by hook or crook or magic spell, to keep odium boiling about the throne of Serbia, to corrode Milan's relations with his wife, to bring about a divorce if she could and reign as Queen of Serbia; but whatever she did, to destroy King Milan.

Throughout these addled years affairs of state had not come to a standstill. They were administered by means of cabinets crashing and recombining, ministers resigning or being summarily dismissed, by edicts written out and waved about and then locked away in a bottom drawer. In the Skupshtina members glowered and shouted at each other across their quaint Turkish assembly hall. When outright insurrections occurred, Milan, with relief, rounded up large numbers of Serbs and threw them into jail.

Meanwhile, the Russians sent pious peddlers into the country districts to sell holy ikons to the peasants, and everywhere they went murderous secret societies came into being whose mission was to make certain that every live Serb belonged to the Radical Party, which was fat with the adherents of Prince Peter Karageorgevich and solid for the "Slavonic Cause," the "Serbian Dream," Mother Russia, and the tsar. This party was henceforward to be the dominant one in Serbia.

Staunch friends and loyal supporters of the Obrenovich dynasty stood by Milan when he was at bay. One day he said to one of them: "You have the reputation of being an intelligent man, but you are very dense indeed when compared to that wonderful woman, Madame Artemesia. She is the only one who understands me."

He then confided to the horrified minister his intention of divorcing Natalie. To divorce a queen! No more arrogant an idea was formulated in these last decades of the nineteenth century, when even ordinary divorced persons might not enter a room occupied by Queen Victoria. Even Milan quailed, and he had to be fortified again and again by Dutch courage offered by his mistress. Artemesia now had a pressing personal reason for urging this sacrilegious course upon the king. She had borne him a son.

With the arrival of this child upon the scene Monsieur Christich had obligingly divorced Artemesia, without however relinquishing his post as Milan's secretary. Artemesia's ambitions became clear when she gave her son a name fit for a King of Serbia: Obren.

Clearing Natalie out of her way had to be plotted with care. Shrewishness is not grounds for divorcing a wife in the Orthodox Church. Adultery would have served, but Natalie's chastity was world-famous. Moreover her popularity among the Serbs was such that no move could possibly be made against her while she remained on Serbian soil. A means had to be found of persuading her to leave the country of her own free will.

Sasha was eleven years old. It was high time that he begin acquiring the princely polish that is achieved only by studies in the fashionable capitals and watering spots. With this ostensibly in mind, Milan suggested to his wife that she accompany their son abroad and take charge of his education, living with him or near him. From time to time he would pay them visits. This arrangement would continue until Sasha's majority.

Natalie gladly agreed. The plan would give her complete control of Sasha, who would grow up to be a "good Russian" like herself, and it would furthermore keep him clear of his father's theater of scandalous activity, which the boy was "beginning to understand." She had long since come to terms with her husband's polygamous desires; all the love of her possessive nature was concentrated on her son. Innocently she left Serbia, comforting herself with the fact that her Serbs detested Artemesia. By this time it was common knowledge that she was in league with the Devil, and they called her "the accursed one."

Natalie established herself in Wiesbaden, a pleasant German watering spot, where she arranged for Sasha to pursue his studies with competent tutors, while she enjoyed a tranquil social existence among the distinguished visitors to the resort who highly praised her beauty and her cordiality. By and by troublesome rumors began to seep through from Belgrade. It seemed that the king had transferred his private office to Artemesia's seraglio and that the favorite was reigning, in effect, as Queen of Serbia. Odious stories were being promulgated about Natalie herself: that she was sexually unresponsive, and that after the birth of Sasha she had refused to spoil her beauty by producing secondary heirs to the throne. In increasing trepidation Natalie began to write letters to Milan which were almost conciliatory, requesting permission to return to Serbia. But Milan had determined that Natalie should never return to Serbia again, and his replies were churlish. Eventually they ceased.

On June 11, 1888—only a few months after she had gone abroad—Natalie received a letter from the king containing the following words: ". . . I have accordingly to inform you that this day I have sent in my application to our Holy National Church for permission to dissolve our marriage."

At first she did not perceive her fate. She replied contemptuously, not forgetting a dig at Artemesia: "Serbia is not a country in which a wife can be thrown aside as if she were a mistress."

But on the heels of the first communication came a second in which the king issued a command: she must return to him his heir. Now the terror of her situation burst full on Natalie: she was to be discarded as queen, wife, and mother all at once. In fear and fury she wrote letters, and not only to her powerful friends; to her political enemies she wrote, imploring their assistance against the terrible injustice that was being done to her, and heartbreakingly she wrote to Milan: "My fate is worthy of compassion, and should draw tears from the very stones." But Milan, no less eloquently, was composing letters to the church authorities that the queen's hatred toward himself was "a chalice of bitterness, which I, the king, had to drink to the very dregs."

Public opinion raised a mighty outcry on Natalie's behalf; every chivalrous heart in Europe and every mother's heart beat with her in her distress, and the press in all capitals poured forth vituperations against Serbia's execrable king. Kaiser Wilhelm II shone above them all like a Galahad: in his noblest voice he proclaimed that never on his soil would a son be dragged from his mother's side. But when a Serbian general arrived in Wiesbaden to take Sasha home and Natalie appealed to the kaiser for his protection, none was forthcoming. No doubt some hard-headed Teuton had represented to the kaiser the impossibility of retaining on German soil the heir to the throne of a friendly country. Natalie now telegraphed frantically to Milan, begging to be permitted to keep her son but another month at her side. The king replied cruelly, not to her, but to Sasha's tutor: "The Crown Prince of Serbia is to return at once to Serbia."

The general called at Natalie's residence. He had brought with him a number of German policemen, and she watched them arrive from a window. She grasped well the plot now: Sasha was to be taken to Belgrade, and there Artemesia would contrive to poison him and have her own son, Obren, recognized as heir to the throne.

When the general entered her chamber, she was clutching Sasha to her bosom with one arm and flourishing a revolver with the other. "Advance and I fire!" she screamed. The general commanded his troops to attack Natalie in a pincers movement, brandishing their sticks, and disarm her; while he, in a brusque forward dart, disarmed of his mother her utterly distracted and despairing little boy.

It is impossible to exaggerate the disgust that these unroyal happenings aroused in Europe and in Serbia against Milan. The Serbs had been very recently a patriarchal people: that is to say, they honored their fathers and their mothers. Milan himself had been obliged to become reconciled with his detestable mother in order to satisfy this national foible. When he had his own son torn by force from his mother's arms, the Obrenovich faction in Serbia became disorganized with shame and shock. The demoralized king began to behave like a lunatic. He browbeat the church council who were reluctantly considering the divorce; then he disbanded them and announced his intention to seek a reconciliation with the queen. Pulled up sharp by his mistress, he again publicly denounced his wife. Artemesia must have spent an exasperating few weeks, heartily wishing that she were back in the Sublime Porte, where in the sultan's seraglio unwanted wives had only to be sewn up in sacks and thrown into the Bosphorus. Surely acts of such Byzantine simplicity were workable also in a country that Turks had ruled for five hundred years!

Quite right. They were. Historical research was brought to bear on the situation and it revealed that in the past the Orthodox Church had assisted certain tsars in disposing of their wives by a sultan-like wave of the hand. The Serbs had a proverb, "Even the Holy Patriarch, when hungry, will steal a loaf of bread." The Metropolitan of Serbia, Theodosius, was hungry, and he found it possible to pronounce Milan and Natalie divorced.

But the sheer brutality of the act disgusted the Serbs. Whatever dream Artemesia Christich cherished of reigning as a queen with Obren instead of Sasha as heir to the throne collapsed under the execration that poured upon her head. She was unable to leave her house unless escorted by a guard of armed policemen. If she was acting as a tool of Russia, the tsar's diplomats must have advised her that her only hope of organizing her life and that of her son lay in inducing Milan to abdicate.

Shortly after the divorce, Milan called his ministers together and told them that he intended to abdicate his throne. This news fell apocalyptically upon their ears. These ministers had stood by him through thick and thin, had staked their careers on making a king out of him. Now here he was proposing to resign his post as if he were a mere politician instead of an anointed ruler with a sacred destiny. They expostulated with him, but with unsatisfactory results. Milan was behaving wildly, for all the world like a man struggling in the toils of a sorceress. He kept bursting into tears and promising that he would cure himself of his fatal passion for Artemesia, that he would collect his nerves and build orphanages and old people's homes, apply himself to repairing the prestige of his dynasty. Now and again he even promised to blow out his brains. But all of his good resolutions were quickly disposed of in Artemesia's incensed lair, and he would call another cabinet meeting and reaffirm that he must abdicate.

"She considers that my resolution is right," he told his exasperated ministers, "that I will be doing an act of grand and noble duty, that I will win the respect of my enemies, and that only then will our country appreciate what I was to my people."

One day he brought to an end a passionate session with his cabinet by flinging out of the room, shouting over his shoulder, "I am astonished that Mijatovich, who knows well that my abdication is unavoidable, should attack me with such fierceness, calling me a coward and an unworthy Obrenovich!"

After the king had slammed the door Minister Mijatovich was pressed to explain this enigmatic remark. He was obliged to confess that many years earlier he had aroused Milan's curiosity about the "Black Prophecy" of the peasant Matha; that Milan had caused the secret scrolls to be brought from Ujitsa to Belgrade and had examined them, and that he had found his abdication predicted there.

Ignoring, if we dare, the tight threads the Fates spin, it may well have seemed to Milan, in view of the fact that almost every Serb was thirsting for his blood, that abdication in favor of Sasha was the only way that he could preserve his dynasty. Serbs are not savages: they would not assassinate a helpless child. By the time Sasha reached an age when he would be eligible, as it were, for assassination, all of Milan's misdeeds would have been wiped off the slate and Alexander of Serbia could begin anew.

In a final irresponsible action, as a conscience-present for the Serbs, the king wrote out a new constitution, far more liberal than they needed or deserved, the sort of document for which much more stable populations would still have to spill their blood and do to this day. Then, on March 22, 1889, he called all the important people in Belgrade to the great hall of his fine New Palace to watch him abdicate. So crowded was the hall that many people were obliged to stand outside. But in the immediate audience Chedo Mijatovich noted that a place had been found for the witch Artemesia, and when the king began to speak, a possible significance in this at once occurred to him: "I was standing on the left of Milan . . . looking vaguely at the glittering group of foreign ministers. Suddenly I was struck by the voice of the king. Decidedly it was not his usual voice, but much deeper and hollower. I raised my head and looked at the king's profile. Yes, it was he who spoke, but not in his natural voice."

Afterward persons who knew Milan well, but who had stood outside the hall while he was speaking, asked Mr. Mijatovich who had pronounced the abdication speech. They were astonished to hear that Milan had done so, for they intimately knew his voice. In this way it was embedded in the minds of many Serbs that to the last minute King Milan was behaving under the influence of hypnotism or magic operated by the accursed one, and that this was done under the direct orders of Tsar Alexander III far off in St. Petersburg.

And yet, for all her arts, Milan did not marry his mistress, nor complete Obren's name with that of Obrenovich. To the amazement of his friends, directly he quit the throne the affection that had held him so tightly dissipated like a spell lifted.

For several years, as he jaunted from one gay capital to the next, Madame Christich listed after him reminding him continuously of all that she had sacrificed for his sake. In her baggage she carried a large packet of letters the king had written to her, containing not only his secrets of love but secrets of state; and with these she sought to blackmail him. As if it were possible to blackmail such a gypsy! Eventually Artemesia lost heart and drifted back to her native city, the Sublime Porte, where she is said to have sold her collection of interesting historical documents to the sultan, and in the old archives of the Ottomans they perhaps still rest, containing all that is left of this woman who, when all is said and done, was no witch, but a person of singular character.

The last that can be said of her is that in 1906 she went back to Belgrade where she vainly tried to drum up enthusiasm for making Obren pretender to the Serbian crown.

A possible explanation for Milan's change of heart is that white magic must always prevail over black. For the ex-king did not go straight from his abdication to the Magnates' Club in Budapest as one might have expected him to do; he went instead to the Holy Land.

All of his life Milan had been an atheist. Once he had commanded two of his ministers, one an atheist and the other a believer in God, to debate their opposing points of view in his presence every Thursday evening. Alas, Thursday evening is the Witches' Sabbath, and the atheist had spoken more convincingly.

Now on this visit to Jerusalem he fell into the hands of a tough-fibered Patriarch who lectured him eloquently on the subject of his faulty character. He did not succeed in effecting any improvement in the ex-king; but he did manage to scare him out of his wits. For standing before the Holy Sepulchre, at the very core of the Christian world, he solemnly informed him that there was indeed a God and that it was altogether possible that He would decide to punish him for his sins by punishing his son. At this, Milan burst into tears. He threw himself upon the shoulder of the priest, crying aloud, "Oh, no, no! Let God punish me, but let Him not punish my son!" Very likely he vowed on the spot that while he was not strong enough to sacrifice his little sins for Sasha's sake, he could at least sacrifice his big ones: Artemesia and her son, Obren.

Yes, Milan used to say that he loved Sasha far better than his own life. On abdication day, in the course of the amateur theatricals he had staged, throwing himself upon his knees before Sasha and hailing him as "My Sovereign Lord and King!" while shedding tears with his hand on his breast, possibly the only moment that had seriously shaken Milan's heart was when his silent, unmoved child looked at him and said, "*Papa, quand pars-tu?*"

2.

The Dear One

The people of those times were hard on children. It was unkindly noted on the day King Milan abdicated his throne that while distinguished persons around him were sobbing loudly, Alexander of Serbia, twelve years old, remained unmoved. "Has he heart? Has he nerves?" were the questions asked.

Three regents had been appointed him by his father: the important one was Jovan Ristich, who had been Milan's regent during his minority and in succeeding years a premier of praise-worthy endurance. He had been Serbia's strong man, but now he was getting old and had no patience left for boy-kings. Boy-kings in his view were to stick to their books, keep still during Cabinet meetings, and sign where they were told; in the par-ticular case of Alexander, he was to refrain from mooning about his parents, especially his Frenchified mother who had intro-duced splashy frivolities into their simple but happy country. Sasha mooned about her however. He had a miniature painting of Natalie which he kept like an ikon, hidden among his papers and schoolbooks, and he wondered if she still remembered him.

Natalie, ever since her forcible separation from her son at Wiesbaden, had been seething about the capitals and watering spots of Europe, dominated by one desire, and after the abdica-tion of King Milan, by two of them: the first to be reunited with her only child; the second to replace Ristich as his regent. No sooner had Milan left Serbia than Natalie opened communica-tion with Ristich, announcing her determination to return to Belgrade and settle down. Now Ristich and his fellow regents had received their appointments from Milan on the strict con-dition—fortified by oaths—that they would not permit Sasha to communicate with his Russian-controlled mother except on infrequent circumscribed occasions. An acrimonious correspon-dence ensued between the regent and Natalie which, on Ristich's side, shows signs of increasing panic. He even sent a minister to reason with the queen, but Natalie only laughed. "I should like to see who would dare to prevent a mother from seeing her child," she said.

She returned to Belgrade, traveling by boat on the Sava River, and the Serbs went wild for joy. They poured out of their farms and mountain hideaways dressed in lovely Sunday brigand out-fits stiff with sequins and artificial pearls, and they jammed the river bank, bearing festoons of flowers. When her ship was sighted, a piercing shout went up and as she tripped across the gangplank they wept to see their voluptuous, vilely treated queen again.

But where were the men in top hats and uniforms? Where were the priceless carpets of state that ought to have been spread beneath her feet? There were none. Her private carriage was drawn up. The queen mounted it and bade the driver to take her to the palace. He drove to the front gate, but it was locked and a double guard was stationed at the door. The crowds swarmed about the palace, howling with sympathy for Natalie, while inside a boy was stammering over his lessons, his eyes rolling toward the windows, where greetings for his mother were to be heard from all of Serbia; but not from him, the king of it.

Natalie took a house nearby on Prince Michael's Street at a spot where every day her son, surrounded by guards, must ride past. Daily she rode back and forth and around the palace, past the nerve-wracked sentinels; and daily at evensong she came on foot to press her tear-stained face between the bars, desperately scanning the windows in the hope of seeing one beloved face. Not only Serbia's eyes but the eyes of Europe were fixed on this melodrama, and Natalie always gave people their money's worth. The names of Ristich and those of the other regents were widely execrated.

In the end they had to give in. A wire was sent to Milan in Paris, appealing to him to permit the child to meet with his mother. Milan balked for a time; then he telegraphed: IF YOU CAN RECONCILE IT WITH YOUR PLIGHTED WORD AND YOUR MANLY DIGNITY, THEN YES. Thus Sasha was enveloped once again in his mother's arms.

If only Natalie had been content to have her heart whole again, to see her son daily, shower him with kisses, stuff him with sweets, and replenish his toy cabinets which Ristich had emptied! But her imperious political ambitions necessitated the removal of Ristich, and to this end she began to fill Sasha's ears with violent abuse of his regent. She wrote long articles to the newspapers, recounting the wrongs she had suffered at the hands of the minister throughout her life; she became cronies with a Russian journalist to whom she passed along state secrets, and if she did not know any, she made them up; and she publicly accused Ristich of having permitted the boy Sasha to be introduced to abominable vices at an early age with a view to corrupting and gaining sinister power over his mind. In short, Natalie behaved as disruptively and malignantly as she had ever done when her husband had been King of Serbia, and the regent became no less eager than his former master to be rid of her once and for all.

But it was not easy to dislodge Natalie now that she was entrenched on Prince Michael's Street. Not only did she have political weight among the opposition party, the Radicals, but she had social weight among the ministers' influential wives; to say nothing of popular weight among the people of Belgrade who loved to see the charitable habits of their beautiful queen as she visited the sick, showered gifts upon the poor and old, and everywhere she went collected ragged urchins to take home and feed and clothe. No worthy or patriotic appeal was ever made in vain to Natalie's power or her purse. For example, there was the case of the widow, Draga Mashin.

The Widow Mashin had a unique history. Her grandfather had been a rich pig farmer in the time of Milosh Obren, the founder of the Obrenovich dynasty, and when the leader had been in dire need of money to buy arms with which to fight the Turks, this farmer had given all he had. In gratitude Milosh Obren had adopted him, under Serbian tribal law, as his *pobratim*, his brother. For some reason, though, he did not follow up this token of deep personal regard with the return of the borrowed money, with the result that the farmer's family sank back to peasanthood and poverty. The son of this patriot was prefect of his district, but he remained a poor man. He had time only to produce a large family of children before he went insane and was shut up in an asylum.

Draga was one of the eldest of the abandoned children, and she had acquired some slender education before her father's madness brought tragedy upon her family. When she was seventeen, being very pretty, she managed to snare a husband some years older than herself named Svetozar Mashin, who was respectably placed in the civil service but was far gone in alcoholism. After a wretched year Mashin died in some inebriated fashion.

In a society that still honored tribal ways, it ought to have been the duty of her husband's brother, a rising young army officer, to take Draga under his wing. But Alexander Mashin would have nothing to do with his young sister-in-law. He hated her bitterly. The reason has not been reliably established. It is sometimes suggested that he was convinced that Draga had poisoned his brother; again, that he believed her wanton behavior during the marriage had driven his brother to a drunken death. A more likely crime of Draga's would have been that she had milked the Mashin family coffers dry in order to support her numerous destitute brothers and sisters, to whom she was devotedly attached.

Some mystery lies here, perhaps never to be solved, but like a tiny shadow at sunset it lengthens and lends its blackness to the night. Whatever may have been the truth, Draga was cast into the world to shift for herself on a small pension, and here a second shadow crouches against the other: did she eke out her existence by lovemaking? In later years it was taken for granted that she had made her living licentiously; and looking into those great heifer eyes of Draga's, in which kindness did not live so much as a huge receptiveness, we may suppose that she accepted lovers from whom she would receive with gratified squeaks small luxuries and spending money, and perhaps a "loan" for her family's sake.

But it is impossible to see this most fatal of women as a *femme fatale*, or as a careerist of the bedchamber, or as licentious or even immodest. Belgrade was a small town then; what it contained of interest, everybody knew. It is significant that no one came forward to impugn Draga's character when, after she had lived insecurely for years, she plucked up courage to approach an influential gentleman and appeal to him for advice as to how she should make her living. He suggested that she should become a governess. Draga opened her eyes wide at this and exclaimed, "I, a governess? But what should I teach?"

Really, it was a shame, the influential gentleman thought, that this granddaughter of a patriot to whom the entire Serbian nation owed a debt should be in the position of a supplicant, and he expressed this opinion to Natalie, who agreed with him. The ex-queen summoned Draga and was pleased by her good looks and unobtrusive manners. She waved her magic wand, and straightaway Draga's dim existence ceased. She became lady-in-waiting to Her Majesty the ex-Queen of Serbia. She wore dresses with frills and capelets trimmed with narrow rims of fur, and stuffed birds perched amid the bows on her tall bonnet. Teachers came daily to cram her with French, German, and bézique, and to drill her in points of etiquette and the contents of the *Almanach de Gotha*. Better than all of this, she could pack a trunk for her young sister whom Natalie was sending at her own expense to be educated in Paris, and she could polish the buttons of her two brothers who were receiving commissions in the army. Surely favors overflowed for all of Draga's deprived brood, and surely, when she daily walked beside the queen, some knowing person would have had the goodness to whisper a few words into the queen's ear, had her protégée lacked virtue. But nobody did.

By this time Natalie was locked in mortal combat with Ristich, who had the additional anxiety that if he could not induce her to leave Serbia, ex-King Milan would feel obliged to come home. The regents had managed to avoid paying him his yearly allowance—which had been agreed upon at the time of his abdication—and he was dunning them unmercifully. At any moment he might bustle down on them from Paris, push them out of the way, and reassume the reigns of government long enough to deal with Natalie and rifle the public treasury. Natalie must positively be made to go.

Mr. Ristich began by requesting her to leave. She said that she had no money. The regent said that he would gladly supply her with the money, to which crude suggestion, smacking of bribery, she replied with the contempt it deserved.

Next a decree of banishment was passed through the Skupshtina, neatly written out, and respectfully submitted to the queen. She read the document and thought that it was a very funny Act of Parliament indeed.

The regent now hit upon a promising scheme. From Hungary a great magnate was invited to visit Belgrade: Count Hunyadi, a man of such countless quarterings that they glimmer like splintered starlight across the dim reaches of Central European history. He also had a current of royal blood running in his veins. It was believed that he would take Natalie in hand and give her some badly needed instructions about the conduct of a queen. He came, and the society ladies of Belgrade fell over their court trains in order to lionize him. Natalie, however, remained aloof. After all, she had been to Biarritz and seen Hungarian magnates in their bathing suits.

But Ristich had a last trick. He commanded that Sasha be taught a little speech; then he placed the decree of banishment in the boy's hand and told him to repeat the speech to the queen. In stunned obedience the boy spoke the unthinkable words which begged his mother to bow to the Skupshtina and leave the country. Silently Natalie listened, and afterwards she asked to be given the decree. Sasha held it out to her and she read it slowly. Then she said: "I will yield only to force." When she was asked what could be more forceful than a parliamentary resolution, she made it clear that she meant physical force.

On a May morning of 1891, the prefect of police, together with several police officers, waited upon Her Majesty. She was *en négligée*, and she dressed reluctantly, impeded by heaving and sobbing. She demanded to be allowed to say good-bye to her friends. Messengers were despatched to summon them, but when the queen's list of friends seemed endless, the prefect brought it to an end. Natalie then began to direct her maids in their packing, but she changed her directions so frequently that no progress was made.

The prefect waited stolidly throughout these painful hours, but at four o'clock in the afternoon he stepped forward and laid forcible hands on the queen.

Throughout the day, outside Natalie's house, Prince Michael's Street had become the scene of an unexpected carnival. Traffic had been suspended and so had all tiresome work. The people of the quarter had gathered as if to some gala event, and hawkers of delicacies were plying their trade. Little groups of fine ladies, Natalie's female friends, stood about her door, and every so often they rushed the guards, weeping and battering their fists against the stalwart chests of the policemen, while happy crowds cheered them on. The queen's carriages were drawn up before her door.

Natalie emerged from her house in the center of a little trap of policemen and got into a carriage.

At the sight of her the mild-tempered, even merry crowd was flicked to indignation. As if compulsively drawn they began to move and congregate in a dangerously buzzing hive around their queen. A little rush of men broke forth to hang on to the carriage wheels; some more seized the horses' heads; others leapt onto the box, tussled with the driver, and toppled him down. Now mighty waves of sound were echoing between the villas: "Long live the queen!" and some stalwart Serbs leapt into the carriage and plucked her neatly out, like a nut from a shell, putting her down with tenderness on the cobbles behind them while they turned to pick up sticks and stones and face her persecutors; and Natalie ran everywhere weeping, grasping the hands of the men of Belgrade and covering them with kisses, enfolding the women in her. arms.

The police were armed. In time they beat back the crowd with the butts of their guns. They managed to recapture the queen and in one speedy operation tumble her into the carriage, slam the door, and get the equipage cracking down the street, leaving the mob behind. But the people were rebellious now, for there had been injuries and beatings, and this mood was spreading into the adjoining streets faster than horses can trot. By the time the queen's carriage arrived at the Serbian Crown Hotel, a crowd of teen-age boys was waiting, spoiling for a fracas. Some rebuilding was being done to the hotel and large lumps of plaster were ready to hand with which to greet the police; other lads detached the horses from the queen's carriage, harnessed themselves, and drew Natalie back to her residence with a grand racket.

The regents were paralyzed with astonishment. The windows of public buildings and of their own houses were being broken, and a formidable number of Serbs were coming together to march upon the old castle where the ministerial offices were installed. Apparently it was their intention to set it on fire, lynch the regents and Cabinet members, and give Sasha back to his mother. That old castle had withstood six centuries of Turkish sieges; now Serbian rulers trembled in the twilight and gave orders to shoot on Serbs. Somewhere among them, forgotten in a corner, was a wretched boy.

As it happened, although shots were fired here and there and some lives were lost, no serious riots developed, and as night fell passions subsided. Many of the rioters were beginning to want their dinners, and teen-agers had bedtimes in those days. Natalie was back in her house with a force of loyal men to guard her. The town resumed its aspect of tranquility—except at the ministerial offices where regents and Cabinet ministers and high-ranking military men, united for once in strong purpose, deliberated how they could possibly rid themselves of Queen Natalie. From their midst a stout general arose and spoke. He said, "I will conduct the queen over the frontier tonight if she is only in her nightdress."

Over the rooftops of the houses of Prince Michael's Street at two o'clock the following morning, with no more of a rustle than rats or cats would make, crept a detachment of soldiers commanded by this general, and when they came to Queen Natalie's house their clever mountaineers' feet found invisible ledges to drop down the walls into her courtyard. Three hundred men were shut up in that house with Natalie, determined to fight for her with their lives. It took more than comic courage for that general to beat upon her door and shout, "Open in the name of the law!" The door opened. Three men and a boy stood there. Everyone else had gone home to bed. Perhaps Natalie had sent them home. She was not a wantonly vicious woman, only stubborn and unbridled, and she had been thoroughly shaken by the previous day's bloodshed on her behalf. Weeping and moaning, she allowed herself to be packed into a common, dirty cab and taken to the railway station, frequently raising her head from her handkerchief to remind her captors of the various battles of history in which the Serbian militia had suffered sore defeat. Shortly thereafter she went to live in Biarritz, where she built a beautiful villa and named it Sashino—"little Sasha's house"—and she covered its walls with countless large and small pictures of her darling boy.

With her lived Draga Mashin as *dame d'honneur*.

Once in the years that followed, during a shopping trip to Paris, the queen, for fun, visited the famous clairvoyant, Madame de Thèbes, accompanied by Draga. The fortuneteller said to her, "You are nourishing a viper in your bosom, don't you know that?"

And when, after some little talk, Draga inquired, "Now what about me?" the clairvoyant replied, "Ah, you! You will marry the highest in your land, but you will be the ruin of him, and you will perish with him."

The regents now drew up an iron-clad bill which was hastily passed through the Skupshtina, banishing Natalie from Serbia forever and a day; and while they were about it, they banished Milan also. The defeated queen acquiesced to this, but Milan charged them one million francs for not contesting or defying the bill.

Now Alexander was truly alone. Miles deep the frozen fields

of silence lay about him, and he had not even guilt to companion him in this imprisonment. No one was angry with Sasha; he was simply condemned to live in the silent eye of fury which no expiation of his could dispel.

No communication whatsoever with his parents was permitted him. His equerries, valets, and aides-de-camp were enjoined to make sure of it, and they searched his room daily so that no small secret of his heart could ever be written down, but had to be thrust in with the rest of the squirming troubles that jammed the corridors of his soul. A servant slept nightly across the threshold of his room.

Twice a week he was permitted to ride in a closed carriage from which he might see the trees of fateful Topchider pass by, if he chose to squint past the interfering bodies of guards-men who on either side of him galloped their horses back and forth, back and forth, guarding him from assassination. He would not have seen much, in any event. Sasha was myopic and he peered out from under the arched eaves of his brows like a timid animal of darkness. He wore glasses over his disturbed sight.

His studies were grim. One or another of his regents was constantly in the room, watchful that his tutor spoke no word against the existing government. Once, during a French lesson, the regent was called from the room, and the boy had time to turn a piteous face to his tutor, whispering, "For goodness sake, talk to me for a minute!"

After eons of time, the rules were lifted somewhat. The lad was permitted to go walking at Topchider with his French tutor, and there, with a young American journalist and an English diplomat, he learned to swim and loved it, little knowing that anything he chose to love was but a heiroglyph for tragedy. To the disapproving Frenchman he said, "Don't tell my regents I am having swimming lessons. Just tell them the king can swim."

The foreigners must have gossiped rudely about Alexander's runty physique, because the French tutor wrote of him as he was at fifteen: ". . . those who recently spoke of his under-developed and rachitic body would perhaps sit down *brusquement* if the king should let his hand rest on their shoulder!" Sasha had indeed inherited his father's muscular development about the arms and shoulders, and his hands were very strong; but the lower half of him dwindled, pollywog-fashion, to meager loins and thighs, and he had knock-knees. Even his loyal tutor recognized a curious disharmonic note in his voice, "high-pitched and yet veiled," a shrouded ghost emanating from some miasmic depths of him, which spoke in plaintive pronunciamentos: "I am an orphan whose parents are alive." In 1893 when his ministers came to wish him Happy New Year, he said, "Keep your good wishes. I am the most miserable of Serbs."

One evening Alexander confided to his French tutor his private terror: he had a morbid fear of any reminder of the fact of death. Every morning his valet had orders to scan newspapers and magazines before presenting them, lest any drawing of skeleton or skull or other sepulchral device should be lurking in the pages to jump out at Sasha. On a recent trip to Moscow a hideous thing had happened. The Grand Duke Sergei had kindly taken him to the chapel of his name saint, where the bodies of many holy saints lay embalmed in shrouds. When distinguished guests were present, these bodies were unwrapped so that they could be kissed. Sasha's myopia had saved him from making a fool of himself. He quickly removed his glasses and kissed haphazardly wherever he was told. And he did not resume his glasses until the saints were safely packed out of sight.

On telling this story, Alexander began to tremble. Suddenly he arose from his chair and began to run about the neighboring rooms. Returning, he said shamefacedly to his tutor: "I just wanted to see how I'll cross these dark rooms when I've left you to go to bed."

The Frenchman suggested that Sasha search his memory for some foolish childhood event that had engraved these irrational fears upon his mind. The son of King Milan thought hard: well, he could never forget an illustration of Gustave Doré to Dante's *Inferno*. It represented a monster called "Sovereign of the Kingdom of Tears."

Yes, Alexander was growing up morbid, withdrawn, and fearful, and being fearful, sly. Ristich found occasion to complain of him: "Not one word of truth comes out of the mouth of this deceitful boy!"

The French tutor, however, found that everything about the

king squeezed his heart, and soon he was up to his ears in a conspiracy to rescue Sasha from his durance vile.

Ex-King Milan, on the fortune that had been granted him, if only he would keep away from Serbia, had been living a high life in Paris and Vienna as the darling of actresses, croupiers, and race-track touts, the lavish friend of struggling artists, the man door openers and hat takers worship as a god. Some of his entertainments reputedly cost him—or at least cost his caterers—fifteen thousand pounds in a single night.

But now the fat years were at an end and the lean years had followed upon them. Milan had dipped back into the pockets of his beneficiaries as far as he could go. There remained the affluent Natalie, his divorced wife. He wrote her an abject letter in which he confessed all of his faults and begged her, for the sake of Sasha's honor, to lend him 350,000 francs—otherwise he would have to blow out his brains.

Natalie's response to this letter was cruel. She sent it to the French papers, which gleefully gave it the widest circulation together with Natalie's majestic reply: that Sasha's honor demanded that his father pull himself together, live properly, and not commit suicide, "like an actress."

Still some understanding—sufficient at least for a conspiracy —seems to have reunited the pair in 1893. There was indeed an urgent reason to join forces if they wished to save their son's throne. For another, even more damnable document, signed by Milan, had recently been published in the French papers. It was nothing less than that famous secret treaty with Austria-Hungary, long-suspected but never quite a certainty, which some acute enemy of the Obrenovich dynasty had now unearthed and made public, showing that for years Milan had been laughing up his sleeve at Mother Russia, the tsar, Pan-Slavism, the "Slavonic Cause," the "Serbian Dream," and at all of his long-suffering brother-Slavs.

The consternation in Serbia when this treachery was divulged can scarcely be imagined. There followed a time of national agony with arrests by night and mysterious screams emanating from between the cracks of dungeon walls; with touch-and-go escapes across the border and strange corpses thumping over crystal waterfalls. In the Skupshtina ferocious members of the

Radical Party jumped up and down demanding the restoration of the Karageorgevich dynasty.

Throughout this excitement Sasha's French tutor traveled back and forth carrying messages between ex-King Milan and Natalie in France and power-hungry Radicals in Serbia. For once both parents submerged their differences, and Milan did not hesitate to conspire with his former deadly enemies, the Radicals. It was clear to him that unless the regents' government were to come crashing down, carrying Sasha with them, Sasha had to be instructed to turn on his regents and defy them.

Sasha was sixteen years old. On April 12, 1893, he invited his regents, ministers, and certain high-ranking military men to dine with him. At first they demurred. There was nothing to celebrate, and so why should they dine with Sasha? But he insisted and they humored him. It turned out to be quite a jolly dinner, with homey Serbian dishes and fiery Turkish drinks, and many a good joke flew about at the expense of the Radicals at which the young king did not laugh—but then, Sasha never laughed. He was always silent, pale, and cold. Quite late an aide-de-camp entered and whispered something into Alexander's ear. The king then arose. Since the toasts were over, his guests stared in puzzled silence.

"Gentlemen," said the boy-king in a voice which betrayed not the slightest nervousness, "it is announced to all the garrisons of Serbia, to all the authorities and to the people, and I announce it here to you, that I declare myself of full age, and that I now take the government of the country into my own hands."

When these words had begun to unhinge the jaws of the assembled gentlemen, Alexander continued, "You will not be be allowed to leave the palace tonight. You can remain here as my guests, but if not, then as my prisoners."

Stunned silence. Then Ristich, trembling and whitefaced, raised his voice and solemnly rebuked Alexander. A general, making explosive noises, rushed out of the room. He was stopped by an aide-de-camp with sword drawn. The doors to the dining room had opened and lines of soldiers were revealed with glittering bayonets.

There was nothing to be done. The conspirators had won the army to the king's side and the people of Serbia woke the following morning to find their familiar ruler, Ristich, discarded and in his place a boy of sixteen. Throughout Europe the news sped, and oddly enough the poetic irrealism of Alexander's dinnertime *coup d'état*—although surely it was the rudest practical joke he had yet played—gripped the imagination of people everywhere. Leading the applause were the staid English who at the very nerve roots of their race found a romantic precedent: Arthur, drawing the sword out of the stone.

At any rate, Sasha got away with it. Serbia was caught in the backwash of the approving wave, and a joyous crowd, with bands playing and flags flying, gathered outside the palace and called him out. He made a regal speech in his frigid fashion, from a balcony, saying, "Let my first greetings on this occasion go out to my mother and father."

He had already dug out the miniature of his mother from among his papers; it was replaced by a large photograph of her. As soon as the new Radical Government—which hailed him as Alexander the Great—could bear to part with him, he appointed a numerous retinue and set out with them for a visit of state to Biarritz, to Sashino.

A universal belief exists that dogs and children have an uncanny recognition of the balance of good and evil in the persons they meet, in spite of everyday observation which proves that dogs know only where their biscuits come from, and children are equally dense. Queen Natalie had a collection of noble Roumanian nieces and nephews whom, for want of Sasha, she loved to invite for the holidays at Biarritz, where she showered delights on them. When the children became peevish, she could always relinquish them to the bored supervision of her lady-in-waiting, Draga Mashin.

The children worshiped Aunt Natalie and intuitively grasped of what inferior material Draga Mashin was made. Cleverly they noted her nervousness in distinguished company, her little airs and spurious graces, her false elegancies whenever she was addressed by the highborn, her squeaks and squeals when they teased her. Everybody teased Draga "just because she was a little bit pretentious, a little bit silly, and also, probably without knowing it, because she liked to be teased": thus, when she was grown, little Princess Marthe Bibesco was to write of the pale lady who gladly allowed herself to be mocked if only someone would deign to notice her. Her position in Natalie's household was partly that of an upper servant: she would mend a little, chat a little, be dismissed and then recalled, summoned for walking, sent back for a cloak, be excused and then required to come and pour the tea. The years were an endless prairie made of silken cushions which had somehow to be traversed, and Draga found relief in reading lurid novels. One of them was called *The Red Death*.

Meanwhile her bloom passed, and she became plump. She was still pretty but far from seductive; certainly she seduced none of the idle noble or rich men who flocked to this resort in the wakes of the courts of Queens Eugénie, Victoria, and Natalie. She was secure, and her family were secure. She was well fed and clothed. No doubt Queen Natalie's dresses were fitted down for her—for Natalie's striking shape was now enhanced by majestic fat.

The fashionable persons who inhabited Biarritz had been following the fortunes of the house of Obrenovich for their lives long, and they knew more of the wrongs and rights of things than we can ever recover from dusty memoirs. The news that the poetic boy-King of Serbia was about to visit their community, that haven of prissy queens, set them into frantic motion as they prepared to pour forth their substance on *petits fours*, *blancmanges*, picnic punch, and other comestibles suitable to a growing lad. Such was the crush of people who wished to be presented to Alexander that Natalie was obliged to set up a kiosk on the beach, and when he came with his regiment of servitors, she stood beside him and lived some illuminated hours watching the smart people of her world gather into stately procession and wait their turns in the gritty damp to bend the knee and scrape the toe and sweep gorgeous summer skirts upon the sand before her son, the sovereign king.

The children hated him at once. "He was a dark, sulky-looking little fellow with a little black moustache, of medium figure, badly clothed in a common white flannel suit with blue stripes, wearing an out-of-date foolish little straw hat, with a string to keep it safe against the sea winds; and over his frowning black eyebrows, over his short-sighted small black eyes, half shut, he wore a disgraceful, a detestable pair of eyeglasses, fasted with a golden chain. . . ."

To the children's disgust their cousin Sasha did not care for the parties that were being given in his honor. In company "he seemed taciturn, dull, with an expression of mistrust on his face and looked like an owl in daylight." As soon as he was able, he would leave the throng and gravitate toward that lonely part of the beach at the end of the terrace where the children played under the eyes of Draga. "Dirty Serbian!" they yelled at him, and he responded in correct litany: "Dirty Roumanians!" It seems obvious that he wanted to make friends and play. But his cousins would not play with Sasha. They might have arrested the cruel comment of stars, but they turned their backs on him. The best he could do for himself was drop down with a shy smile beside the lady-in-waiting underneath her beach umbrella. What was she reading? *The Red Death?*

Sasha became devoted to this portion of the beach and he spent less of his time munching Natalie's ornate meringues and more of it crouching under the umbrella with the squealing Draga, while the children bombarded them with crabs and other monstrosities. Whenever possible he joined them on their cycling expeditions, picnics, and jaunts in the carriage. Natalie was severely blamed afterwards for allowing these carryings-on, but it is hard to see how a queen of spotless virtue could have expected mischief to arise between her carefully genteel, not-so-young lady-in-waiting and her teen-age boy. In fact her trust was not misplaced, because Draga did not take advantage of Sasha's innocence. Long afterward, furious at some ugly imputations against her character, Alexander told one of his ministers that he had every reason to know her blamelessness, because for no less than three years Draga had foiled every one of his ignoble designs upon her. Once, he said, when in his youthful passion he had crashed into her bedroom at Sashino and pounced on her, she had taken him firmly by the shoulders, pushed him away, turned him around, and marched him out of the door, turning the key afterwards in the lock. "She did this to me!" he cried in recollected mortification. "Her king!"

The children witnessed another of Draga's narrow escapes. They were up to some nefarious business close to the roof of the villa near Draga's attic room, when they froze to stillness at the sound of feet thumping up the stairs. "From our shelter we could see quite clearly the long-lighted passage. The form of a woman dressed in black appeared at the entrance, coming from the staircase. It was Draga, running, panting; and running after her was King Alexander. What game were they playing? He caught her at last and pushed her against the door of her own room. We saw him trying the door furiously, but it was locked. He put his arms around her, making her his prisoner. Draga gave one of her shrill little screams. He closed her lips with his—to silence her, I believed. . . ."

Daily the fashionables of Biarritz converged upon the little village of bathing huts which stood at the edge of the tide and there divested themselves of their complex costumes, emerging waist deep in the frolicsome waters. Sasha would have none of this. He insisted on swimming at the lonely part of the beach where Draga sat, although he was warned that there was a dangerous hollow there in which a treacherous undertow frequently developed. However, he pigheadedly trusted to himself and his *baigneur*, a local Basque sailor, born to the waves.

One day when he went swimming, both Alexander and his *baigneur* were turned upside down by a mighty wave and they did not bounce up again. After an awful interval during which his watchful aides-de-camp came running, another wave crashed in carrying Alexander, and it cast him unconscious upon the sand. In the presence of a large company of shrieking guests from the terrace, the king was tenderly scraped up and carried to his distraught mother, and eventually he was revived and put warmly to bed. But the *baigneur* was drowned and all festivities had to end while his body was recovered and regretfully returned with suitable recompense to his wife and children.

The oddest thing about this episode was that while all the other ladies on the spot had behaved themselves usefully, rendering prayers to Heaven and advice to aides-de-camp, the lady-in-waiting had remained at the edge of the hubbub and fainted dead away.

It is a glorious thing to be a king and have the power to declare one's parents' divorce null and void, to command them to love each other. Milan and Natalie enjoyed a short period of truce, and the queen established herself in Belgrade, where, helpful to Sasha, she caused all state documents to pass through her hands; and she held court over a group of ladies whom Milan called "the queen's bodyguard." With these ladies, at long last, Natalie came into her glory. Daily, over their tea and cakes, they would discuss all manner of social questions, debating back and forth, proposing measures, drawing up resolutions. When they had a document prepared, it was sent to the palace for Sasha to sign, whereupon it became law. Natalie's boudoir became a "Woman's Parliament" of the kind that would have rejoiced W. S. Gilbert, and it was a comic achievement indeed, except that for such trivial radiance Natalie had wrecked her husband's policies and her son's life.

It must have been at this time that Draga gained the reputation of being the mistress of ex-King Milan, for she was frequently seen in and out of the palace, and this explanation sprang naturally to the mind. It is a curious fact that to this day there are Serbs alive who have heard the scandal from their fathers, and insist that the notorious Draga Mashin was Milan's mistress. And yet the memoirs of a close friend of Milan's state categorically that the ex-king disliked Draga on sight, that he had an instinctive mistrust of the unobtrusive woman with her cakey smile and too receptive eyes.

Besides, Milan did not pay more than brief visits to Belgrade at this period; he was far more likely to be found in Paris with his son as guest, arranging for Sasha entertainments of quite a different nature from those of Natalie at Sashino. Unlike the queen, Milan had been miserably disappointed in his son's physical appearance. It troubled him also that in the presence of the prettiest actresses Sasha was not merely gauche and impervious to their influence, but uneager to take lessons in social address from his father. Milan began to wonder if his son was sexually defective. This rumor, perhaps started by his garrulous father, persisted throughout Alexander's life.

But one day in Paris when Sasha went walking with a confidential friend, they stopped at a jeweler's shop and the young king asked his companion to lend him money to pay for a gift he had previously ordered there. It was an elegant golden cigarette case on which was worked in diamonds: DRAGA.

The word *draga*, knobby as it sounds to English ears, in some Central European languages makes the best sound in the world, the first a man hears in the clasp of his mother's arms, and if he is lucky, the last he will hear before the grave enfolds him: *draga!*—dear one!

So Alexander's friend smiled to see this name written in diamonds and said suavely, "She is dear to me, too, since she provides me with the occasion of lending money to my king."

In Serbia, Alexander's *coup d'état* had brought the Radical Party to power, and after they had shot or incarcerated their most vexatious opponents, they had an easy time of it. It was only necessary to point to the helpless youth of their king and his urgent need of the support of all Serbs to reduce what remained of the opposition party to acquiescence. For a while Sasha played the role of the totemic idol who reconciles within himself all the conflicts of his tribe. Possibly he derived too great an opinion of himself. Before long his ministers began to have enough of Sasha. They told him flatly to stay out of Cabinet meetings, and that they would call him when they wanted him. When they needed his signature on a document, they did not bother to explain it: they simply banged on the table and swore at him until he signed. Because Sasha hated roughness of any kind, was in fact frightened of any show of masculine violence, he sometimes burst into tears and ran out of the room.

Clearly Alexander of Serbia had not the stuff of which parliamentarians are made. He conceived a deep hatred for parties, parliaments, and their squabbles, and formulated for himself a simple political philosophy: Serbs were disorderly, unstable, and intolerant, and did not deserve freedom; they would be much better ruled by one righteous man whose word was absolute, none other than Alexander the Great.

Alexander, therefore, plotted a new *coup d'état*, again probably with the complicity of Milan. One midnight, having scraped together a subservient cabinet, he rescinded the liberal constitution which Milan had presented to his people on abdication day, and replaced it with the one that had been in effect before; this placed sufficient power into the sovereign's hands so that if anyone was going to run out of Cabinet meetings in tears, it would not be the king. This second practical joke of Sasha's again met with admiration from conservatives in Europe who did not hold with constitutions. "A monarch of great determination," he was called, "resolved to govern as well as reign."

Sasha perceived also that his mother's teatime parliament was bringing a certain amount of ridicule upon him, and so, gently, for the second time he asked her to leave the country, doubly regretting to see her go with the dear, and still cruel one in her train.

At nineteen Sasha was "a quiet, prematurely grave young man . . . his manners are amiable; he meets you half way. The smile on his lips is somewhat flickering and might be called feeble. He has a friendly shake of the hand for those he knows, but what he really thinks lies buried deep down in his heart, and no one of his entourage has been allowed access to this secret chamber. . . ."

Sasha not only nursed a secret chamber but he lived in it, peering at the real world through a narrow window; or else he would have perceived that Serbs were the last people on earth to put up with his dictatorial ambitions. Egalitarian to the bone, the least of them disliked taking work as domestic servants: menial positions were usually filled by such lesser brother-Slavs as Bosnians or Croats. Even the deplorable party strife and the wild battles in the Skupshtina may be seen as what Emperor Francis Joseph called, in no friendly mood, "their democratic tendencies." But Sasha's masterful tricks had succeeded so well thus far that it seemed to him at the time that the world was not too huge to conquer.

Besides, in the summer of 1896, the stranger, happiness, had come whistling into his life: on a visit to his mother at Sashino, one of his forays against her lady-in-waiting had ended in decisive victory.

Of course the silent Sasha did not confide this event to anyone; his mother had not an inkling. But after his return to Belgrade some tender love letters passed between the guilty pair, and one of them fell into the hands of the queen. For her chaste mind it was an agonizing shock, and she reacted as unwisely as possible. She cast Draga Mashin out of her house, set her adrift upon her own tiny resources. Then Natalie sat down to write letters to all her friends about the ingratitude of the younger woman, the vileness of the viper she had nurtured in her bosom.

Some years later Draga told a friend about a time when she was alone and helpless and had prayed to God to send her a protector; and the same night, when she climbed into bed, she prayed again that if it was His will, He should let her see in a dream the image of that man. She dreamed: she was standing in a garden looking toward the blue sky, when suddenly she noticed something slowly descending from the clouds. It was a golden picture frame and it floated in the air. Inside it was the likeness of King Alexander of Serbia.

Alexander had been a small boy when Draga had previously been a young widow in need of protection; the dream, therefore, if it occurred at all, must have come to her at this time when she was banished from Sashino. A touch of verisimilitude is lent the story by the picture frame: Sashino was full of pictures of Sasha, splendidly framed, which Draga had no doubt dusted for years.

Homeless once again, Draga had only one place to drift to, and that was Belgrade. Shortly after an announcement appeared in the papers that the court lady of Queen Natalie for reasons of bad health had been at her own request relieved of her duties, the citizens of that town saw an interesting sight: their king, off for his winter holidays in the Tyrol, and at his side, abloom with health and ornately dressed, a lady of uncertain years. Some said she was in her late twenties, others guessed she was as much as fifteen years older than the king.

One day they would loathe her. Not the accursed Artemesia nor the most villainous Roman empress was so abominated by her countrymen as this soft, gelatinous Draga Mashin. In life there are people who cannot talk back, and in history persons whose characters were so unassertive that they are condemned to be understood through reflection, as if caught in a maze of crazy mirrors. Draga is one of these, and we gaze all the more curiously at the only mute defense she has left behind her: her photograph. We see a youngish woman, running to fat, with pretty delicate features rather heavily framed with peasant bones and pads of flesh. She has huge soft eyes, but they hold no active sparkle or intelligence; they are indolent, even stagnant. Like a person lost in the world's stage machinery, she holds her head habitually to one side with a saccharine smile. She certainly does not look diabolically clever, shrewd, and ambitious, still less licentious, and in fact not one of her reliably reported words or actions bears out this enduring view of Draga Mashin. She seems more like a harmless, sluggish animal which, when touched on a tender spot, might lash out destructively.

Draga had a tender spot: her love for the younger orphans of her family, for whose sake, since she was a child herself, she had made occasional little stabs at fortune.

A domineering yet deprived orphan like Alexander naturally loved this passive and genteel woman. In her there was no roughness to dismay him, no turbulent emotion, no criticism, only boundless acceptance. His sexual organization seems to have been infantile. Indeed, he ruled Serbia by means of infantile tantrums and tricks. But Draga, like the most doting mother, like Natalie, would have praised the statesmanship of everything he did.

It is not quite pleasant to visualize these two wrecked personalities engaged in the sacrifice of love, but healthier persons may feel rebuked by the sheer completeness of the gifts they exchanged. They placed not only the best of themselves at each other's disposal, but the worst, all their foolishness and bad judgment, their vanity and their utterly false grasp of their responsibilities: an abysmal pool, but shot through with the brightness of their love.

Shortly after Draga became his official mistress Sasha again astounded the world with a feat of prestidigitation: he revoked the decree of banishment against his father and invited Milan to return to Serbia to reorganize the army, as commander-in-chief.

Queen Natalie, however, was not invited to Belgrade. Her treasured son cut her out of his life, and he never saw him again.

Nicholas II, who in 1894 succeeded to the throne of Russia, inherited not so much his father's Pan-Slavism as his foreign policies. He could not, like Alexander III, tie knots in silver spoons with his bare hands, but probably his ambassador to Belgrade tied some when he learned that Milan was returning to Serbia in a position of highest responsibility.

For the ex-king his son's offer of a job was a sign that Heaven had at last switched to his side, for his debts were climbing, and all he needed was to be placed in charge of that branch of government which then, as now, received the most sap. Milan was not an entirely worthless individual. In middle age he was one of those ebullient stout men who sometimes do not organize themselves well but know exactly how to organize others. His first act in his new post was to make a rule that whatever else went unpaid in Serbia, her armed forces should receive their salaries on the dot and in full, from commander-in-chief down to the last batman. After that it was a simple matter for him to whip up an army which ate out of his hand and was widely praised for its vim and sparkle.

Back in harness Milan placed as many Russophile Radicals as possible in jail on trumped-up charges, and studied how to draw the country back under the giant wing of Austria. The Russian ambassador turned pale with rage whenever he passed Milan in the street, and at court receptions refused to stand in the same room with him. Eventually he had to be recalled to St. Petersburg and replaced by an urbane individual who played cards with Milan and kept his feelings to himself.

Milan was dismayed by the capricious and deceitful character of his son: "There is no dependence to be placed on Sasha. He goes from one extreme to the other; and he is quite capable of pursuing, with the same deadly hatred which he shows to the Radicals, the very people he now pretends to admire." He perceived that if Sasha was to be induced to cleave to his own Germanic policies, he must be persuaded without delay to marry a Germanic princess.

Efforts to make Sasha marry had been in progress for years. Once, when he was a mere lad and the Radicals had been in power, they had virtually kidnaped him into Montenegro in order to force him to propose to one of the Serbian princesses of that land; but Sasha had thrown a tantrum and they had been obliged to remove him from the scene. Natalie, in her days of influence, had lined up a number of noble Slavic ladies like herself; but he had managed to make himself obnoxious to all of them. Now, in order to thwart his father, he drew up a list of specifications for Milan to present to the Austrian foreign minister in Vienna: the aspiring Queen of Serbia had to be young, very beautiful, and of such personal charm as would win Sasha's love; politically well connected with family relationships in the first-class courts of Europe; highly cultured and gifted, and fabulously rich. The Austrian foreign minister could only respond that such a paragon would hardly wish to bury herself in Belgrade.

His father's newest onslaught against his bachelorhood was especially unwelcome to Sasha because he was madly in love with Draga Mashin. He had installed her in a house on Crown Street, not far from the palace. It was an unpretentious cottage, but Draga, now that she had the king's uttermost resources at her disposal, was showing a flair for splendor, and she furnished it magnificently with every royal luxury, and in the heart of it, clothed in shimmering brocades and rare laces, like a plump odalisque she ensconced herself, surrounded by her siblings for whom she arranged distinguished marriages and careers in the army and diplomatic corps. Now for the first time in her life she had friends who appeared to admire her, who courted her, and did not dare to tease. One of them was the new, urbane Russian ambassador.

There were detractors, too. Various lively Serbs come forward at this time with love letters which purported to have been written by Draga when she was a young widow, and these were passed about the city from hand to hand. If they were not forgeries, they must have been full of pathos, the begging letters of a teen-age girl with ten children to support, artlessly beseeching love or money. Draga was not a vindictive woman, and she did not move against these calumniators. She did not even move against her chief vilifier, her brother-in-law, Colonel Alexander Mashin, who as a confidant of Commander-in-Chief Milan was now at the peak of his career, and whose fall would have been spectacular had Draga chosen to bring it about. But she did not. She simply gloried in her home, where by day she dispensed sticky Near Eastern hospitality to flatterers and by night preened and beautified herself for the pleasure of Sasha.

"You beautify yourself too much, Draga," one of her new friends said to her, "and it is no wonder that the king is so much in love with you. But surely you will not turn his head so that he might make you Queen of Serbia?"

To this suggestion Draga replied indignantly. "What do you think I am? I hate you for talking nonsense. You know I adore Sasha, and just because I adore him, I shall never stand for a moment between him and his duty. He must marry a foreign princess. . . ."

Who was this so-called friend, setting dangerous notions to simmer in the silly head of Draga? She was a Roumanian woman who had recently settled in Belgrade with her husband, a Russian general, and they had both courted the company of the mistress. The Roumanian lady told Draga that she herself had once been but the mistress of her husband, that "the general had never meant to marry her until she heard of an old witch who dwelt somewhere in the neighborhood of Ploesti. For a few napoléons d'or she obtained from her a charm which she was told to give the general to drink in a cup of coffee." Not quite two weeks after that coffee the general had wakened one morning in a melancholy frame of mind. "What is the matter?" his sweetheart asked.

"A great deal is the matter," replied the general. "My conscience is telling me that our present relations ought not to be continued and that if I am an honest and honorable man, I ought to make you before God and before man, my lawful wife."

Following the instructions of the old witch, the lady had laughed at her general for seven days, but on the eighth she had consented to marry him. Furthermore, she told Draga, the marriage had been a happy one in spite of her own humble origin. She promised that if Draga would bring her a few hair combings of Alexander's and some napoléons d'or, she would gladly make the trip to Ploesti on her behalf.

There were many who said afterwards that the real witch in the case did not live in Ploesti but in St. Petersburg, where the tsar—or his foreign minister—was now furiously bent upon the destruction of the dynasty, applying "methods of such intensely Asiatic Machiavellism that the mind and morality of western Europe can hardly realize that such actions would have been possible at the end of the nineteenth century." The Russians were closing around Draga, seeking her influence to drive a wedge between Alexander and ex-King Milan, and working upon her passive peasant mind to encourage Alexander's capriciousness and dictatorial follies.

Milan, in spite of his dislike of Draga, did not interfere with his son's love affair, perhaps relieved to see that he was capable of one. But he was beginning to perceive her as an enemy. "The Mashinka is running him to earth," he said. "Since this creature has got influence over him, Sasha is not recognizable." He bore hard on Sasha to marry, pointing out to him, and truly, that until he produced an heir to strengthen the dynasty, his life was not safe.

Assassins were indeed at work. In 1899 one of them had shot at Milan as he rode in an open coach and all but failed to miss him. The culprit was seized, and after persuasion he confessed that his gun had been given to him in Bucharest in a certain house which was known to be a headquarters of the Russian secret police.

One day, the chief of police of Belgrade paid a visit to the prime minister, Dr. Vladan Georgevich. He said he felt it in his bones that Draga Mashin was going to cause terrible misfortune to the dynasty.

"Why?" asked Dr. Georgevich.

"She has made the king perfectly blind so that he cannot see anything but her. He spends every night with her. With the magic drinks she gives him, she has made him so foolish that he spends hours under her window, begging her humbly to let him in. Have you never thought that the king, waiting under Draga's windows in that deserted street might be murdered or catch a serious illness in wet and cold weather?"

Dr. Georgevich had never thought of it, although he was a physician. He remarked that the king was always accompanied on his amorous maneuvers by a colonel whose sword and revolver were worth a squadron of guards, and he advised the chief of police to hide a few extra policemen in the bushes underneath Draga's windows and to forget about her, as no doubt the king soon would, for the affair had been dragging on for three years, and now marriage plans were well under way. He confided to the troubled policeman that Alexander had solemnly promised that he would marry within the year.

The chief of police would not be comforted. "Mark my words," he told Georgevich, "If he has promised to marry, then he intends to marry none other than Draga Mashin."

The hunches of this simple peasant were not taken seriously by the prime minister who had joined forces with Milan to put his king into a corner. Milan had wheedled Wilhelm II, the German emperor, into yielding up one of his less important German princesses to Serbia. She was nubile, willing, and waiting. Dr. Georgevich had told Alexander that if he did not marry her within the year, he would resign his government. Sasha was cautious. "I cannot decide before I have seen her personally," he said.

But his tormentors would not let him be. He must marry or else be abandoned by both of them. At length Alexander came to his senses, and upon his solemn word of honor, given before several ministers, he promised that he would marry before the year 1900 was over. His father was so pleased that he jumped up and kissed him.

"Of course, some delay is unavoidable," continued Alexander. "Papa has been unwell. You think he looks well, but in truth he is ill. He hardly eats anything. He must go to Carlsbad. Dr. Georgevich too has made a wreck of himself in untiring service of his country. He must go to Marienbad, and afterwards to the Exhibition in Paris. Now we can't all three be absent from Serbia at once, can we?"

It was arranged that both of the ailing gentleman should visit their respective watering spots, and when their constitutions were on the mend, Dr. Georgevich was to return to Serbia, whereupon Alexander would join his father in Carlsbad and together they would travel to Germany to make the acquaintance of the princess.

One June 7, 1900, Milan left Belgrade for Carlsbad. On June 8, Dr. Georgevich departed for Marienbad.

One month later, on July 8, Dr. Georgevich's *chargé d'affaires* in Belgrade wired his chief in cipher that a terrible misfortune was about to fall on Serbia and begged him to come home immediately. The same message was sent to the ex-king Milan.

Both gentlemen reached at once for the cipher books which Alexander had personally provided for them before their departure. Unfortunately, they appeared to be the wrong books. They could make nothing of the messages from Belgrade. They then began to wire back and forth to each other in cipher, but it seemed that not only were the books faulty, but they were faulty in different ways. They didn't match. After much time had been lost deciphering gibberish, they began to communicate in plain Serbian. It then became clear to them that Alexander was preparing to marry his mistress, Draga Mashin.

Dr. Georgevich wired Alexander: MOST HUMBLY I PRAY YOUR MAJESTY TO LET ME KNOW IF THIS FATAL DECISION

FOR SERBIA AND THE DYNASTY IS A DEFINITE ONE. To which Alexander replied, YES. Dr. Georgevich then resigned his government.

Milan wired his son, resigning as commander-in-chief.

Meanwhile, in Belgrade, Alexander had been calling everyone he knew into his office, where he obliged them to swear an oath of loyalty to him on a holy ikon which he kept in his pocket. A certain minister, Mr. Petrovich, refused to take this oath. He said he did not believe in ikons. The king began to work himself into one of his whimpering tempers. He said, "Now listen to me! You know that I have had neither childhood nor youth like other men. The eternal quarrel between my parents made my life bitter . . . killed in me every sentiment. I have never had any ambition, not even the ambition to reign as king.

"You and your colleagues have always pressed me to marry. I have now decided to do what you have wished. . . . I found that none of the great sovereign courts was willing to give me one of their daughters for a wife. I am really not disposed to marry a princess belonging to a branch line and to a little court. Therefore I have decided to marry a Serbian, a daughter of my own people."

Choosing his words with greatest caution, Mr. Petrovich agreed that this was an admirable scheme which would certainly not be opposed by anyone if only the lady were of respectable family, younger than the king, well-educated, and pure as an angel.

After an awkward pause, the king continued: "The difficulty lies just there. There exists already a woman whom I love more than anyone in this world, the only woman with whom I can be perfectly happy, and only then can I consecrate my whole life to the interests of the people if she becomes my wife. In the whole world there is only one woman who can make me forget the bitterness of my past life and make me feel happy. That woman has hitherto been my good angel who gave me the strength to bear patiently all that I had to bear."

Then the king said, "That woman is Madame Draga—I am inflexibly resolved to marry her!" The minister, Petrovich, immediately tendered his resignation. He told Alexander that Prince Peter Karageorgevich would gain more in Serbia from such a marriage to a woman of ill-fame than if he distributed napoléons d'or; that not a single European court would receive him with such a queen; that his ministers would be boycotted by all sovereigns; and that he would bring his country low, into irony and contempt.

The king's eyes filled with tears of rage. He took off his spectacles, rubbed them, fixed them again, jumped to his feet. "Do not insult me by attacks on her," he cried. "She is an honest and honorable woman, and only her enemies speak badly of her! Only after she knew that I could not live without her did she sacrifice herself to me!"

He insisted that Draga was but eight years older than himself. "I am passionately in love with her and without her I cannot live," he cried. "I gave her twenty thousand pounds that she should not leave me. I surrendered myself to her, body and soul. . . . She persistently refused to become queen. And now, after I have at last broken down her resistance, you come and make difficulties. Have you no pity for me?"

Thus did Alexander fling wide the doors of his secret chamber to Petrovich. He had yet to face worse arguments, that of loyal friends of the dynasty who had staked their lives on service to the Obrenovich; of influential citizens who formed clubs and groups to wait upon the king and expostulate with him; of his ambassadors who were frantically telegraphing from abroad. His Cabinet had resigned; affairs in Belgrade were near anarchy. There were strikes, and the public services were disrupted. Every morning people woke up to some new rumor: that revolution had broken out; that Milan was on his way to resume the reigns of government; that Prince Peter Karageorgevich had invaded the land at the head of the army; that Alexander had been assassinated.

The former Cabinet confronted Draga at her home. They appealed to her love for the king, her loyalty to her country, and to her purse, promising to reward her richly if she would leave the country at once—and if she would not, they were prepared to remove her forcibly. Calmly Draga agreed: she said that while her maid was packing, she would hide at the house of a friend. Her carriage was called, and under the gratified stare of the ministers she mounted it, assisted by her younger brother. To him, she whispered the name of the friend with whom she was taking refuge.

What had become of her former patriotism and concern for

the king's prestige? Even if in some dream image of herself she had intended to step lovingly aside to make way for a royal queen, Draga was in reality incapable of this noble act. Very likely her Russian friends had urged the disruptive match on her; without doubt her family dreaded the loss of their social position; and as for herself, Draga loved Alexander, and she was probably aware that he was not capable of being a husband to any other woman except herself.

It is not known that she took advantage of the services of the witch of Ploesti, but her behavior in steadfastly refusing the marriage and then suddenly acquiescing to it was observed to follow closely that of her Roumanian friend. However, we need not turn to witchcraft to explain why a panicky fat lady, faced with immediate loss, should choose to risk future catastrophe.

And so, within two hours after she left her house on Crown Street, Alexander, summoned by Draga's brother, came to her rescue. He took her home again, and there placed upon her pudgy finger an enormous diamond ring.

And after all, there was no revolution in Serbia or outcry for Karageorgevich. For to the stunned astonishment of Serbs, a telegram arrived from the haughtiest and most decisive of sources, from Mother Russia. In it the tsar sanctioned the marriage, congratulating Sasha upon his choice of a bride, and he promised to act as *kum* at the wedding. This position of chief witness is in the Orthodox Church an extremely sacred one, signifiying a godparent, a sponsor, a guarantor of the sacred character of the marriage.

Milan wrote from a tearing heart: "Nothing remains for me but to pray to God for our fatherland. I shall be the first to cheer the government which shall drive you from the country after such folly—Your father, Milan."

The ex-king never saw his son again. Alexander restored the decree of banishment against his father, and he gave further orders to his army that Milan was to be shot "as a mad dog," should he ever be seen in Serbia. Milan died one year later, aged forty-seven, in Vienna in mysterious circumstances; some believed as the result of a gambling brawl. His debts were enormous, his pocket was empty, and his possessions were few. There were some stacks of canvas containing the senseless daubs of his modern artist friends, such as Cézanne.

The marriage of Alexander of Serbia with Draga Mashin took place in a blaze of light and a cloud of incense at the Cathedral of Belgrade. Acting as *kum* in proxy for the tsar was the urbane Russian ambassador. Afterwards he had nothing whatsoever to do in Belgrade but sit back and watch how the skein of intrigue, spun for decades around the Obrenovich dynasty, would tighten at last and strangle it. His embassy was directly across from the Old Palace where Draga reigned as queen, not unwounded, we may be sure, by the secret contempt of her ladies and of the *nouveaux riches* as they swept their curtseys before her; or by the fact that at the mention of her name Serbs spat in the street. "I pray to God," she once said, "to enable me to perform all my duties properly and thoroughly in order that all Serbs . . . may one day honestly say that after all, the king did well in marrying me."

But no scapegoat chosen by a mob ever escapes its ritual destiny. The Serbs were a people of unique pride. A nation does not fight a just cause for five hundred years at great sacrifice without emerging from it with a sense of being seared and stainless. In a similar mood must the Children of Israel have entered their Promised Land or the Pilgrims demolished their first Thanksgiving turkey: with the godly feeling that they had caused a brilliant day to shine for their children.

But ever since Prince Michael had incautiously picked out of a foreign courtyard a grimy youngster of questionable origin and made a prince of him, miasmas had spoiled this Serbian day, and the nation had cringed under one humiliation after another at the hands of the Obrenovich: the vulgar scandals of Milan's reign, the debauchery and unroyal brawls, the financial hocus-pocus and brutal party strife were now rolled up into a club of hatred and visited upon the unstable Alexander, who fancied himself a dictator, and his queen, the harlot Draga.

One palliative exists for an unpopular royal marriage: the expectation of a rosy royal heir. Queen Natalie removed it. For three years, obsessed with hatred and grief, she had occupied herself at Sashino with writing slanderously about Draga, often on open postcards, to her friends in Belgrade. By this means she spread it abroad that Draga had undergone an operation that made her incapable of bearing a child. Here was the crowning sin of a king against his people: he had given them a barren Lilith for a queen.

Consternation rather than jubilation was therefore the mood in Belgrade when it was announced from the palace that the queen was pregnant. This news was confirmed by the gossip of her maids and ladies-in-waiting, and by a fashionable Parisian doctor who came to add his voice to all the others that Draga was indeed expecting a child. But such was the loathing in which the queen was held that none of them was believed. A sister of Draga happened to be pregnant at the time. A rumor was circulated that she intended to simulate an *accouchement* and smuggle her sister's abominable offspring into her bed as a royal child. These uneasy mutterings soon reached the ears of the tsar who, as *kum* for the wedding, was by custom expected to stand *kum* for the first child. Since he could not afford to be brought to ridicule by Balkan skulduggery, he sent his own physicians to examine Draga. They arrived—two of them. They examined her and told her she was not pregnant. They publicly announced—perhaps in sheerest kindness—that she had a gynecological condition that might easily have misled her into believing that she had conceived a child.

But now the Serbs made themselves sick with hatred. No hopeful speech of Draga's, no good intentions, or pretty looks or sweet smile could change their hearts, for indeed the more appealing the scapegoat, the more voluptuous the hatred. There was one man above all who had perhaps watched Draga for years with the burning eyes of a malignant lover: Colonel Alexander Mashin. Like many of his fellow officers who had spoken out against the royal marriage, he had been obliged to retire from the army; but no fiercer measures than this were taken against him.

We will perhaps never know if Draga and Alexander had indeed conspired to foist a changeling prince upon their people. It is useless to defend them of the charge because they were both such formidable fools. Draga, unable to comprehend the dangerous demons that were rearing up around her, had bestowed flagrantly undeserved honors on her family, not only upon her brood of brothers and sisters but on every country cousin who came to Belgrade clamoring for rank, uniforms, and high decorations, and she seems to have had an almost pathological need for their gratitude. Often, on summer evenings, while the sound of music from the palace orchestra trembled on the air, Draga and Alexander would appear on a low balcony to greet the citizens strolling past the palace gates; and all of Draga's bedizened peasant relatives appeared there also, graciously acknowledging the courtesies paid to the royal couple. Serbs are egalitarian, but nobody is as egalitarian as all that.

Draga's two young brothers were particularly arrogant. They had high army commissions and they insisted that upon their arrival at barracks they were to be greeted with royal state and the orders of the day presented to them. When they visited a café, the orchestra was to break into the national anthem. Musicians sneered; but the army seethed with rage. Alexander had not his father's gypsy charm which again and again had won him the forgiveness of military men. He was repelled by the heartiness, the coarseness, indeed by the manliness of soldiers. Urged by a loyal counselor to conciliate them, he replied, "These men do not understand kindness and generosity. They would interpret it as proof that I am afraid of them and that I wish to bribe them."

He had tried shortly after his wedding to bribe his people by restoring to them the liberal constitution; but in vain. An outbreak in favor of Karageorgevich occurred in 1902. By a midnight *coup d'état* Alexander again withdrew this constitution and declared the country under martial law. Citizens were fired on; there was a roundup of all persons Alexander considered his enemies, and they were shot, imprisoned, or exiled. Now he was absolute master of Serbia, and he ruled with the aid of a military dictator, General Tsintsar-Markovich. To be sure, even Alexander realized at length that he had gone too far, and he restored their liberties to the Serbs. But by the time he did they were planning a midnight *coup d'état* of their own.

Portents and prophecies were becoming popular in Belgrade, all of them black. The dismal predictions of Madame de Thèbes about Draga were published in the journals. The editor of Serbia's most important newspaper, Todorovich, began to write a serialized novel based on the "Black Prophecy" of the peasant Matha, that mysterious blueprint of the future which everyone had heard of but so few had read. Did it not foretell some ghastly end for the Obrenovich? The king called in Mr. Todorovich and asked for an explanation. The journalist had one ready: he said that he intended to give his last chapters a hopeful twist which would have the effect of allaying popular fears. The king did not accept this. He insisted that the serial cease. He said, "As regards myself, I do not care so much . . . but the queen is very much annoyed."

The queen was indeed annoyed; she too summoned Mr. Todorovich, and she received him stiffly, standing. She said, "Whenever I take your paper into my hands I tremble with fear lest I find you discoursing on that cursed prophecy. For myself personally, I do not care. I have hardened my heart against all sorts of annoying stories. But my heart bleeds for the king. . . . I'm afraid he will be ill . . . he gets no sleep."

She then explained to him Alexander's unhappy childhood secret: "You must understand he hates to hear anything about death. The moment anyone mentions it, he changes color, shivers, and is terribly disturbed as some persons are when they see a snake. It is not fear. It is a sort of sickness."

Regretfully, Mr. Todorovich promised to lay aside his novel. Draga became more friendly then, and she urged him to tell her what actually had been prophesied by Matha. He cruelly told her that it predicted the death of the king before his thirtieth year. She sighed deeply, saying, "Oh God, is it possible?" But she could not resist wheedling out of the journalist Matha's predictions about herself. He replied, "So far as I know, your Majesty, the clairvoyant said only that the king would marry a Serbian lady, his own subject, and that she would share with him his destiny."

"Oh, my God!" replied Draga. "What I am praying for is to share with him his destiny. It seems to me that poison would be sweet to me if only I could drink it with him."

Draga did right to sigh for the poison cup, and the king to lie watchfully awake at night. A rumor had gained credence as a possible explanation for the lunatic conduct of Draga's brothers that the king wished to name the younger one as his successor, and that one day the people of Serbia would wake in the morning to find that by one of his midnight miracles,

Alexander had transformed the loathsome young man into a crown prince. Hatred now turned into barbaric ferocity, and as the year 1902 drew to a close, the couple lived in purgatorial fear. Conspiracies grew in their path like nettles, and from all foreign capitals there arrived from Alexander's ambassadors warnings of grim rumors. The Serbian ambassador in London had a pet spy who had built up a panel of mistresses among the chambermaids of all principal embassies, and he thus had access to the best gossip in Europe. He communicated that a public meeting was to be organized which, while marching past the palace, would suddenly break ranks, rush into the palace, and slay the king. Shortly afterward a demonstration of shop assistants which had the misfortune to walk past the palace was shot at by the royal guard.

On Palm Sunday, April 6, 1903, it was planned to surround the king and queen at a religious fête while the *Te Deum* was being sung. They got wind of the plot and did not participate in the fête. Again they learned they were to be killed while attending a circus performance; or while laying a foundation stone; or that they would be ambushed while riding. A kitchen boy in the palace was detected by the cook putting poison into their dishes, and he committed suicide. Again and again plots were laid, or half laid, and as one failed, another would spring up to take its place, and for months the king and queen lived like prisoners condemned to death, commanding by day the company of friends or loyal partisans of the dynasty, but at night alone and embattled by restless shadows. They no longer left the palace. "The bear has withdrawn into his cave; but we will go and find him there," said an enemy. It was Colonel Mashin.

"One night," Draga told a friend, "the king came to me just as I was beginning to doze. He took my hand in his, kissed it, and said in a very, very sad voice, 'Queen of Serbia, whom hatest thou?'

" 'What do you mean, Sasha?'

" 'Whom hatest thou, Queen of Serbia?'

" 'Oh, my dear Sasha, what is the matter with you? Why should I hate anyone? I do not hate anyone.'

" 'Nor do I hate anyone. And yet, we are hated. And hated just by those to whom we have done so many kindnesses. And why do they hate me? Is it because I am the son of a king and a king myself, and not the son of a fisherman, born in a hut somewhere on the Danube?'

" 'But if kingship is my crime, what have you done to them, you a weak woman?'

"He was pale, his hands were cold as ice, and tears were rolling down his face."

On March 20, 1903, the Serbian ambassador accredited to the Court of St. James received in London a message from the distinguished journalist W. T. Stead. It advised him that his presence would be welcome that afternoon at the offices of the *Review of Reviews*, where a gathering of people would witness a demonstration by a newly discovered clairvoyant. The ambassador was requested by Mr. Stead to bring some obscure Serbian object with him, and so he tore off from a letter a signature of King Alexander written in Cyrillic script. He put it in an envelope, which he sealed.

The clairvoyant was a complete failure. She was a respectable matron from the north with twelve children, and the crush of smart Londoners with their busy vibrations discomposed her. Mr. Stead resigned himself to buying her some dinner and sending her home. He therefore invited her and about ten friends and two other mediums who were present to dine at the Norfolk Hotel nearby. The Serbian ambassador did not join this company; he had an engagement at Buckingham Palace. But he left his envelope with a fellow guest who privately examined its contents, but afterwards sealed it again.

It seemed that what the medium, Mrs. Burchell, had needed was a good dinner inside her, because after she had dined she began to feel more at ease, and she returned with the dinner guests to Mr. Stead's offices where, without effort, she gave several demonstrations of her queer talent. The person who was holding the Serbian minister's envelope now gave it to Stead, saying, "Try her with that." Stead, who had no idea what was inside the envelope, handed it to Mrs. Burchell, who told him that she was getting tired. Nevertheless she took the paper, languidly turning it in her hand, and she said, "Royalty. An important person. A king."

She did not seem to be in a trance, but spoke normally, quietly at first, then with growing excitement. "He is young. Dark

Stout body and long neck. With him is a lady, the queen—a brunette.

"Terrible! Terrible! It is all bloody! I cannot bear to look! Oh, it is terrible! I cannot bear it! I see a very dark man rushing into the chamber. He tries to kill the king. The lady implores them to spare him. Oh!—"

Now in a state of breathless horror, poor Mrs. Burchell threw herself from her chair to the floor so that Mr. Stead put out his hand to spare her from injury. But she did not fall. Instead, she went on her knees, clasped her hands and continued in a voice of agonized entreaty: "They are killing him. Oh, save him, save him! The queen falls on her knees and implores them to save her life—they will not listen. Oh, what tumult, what bloodshed! How terrible! They kill him! She pleads in vain. Now they fling her on one side and stab her with a dagger . . . and oh—and oh—and oh!"

Now the medium fell sideways to the floor.

In the excitement of these events the other two mediums who were present, a Mrs. Manks and a Mrs. Brenchley, had fallen into trances and were having exactly the same experience as their colleague. Mrs. Manks, who had traveled in Russia the previous year, was able to add a curious detail: "They seem to me like Russian uniforms—*kalpaks*—but it is dark and I cannot see them clearly. Now the king is dead. But oh, what confusion, what bloodshed!" Mrs. Brenchley, not so well traveled, contented herself with doleful symphonic sounds: "Yes, yes, I get it in the air! They are killing him! I see it! Yes, yes! She is quite right!"

Mr. Stead later wrote down the account of this extraordinary occasion and published it in the *Review of Reviews* together with the signatures of most of his guests. One who did not sign was Mr. Stead's private secretary. This individual had been present throughout the excitement, but for some reason he said afterward that he had seen and heard nothing. We shall ignore this blind, deaf, nameless, and indeed probably very soon jobless Victorian wage-slave, since we have the signatures of a dozen people of assured income—especially as it later transpired that all of the best mediums and clairvoyants in Europe had been seeing exactly the same vision, to the point of tedium, for weeks.

. . .

In Belgrade the army conspiracy was congealing around Draga's brother-in-law, Colonel Mashin. He was not the best organizer in Serbia, but he organized well enough. No fewer than 80, and some say 150, army officers were implicated, and they discussed their plans openly. Yet their plot, like Edgar Allan Poe's letter, was hidden well, because there were so many plots. It was as if plans for murdering the king and queen had become a favorite café-table game.

Draga was haunted by presentiments. The day before her death, she wrote, "At night I seem to see the terrifying picture of Michael in his death agony, stretching his bloodstained hand toward his murderers and crying, "Stop, my brothers! It is enough!"

June 19, 1903, was a steaming hot and sultry day. A diplomat just home from abroad called upon the king. In the waiting room of the Old Palace the equerry on duty was a certain Naoumovich, a favorite of Alexander who only a few days before had presented him with eight hundred pounds to pay his gambling debts. He was collapsed in an armchair, unshaved, and spending the last day of his life, as a traitor should, in a state of depression which he was trying to cure with brandy.

Not so the king's first aide-de-camp, a man they called Handsome Laza because of his trim looks and gleaming teeth. In great spirits he chatted happily with the visitor, and thus he deserved to spend his last day.

Alexander invited his visitor to dinner with several other guests, including Draga's brothers, and the former military dictator, General Tsintsar-Markovich. They gathered between seven and eight that evening, but they had to wait a long time for dinner while Alexander in his vague way meandered on and on about some unrealistic military plans. At 10:30 the premier interrupted him, saying that Draga was hungry. Alexander rose at once and went for the queen in her rooms. Together they descended the stairs to the huge entrance hall where the musicians of the guard were waiting to play during supper. Here Alexander noted that his equerry, Naoumovich, was looking ill. "Why didn't you ask to be relieved of duty tonight?" he kindly asked. But Naoumovich had a duty that night from which he could not be granted relief. In his capacity of equerry he had ordered large quantities of strong wines to be taken from the king's cellar to the officers' room, and there a young lieutenant was filling the glass of the commander of the guard. Eventually, whether from wine or drugs, the commander fell into a deep sleep.

In the meantime, outside in the city streets, the citizens of Belgrade were crowding the cafés and beer gardens, for it was too hot to go to bed. In the little garden restaurant in front of the Serbian Crown Hotel a group of officers were getting drunk on *slivovitz* and shouting to the gypsy musicians for a *kolo*, the Serbian national dance. What *kolo* did the gentlemen desire, the gypsies wanted to know. "Queen Draga's Kolo," of course, they shouted, roaring at such wit, and again and again they demanded the tune that had been composed in compliment to the queen, and they danced to it in a tight circle, entwining their arms about each other's shoulders, swinging their bright boots, swaying their hard hips. One of them was named Dragutin Dmitrievich, but his comrades called him by the nickname Apis.

Colonel Mashin was not drunk. He was visiting a former fellow-officer who like himself had been retired from the army after having protested the marriage of the king. In the late evening the colonel took leave of his friend, but he was soon back again, and this time he was wearing his old uniform. He explained that the same night Alexander would be murdered and Peter Karageorgevich called to the throne. The friend implored Mashin not to proceed with the plot, but the colonel's mind was fixed. He only asked that if he did not live through the night, his friend should execute his will and protect his wife and children.

The colonel then went straight to the barracks in which Alexander's own infantry regiment was quartered, but its commander was one of the conspirators and he turned the regiment over to Mashin, explaining to officers and men that this was done by the orders of the king. Mashin ordered the entire regiment to arms, and sent various detachments to arranged destinations, while he took command of one of them and led it toward the palace.

It was after midnight now, and the royal supper party had broken up. Alexander and Draga had retired to their double bed in the Old Palace, but perhaps the king was reading. The citizens of Belgrade were seeking their rest, and from the cafés and gardens groups of drunken officers were emerging in booming spirits and staggering in groups along the avenue that led to the palace.

The noise they were making by no means startled the urbane Russian ambassador. He had been apprised of the conspiracy several days before, and he was already ensconced at an upper window of his embassy, regarding with interest the heads of troops from the fortress who were bunching in the narrow street below, and across the way pressing upon the railings that enclosed the small garden of the Old Palace.

The police commissioner, on the other hand, was alarmed when, roused from his bed, he saw troops moving toward the palace. He telephoned the chief of police who, having just dropped off to sleep, was peevish. He asked the commissioner why he did not address himself directly to the Central Police Station which was next door to the palace. The police commissioner called the Central Police Station. Unfortunately the officer in charge had stepped out for a few hours to enjoy the night air in a beer garden, leaving the station in the care of a clerk. This young man telephoned the palace, but he received no answer because the wires had been cut. Not knowing what else to do, he did nothing.

Mashin, who was late, appeared last upon the scene with his detachment, which he disposed in such a way that the palace was completely surrounded. The men who lined the streets and most of their officers had not a notion of what they were doing. They were now told: the king had decided to bow to the people's will and rid himself of Queen Draga. They were there to guard the peace, prevent public demonstrations, and see to it that she was removed quietly from the palace and conveyed over the border.

But upstairs in the Old Palace the king had lain face down on the night table his book, and he had put his hand on the shoulder of his dear one to waken her. Whispering and wondering, they arose from bed and must have peeped from a window at the commotion below which now lacked but a military band. They then hid themselves in Draga's dressing room. This room was really a large closet off the main bedroom, and

whether by a decorator's whim or by design, it was separated
from the bedroom by a door flush with the wall and covered
with matching wall paper. In dim light the outline of the door
was invisible.

The hour of the drunkards had now struck. Twenty of them
appeared at the south gate. Inside, the young lieutenant who had
poured drinks for his commander and robbed him of his keys
after he fell asleep opened the gate. The conspirators raced
up the carriage drive with such thud and racket that they woke
the sergeant on guard duty at the front door of the palace.
"To arms! To arms!" he cried to his companions, but one of
the approaching drunkards drew his revolver and shot him.
Other guards rushed out of their rooms, which flanked the
door, but the young lieutenant came forward, drew his sword,
and said, "The king's orders are that you do not move from
here no matter what takes place around you."

Handsome Laza, the king's first aide-de-camp, now appeared
on the scene, demanding what the noise was about. He also
was shot, but the conspirators were at once contrite, because
he was a popular man. For a while they stood shuffling about
in the entrance hall while someone found a scarf and bound up
Handsome Laza's wound. This done, they rushed eagerly upon
the inner door, expecting to find it unlocked, because Naoumovich was to have seen to it. But he was fast asleep by now, having
taken too much of his curative brandy. By good fortune someone had brought along a dynamite cartridge, and this was used.
A great detonation shook the palace, and it was heard throughout the quarter of the town. People poured out of their houses
into the streets and pressed toward the palace. Even Naoumovich awakened and came staggering to his duty, but the man
they called Apis shot him dead. Apis was the lover of Naoumovich's wife.

The policemen of the Central Police Station, who had been
waiting for some time to be told what to do, were beginning to
worry that all was not right at the palace, and seeing crowds
standing about in the darkness, they began to fire on them. But
these crowds were armed soldiers who fired back, and for about
ten minutes battle raged. Several men had been killed before it
was explained to the policemen that if the king was ever to

disembarrass himself of Draga Mashin, they must go back to their station and resume their night's rest.

The drunken band had now gained the inner rooms of the palace, but difficulties still plagued them. The dynamite cartridge had somehow broken the electrical system of the palace, and every light had gone out. For some time the conspirators stumbled and crashed around the rooms, those very rooms where once a boy had groped to mark out his way to bed, and they shouted for servants to come to their rescue with candles. A few terrified lackeys were finally rounded up, and they stammered that they had no candles. Well, then, they must borrow some from the neighbors! Several were dispatched under the command of one of the officers to the house of a nearby doctor who gladly obliged them with candles. Lighting these, they assailed the upper floors and at length found the royal bedchamber, where in the trembling light they gazed upon the bed which had been occupied but was no longer, and the king's book lying open beside it. Enraged, they lay about them with their swords, ripping and ravaging the curtains and the bed, and striking the walls in order to detect secret chambers, but they failed to detect the door to Draga's dressing room; baffled, they at last abandoned the bedroom and returned to lumber about the palace for an hour, slicing and breaking everything in their way, shooting at the walls and smashing down every locked door.

Handsome Laza was bleeding to death. He had been popular before, but he was popular no longer. They told him that they were going to kill him, but that they would spare his life if he told them where the king and Draga were hiding. He said that he did not know. They beat him with their swords, kicked and pummeled him. At last he suggested that they search the New Palace which King Milan had built in the same courtyard, adjacent to the older structure. They hauled him to his feet and kicked him before them down the stairs toward the front door, but he protested all the way that it was wicked of them to force him to accompany them into the night air because he had a bad cold and had lost his hat. One of the young lieutenants took off his own hat and put it on Handsome Laza's head. Then, gripping him firmly, they dragged him outside, where they came face to face with their furious entrepreneur, Colonel Alexander Mashin,

who after more than an hour of standing about with his cohort
in the street had finally obeyed the promptings of his tattered
nerves and was running into the palace with other impatient
officers to find out whether his plans had come to fruition. When
he learned that they had not and that Handsome Laza was leading
everyone on a wild goose chase to the New Palace, he went into
a towering rage. "You fools!" he bellowed, "Can't you see this
rogue is fooling you? Go back, and we'll all come with you."

Considerably fortified now by sober heads, the murderous
band returned to the search for the king and queen.

For almost two hours the royal pair had cowered in the back
of Draga's closet, listening to the firing in the yard and in the
palace, the screams and entreaties of servants in the corridors,
the threats, blasphemies, and violence done. The windows were
open. The Russian ambassador could also hear these
sounds. Now as he stared entranced at the fantastic culmination
of diplomacies, he might have seen at a tiny window, close to the
window of the royal bedroom, a woman's anguished face peer out,
straining toward the Russian Embassy, searching for those troops
of the imperial guard who would soon come marching out to
restore order, calm madness, and claim the lives of the people
for whose marriage the tsar had stood *kum*. But the urbane ambassador commanded no such troops to leave the embassy.

Draga, making so bold as to lean out a little from that window
and search for a friend, saw one: down below in the courtyard
was the familiar face of a guards officer, and some others, and
she called down, "Soldiers! Your king is in danger! For God's
sake, to the rescue!" The guards officer looked up and saw her.
He drew his revolver and shot at her. She drew back dismayed,
but whooping with triumph, the officer flew into the palace and
up the stairs, shouting for Mashin to tell him where the king and
queen were hiding.

They all crowded back into the bedroom, but they could not
find the door to the closet. An axe was brought, and with this
they began to hack down the wall. In the meantime, someone had
persuaded Handsome Laza that they had not come to kill the
king, only to insist that he sign a writ of abdication; indeed,
some of the soberer persons had such a document prepared and
with them, and they showed it to the aide-de-camp. Handsome
Laza said, "Do you give me your word of honor that you will

spare the life of the king?" They gave him their word of honor. Laza knocked at a certain point in the wall and cried, "Sire, sire, open! I am your Laza! Here are your officers!"

The door to Draga's wardrobe opened and the king and queen stood there. They had been trying to dress themselves. The king had thrown a robe of Draga's over his nightshirt and his poor dwindling legs, and Draga, with awesome modesty, had put on some satin stays and a petticoat and yellow stockings. The king stepped in front of her and confronted his murderers, blinking at the candlelight and the muted blue menace of guns. One of the sober leaders asked him if he would abdicate, and he refused. Then several men at once shot the king. He fell back into Draga's arms; for a moment she stared at her murderers in ghastly surpise before they shot again. Then both the king and queen fell to the ground.

The assassins clustered around. They emptied their revolvers into the couple jerking and bleeding upon the floor. Then they seized them and stripped them. They ripped off Draga's stays and other clothes, and drew their swords and daggers on her. They hacked her body obscenely, slitting her belly and plunging their blades into her thighs and breasts. While they were about this abominable artistry, someone shouted that the king was not dead, that he was stirring in his blood. They shot him again, stabbed him and stripped him of his clothes.

Then the assassins remembered their comrades outside the palace who were ignorant that the deed had been accomplished. They hauled the corpse of Draga to the window, picked it up and dangled it outside in its crimson indecency for all to see, and a shout that shuddered between horror and joy tore loose from the nearby soldiers and spread into the streets where the troops broke their ranks and came running. The assassins let the body drop down onto the grass of the little garden, and stood aside to give place to their companions behind, who were dragging up the body of the king to raise and swing it out of the window—but the momentum of that swing was arrested suddenly. The king was not dead. His hands, his strong hands, had caught at the window frame and he was clutching for his life. Someone flashed up his sword and the fingers went flying. Then they flung Alexander to the grass with such furious force that one of his eyes burst from its socket, and he lay sprawled beside

Draga while troops rushed up to spit upon the corpses and befoul them.

Inside the palace, the murderers were seized with exultation. They screamed and danced about the rooms, firing their revolvers frenziedly at paintings, mirrors, candelabra, not forgetting Handsome Laza. They looted whatever they could find, tore at walls and cupboards for the queen's jewels and the king's cash and *bijouterie* of watches and rings. Meanwhile, Draga's brothers had been taken from their houses, placed side by side and shot, and their bodies plundered of ornaments and money and their shiny patent-leather boots. General Tsintsar-Markovich was called upon at his home and shot in the back as he turned to order refreshments for his guests. All of Alexander's Cabinet and Draga's relatives and favorites were murdered that night except those who, warned in time, escaped across the River Sava. And in the streets desultory riots and skirmishes took place between regiments whose commanders were loyal or disloyal to the Obrenovich.

A light rain fell during the night, alleviating the sultriness and the tainted air where the bodies of Alexander and Draga lay, and cleaning them. Close to dawn the Russian ambassador left his window seat, threw a cloak over his shoulders, crossed the road into the garden and looked down on the dead. A high-ranking officer approached and clicked his heels. It was Colonel Alexander Mashin, proudly saluting. The ambassador turned to him a face full of sick contempt, and pointing to the bodies, told him in the name of God to get them out of sight before the day broke. Soldiers were called to the task. The body of Alexander resisted them: they had to tug his good hand clear of the clump of grass between his fingers. This king had never known why life had been given him, but he clung stubbornly to his mother earth.

The ravaged bodies were carried into the ravaged palace, where a tranquil object remained in the royal bedroom: the king's book where he had left it. It was a novel by Stendhal, *L'Amour*. It contained the words, "The remedy of love is almost impossible to find." And opposite this statement Sasha had written, "Why look for it? Since one has only one desire, to love and be loved."

.   .   .

On June 16 a *Te Deum* was sung in the Cathedral and the Metropolitan Innocent thanked the army for its patriotic deed. Soon afterward there came from Geneva the slight, stiff, elderly man, grandson of Kara George, for the sake of whose ancestral rights Serbs had been murdering each other for almost a century. Peter Karageorgevich is not known to have taken direct part in bloody plots against the Obrenovich kings or to have interfered dishonorably in Serbian affairs. He had but sustained his claim to the throne throughout his life. He had lived austerely, almost ascetically, sometimes hard pressed to feed himself and his children, for he had taken no money from his partisans in Serbia, nor from the tsar any favor except that he had allowed the Russian sovereign to educate his sons in St. Petersburg.

Now he was dressed in the robes of a king and taken to the Skupshtina, where martial buntings in the national colors streaked across Turkish exquisiteries and a throne had been erected. Before it stood King Peter I of Serbia to take his oath. Suddenly a tumultuous cheer broke from the assembled gentlemen, a thunderous ovation, and they leapt to their feet and shouted out their triumph to roof and sky. Peter Karageorgevich stared at them. He had known that he would have the task of restoring the prestige of a people whose ambassadors dared not show their faces anywhere in Europe, a race degraded. And now he knew that he would have to do it with the assistance of murderers.

So he looked about him saying in his thin voice, "God help you, brethren! God help you!"

DIE FREUNDIN

1.

The Young Emperor

The nineteenth-century people who followed the royal *chronique scandaleuse*—and they included almost everyone with time to read and talk—depended for much of their daily fare upon Austrian archdukes. These princes were not precisely Austrians; they were Habsburgs, members of a family in whose veins ran the blood of every Catholic royal dynasty and which for centuries past had given to Europe her Holy Roman Emperors. They stood above races, nations, and laws, and taking full advantage of this fact, they were continually bursting into the limelight in a mad explosion of Mitzis, Fritzis, family jewels, furious archduchesses, irate innkeepers, faithful valets, and bad checks. Their lively ways and hedonistic tastes brought into being the cultural complex we call Gay Vienna.

As far above them as they were above others was the head of their family, Emperor Francis Joseph, a man whose awesome royalty, fortified by his personal dignity, sobriety, and industry, set him apart not only from other Habsburgs but from other sovereigns, and certainly from Gay Vienna.

He had indeed no chance to become an ordinary archduke, or even an ordinary monarch: he was marked out from birth to rule over the vast feudal domain known as the Habsburg Empire, which sprawled across the richest Danube lands and sustained many different ethnic groups of people who did not care for each other much, and for the Habsburg emperor even less, but who expected him nevertheless to be, next to God, their transcendental father. From earliest childhood he sandwiched a taxing course of learning between his military exercises, and he spent his Sunday afternoons with old Chancellor Metternich, listening to his precepts for managing Europe.

By the time he was seven he wrote a disciplined Gothic hand. Sometimes when he wrote a letter, he would scribble on it drawings, for instance of soldiers, and they were so perceptive and funny that they might well have been signed by the youthful hand of a famous caricaturist, rather than by that of "Franz."

In 1848, when he was eighteen, the Hungarian provinces revolted under Kossuth, and the Austrian mobs were behaving themselves so savagely that the imperial clan was forced to flee their castle in Vienna. They took refuge in the Moravian fortress of Olmütz (where Lafayette was once imprisoned). There they persuaded their poor, weak-minded, epileptic Emperor Ferdinand that he was to blame for the catastrophe and that the best way he could serve his dynasty was to relinquish his crown to his nephew, Franz. The clan gathered in the dining room of the archbishop's palace at Olmütz to witness the ceremony. There were no public theatricals. Habsburg affairs were no business of the people they ruled. When it was over, the deranged monarch stroked his nephew's cheek, saying, "Bear yourself bravely—it is all right." Then Emperor Francis Joseph went to his mother and wept.

There was to be no more youth for this boy, and never again would he put a fanciful stroke upon a sheet of paper. Instead a strange canvas was placed before him upon which, like his ancestors, he would have to paint the history of his age. He did this, as he had been taught, with mystic self-assurance, and so intent did he become upon his task that even those who worked most closely with him remained ignorant of his private character. He would be called insensitive, cold, calculating, a man with "the mind of a provincial postmaster" who had no emotion at all; a machine fit for nothing but signing documents, with no artistic or intellectual sensibilities, no appreciation whatsoever of the genius that arose in his surroundings.

But his private correspondence, published in the decades since his death, opposes this traditional image of Francis Joseph. It has become clear that though he was above all else, he was not above the torments usually reserved for a man who has a wife and a mistress.

Still, his case differed from the ordinary. For it was Francis Joseph's meretricious wife who was his true mistress, and his virtuous mistress who was his true wife.

The Kossuth Revolution was put down for the young emperor by the Tsar of Russia, Nicholas I, who kindly sent to the rescue his General Paskiewicz—this was the same man who as Viceroy of Poland had tried to outrage the innocence of young Lola Montez. He had far better luck with the Hungarians: he brought them to their knees. After he had turned them over to Habsburg vengeance, the young emperor ordered the chief rebels to be hanged.

No doubt this harsh measure was urged upon him by his mother, the Archduchess Sophie, a despotic woman of whom it was said that of all the Habsburg archdukes, she was the only man among them. She was determined to refashion the disturbed realm into an archaic autocracy whose only parliament would be seated in the conscience of her son. She made certain that his first act was to deprive all of his people of all of their rights. For the next few years Francis Joseph's mother was, in effect, emperor, and she permitted him to enjoy some relaxation from his endless studies and heaps of documents by sowing mild wild oats among the girls of the Vienna stage. When in his early twenties he began to flirt with court ladies, she chose for him a pliable wife, one of his Wittelsbach cousins of Bavaria, Helene. A family meeting was arranged in which Francis Joseph made the acquaintance of this young lady, whom he agreed possessed every possible quality of beauty, gentleness, and elegant bearing. However, he found that he could not tear his eyes away from her fifteen-year-old hoydenish sister, Elizabeth.

For the first time in his life the young emperor defied his mother. There was a private row between them in which he made it clear that he would marry Elizabeth and no one else. In making this choice, he deserves full marks as a connoisseur of women, for portraits of the young Duchess in Bavaria as he first saw her do not give promise of Elizabeth of Austria's superlative beauty. The empress had hair of light auburn shot with gold, and it was so long and thick that no matter how high she piled it in castellations about her head, swathes of it were left to go rushing down her back. Her eyes were gray with flashing amber lights, and slanting slightly, they had the fey and sidelong glance that some wildflowers have—and some touchy horses too. Her delicate straight nose and curving lips left no room for improvement. Her posture reminded people of swans, lilies, and gazelles.

She had spent her childhood running about her father's modest country estate as little more than a member of a pack of dogs. She now came to the stilted world of the Hofburg whose carefully ceremonious ways had become fossilized in centuries past and in which an empress could not move from one spot to another without setting into motion, as in a German mechanical toy, a host of figurines: ladies-in-waiting bustling, courtiers mustering, chamberlains bellowing, soldiers stiffening, doors opening, drums rolling. She faced the unkind authority of her all-powerful mother-in-law, who viewed vengefully this "little fool from Bavaria" her son had disobediently married and who took every opportunity to diminish her. The court cliques drew around the archduchess and away from the child-empress who, since she had not been allowed to bring one lady from Bavaria to keep her company, was left to grow up in lonely, hostile dignity.

A daughter was born, and then another, Gisela. In 1857 Elizabeth was delivered of an heir, the Crown Prince Rudolf. In his joy Francis Joseph immediately made him a colonel and decorated him with the Order of the Golden Fleece.

All of these children were removed from Elizabeth at birth by the archduchess who said that Elizabeth could hardly be expected to bring up royal children when she could not bring herself up. Elizabeth appealed to her husband against this crushing treatment, but fruitlessly, because obedience to his mother was ingrained in him. Besides, he was at that time developing those pedantic work habits that were to make him the Emperor of Bureaucrats, and he had little time or nerves left to deal with his wife's glooms. He treated Elizabeth with tender affection, and he was bound to her by holiest bonds, but he had not really become aware of her. She had matured into a woman of rich, progressive intellect. The Archduchess Sophie understood that if he were to become addicted to Elizabeth's lively companionship, she might lose her son forever, and her empire too. She therefore encouraged Francis Joseph to seek again his relaxation with the ladies of the Vienna stage.

In the first half of Francis Joseph's reign, two mighty changes were taking place on the map of Europe, both to be effected at his immense expense. The first was the unification of Italy, of which he owned the rich northern provinces. We have seen how the subtle Cavour, with the aid of the Countess Castiglione, inveigled Napoleon III into fighting his battle with the Habsburg emperor. The decisive encounter took place at Solferino, where Francis Joseph's cavalry, aglitter with buttons and clean swords, fell into the mud before Napoleon's fire. Throughout this campaign, which the emperor commanded in the field, he received letters from Elizabeth, the letters of a young woman in love, desperately fearful for his life, longing for his company, and desiring to join him at the front and share his flea-bitten military discomforts. "Do you love me still?" she wrote. "If you did not, then whatever else might happen I should not care." On his return from Italy, having lost most of his provinces there, he was greeted glumly by the Vienna crowds but by Elizabeth as if he were a conqueror.

One year after this affecting reunion, in 1860, Elizabeth left Francis Joseph. There was a family quarrel, a Habsburg family row about which no detail was ever divulged by the participants. Then Queen Victoria's yacht, the *Osborne*, was hurriedly borrowed, and it carried Elizabeth to Madeira, where in a rented villa she spent much of her time locked in her room, crying her heart out. For almost two years she could not be persuaded to return home.

Elizabeth's odd conduct was at first explained in Vienna by an official report that she had fallen gravely ill, but this had to be modified when she was seen to be, apart from her melancholia, in fair health. Historians generally state that the long tussle with her mother-in-law had ended in a nervous collapse. The gossip of those times, however—and it remains to this day fixed in the minds of people who drink their coffee with whipped cream on the top—suspected that Elizabeth had contracted a venereal disease from her husband. Such gossip cannot here be ignored, for it provides a credible explanation for the sudden wreckage of this marriage and for the imperial couple's future relationship.

It seems quite certain that some deep offense had been offered to Elizabeth's femininity, and that she had been faced with evidence of Francis Joseph's infidelity in a particularly intolerable form.

Elizabeth was one of the handful of people on earth entitled to speak to Francis Joseph on equal terms and call him by a familiar name, and he lost her when he was thirty. He lived out decades in helpless expiation of his crime against her. No one can read the emperor's letters to his wife without feeling deeply moved by his obvious longing and loneliness, and perhaps his renowned self-mastery and self-abnegation was as much the product of his hopeless love for Elizabeth as of any other stricture on his life.

The second event that shaped the world of Francis Joseph was the unification of Germany under Bismarck. The decisive battle took place at Königgrätz in 1866, where the Prussians cured the young emperor forever of any ambition he may have had to be a lion in battle. The disaster marked the end of his autocracy and the downfall of Archduchess Sophie as a politician. All of his people rose up desiring an end to despotism and in its place constitutions, an unmuzzled press, freedom of speech, and trials by jury. He spent the rest of his life giving way to these demands inch by inch, and—whenever he could—persuading his parliamentarians that it was better to go waltzing than to disagree with Francis Joseph.

Elizabeth, so far as her official duties permitted her, lived apart from her husband. For a while she amused herself with Hungarian politics, and also, it was rumored, with a succession of handsome Hungarian magnates. Much as they disliked the Habsburgs, the Hungarians came to adore Elizabeth, and she was able to bring about a compromise—*Ausgleich*—between the emperor and his most turbulent province, whereby the "dual monarchy" which we know as Austria-Hungary was created. The event was celebrated in Budapest by the formal crowning of Francis Joseph as king and Elizabeth, in the full blaze of her beauty, as queen, the "noblest creature on earth" as the grateful Hungarians called her. After this, she lived almost exclusively on her Hungarian estate of Gödöllö.

Francis Joseph kept his distance from his wife's private life, except when she gave him the pleasure of being included in it. But he watched anxiously her multiplying eccentricities. At

Gödöllö she surrounded herself with a malodorous band of gypsies of whose wild, heart-rending music she never tired, and whom she often fed in her own halls, uncaring if they stole her valuables and peeled the gold leaf off her walls. She had a private circus ring in which she trained herself and her magnificent horses in the most advanced and dangerous arts of the *haute école*. When she heard of a horse that was untameable, she tamed it. She rode with the *csikósok*, the Hungarian cowboys, and she could ride three horses to a standstill in one day. Presently she developed a craving for excitement and change which drove her to restless travels across Europe and North Africa.

Francis Joseph could not bring himself to deny his wife any whim or to curb her abandoned extravagance. He refused her nothing, or almost nothing. Once when he asked her what she wanted for her birthday, she wrote, "Since you ask what would give me pleasure, I beg for either a young royal tiger . . . or a locket. What I should like best of all would be a fully equipped lunatic asylum."

As the years passed, and Elizabeth grew older, her amusements grew more and more reckless, even suicidal, as if she were controlled by a death-desiring force. Her great beauty remained, but the devastating sweetness of her youthful expression was pulled into cynical, bitter lines.

By the time the emperor was middle-aged, his life had become a lonely, monotonous ritual, devoted to his work. At three-thirty every morning, he was awakened by his valet with the words, "I am at your majesty's feet"; to which Francis Joseph always replied, "I thank you." He then arose and retired to a tiny anteroom, where he was bathed by a bath attendant in an old rubber tub; or else he washed himself at a rickety washstand from which he frequently got splinters in his legs. He was dressed in underwear of coarse cotton—his valet did not envy it—and in the plain uniform which best became his strict mind and slight figure. His boots were slender too; they gave him corns and bunions.

First to his prie-dieu for a talk with his immediate superior, God; then his physician waited on him for a brief peering and tapping. Afterward he sat at the small desk from which he ruled his empire. His documents, piled up from the evening before, were awaiting him, and he began to read them at once, carefully annotating the margins.

At five o'clock he ate a breakfast of coffee, rolls, and ham except on fast days; in mid-morning, biscuits. While eating, he did not look up from his documents. His house servants appeared to dust and sweep, but he did not look up. Once he had a tooth drawn at his desk, and once he drew one out himself, resuming his work immediately afterwards. He bore pain without moving a muscle, and he never complained about anything or asked for any extra service. Whatever service he received from however humble a servant, he always acknowledged with the words, "I thank you."

The rooms he occupied at the Hofburg and at his other residences were always the most modest and uncomfortable. Iron objects such as old bullets and cannonballs decorated his mantlepieces; or statues which kept breaking and were glued together again clumsily by servants. His were the surroundings of a man whose wife did not care for him much.

He lunched at his desk, not raising his eyes, and worked all day. Ministers and aides drifted in and out as they were summoned. Sometimes his meticulous and pedantic hours were relieved by his valet intruding with an inhalation for his incessant colds; a religious ceremony might be scheduled, or his great joy, a troop review. Sometimes the artistic Archduke Franz, long buried in him, would have the pleasure of redesigning the uniforms of one of his regiments. But the emperor's only real recreation was hunting, though he never took his gun in hand before he had finished with his daily documents.

Two afternoons a week he received in audience the people of his land—those who had some complaint or problem whose solution was not adequately dealt with by ordinary courts. Petitioners crowded around him everywhere he went, often trying to kiss his feet and knees as they handed him their agonies in writing, and he took them with his own hands even in areas blighted by cholera. He set aside $12,000 a month of his privy purse for their financial assistance. People of all grades, in all sorts of national costumes, or no costume at all except the rags they lived in, waited to see him, but such was his sacred character in their eyes that many who came before him could only sink to their knees, dumfounded. "No one should kneel to me," he would admonish them and rise to help the women to their feet. Few who saw him could remember a detail of the interview—only that in a shimmering dream they had seen the face of the All-highest.

"I sometimes think that my uncle's fortune was in his face," wrote a niece of Francis Joseph, wishing to imply that he was not as kind as he looked; and indeed, to the Habsburg clan, that state within a state of which he was the absolute ruler, as well as to his ministers and generals, his aspect was often that of a God of Wrath. And yet the wrinkles that were being engraved into his face in middle age show an habitual attitude of kindliness. His whiskers, crowding bushily around his upturned nose, giving to his face the general outlines of that of a tomcat, hid full curved lips, and cheeks padded with childlike fat. Only his close-set tense eyes of palest blue suggest the anxious pedantic man, explosive and harsh, who struck terror into the hearts of mischievous archdukes. But his servants never saw him even slightly ruffled, and on those occasions when he came face to face with his subjects, his strained cold eyes withdrew into the background of his fortunate smile, and he would blush with pleasure and shyness.

He was not loved by his people, although he wished to be loved. He was too mystically enshrined. Besides, he stood rigidly against their serious political aspirations, appeared to take no interest in their arts and sciences, and had no identification with their daily pleasures. He was wedded to them by bonds most holy, but he had never really met them. They were distinguished by *Gemütlichkeit* and *Schlamperei;* he was distinguished by extreme reserve and was the slave of duty.

If he had been an idealist like Napoleon III, or a genial man like Edward VII, or possessed of any flamboyant quality or fault, he might have moved into the future more spectacularly. But he came so modestly, on such a private road, that his role in the immense motion of history is almost imperceptible; his unstable son, the Crown Prince Rudolf, comes forth clearer to modern understanding. And yet Francis Joseph, with his courtesy to humble people, his meticulous and fair consideration of their obscure problems, his industry and selflessness, had natural qualities that all of today's elected politicians must make a show of. More than any other monarch Francis Joseph was his people's civil servant.

He served at his desk all day and dined at a table pulled out from next to the wall of his office. He went to bed at eight-thirty and disliked anything that prevented him from doing so, such as a ball or banquet. Occasionally, as duty obliged him, he attended a performance at his private theater, the Burgtheater. Growing old, his interest in pretty women was completely discreet, and after his break with Elizabeth, scandal did not again assail his name. But after 1883 he particularly enjoyed watching the new star of the Burgtheater, Katherina Schratt, romping through some light comedy with a rustic background, clothed in a national peasant costume. She was a type of girl the empress called contemptuously, a "geranium," that is, she seemed to exude all homelike virtues. However, the emperor approved of these virtues in a woman. It is likely that they seemed improbably exotic to him.

Golden happiness threaded through his life when Elizabeth came to the Hofburg or spent some weeks with him at the imperial summer villa at Ischl. But she was cruelly impatient with his company. When he called at her apartments in the Hofburg, she had a trick of ordering all windows and doors opened, knowing that he hated draughts and was susceptible to colds. It came to be understood gradually by their contemporaries that Francis Joseph was far too dull and unfeeling a man to interest such a sensitive free spirit as his wife.

But there were times when Elizabeth could not avoid his company, and she was forced to be his captive audience while he sought to fix her attention on his troop reviews, his maneuvers, the latest royal children born, the latest chamois dead; and the latest hit of Kathi Schratt at the Burgtheater. The middle-aged Elizabeth would sit with acidulous lips turned down, hardly mumbling a response, and never pleasing him by repeating a remark he had not understood. Far gone in egocentricity, she inhabited an eerie dreamworld of her imaginings, and not long since she had begun a love affair with the dead Heinrich Heine. His ghost had appeared to her one night and struggled with her for the possession of her soul.

She was one of the "mad Wittelsbachs." People called her "the fairies' child," not only for her fragile beauty but because of her fey ways. Probably she lived in fear of madness. She longed to retire to the island of Corfu, there to build a villa in which she would find solitude and a quiet mind. But in order to do this she would first have to escape from the monotonous prattle of her husband and from all the demands of his endless abject love.

Deep in this suffering woman was buried a darling Elizabeth, a generous person with insight and sympathy. She was quite aware that while Francis Joseph had spoiled her youth, she had deprived his life. Now he was fifty-three, an age when a man must be renewed or drag his shackles to the grave. It was evident that he admired the court actress, Katherina Schratt. In 1884 she was one of the Burgtheater company commanded to present a gala performance before the emperor and his guest, Tsar Alexander III, and afterward the actors had shared a buffet supper with the monarchs. The Crown Prince Rudolf had found this arrangement "strange." Again, at the Industry Ball of 1885, when the emperor received his captains of industry and professional vassals at the Hofburg, people noticed that he spent some time in jovial conversation with Kathi Schratt.

But the empress realized that however the emperor might admire the actress he would never break the pattern of his rigid habits and early bedtimes to pursue this admiration unless he were prodded by the only person on earth who had the right to prod him: herself.

One day in 1886, in a mood of tenderness or exasperation, Elizabeth summoned to a private audience Frau Katherina von Kiss-Schratt, and in this interview, it is said, the "fairies' child" and the "geranium" entered into a secret compact.

Kathi Schratt was twenty-nine years old when the empress turned her life upside down. For many years she had been a favorite of the Vienna masses as a theatrical star, and she was also to be seen on the chief float of every carnival, wielding a cornucopia, dressed as Fertility or some other desirable abstraction. In her own person, indeed, she was something of an abstraction, being the image of her race's rustic ideal, and whoever has opened his eyes in some south German country inn to see a *süsses deutsches Mädchen* shining in the morning sun and laden with coffee and *Kugelhupf* has seen the shape of Kathi Schratt. It doesn't matter whether such women are beautiful: they seem to be compounded of the firm rocks, the rich soil, and the clear air of their land.

Next to the lyric grace of Empress Elizabeth, portraits of Kathi show her as heavy-boned and overfed, yet she must have had unusual qualities to have played her captivating historic role, and we sense them in the friendly strength of her direct and honest gaze. She had also a singularly clear voice of a timbre that lifted the heart of those who heard it.

She was born in the small town of Baden, near Vienna, where her father was a haberdasher, and in later years she herself wrote of her first appearance on the stage, when she was eleven. She had a friend whose father managed a local theater, and through him she obtained an insignificant part. Her father got wind of this, and invading the theater backstage, took hold of his daughter, and dragged her home in very bad odor. She was then immured in a convent, where she did well enough in her lessons. But one night, after Vespers, when the girls had been safely tucked in bed, Kathi arose to give them a solo performance of one of Grillparzer's plays, using as costume a bedsheet draped toga-fashion with a corner flung over one shoulder. Just as her clear voice was hitting form, the door opened: *enter* MOTHER SUPERIOR, *with a flourish.* She put Kathi on eight days of bread and water and wrote to Herr Schratt: "There is something about her that lowers the reputation of this convent and distracts the pupils from the usual course of good behavior." She requested him to come and take his daughter home.

In those days—the Gaudy Empire in France was just whirling to its full stop—most actresses were part-time *horizontales;* they were expected to live in a style far above their incomes. On one side of their path stood a debtor's prison, and on the other an aristocratic love nest, with more squalid residences down the lane: a solid burgher like Herr Schratt had every reason to protest his daughter's enchantment with the theater. But beside him flowed the beautiful blue Danube, and around him the houses were filling up with furniture in the style of Biedermeyer; Johann Strauss had just donned the black coat and white tie proper to the ball master of Francis Joseph's court: Gay Vienna was taking shape, and Herr Schratt could not guess that it lacked only hundreds of plump middle-class girls like Kathi—and her most of all—to flock to the *Kaiserstadt* and give to it their special rubric of natural good manners, kindliness, and ingenuous coquetry.

In the end she persuaded him to permit her to study acting in Vienna, and he sent her off with such strict advice that the first time a director tried to kiss her she burst into tears and ran from the stage.

By the time she was seventeen she had secured an important role with a company playing in Berlin, that of Joan of Arc; and in the following year, 1873, which was the twenty-fifth anniversary of Francis Joseph's rule, she had the honor of a part in a most inappropriately chosen drama to be played before the imperial couple: *The Taming of the Shrew*.

She became a member of the company of the Stadttheater, a private enterprise managed by Heinrich Laube, but almost immediately afterward a stock market crash ruined him. Kathi is said to have come to America at that time with Herr Laube and other members of the Stadttheater and to have played to empty houses in Baltimore and elsewhere, before their agent absconded with the moneybags, leaving them all to make their way home as best they could. Eventually Herr Laube got his players back to Vienna, and in the next years Kathi became an increasingly familiar and popular figure of stage and carnival because she looked like the Spirit of Austria; but her reputation remained spotless.

In 1877 or thereabouts she married a Hungarian of an impoverished noble family named Kiss, and one year later they had a son, Anton. Like almost any girl who marries a Hungarian, she immediately found that she had political problems: her husband's grandfather had been involved in the revolution of 1848 and was hanged by order of Francis Joseph. The Kiss family now employed Kathi to take her pretty looks to an audience with the emperor in order to petition for the return of their confiscated fortune. This may have been the first time she met the emperor face to face. He did not grant her petition, and though he must have found her attractive, his thoughts did not rest upon her. In 1879, when in honor of his silver wedding she played Puck in *A Midsummer Night's Dream*, he wrote a letter of thanks to Herr Laube in which he did not mention the name of Katherina Schratt.

Kathi's marriage into a good family had elevated her position in life; the right to place "von" before her name carried with it respect and privilege. And so, although she was an actress born, after her marriage she resigned her position at the Stadttheater. As it turned out, her admirer, German ambassador Philipp zu

Eulenburg was right when he said she had committed a *Dumm-heit* in marrying Kiss. He engaged in reckless speculations with his own and his wife's money and fell into the hands of usurers. The young couple got to such straits that the bailiff came and took their clothes away. Eventually Kathi tore loose from her husband and they were separated, though never divorced. She returned to the Stadttheater and later was graduated to the emperor's own Burgtheater. Anton was placed in a military school. No evidence has come to light, not even gossip, to charge that in these years of her young womanhood Kathi had ever transgressed the excellent commands of Herr Schratt.

In the eighties, before the heroines of Ibsen, Schnitzler, and Gerhart Hauptmann had walked upon the stage imprisoned in social significance, the dramas presented at the imperial theater were such that some called it the *Comtessentheater*—fit only for the consumption of delicately reared young girls. A special censor was employed by the imperial house to keep God in his Heaven at the Burgtheater and Francis Joseph on his throne. No implied criticisms of the Habsburg dynasty were permitted, or of the aristocracy, or the church. No monk in his robe might be shown. That princes had mistresses might not be suggested, although the actresses might have been in real life the mistresses of princes. Ladies of standing were not allowed to commit dramaturgical adultery, nor were heroines of the lower classes permitted to wind up in the last act married to handsome noblemen.

Probably Francis Joseph himself was the chief culprit for this dull theater, and no wonder. His life was a tangle of socially significant problems. His wife collected anarchistic literature, his son consorted with Hungarian dissidents, his relative, Archduke Johann Salvator, wanted to marry a girl named Miltschi, his ethnic groups were crying out for dominance over every other ethnic group, his young Jews wanted to be barons, and his young barons wanted to emigrate to the American Wild West. Francis Joseph supported the Burgtheater out of his own privy purse, and when he went there, he wished to see girls in peasant costume enmeshed in country complications with goatherds.

In 1886 it became known that Empress Elizabeth had commissioned the court painter, Heinrich von Angeli, to paint a picture of Katherina Schratt as a present to Francis Joseph from the empress herself.

On May 20 Angeli received a note from Francis Joseph: "With the empress' permission I should like to come tomorrow at one o'clock to your studio, to see the picture of Frau Schratt which she has commissioned you to paint for me."

A few hours later a second note arrived: "The empress will accompany me."

The next day when Kathi arrived for her sitting, she was informed of the impending visit of the imperial couple. Although she had by that time concluded her secret treaty with the empress, she now got cold feet and wished to cancel the sitting for the day. But Angeli dissuaded her. Francis Joseph was highly regarded by artists, because they were among the very few persons he permitted to stand before him attired contrary to etiquette in their old smocks; and when he sat for his portrait, he always took pains to chat informally with them until their fingers stopped trembling and they could hold their brushes properly. Angeli, a favorite court painter, was accustomed to the concentrated majesty of the *Kaiserpaar*, and he managed to keep Kathi sitting on her perch.

The emperor and empress came and went. The portrait no doubt delighted Elizabeth, for it shows Kathi even fatter and more roguish than she really was. It is possible that in the artist's studio some mechanism regulating the future relationship of these three people was tacitly set in motion, for two days later, on May 23, the actress received the following letter from the emperor: "Madame: I ask you to accept the enclosed token as a sign of my deepest thanks that you have taken the trouble to sit for the portrait by Angeli. Again I must repeat that I would not have permitted myself to ask this sacrifice of you, and that therefore my joy over the cherished gift is all the greater. Your devoted admirer."

The token mentioned was an emerald ring, and the joy so eliptically referred to may indicate an understanding that Kathi was to become the emperor's *Freundin*, woman friend. This term, happily coined by the empress, does not necessarily carry the sense of "mistress" or any imputation against Kathi's honor. Elizabeth tactfully and hopefully left this aspect of the affair in the hands of Francis Joseph.

Two weeks later, Kathi learned what it is like to be wooed by a bureaucrat: "Madame: Forgive me for daring again to address a few lines to you. Only because I do not know when you leave Vienna, because I should like to know exactly where I can find you at Wolfgang and . . . the name of the house where you will spend the summer months. . . . I ask you to write for me on a scrap of paper the answers to the following questions:

"What is the name of the house or villa?

"How long a walk is it there from Wolfgang?

"Will you be already there by the beginning of June or arrive later? . . .

"Again seeking forgiveness for this importunity, your devoted Francis Joseph."

Throughout the summer many meetings took place between the emperor and the actress, most of them in the presence of Elizabeth and the Archduchess Valerie, the empress' favorite daughter. Elizabeth was determined that her promising scheme should not be muddied by gossip and that the position of *die Freundin* should be firmly founded upon her own approval. There was, of course, some smothered muttering, much to the discomfort of Archduchess Valerie, a morose and taciturn girl; but even she was not immune to Kathi's gay and wholesome presence. By the end of summer a *Kaiserquartet* had developed, so apparently *gemütlich* that scandalmongers had little to feed upon.

Having thus discreetly threaded her husband's life to that of the actress, Elizabeth felt free to travel the following winter to the Levant to see the Homeric cities. The emperor bade her farewell in a mood of sad tenderness, like a man who sees a most exquisitely confectioned dessert melting before his eyes and resigns himself to finishing his meal with fruit and nuts.

In his letters to Kathi his wooing may be traced through the winter freeze. His first approaches were as awkward as those of a second lieutenant to his love. He informed her that his days were passed with "deep worries and a lot of work"; that the recollection of days passed (in the country) and the hope of their return were high points for him. All he wanted of her, he said, were "kindness and friendship." About the susurrating gossip he wrote, "your honor and your reputation are sacred to me." He felt embarrassed that he had to bring up such a delicate subject, and apologized if he had ever used indelicate expressions in connection with it in her presence.

On the last day of 1886 he wrote to Kathi, begging her to preserve for him during the coming year her friendship, forgiveness, and kindness, and he signed himself rather warmly, "In faithful friendship, your devoted Francis Joseph."

He began to spend his evenings at the Burgtheater, reckless of bedtimes, and to take delight in her costumes. He assured her that he preferred to see her in ladies' toilette rather than dressed as a cadet, wearing a uniform. Examining Kathi minutely through his opera glasses, he noted with gratitude that for his sake she had stopped wearing earrings—a feminine custom he deplored.

In February of 1887 he took his first infinitely considerate step to assure her that he had her financial needs under advisement: "Carnival is nearing its end, it requires beautiful clothes, these are costly, you should and must contract no debts, and so I would be obliged to you in deepest gratitude if you would accept in friendship the small contribution enclosed toward the cost of your attire. I consider you a distinguished and talented woman, but I am not yet quite convinced of your financial talents. . . ."

He explained to her that his imperial relatives found it eminently practical to receive financial favors from him and that he wished to be "candid and practical towards you, my dear Madame, and I hope that you are not offended with me."

Never in his letters did the emperor address his *Freundin* as "*du.*" This familiar mode of address was reserved exclusively for members of the imperial family. Furthermore, most of his letters to Kathi seem to have been written with the heavy thought that one day strangers, like ourselves, might set eyes on them. Such careful courtesy did he show her that we could not guess from his written word that there was a love affair at all. Indeed, many people, even today, insist that there was not, and no evidence has come to light to prove them wrong.

But even less evidence exists to prove that Francis Joseph did not know why God made pretty women. The forty million inhabitants of his empire entertained no doubts on this score. The affair became an organic part of their society. They spoke of it beneath their breaths and brought up their children to do the same. The winter of 1888 found Kathi's virtue under serious assault, for on February 14, St. Valentine's Day, the emperor wrote to her an extraordinary confession: "That I adore you,

you surely know, or at least feel, and this feeling has also grown constantly in me since I have been so fortunate as to know you.

"You say," he wrote, "that you will control your feelings. I too shall do it, even though it will not always be easy for me, for I will do nothing wrong. I love my wife and do not intend to misuse her confidence and her friendship for you." And he told her in the ancient syllabary of an aging man who is falling in love with a young woman, "As I am too old for a brotherly friend, permit me to remain your fatherly friend. . . ."

Kathi's replies to these letters (though they may repose in some corner of the Habsburg Archives in Vienna) have not been published, and so we do not know how she responded to her sovereign's passion. We only know that this *süsses deutsches Mädchen* became a necessary fixture in Francis Joseph's life and that she walked into the cimmerian shades of the Hofburg, seeming to bring with her the country sun, so that the inhabitants of the great castle who were set to move only within the limits marked for them by etiquette and tradition paused to smile at her. Never was a royal favorite more liked that Kathi Schratt.

A mythology exists full of tales of how Kathi played the part of good angel in the manifold scrapes, amorous, scandalous, financial, political, and bacchanalian, in which Francis Joseph's large and eccentric band of relatives were continually involving themselves. His nephew, Archduke Otto, aroused the ire of multitudes when he jumped his horse over the coffin in a peasant funeral procession; on another occasion he was seen by the British Ambassador's wife rushing about the corridors of Frau Sacher's hotel, naked except for his Order of the Golden Fleece. The emperor's brother, Archduke Ludwig Victor, made a nuisance of himself at the Turkish baths and had to be banished to a country castle with only female servants to wait on him. Archduke Johann Salvator whisked Miltschi off to his castle, and after having married her in his private chapel, had no idea what to tell his mother, still less the emperor, without Kathi's good advice.

If Kathi actually became a buffer between the emperor and his egregious clan, it is something of a marvel. Francis Joseph had a unique dynastic sense, and to him Habsburgs were sacred, if insufferable. But it is very likely that her sound common sense helped to assuage his wrathfulness, and that his escape from his fakir-like existence into Kathi's gay company softened him. By changing the framework of his life, she must have subtly changed the man, called forth in him the *Gemütlichkeit* so characteristic of the world he had permitted to flourish around him, but from which he was cut off. Kathi was horrified to find that Francis Joseph gave no tip or present to any of his personal servants on Christmas Day. There was no question of parsimony. He looked after them and their families in sickness and in health and educated their children out of his own pocket. But it had never occurred to him to reach, even symbolically, across that chasm that separated a Habsburg emperor from his people in honor of Christ's birth. However, he learned to give Christmas presents under the rule of the good Kathi.

Now side by side with his bits of iron, silver and crystal ornaments appeared on his mantelpieces and flowers in plenty. Rickety furniture was removed and replaced by objects that glowed with polish. Frayed cottons gave way to silk. Decent bathroom appointments, comfortable chairs, a desk of convenient size were placed in his private quarters and screens arranged across the path of draughts. A warm robe and cap were hung in the empress' apartments so that when he visited her, she might open the windows as wide as she pleased. It is quite certain that the subdued opulence that appears in the photographs of Francis Joseph's apartments at the end of the century was the product of a long and subtle conspiracy between his valet, Ketterl, and *die Freundin*.

They did not always get away with it. A worn-out carpet they removed had to be rescued and relaid. He said that the holes in it helped him to think. But he was gently indulgent to Kathi's efforts toward his comfort and grateful for them.

The Empress Elizabeth deserves praise for her correct instinct in choosing Kathi Schratt as a companion for her husband. Still, she was not a woman to view her achievement with pleasure unpoisoned by spite. She observed with satisfaction that the figure of Kathi, twenty-two years younger than herself, could not compete in girlishness with her own, which, with her swan-like posture, had caused the Greek fisherman on her recent voyage to compare her to the lovely figures they carved at the prows of their vessels. With inner amusement she watched Kathi overdoing herself at luncheon and tea with butter and cream; and presently she made Kathi a malicious gift of a dear little silver butter churn, which she could carry about with her to make fresh butter out of *Schlag*.

Katherina Schratt, on her side, was not merely a simple child of her native soil. She was an actress, and every known fact of her life suggests that she was a born actress, an immensely impressionable person, whose fundamental solidity of character was shot through with sensitivity of a rare sort. Her sudden elevation into intimacy with a man so sacred that his worn-out socks and underlinens were never thrown away but sold at public auction, must have been for her a stunning experience, and she is very much to be admired that she eventually learned to manage him in a way that a woman ought to manage her lover, without offense to his imperial dignity. But Elizabeth, the "noblest creature on earth," must have stumped Kathi's good judgment, especially as Francis Joseph himself was never tired of pouring out to Kathi his aching admiration for his wife: ". . . I can assure you that she likes you very much, and when you know this wonderful person better, you will have the same feeling towards her."

And so Kathi became infected with a very common disease among men and women alike: Elizabeth-worship. In her confusion of mind, she must have begun to try to improve herself, her hair, her dress, her manner and habits, by imitation of her heroine. Her efforts did not escape the empress, whose private papers contained this poem:

> Your buxom angel comes anon
> With roses quite an armful;
> Be patient, then, my Oberon—
> Excitement might be harmful!
>
> She brings along her little churn,
> She'll never go without it;
> She likes her butter to a turn,
> There're no two ways about it!
>
> Her corset is so tightly bound,
> The stays are almost breaking;
> The while she stiffly walks around,
> Her poor old ribs are aching.

Imbued with aping mania,
Despite her pounds of fat,
She longs to be Titania . . .
That Katherina Schratt!

Titania was Elizabeth's fantasy name for herself, and she had acutely recognized the actress's emotional dilemma. But did she recognize her own? In the spring following the first winter of Francis Joseph's wooing, the empress had gone walking in the park of Schönbrunn with the Archduchess Valerie, and they had met Kathi Schratt carrying a bunch of violets which she immediately offered to the empress, explaining that as it was March 1, violets given on that day would bring good luck.

Elizabeth enmeshed herself in superstitions and presentiments, most of them gloomy and rotten as cobwebs; here for once was a superstition with charm, and she welcomed it. From that time, side by side with her royal contempt, there grew in her the notion that Kathi and everything about her stood for luck. The two women became entangled in love and hate, and Kathi, unable to tolerate hatred in her mind, camouflaged it by adoration of the empress.

Elizabeth for her part began to treat her husband more winningly than she had done in years. On the New Year of 1889 the emperor wrote to her: "My best wishes to . . . you, my beloved angel. . . . The blessed feeling that your love . . . increases with the passing years, instead of growing colder, causes me the warmest gratitude, and makes me infinitely happy."

To Kathi he gave gifts: a charming and appropriate villa on the Gloriettegasse, not far from his palace of Schönbrunn, where he took to spending most of his time; also an apartment close to the Hofburg which was equipped with a special elevator for His Majesty's use. At Ischl, close to the Kaiservilla, she became the owner of the Villa Felicitas, a sort of giant chalet. She also received from him a long procession of valuables which were to mean much to her in the troubled future.

He gave her a jewel of swallows wrought in diamonds. He wrote after an evening spent with her, "I must thank you . . . for wearing the swallows in your hair." A few days later, after attending the theater, he wrote, "I was happy to be able to admire you the whole evening, and I thank you most heartily for the friendly glance from behind scenes."

So merrily did the friendship develop that by the end of the year 1888, the emperor was writing to Kathi in tones of rare mischief: ". . . the maneuvers ended splendidly in glorious, not too hot weather. . . . By trotting and galloping I took pains to shake off the Prince of Wales* from my vicinity, but I could not do it; the fat man was always with me and held out unbelievably, only he . . . tore his red Hussar trousers, and as he had on nothing beneath, it was rather unpleasant for him."

And again he wrote, "I would so have liked to see you in the yellow wig and with spectacles. . . ."

It is touching to watch these fragile gaieties shooting forth from the arid emperor, while close at hand fresh calamity was gathering to overwhelm and cancel them.

2.

The Crown Prince

Francis Joseph's administration, as it became stabilized in the seventies, was a police state and bureaucracy, a form of government we assume to be a vessel of human misery. But the people of Gay Vienna—and Budapest—were not miserable except when weeping to the tune of gypsy music. Whatever explanation political scientists have for this anomaly, one can't help observing that the sheer vastness of the governmental organization could have been at the bottom of it. To become public officials was the object of most schooled young men of the middle class, aside from Jews who kept the industry and trade going or else were intellectuals and professionals. These bureaucrats, these police-men, these Jews *were* the people of Gay Vienna and Budapest, and far from oppressing one another, they spent endless hours developing their wit over café tables; they waltzed and clicked

---

* The future King Edward VII.

their heels and called each other by wondrous flattering titles. Most of them had deep-seated political yearnings, but with Francis Joseph taking care of everything, they wisely practised *Schlamperei*, the art of happily letting things slide.

But a police-ridden and bureaucratic state has callousness and mendacity built into it, and in 1889 these devils waltzed at Mayerling.

The story of Crown Prince Rudolf and his heroine, Marie Vetsera, has been told in several flatly contradictory versions, all by people who were convinced that they had the facts. Yet the documents that once contained the facts may no longer exist. They were said to have been rolled up by Francis Joseph himself and placed in a large black bag which was sealed and handed down from prime minister to prime minister through the years; but when that bag was opened after the empire fell, it was found to contain nothing but blank sheets and old newspapers. A few police records remain, however, and they are grim testaments to find at the heart of a legend of high romance.

Rudolf, as we have seen, was the child of cousins, as was his mother, and both of his family tributaries brought him a heritage of mental instability along with his exalted destiny. He was a nervous child, and his tutor, appointed by his grandmother, Archduchess Sophie, tried to toughen him by shooting off revolvers in his bedchamber while he slept; or he locked the boy alone in the zoo while he hid himself in the bushes, crying, "Here comes a wild boar!" Elizabeth, in defiance of her mother-in-law, wrote an ultimatum to Francis Joseph, insisting upon a new tutor of her choosing. The emperor gave in, and Rudolf was placed under the governorship of Latour, a gentle man with secret liberal sympathies. Under his charge the crown prince in his teens wrote compositions so critical of his father's government that they had to be locked up out of the emperor's sight.

As he grew two criminal faults—for a royal person—were noted in him: he was unsteady on horseback and he was a bad shot. His mother was obliged to forbid him to ride with her in England because his clumsiness disgraced her own superb horsemanship. His father wrote a letter advising him that when out hunting, he must be perfectly certain from the start that he was going to kill something. That Rudolf had his mother's love of nature and might have preferred to study animals rather than shoot them cut no ice with Francis Joseph because natural history was not the *métier* of the heir to the Habsburg throne. And so Rudolf developed into a bloodthirsty wasteful huntsman.

None of his father's stolid, steady qualities were in him, nor even Elizabeth's fanatical perfectionism. He had wide-roving interests, but they were fickle and perverse. Much sympathy has been given him by his biographers because his father did not appreciate his son's intellectual quality and granted him no responsibility in government aside from dog's work, like entertaining visiting royalties and inspecting remote garrisons. But this was a fate Rudolf shared with his contemporaries the Prince of Wales and Crown Prince Frederick of Prussia. A nineteenth-century monarch was, after all, not a practical politician but a demigod who wore a perfectly circular halo. Few of them were willing to let their young try it on and bend it out of shape.

Francis Joseph gave to his intelligent son unusual latitudes: he permitted his friendship with such scholars as the great zoölogist Alfred Brehm, and other scientists not formally acceptable at court; and also with Jewish intellectuals and newspapermen, some of whom were political radicals. Since the emperor must have known the direction of his son's politics, it is surprising that he put him to work in an infantry regiment whose officers were drawn from young men of the middle class.

It is in this period of Rudolf's young manhood that his reputation as a Habsburg Hamlet rests, when he was comrades with the infantry officers and spent his spare time writing—in excellent literary style—political articles for the *Neues Wiener Tageblatt*, owned by his friend Moritz Szeps. In these articles the crown prince indignantly pointed out the many injustices and faults inherent in his father's government and, at his best, he looked abroad to the politics of Europe foreseeing times to come, even some of the illnesses of our own times. One of his famous flashes of inspiration, written in 1888, concerned the newly crowned German kaiser: "Wilhelm II progresses. Soon he will be ready to stir up a first-class muddle in old Europe; he is just the man to do it, too."

Undeniably, Rudolf was a man of brilliance and insight, but his articles were written anonymously, and he did not run the same risk as Szeps ran in printing them; if he had run such a risk, it is hard to say whether he would have been braver than he was when sitting on a horse. That such doubts of himself occurred habitually to him is written plainly on his face, in the quivering, imploring glance of his eye. Rudolf resembled his mother, but her fragile beauty was translated in him into the physical signatures of weakness. He hid them by growing a beard and mustache cut into a princely shape, so that at first glance women thought he was not Hamlet but Prince Charming.

Beneath the glamour of his youth lurked the somber spell of death. He wrote a will in his teens and became attached to his mother's favorite cousin, the ghostly and suicidal King of Bavaria, Ludwig II. During his young years with the infantry in Prague he had an odd adventure. He had visited the ghetto, that ancient place where the Golem stands immured, and there a cantor's daughter had laid eyes on him. Like other teen-agers of her time, she promptly fell in love. Her family sent her away at once to visit relatives in another town, but she escaped from them, and in the dead of winter made her way back to Prague. Underneath the lighted windows of the military barracks where she supposed Rudolf lived, she huddled worshipfully throughout the night. She caught pneumonia and died, and was buried in the old Jewish cemetery.

Rudolf thought that this was the most beautiful thing that had ever happened to him. He said the cantor's daughter was the only person on earth who had ever really loved him. He looked for her grave and laid flowers on it, and though he had not known her, she was perhaps the only girl he ever loved and then only because she was dead.

Few young men in the world could have been so abused by women as Rudolf. His favor could make the greatest lady greater; his admiration for a woman could have ensured preferment for her husband and father. Beyond the women of his immediate circle were the social climbers, persons who by whatever indignified means must raise their positions in life. At the age of twenty the crown prince was pursued by a Baroness Vetsera, a Levantine woman with "beautiful, interesting eyes," who though she was a widow of uncertain years and had two growing daughters, did not hesitate to push presents and blandishments upon him, so that even the preoccupied emperor remarked upon her impudence.

The crown prince kept track of his love affairs by meticulously bureaucratic methods that his father would have admired with reservations. He compiled a "Register of Conquests" containing the names and particulars of all the ladies who had enjoyed his favors, with the virgins entered in red ink, including his wife. What's more, he had on hand a huge stock of silver cigarette boxes which he distributed as mementos of every happy occasion, and they were inscribed in a way that does not sustain Rudolf's historic image as a "democratic" prince. Women who belonged to the great families, equal in official status to the Habsburgs though non-reigning, received boxes engraved with Rudolf's friendly signature. Ladies of the highest nobility were given boxes bearing Rudolf's name with his imperial and military titles. Very noble women whose blood was somehow flawed by an ancestor's inconsiderate marriage to a commoner had to be satisfied with the simple initial *R*, accompanied by the archducal crown. Those still lower in rank received boxes with the crown only, while ladies of the lesser nobility and commoners were presented with boxes on which was engraved nothing but Rudolf's coat of arms.

As time went by and these ladies compared notes they found that aside from cigarette boxes, they had very little to talk about.

One girl above all seems to have claimed the fancy of the crown prince. Her name was Mizzi Kaspar, and the police records refer to her as "a woman of doubtful reputation," in fact an *horizontale*, but Rudolf nevertheless entered her in his "Register of Conquests" in red ink. Mizzi was frequently glimpsed in his tent when he went on maneuvers and in his hotel rooms when he went on inspection trips. She accompanied him to Brussels when he went there to ask Leopold II, King of the Belgians, for the hand of his daughter, Stephanie, in marriage, and upon being discovered in his apartments in the royal palace, had to be tossed out by Leopold with a roar. This evidence of Rudolf's cynicism did not prevent the King of the Belgians from trying to foist his daughter on the crown prince before she had reached a practical state for marriage.

These imbroglios and Rudolf's growing reputation as a lascivious wastrel so horrified Queen Victoria that when his marriage with Stephanie of Belgium finally took place, she was dead set against the Prince of Wales attending it.

Yet as a young husband Rudolf glowed again briefly. In his teens he had written, "Love is certainly the most beautiful thing in the life of all organic beings. . . . In this [man] comes into accord with nature itself." He seems to have made a genuine effort to achieve this harmonious state with his wife and to interest her in his intellectual pursuits; indeed he even took her to the gay cafés, incognito. But his wooing was lost on Stephanie who had inherited her father's critical, harsh, and arrogant nature, without his intellect or wit. The two had nothing in common, and when, after the birth of a daughter, the doctors said that Stephanie would never be able to bear an heir to the throne they began to detest each other. Stephanie organized her own secret police force to spy on Rudolf's activities. Once, when she knew he was visiting a mistress of the moment, she had herself driven to the lady's house and she left her carriage with its imperial crest and golden wheels parked before the entrance, while she slipped out and rode home in a public cab. When the crown prince emerged from his lady's establishment, he found half of Vienna waiting to enjoy the joke.

But Stephanie's beady-eyed hatred enabled her to perceive more clearly than any of the Habsburgs the road her husband was traveling to his tragic destination at Mayerling.

Francis Joseph could not understand lack of self-control in an imperial prince, and a certain estrangement took place between father and son which did not help Rudolf to weather the storms of self-loathing that were beating over him. For by the time he was thirty Rudolf's rake's progress was complete. His sexual experiences were such that he feared he was becoming impotent. He suffered from venereal disease. He was an habitual drunkard, drinking his brandy neat from a teacup at teatime. He had become addicted to drugs, morphine and ether, and was unable to break his dependence on them. And he was a traitor to his father, for he had become involved, perhaps too deeply, with Hungarian separatists. The exact extent of his treason—whether he had simply lent moral support to Hungarian dissidents, or whether he actually planned to depose his father and assume one or both of the twin crowns—we do not know. All documents relating to it—and these, rather than love, may be the heart and soul of the Mayerling tragedy—were confiscated by his father. The slightest treachery on his son's part would have been abhorrent to the emperor and for that matter to the crown prince also, who was weak but intelligent and above all a Habsburg. He must have been perfectly aware that a demoralized drunkard and drug addict, however politically progressive, was not a proper substitute for, or successor to, the Emperor Francis Joseph.

In the last year of his life he became irascible, rude, explosive, and morbid. He studied cases of suicide and kept asking his friends "Are you afraid to die?" He probed them for their opinions about life beyond the veil. His wife, Stephanie, alarmed by his drunken threats to shoot her and then himself, tried to interest Francis Joseph in his son's behavior. But the austere life of Francis Joseph had recently become lively with the presence of Katherina Schratt, and he therefore did not attend to Stephanie, that "obelisk of tactlessness" and chronic complainer.

And so Rudolf, like his mother, became enamored of death; and yet his heart was not in the flirtation. He would not have dared to sail his yacht through tempests like Elizabeth or to go walking alone in regions infested by anarchists. Elizabeth teased death like a bride; but Rudolf, with failure festering in his bones, was but a wretched petitioner, and he had no intention of facing the stern audience alone. He therefore asked one of his aides, a lieutenant, if he would be willing to commit suicide with him. The lieutenant regretted that he would not. The crown prince then approached another officer of his staff, but with the same barren result.

One day in 1888 Mizzi Kaspar visited the chief of police of the city of Vienna. She told him that Crown Prince Rudolf was seriously considering committing suicide and that he had asked her to accompany him to the "Hussar's Temple," a pretty little structure atop a hill in the country, and there die with him. Mizzi hoped, in making this report to the police, that a warning might be sent to Rudolf's father. But the chief of police, Herr Kraus, did not relay her message. He did not dare to communicate such a tale from a "woman of doubtful reputation" to the Emperor Francis Joseph.

On November 5, 1888, Rudolf attended the annual Polish Ball, and there he met a young girl who greatly impressed him with her huge Oriental eyes. Perhaps they made him think of the cantor's daughter of Prague, because on the same night he despatched an aide—that very lieutenant who had refused to commit suicide with him—to Prague to lay flowers on the cantor's daughter's grave under cover of darkness. This pusillanimous person did not dare to enter the old Jewish burial ground, so he engaged a braver man to do it for him.

Rudolf made no move to improve his acquaintance with the young lady of the ball. But the following day he received from her a note in which she told him that she would like to know him better. She signed herself Baroness Marie Vetsera.

The romantic legend has been just as busy with Marie Vetsera as with her Prince Charming. She is customarily described as beautiful. In fact, the beauty she might have one day owned had scarcely begun to blossom: she had just turned eighteen when Rudolf met her, and she is instantly recognizable as one of those plump girls whose moods alternate between bubbling affection and moping depression. Had she been put in a box with a lid on it until she was older and her two natures had made peace with each other, she might have brought to some bureaucrat the enchantment of a submissively amorous and soulful wife with excellent judgment in cooks.

But she was not put in a box, far from it. She belonged to a "coming" family that had not yet "arrived," and Marie's charms were an asset in that tedious climb. She was therefore hustled early into the silks and laces, the braidings and beadings, the feathers and furs of a mature woman, and in obedient response, when she was sixteen she had a love affair with an English army officer in Cairo. When this was discovered, her mother no doubt explained to Marie that her social lapse had been as grave as her moral one. She was brought home to Vienna where her mother made certain that she should form attachments to the right people who could be of use to her.

The elder Baroness Vetsera, who a decade before had amused the entourage of the imperial family by her incongruous pursuit of the young crown prince, had been born a Baltazzi, a Levantine family of humble origin; but they were growing rich as bankers and had gained an informal place in society in both England and Austria because of their fine racing horses—in 1876 a Baltazzi horse had won the Derby—and by their readiness to lend money to such needy uncrowned heads as Edward, Prince of Wales. This whiff of turf and of bribery has given the Baltazzis an unsavory reputation, but they were not the only family of obscure beginnings, caught in a rigid class system, who were trying to achieve the happiness of firm social footing by the only power they had, that of shrewdness and money.

Nor can the elder Baroness Vetsera be justly accused of being an unloving mother in failing to steer her daughter clear of entanglement with the crown prince. Such an Anglo-Saxon attitude was foreign to the morals of the imperial city, where Habsburgs were a race apart, like Olympian gods, and if they no longer enjoyed in a literal sense the *jus primae noctis*, they enjoyed its fringe benefits. A properly conducted romance between Marie Vetsera and the future emperor was exactly what the Baltazzi family needed to put an end to social struggles. Rudolf's lightest word could have procured for Marie an important marriage and another for her sister Hannah.

And so Marie's mother closed her eyes when the young girl took to walking on the Prater through December slush to meet Rudolf and returned with clean boots. Rudolf had a morganatic cousin, Countess Larisch, who appears to have made her way in the world by doing what members of the imperial family told her to do, and she placed her apartment at the disposal of the lovers. And sometimes, with the connivance of her maid, Agnes, Marie would steal out of her house at night, wearing perhaps only her nightdress with a cloak flung over, to a place on the corner where Bratfisch was waiting. This Bratfisch was one of Vienna's famous *Fiakers*, professional singers and entertainers who owned their own cabs and made extra tips by entertaining their customers as Venetian gondoliers do. Each gay young aristocrat had his favorite, trusted *Fiaker* to act as his stout right arm and shield in many an amorous adventure, and Bratfisch—his name means fried fish—was Rudolf's. His present duties called for him to wait for Marie at night and convey her to the Hofburg, where she entered by a side door and was conducted through a warren of passages and stairways to Rudolf's rooms.

In January, 1889, he gave her not a cigarette case but an iron ring with the inscription I.L.V.B.I.D.T., which stood for the words, *in Liebe vereint bis in dem Tod*—united in love until death.

Marie is very touching. She went ice skating one day with

young Duke Miguel of Braganza, of the Portugese royal house, one of those exalted persons her mother so approved, and there amid the winter's crackle and sparkle she bragged to him about her imminent death. She showed her curious ring also to a Count Wurmbrandt, and she assured him that she would leave it to him when she died. She engaged a box at the opera opposite to that which would be occupied by Crown Princess Stephanie, and she attended the performance decked out in a grand parure of diamonds and a diamond tiara, such jewels as only married women wore, and by staring at Stephanie through her opera glasses, she made sure that the crown princess noticed her attire. Plainly she felt exalted to have been chosen Rudolf's bride in the life-to-be, and she could not resist making a proud splash about it in the present one.

Her social snobbishness was certainly unpleasantly exaggerated, but not even the soggiest retelling of her story has ever insisted that Marie was intelligent. She was just a plump girl whose short turned-up nose gave her the look of a pretty little pig, with only her great eyes, like a pair of Saracen mysteries, to suggest that she would ever listen to the ghastly wooing of a mad prince.

Her French teacher, a Monsieur Dubray, recalled afterward that she had been very much excited about a newspaper story of a couple named Chambigas who had bound themselves together with a piece of rope and jumped into the sea. M. Dubray considered both of the young Baronesses Vetsera, Marie and Hannah, to be warmhearted, romantic girls, incapable of purposeful deceit.

On New Year's Day of 1889 Rudolf wrote to his friend Moritz Szeps: "An uncanny quiet reigns, like the quiet before a storm."

On January 25 he wrote about his own mood, that he had achieved "a philosophic calm that nothing can disturb."

On January 27 there was a mighty scene between Francis Joseph and his son, a Habsburg family row of which the subject cannot be guessed; but this has not deterred anyone from trying. The fact that the Cardinal Prince Archbishop Doctor Ganglbauer was present suggests that Francis Joseph had learned with outrage that behind his back Rudolf had opened a tentative correspondence with the pope with a view to divorcing Stephanie, the daughter of a Coburg monarch and the mother of a Habsburg princess.

The question of Rudolf's dissolute life would almost certainly have been raised, and also his new relations with Baroness Marie Vetsera, whose impudence to the crown princess was an open scandal. Not the least of matters to be threshed out would have been Rudolf's suspicious friendships with Hungarian malcontents. Whatever was the main subject on the table, the impassive Francis Joseph is rumored on this occasion to have worked himself into such a state of dread majesty that he fainted. Rudolf left his father's office reeling.

That night the German Embassy regaled the great world of Vienna with a reception in the grand manner, honoring the birthday of their new kaiser, Wilhelm II. Francis Joseph, resplendent in the uniform of a Prussian field marshal, was conversing with Cardinal Prince Archbishop Doctor Ganglbauer when Rudolf entered, also in Prussian uniform. The emperor cut short his chat abruptly and walked over to his son, offering his hand. Rudolf took it without a word, and bowed deeply.

The young Baroness Vetsera was at the reception, and Rudolf spoke to her twice during the evening. Rudolf's friend Count Hoyos spoke to her also and he said something about a "shoot at Mayerling." At some time Rudolf chatted with his sister-in-law, Princess Louise of Coburg, and was moved to confide in her that the person he was fondest of in this world was Mizzi Kaspar.

Returning to his rooms at the Hofburg, he sent his valet in search of Mizzi Kaspar, and she was brought to him. The following morning after she had left he wrote her a letter which one who read it later said was overflowing with love. Shortly before, he had given her a cash present equivalent to $25,000.

The noon of that day, January 28, his carriage waited to take him to his hunting lodge at Mayerling, about two hours' journey from Vienna. Marie met him there, brought by Bratfisch. The lovers dined together that evening, and Bratfisch entertained them by whistling.

At ten minutes past eight on the morning of January 29 two close friends of Rudolf's arrived at Mayerling at his invitation, to go hunting with him that day: his brother-in-law, Prince

Philip of Coburg, and Count Hoyos. Rudolf excused himself from hunting. He said that on the previous day when he had driven to Mayerling, the frozen ground had troubled the horses, so that he had been obliged to get out and push, and he had caught cold. The two gentlemen then went out alone for some meager hunting, but Prince Philip returned early to Mayerling in order to catch the train for Vienna, where a Habsburg family dinner was to take place at the Hofburg. Rudolf was also expected there, but he excused himself again because of his cold.

Around five o'clock in the afternoon Count Hoyos drifted back from the mountains and went to his rooms in a guest house of the hunting lodge. At seven he was summoned to dine with Rudolf. Neither Hoyos nor Prince Philip had the slightest inkling throughout the day that Marie Vetsera was with the crown prince.

Not so Marie's mother in Vienna: when her daughter had not returned home the night before, she knew well enough that Rudolf was the culprit, and she was frantic. For some weeks this woman had taken a lenient view of the affair, hoping to use it to advantage. But perhaps Marie's lighthearted chatter about death had aroused her suspicions. Or perhaps Marie had been talking soulfully to her sister or her maid. For whatever reason, the baroness was now fully alert to her child's danger, and in spite of the social disadvantages of meddling in the crown prince's amours, she plucked up courage to approach Herr Kraus, the chief of police, and beg him to find her daughter. Herr Kraus knew quite well where Marie was—that was his business —but he saw no reason for placing his career in jeopardy by revealing it to the baroness, and he advised her to see the prime minister, Count Taaffe. Count Taaffe too was aware of the delicacy of the situation, but he was sorry for the baroness. He said that the crown prince was expected at the Hofburg that night for a family dinner, and he would try to buttonhole him and bring up the subject discreetly. Marie's mother returned home to spend another night of desperation.

But of course Rudolf did not come to the family dinner. Instead he dined at Mayerling with Count Hoyos, who was surprised by his unusually agreeable and friendly mood. At nine o'clock Rudolf dismissed him, shaking hands cordially, and telling him that he would see him at breakfast the following day promptly at eight-fifteen, by which time Prince Philip would also have arrived on the morning train from Vienna, and they would all have a good day's hunting. The crown prince then retired to his bedroom, where Marie was waiting for him.

By that time, it is assumed, the pair had prepared a number of letters. Most of Rudolf's, indeed, must have been written in Vienna, and some dealt with such weighty matters as his will. Marie's letters were almost frivolous. She wrote to her former admirer, the Duke of Braganza, telling him, "We are extremely anxious to find out what the next world looks like"; and she promised that he should have her fur tippet to hang over his bed. To Countess Larisch, whose life was to be ruined for her part in the affair, Marie made the excellent suggestion that she should follow their example. To her mother she wrote, "Dear Mother: Forgive me for what I have done. I could not withstand love. I want to be buried beside him. . . . I am happier in death than in life. . . ." She added a postscript: "Bratfisch whistled beautifully last night."

She also left a message for Count Hoyos, reminding him about the "shoot at Mayerling."

Rudolf held up his service revolver with its soft lead bullet and shot off the top of Marie's head. He arranged her body on the bed and placed a pink rose in her hand. She was naked except for a light chemise.

United in love until death, they had said. But were they? Marie had shut her great dusky eyes before the thunderclap of his gun; but the moment she was gone Rudolf must have realized that death admits suicides by single file and that after all, he would have to die uncompanioned. We cannot know what thoughts chased about his brain, or if it was cowardice that made him hesitate to turn the revolver on himself and steal hour after hour of life, leaving Marie to waken alone in the unimaginable land. He drank a lot throughout the night, and perhaps he tried to think of an easy way out. At some time he might have recomposed his farewell letter to his mother, for years later Elizabeth confided to the Empress Eugénie that he had written that he did not want to die, but that no other course was open to him, since he was a murderer.

And yet in Francis Joseph's world an imperial person could not be a common murderer. It would not have been impossible for him to clear Marie out of his way and resume life as if she had never been born. And so when Rudolf wrote to his mother that he could no longer appear before the emperor because by his actions he had made himself unworthy of wearing the golden sword knot of an Austrian officer, he was grappling with his self-respect as a man and son, not as a prince.

At six-thirty on the morning of August 30, Rudolf emerged from his apartment fully dressed. He went to the room of his valet, Loschek, roused him, and told him that he was going to doze for one more hour, and that he wished to be reawakened at half past seven. Bratfisch was to be instructed to have his hackney cab waiting at that time.

Accordingly, at seven-thirty Loschek rapped at the crown prince's door. There was no answer. He rapped louder. Eventually he armed himself with a piece of wood in order to make a clatter on the door, but since no response was forthcoming, he went in some alarm to the guest house to fetch Count Hoyos. The count accompanied him back to the crown prince's door, and for some time they stood there shouting and banging. Count Hoyos was now for breaking down the door, but Loschek explained to him that Baroness Marie Vetsera was within, and so, fearing that there might be reason for haste and yet paralyzed by proprieties, the count hesitated. Then to his tremendous relief a carriage drove up to the front of the building bearing Prince Philip of Coburg back from Vienna. The two gentlemen conferred. They decided to take upon themselves the responsibility of breaking down the door, but out of respect for Marie, the valet, Loschek, should be the only one to enter.

The door was crashed down and Loschek entered. He returned to say that Rudolf and Marie were dead in bed and that the crown prince was lying over the edge of the bed with a great pool of blood in front of him. Somewhere Loschek had read that cyanide of potassium caused hemorrhage, and since there was a glass close to Rudolf's hand, he supposed that he had been poisoned.

Stunned by horror and grief, Hoyos and Coburg struggled with their decisions. A telegram was sent to Vienna urgently summoning, without explanation, the royal physician, Dr. Widerhofer. Hoyos was nominated to take the news in person to the emperor. He climbed into the cab so providently ordered for

him by the crown prince, and fighting off the questions of Bratfisch, arrived at the station at Baden in time to intercept the
express train to Vienna; but since the train did not normally
stop at Baden and the stationmaster, deaf to all entreaties, refused to flag it down, the count finally blurted out the truth,
whereupon the stationmaster flagged down the train, and
after he had seen it on its way, telegraphed at once to the
Rothschild Bank which owned the railway, and probably he telegraphed also to all of his acquaintances.

By the time Hoyos arrived in Vienna the city was trembling
with rumors as if before an earthquake, the stock market was
jumping up and down, and so was Baron Albert Rothschild.

Hoyos flung himself headlong off the train and into a cab to
the Hofburg, straight to the apartment of Count Bombelles, the
Master of Rudolf's Household. Count Bombelles said promptly
that only the empress could possibly break such news to Francis
Joseph, and together they went to see Baron Nopsca, the Master
of her Household. Baron Nopsca had not the slightest intention
of approaching the empress with this matter and suggested that
Prince Hohenlohe, the Master of Francis Joseph's Household
should be put in charge. Prince Hohenlohe observed at once
that since Rudolf was a lieutenant general, only the adjutant
general, Count Paar, Francis Joseph's chief aide-de-camp, was
competent to deal with the situation. And so he was. He led
them straight to Frau von Ferenczy, the empress' reader and
secretary, and told her to break the news to Elizabeth.

Elizabeth was having a Greek lesson when Frau von Ferenczy
interrupted and asked that the teacher be dismissed. When he
had gone, Frau von Ferenczy slipped out of the room, seized
Baron Nopcsa and pushed him before the empress.

It is not astonishing that these great officers of the Habsburg
court should have moved, however erratically, to break calamity
over the head of Rudolf's fragile mother. Elizabeth was an un-
balanced woman, but not in a crisis. She wept briefly upon hearing what Nopcsa had to say but then immediately calmed herself.
The affair was to devastate her, but she made sure that her
clothes and face were composed before requesting Francis Joseph
to come to her. He came. He left her apartments with bowed
shoulders.

The empress then remembered that it was the time of morning

when Frau Schratt usually arrived to spend one hour with Francis Joseph, and that she would be waiting, as usual, in the rooms of Frau von Ferenczy. Elizabeth herself went to find Kathi and break the news to her, while she conducted her to the emperor's door. She then summoned the Archduchess Valerie to tell her something that would "blanch her cheeks with horror." When Valerie learned that it concerned her brother Rudolf, she immediately asked, "Has he killed himself?" The empress was astonished at this question. "Why do you think that?" she asked. "No, no! It seems probable, even certain, that the girl poisoned him."

The dolorous news staggered through the court of the Habsburgs, leaving some people shocked beyond words and others, like Crown Princess Stephanie, not at all surprised. Then Frau von Ferenczy, returning to her own rooms, found a woman sitting there, humped up in dread and despair. It was the elder Baroness Vetsera. She had been once again to see the prime minister who had told her, "Only one person can help you. You must see Her Majesty." And so this woman who for more than a decade had dreamed of coming to the Hofburg extravagantly attired under streaming chandeliers to be formally received before the eyes of the court, now came distracted and moaning persistently, "I must see her, I must! I have lost my child!"

The empress came to her, leaving the door open so that Frau von Ferenczy heard the conversation. The baroness in agitation began to explain that Marie had been gone for two nights and that the crown prince must have taken her away with him. Elizabeth cut her short. "Collect all your courage, baroness. Your daughter is dead."

"My child!" cried the baroness. "My dear, beautiful child."

"But do you know," continued Elizabeth, "that my Rudolf is dead too?"

The baroness fell to the ground before the empress and clung to her knees. "My child!" she cried. "What has she done? Was this her doing?"

Elizabeth disengaged herself and left the room. At the door she turned and said, "Remember! Rudolf died of a heart attack."

To outward appearances Francis Joseph had only one thought upon the death of his son: to uphold the reputation of his dynasty.

Not only did the lie about the heart attack go out into the special edition of the *Wiener Zeitung*, but he spent the ensuing hours phrasing that lie over and over as he wrote messages to be sent by telegraph to his fellow monarchs throughout Europe. At the same time quarantine was set on all information leaving the country; and a false statement was sent to a foreign newspaper announcing the death of Marie Vetsera in Venice. Outside the Hofburg nervous sounds were heard, that of crowds shuffling and pressing about the gates as they waited for information of enormous moment to them. But none was given.

On January 31 sickening shocks awaited the emperor when Dr. Widerhofer brought his medical report: that Marie was pregnant; that both Rudolf and Marie suffered from venereal disease. The doctor stumbled through it, and then he said, "I can assure Your Majesty that His Imperial Highness, the Crown Prince, did not suffer for a moment. The bullet entered his temple absolutely straight and death followed instantaneously."

"What do you mean, the bullet?"

"Yes, Your Majesty, the bullet. We found it—the bullet with which he shot himself."

"He? He shot himself? That isn't true. She poisoned him. I repeat: Rudolf did not shoot himself. If you say that, you must prove it!"

The aghast doctor proved it. Francis Joseph now almost collapsed. He began to sob heartbrokenly. Then he gathered himself and asked the doctor: "Did he leave a letter of farewell?"

"Several letters. But none for Your Majesty."

Francis Joseph had now to learn that Rudolf had murdered his mistress. As horror piled on horror, in agony and shame, he cried out, "My son died like a tailor's helper!" The ugliness of his actions increased. He confiscated letters, sealed desks, placed all characters of the drama under police surveillance. He issued an order for the immediate deportation of the elder Baroness Vetsera to Venice.

Then he turned his attention to beating down the church. Rudolf had humbly asked to be buried next to Marie in the burial grounds of the Holy Cross Monastery near Mayerling. There was of course no question of Rudolf of Habsburg-Lothringen lying in a country cemetery like a tailor's helper; he had to be buried honorably in the crypt of the Capucine Monastery, side by side with Habsburgs of ages past, with the full rites of the church. It was therefore impossible for Rudolf to have committed suicide. More lies were necessary. The matter was put to the doctors. They examined Rudolf's brain and obediently found evidence of mental disorder in which, they said, he could have done violence to himself while of unsound mind. The pope accepted this explanation; and Rudolf's body was brought home to lie in state at the Hofburg under the black-draped walls, the candles, the crucifixes, amid masses and chants, with orders and sword. On February 5, accompanied by the hollow sound of drums, his father followed him on foot to the Habsburgs' perpetual home.

Marie was disposed of differently. For two days after the tragedy her body lay where it had been locked out of sight in a small room at Mayerling—it has been said to have been the place where wood was kept. Her family were forbidden to approach her. Officials were despatched to Mayerling, accompanied by a doctor, and commanded to certify that she had committed suicide. Although the doctor was one of those who had previously signed a post-mortem statement that Marie had been murdered by the crown prince, he now signed the false statement, as did Marie's uncles, Herr Alexander Baltazzi and Count Stockau. Having signed, they were permitted to take charge of their niece's body and bury her in a manner directed by the emperor, under cover of darkness in the cemetery of the Holy Cross monastery.

The Baltazzi brothers went to Mayerling by night and found Marie where she had been hidden in the anteroom after the post mortem. She was naked, and death spots were on her body. They dressed her in a fur coat and a large fur hat to cover up the gun wound on her head. They propped her between them in their carriage, her head tied upright to a walking-stick, to look as if she were alive, for the countryside was infested with curious journalists. By obscure mountain roads, through sleet and storm, they made their way to the monastery, sometimes unable to negotiate the hard-frozen slopes, so that the coachman had to stop and screw new spikes into the horses' shoes, and sometimes bogged down in semifrozen mud. Through it all, Marie's body had to be held erect, and it smelled of death.

The abbot of Holy Cross was surprised when so many officials of the Vienna police and a large number of local bureaucrats descended upon him that night, and informed him that a young girl had committed suicide in the vicinity of Mayerling and that her family requested permission to bury her in the monastery grounds, such permission having already been given by the pertinent local and state authorities. Through mercy or through sound common sense, the abbot allowed his religious qualms to be overcome by all these policemen. He ordered that a coffin was to be made for Marie in the monastery workshop, and he sent an extremely reluctant brother into the storm to hack out a grave from the stone-hard earth. The Holy Cross Monastery was noted for its hospitality, and so to while away the time the abbot had a good meal served to his visitors and plenty of wine, so that they became quite jolly while Marie Vetsera swayed through the sleet in the mountains above Mayerling.

Police Commissioner Hawerda was in charge of the proceedings. Upon learning by a coded message what route the coach containing the body was taking, he went to intercept it with Baron Gorup, a policeman of the Hofburg. The coach reached the cemetery gates at the stroke of midnight. "Count Stockau, Herr von Baltazzi, Baron Gorup and I lifted the body out of the carriage and carried it to the mortuary where we placed it in the newly made coffin. After some time we left the cemetery and returned to the monastery . . . the continuous bad weather prevented the grave being ready at the appointed hour. It was only owing to the energy of Baron Gorup, who remained in the cemetery from 7 A.M., encouraging the digger, that the grave was ready by 9 o'clock . . . half an hour before the completion of the grave, I went with Count Stockau and Herr Baltazzi, who had requested the church's blessing, in the most inconspicuous way possible, to the cemetery. The coffin was now closed. The storm and rain made the burial so difficult that the two forenamed gentlemen, as well as Baron Gorup and I, had to lend some assistance."

At nine-thirty on a foul morning Marie was laid in the ground. The gentlemen stole away from her unmarked grave, and a guard was set upon it to make sure that no one should approach it.

And yet in this police state there was always room for *Gemütlichkeit* and *Schlamperei*. In due course Marie's mother was allowed to return from Venice, and thereafter, once a week, the cemetery guards turned their backs when a lady veiled in black drove up in a carriage, stepped out, walked to the rectangle of depressed earth, and laid camellias on it.

Some months afterward the chief of police, Herr Kraus, wrote to Prime Minister Count Taaffe: "I strictly execute the orders given to me; nevertheless I agree with Your Excellency that in spite of all discretion, it is fitting to have regard for a mother's suffering.

"But last Saturday, another lady, carefully veiled, stepped out of an unnumbered carriage and without the slightest hesitation walked to the grave which was marked only by a few wilted flowers. The lady deposited on it a bouquet of camellias. I feel it is my duty to advise Your Excellency of the incident without further comment."

Not long after the visit of this lady whose movements could not be commented upon, a stone cross was erected on the grave. It read:

Marie, Baroness Vetsera
born March 19, 1871, died January 30, 1889
"Like a flower man grows to be broken."
John, XIV:2

Marie Vetsera was made to bear for Rudolf's sake the stigma of suicide. Her mother was socially ostracized in Vienna and was prevented by Francis Joseph from defending herself. By order of the emperor the name of Vetsera could never again be publicly spoken in his empire.

All servants and gamekeepers of Mayerling were given new papers, names, identities, and scattered to the corners of the land. Only Bratfisch defied the sovereign. He flatly refused to leave his Vienna. He was allowed to stay under strict police surveillance.

Francis Joseph, a man of rectitude and piety, has disgraced himself in modern eyes by protecting the honor of the House of Habsburg by lies, subterfuge, arbitrary acts, and ruthlessness. Yet, if for "House of Habsburg" we were to understand the name of a modern political party of which he was the head, we should comprehend his actions without difficulty. His efforts were unavailing. The rumors that shuttled about the city of

Vienna and far beyond it were as savage as anything he could have dreaded: that Rudolf had been arrested for treason at Mayerling and had been beaten to death by the police; that Marie had died in an attempt to shield him from his assailants; that the emperor himself had sent policemen to murder his son.

Her Majesty, Augusta Victoria, the German kaiser's wife, learned the facts in Potsdam from no less an authority than her Viennese hairdresser who, while nimbly threading the empress's flat locks into luxuriant toupées, held forth to a mesmerized audience of court ladies on the subject of high life "horrible to contemplate" in Vienna. It seems that Rudolf had been addicted to revels wherein beautiful girls were induced to disrobe and submit to caresses before everybody. "The crown prince," said the hairdresser, "—I entreat your Majesty and the ladies present not to suspect me of a desire to desecrate the late prince's memory—had arranged a feast of that kind at Mayerling with several boon companions; and when the beautiful Baroness Vetsera refused to disrobe, her lover, drunk with wine and passion, pulled out a revolver and shot her. Then—it was regicide most horrible!" Here the *friseur* let his voice drop to a whisper under the stress of his patriotic feelings, "The army officers who had witnessed the scene drew their sabers and in their anger and indignation cut our prince imperial to pieces!"

In shame, the emperor was obliged to expose his perfidy. On February 2 the *Wiener Zeitung* published the official announcement that Rudolf had committed suicide while of unsound mind, and it carried the doctors' certificate attesting that abnormal mental conditions were printed on his brain. But that was all. There was no mention of Marie Vetsera. And so the rumors did not cease, but multiplied like weeds seeding over a lost grave, and when the noxious ones had run their course, they were replaced by a love-legend. It came to be understood that Rudolf and Marie were lovers who, prevented from wedding by the inexorable Habsburg Family Law, preferred to lie together in death.

The tale just told is more nearly true than the famous romance, but it is not the full truth. No one has explained why the valet Loschek, to say nothing of the inhabitants of the countryside around Mayerling, did not hear the reports of two gunshots; nor what possessed Bratfisch to tell a game keeper at *seven o'clock* of the morning of January 30, one half hour before Loschek said he began to knock on his master's door, that there would be no hunting that day because His Imperial Highness was dead.

If the truth exists on record, it lies in the archives of the Vatican, the full confession Francis Joseph wrote to the pope. But there it will remain, presumably until Judgment Day.

One fable about Mayerling has been dispelled in recent years: that Francis Joseph felt no grief for his son. "Throughout these sad days," the Prussian military attaché wrote, "the emperor did not sign a single military report a day later than usual, even on January 30th." Nor did he mention the name of his son again. It was not understood by those around him that he could not express grief except to the empress and Kathi Schratt. Months later he was still pouring out his desolation in his letters to Kathi, saying that he could think of nothing else, but that to talk about it had "a certain calming effect."

Francis Joseph never conferred upon Kathi Schratt a title of nobility. But when it became known throughout the land that at an evil hour this haberdasher's daughter, one of themselves, had been called upon to comfort the emperor, the people of the empire accepted his own title for her: she was *Die Freundin.*

3.

The Old Emperor

As the emperor approached his seventieth year his pedantically regulated habits were modified to include his *Freundin.* However, the new pattern was almost as rigid as that of former times. Every morning at half past three, upon learning that his valet was at his feet, he arose, and by four o'clock was deep in his documents. At five-thirty his hat and coat were brought to him, and he set out on foot for the house of Frau Schratt, letting himself out of the gardens of Schönbrunn by a little door hidden behind the lilac bushes. About six he arrived at the house on the Gloriettegasse, where the door was already unlocked for him. Once, when Kathi's cook overslept and failed to unlock the door, he simply stood and waited on the doorstep. He did not know that one could ring a bell.

Breakfast, which was taken in Kathi's boudoir, consisted of crisp, newly baked croissants, ice-cold butter, and coffee with fresh *Schlag*. The china and napery were the same as those used at court. After breakfast a cedarwood box containing his special long Virginia cigars was offered to him, and as he smoked his eyes were gently flattered by the dozens of pictures of himself with which she had decorated the walls of her private rooms, showing him in all of his glorious uniforms, or else in his seedy *Lederhosen* standing proudly over the remains of a chamois.

With Frau Schratt he could talk to his heart's content about those interesting troop reviews and royal births and deaths; and, as time went by, about his diplomatic and political problems. Kathi never deliberately interfered in politics, but he came to respect her opinions and to rely on her good sense.

After breakfast he and Kathi walked before he returned to duty at Schönbrunn. But occasionally he would linger in the warm Biedermeier glow of her house, particularly if chicken *paprikás* was being served for luncheon. Next to Kathi's dining room there was a closet in which hung a black housecoat of his own design, reaching to his knees. Next to her fireplace was the "wonderful armchair" she had placed there for him alone.

Several evenings a week he dined with Kathi or she dined with him in his office. He meticulously kept his Master of the Kitchen informed of his plans, so that no cook in any of his hundred and forty kitchens should complain that the emperor was inconsiderate. On days he expected her, he applied himself with conscientious zeal to the selection of the menu, and passed hours in a state of subdued excitement, repeatedly retiring to his anteroom to brush his lamb-chop whiskers and then returning to stare at himself in the little desk mirror she had given him on which was written: *Portrait de la personne que j'aime.* In later years Kathi's banker, Herr Palmer, a Jew who looked "like a rococo statuette," would join their evenings, and he seems to have become the confidential friend of the emperor's old age, *"le Juif de la maison,"* as German Ambassador Eulenburg called him.

In this way Francis Joseph partook of the *Gemütlichkeit* of his world, and the wits of the cafés had their fun with his sudden plunge into the middle class. Once, they said, a delivery man rang Kathi's doorbell. When the door was opened, by the emperor, the rattled man could only drop his parcel, snap to attention, and sing *"God Save the Kaiser."*

Through Kathi he acquired an unslakable appetite for theatrical gossip, and she became a perfect funnel for petitions between her colleagues and the emperor; he established from his privy purse a reserve fund for actors, musicians, and painters in need. At Ischl one summer she took him to see the Jewish comedian Heinrich Eisenbach, who made him laugh so hard that after the performance he summoned the actor and asked what he would like to have as a reward. Eisenbach requested permission to take his snapshot with his own camera, and the next day Francis Joseph graciously posed. But the comedian's hands trembled so that the photo turned out to be a fan of emperors.

Sometimes on the warm evenings of spring and fall, when the lanterns in Kathi's garden were dancing and the guests had assembled around her fountains, the emperor would let himself through the little door in the park of Schönbrunn and walk across to join them. There he could have met Brahms and Anton Rubinstein and Moritz Szeps, the newspaper publisher who had been his son's friend; Edmond Rostand, who had come to Vienna in order to do the research for his play *L'Aiglon,* and it is possible that Francis Joseph, who had been greatly attached to Napoleon's son when he was a boy, had something to say to him. In Kathi's garden, it was said, the emperor would smoke a cigar with the unofficial monarch of his world, his ball master, Johann Strauss. Francis Joseph was curious to know what Strauss did with the hundreds of laurel wreaths that were tossed to him on his opening nights. "I put them in the woodshed, Your Majesty," Strauss told him, "and there they rot."

Strauss was a neighbor of Frau Schratt and her great friend. They shared two passions: eating and gambling; and the pair of them made frequent expeditions to the casino at Baden, or stayed at home consuming quantities of crayfish, goose-liver *pâté*, and Goulet *demi-sec*. Whenever Strauss finished a new waltz, he would bring it with his violin to Kathi's villa for her opinion, and sometimes Francis Joseph participated in these try-outs, although in order not to embarrass Strauss he hid behind a screen. The grand "Emperor Waltz" is dedicated to Katherina Schratt.

Whatever resentment arose in court circles against Kathi Schratt was stifled immediately by the empress, who tended the affair like a favorite flowerbed. She took every occasion to show her favor to *die Freundin*, often walking with her in the parks of Ischl, and kissing her when they met as if she were visiting royalty. Francis Joseph never ceased to marvel, with gratitude, at the understanding view Elizabeth took of his secondary love, and he loved her all the more for it. Perhaps the greatest blessing Kathi brought upon his soul was his wife's new amiability. In 1891 he spent some days with her at Gastein, and he wrote after he had left, "My inexpressibly beloved angel: I am in a melancholy mood and aching heart . . . Yesterday . . . as I drove down the hill and looked sadly and longingly back at the Helenenburg, I though I recognized your white parasol on the balcony, and my eyes filled with tears. Once again, my warmest thanks for your love and goodness. . . . It is seldom now that I pass such happy days."

What could *die Freundin* have thought of this? Perhaps she was not aware of the absurdity of her position, as Elizabeth certainly was. Once the empress confided to her daughter, "I really play an almost ridiculous part." Kathi, as sensitive in her way, might have detested Elizabeth, but she continued to adore and ape her. Occasionally she abandoned the emperor in order to pay visits to Elizabeth at Cap Martin.

Elizabeth's mental condition had deteriorated after Rudolf's death. She put on black and remained in perpetual mourning; her moods of melancholy and cynicism, perhaps of madness, increased in intensity. She had spent the ensuing years frenetically building in Corfu a strange Homeric villa, attached to a cliff at a far-gazing spot over the wine-dark sea, and she filled it with statues, including a remarkable memorial to her ghostly lover, Heinrich Heine. She lavished $12,000,000 on it before discovering that it was not exactly what she had in mind. Finally she abandoned it and went to the Riviera to settle down close to ex-Empress Eugénie—who was a magnet for melancholy royalties—and she spent her days not walking but rushing about the mountain paths as if demon-ridden. She would set off in the morning at a swift pace, followed by one of her "Greek readers"—these were a succession of young university students of the classical languages—and he had a book of Homer or Sophocles in his pocket. After a while the empress would slip behind a bush and take off her petticoat, leaving it for the Greek reader to pick up and carry, and then she would rush onward for hours, with the Greek reader puffing along behind, careful to retrieve the various articles of underclothing she left along the way. Finally she would sink, exhausted, upon a hummock, whereupon the Greek reader would sink down beside her, lay aside his burden of clothing, take out his book, and begin to read aloud in Greek.

In this way she spoiled her health as well as that of several Greek readers, who were nevertheless not deterred from falling in love with her, although she was visibly aging and soon to be a great-grandmother.

These maneuvers were supposed to prevent one ounce of fat from forming on her slender body, which she worshiped with narcissistic passion and sustained by "milk days" and "orange days," in which she would take no other food, and sometimes she ate little else but crushed ice flavored with the juice of violets. When, to her outrage, her stomach would swell—with the symptoms of starvation—she took herself off to some capital to consult a quack. But she would have nothing to do with the reputable doctors Francis Joseph was continually sending to her, regarding them as being old-fashioned fuddy-duddies if not outright spies.

In her letters at this time she constantly begged the emperor, with what seems excessive avidity, for news of Kathi Schratt. She asked him to send her the numbers of Kathi's various houses and of her city apartment so that she could place money on them at the casino. She would have been in despair had Kathi's violets failed to appear on her breakfast table annually on the first day of March. And once she told him that only three threads bound her to her life: himself, the Archduchess Valerie, and *die Freundin.*

But, when Kathi came to visit, Elizabeth could only have watched with joy her alter ego hoisting her solid South German bones about the rocks of Cap Martin and huffing behind her on her wild hikes. The enthralled Kathi strove nobly, however, and for some years she became addicted to rushing about mountain-tops. She participated also in Elizabeth's fiendish diets. A new quack had recently promulgated the doctrine that the best means of removing unwanted fat was to eat sand, and both Kathi and Elizabeth threw themselves gleefully into this *folie à deux*. It was well for Kathi that at Cap Martin she had close at hand the steadying influence of the gambling casinos, but even here she acquired the habit of flinging money away in handfuls after the manner of Elizabeth.

When in Vienna Kathi had a bout of ill health, she made herself so rude and intractable to the doctors that one of them dared to tell Francis Joseph, "That's Empress Number Two." The emperor's valet noticed that when he had occasion to send newsy messages to both Kathi and Elizabeth at the same time, he often worded them alike; but for Elizabeth was reserved the familiar "*du*." The actress' role was indeed a false one, and it was to cause her torment before she came to terms with it.

On September 10, 1899, as Elizabeth walked with her lady-in-waiting from the Hotel Beau Rivage in Geneva toward the lakeside quay, a half-mad anarchist plunged into her breast a dagger made out of a shoemaker's awl, triangular in section. She was taken back to the hotel, where the doctors worked over her, but she was dead. Elizabeth had wasted much of her life brooding upon death. Among other things, she said, "It is useless to seek for a charming death; it is enough to know that the soul has died in beauty."

Despite the squalid cruelty of the instrument, a charming death was given to her. Nothing but a tiny triangle, like a jewel, was on her breast, and from her face the marks of cynicism and malice disappeared, leaving her lovely, the image of Titania carved in alabaster.

A message was telegraphed to Vienna. The emperor read it: HER MAJESTY THE EMPRESS HAS JUST PASSED AWAY. He sank to his chair sobbing, "So nothing at all is to be spared to me upon earth," he moaned and laid his head upon his hands, weeping. Then he said, "No one knows what that woman was to me."

Within seconds he collected himself, straightened, and gave abrupt orders that his two daughters, Valerie and Gisela, were to be notified. A few days later, in cold self-command, he followed the empress' coffin to the Capucine crypt. Francis Joseph was not heard to mention her name again. Only in his letters to Kathi Schratt he mourned his wife without cease. And he told Kathi that he was happy only in her company, for it was only with her that he could speak of "the one I can't forget."

In March, 1900, hardly six months after Elizabeth's assassination and at a period of the emperor's blackest misery, Kathi left him.

Her precise reasons are not known. But for thirteen years the empress' patronage had allowed her to play her role with dignity. The affair had been a tripodal one, and when one of its supports was removed, the structure collapsed. Kathi had been *die Freundin*, even "Empress Number Two." Now she was in the position of a mistress, and a few incidents that occurred directly after Elizabeth's death served to show that the emperor was painfully conscious of that fact.

As 1900 began the manager of the Burgtheater who had been complaining for some time of Kathi's frequent leaves of absence, refused to renew her contract. His explanation was that the new plays that were finally being permitted to come on the boards, by Ibsen, Schnitzler, and Gerhard Hauptmann, called for a different type of heroine. This was true. It is perhaps unjust that socially significant heroines are invariably thin and hollow-cheeked, but such is the case. The emperor, however, could have overruled this truth in favor of fat actresses by a stroke of his pen. But to Kathi's indignation he did not do it because he did not wish to provoke gossip.

With the same fine sense of propriety, he refused to bestow on Kathi the Elizabeth Order, a newly created decoration which the empress herself had promised that *die Freundin* should be the first to receive. And when the town of Salzburg raised a memorial to Elizabeth and requested that Frau Schratt should recite a poem at the unveiling of it, the Archduchess Valerie raised such an outcry against the incongruous situation that the emperor forbade Kathi to accept the invitation. Obviously he did not know what to do with Kathi, except to hide her and perhaps use her as a wailing wall for endlessly prolonged mourning.

Kathi might indeed have remained to mourn with him for quite a time. But her false self-image as Empress Number Two as well as her genuine feelings for Elizabeth must have suffered outrage when she was presented with the empress' vile bequest: a gold piece mounted on a brooch. The imperial family always tipped lackeys and even beggars with gold pieces.

And so there was a quarrel at Kathi's Villa Felicitas at Ischl, a Habsburg quarrel of which no detail has been divulged by any servants who dared to listen. The following day Kathi re-received this letter: "My dear good friend: Actually I do not know if I may still use these words, or if I should not write: *'Gnädige Frau'* [Madame]. But I cannot give up hope that yesterday's black thunderclouds will disappear and the old, happy relations of friendship will be restored again. You rejected so obstinately and passionately my earnest, well-meant remonstrances and pleas, made in our mutual interest, that I let myself be overcome by a vehemence that I regret and because of which I ask your forgiveness with all my heart. I mean also to forget the hasty, insulting, and to me deeply painful manner of your departure yesterday. . . . We must find each other again. Think of the long years of our serene friendship, of the joy and sorrow we shared, which you helped me bear. . . ."

If Francis Joseph had meditated on those years in the proper spirit, he might not have added these fatal words: "Think of our dear *Unvergessliche* [unforgettable one], whom we both loved so and who hovers over us as a guardian angel. . . ."

Few men of power have lived upon this earth so long and failed so dismally as Francis Joseph to impress their personality upon those around them. His letters to Kathi Schratt when she abandoned him set alight the cold, colorless, historical phantom, as we hear his despairing voice and relive his old woe: "I am unspeakably sad, for the thought that I, amidst all my troubles, should lose my solace, she who keeps up my courage, with whom I could discuss everything, is too terrible. Early in the morning upon arising you were always my first thought; the prospect of being able to see you . . . brought my frame of mind into proper balance; if trouble and care oppressed me, there was the hope of seeing you, your dear company was the comfort that gave me strength and courage, and now if all that should change, I should live on lonely in the days of my old age. You cannot want that, your kind heart will not allow it . . . give me a sign which will let me hope that all can be well again. . . . God protect you and guide your heart to mercy. . . . My feelings for you continue always. . . ."

This letter elicited a soft response from Kathi, but she refused to see him again, and in spite of his entreaties she abruptly set out upon her Elizabeth-like travels from one curative resort to another, followed, as once the empress had been followed, by a paper-trail of letters. In August she had the grace to return to offer him congratulations upon his seventieth birthday. But on the following morning, the emperor with tears in his eyes, informed his astounded and not at all triumphant daughter, Valerie, that he was going to call on Frau Schratt for the last time. As he returned from this farewell visit, walking in stunned desolation back to the Kaiservilla, he happened to see a chimney sweep, and he made swiftly for his office to write to Kathi and ask her hopefully if she did not see in this a sign of luck. "Luck, for me, means to see you again," he told her. In writing this aching letter, he forgot, for once, that strangers might one day read it. He did not call Kathi his *Freundin*, or his Dear Madame. He addressed her with the endearment once reserved for Elizabeth: she was his "passionately beloved angel."

Hope, in fact, was lively, but it had nothing to do with chimney sweeps. The intrusion into his affairs of an individual named Felix Weiner was the emperor's good luck charm, had he been able to read the signs properly.

In those years at the century's turn, Kathi Schratt was the leading lady of her operetta society, and as such, although middle-aged and plump, she was an object of popular adoration. Young men followed her about with flowers and sighs and in the worst cases dedicated their poems to her. Herr Felix Weiner had first intruded himself upon Kathi in August, 1899, shortly before Elizabeth's death, and perhaps the emperor had overlooked him during the weeks of shock and grief. But his name might well have been raised during the renowned quarrel at the Villa Felicitas, because shortly after Kathi first left him—leaving no forwarding address—she received a snappish communication from Francis Joseph: "In yesterday morning's edition of the *Fremdenblatt* there was already the notice of your arrival at Mendelhof and so it will not be difficult for Herr Felix Weiner to find you. I am curious as to when I shall receive your requested telegram with the anouncement of his arrival. . . ."

Herr Weiner was not his only agony at that time. His relative, Countess Larisch, had just prepared and printed for publication a scandalous book divulging that Elizabeth had been a lady of many love affairs. It was absolutely necessary to suppress this book, and with the assistance of his banker friend, Herr Palmer, he was negotiating with Countess Larisch to buy up the entire edition so that he could burn it. Not until May 13, 1900, when Kathi was at Carlsbad, did he return to a nagging pain: "I forgot to ask you to telegraph as soon as Herr Weiner arrives in Carlsbad. Perhaps you will be kind enough to satisfy my curiosity, or actually my interest. It would really be best if he remained in Vienna. . . ."

Kathi must have satisfied his curiousity, while adding considerable fuel to his interest. A few days later he wrote, "Your dear telegram yesterday, for which I thank you most heartily, makes me quite concerned, as I fear that Felix Weiner's audacity will destroy the whole result of your cure. . . . I am *désperat*, that you can get no peace from this unspeakable person, and and that the police do so little to obtain it for you. I only hope that you yourself had nothing to do with the incredible scenes of which you write and that Weiner really left Carlsbad yesterday."

Not long afterward, he had the pleasure of indulging in unpleasant gossip at the expense of his friend Weiner: "My thoughts are constantly with you and in my mind I recall every happy and sorrowful moment that we have spent together. . . . I am glad that Herr Felix Weiner did not annoy you at Gastein. As Prince Liechtenstein told me, that happens because the impudent youth has no more money, so that he intended to borrow of Baierl*. . . . Really just as shameless as naïve. . . ."

Almost as an afterthought he informed her in this letter that he had just finished making a huge bonfire out of the Countess Larisch's wicked books.

From Paris to Stuttgart to Rome wandered Kathi. With mal-

---

* a policeman

ice, one supposes, she did not return to Vienna for Christmas. Instead she threatened to visit Egypt, and in the same letter mentioned another matter of interest. Francis Joseph's reply: "I was shocked at . . . Felix Weiner's incredible impudence. The man must really be a fool, who might also be dangerous however. According to your telegram he seems to have stayed at St. Gallen until your departure, and I just hope that he does not annoy you also in Paris or Munich, and that Hawerda, to whom I have put it very strongly, will be successful in rendering him harmless. . . ."

The rearing up of Hawerda, who was the policeman in charge of the burial of Marie Vetsera, brings a sinister note into the affair, and one begins to worry where Felix Weiner will turn up next, if at all. On February 27, 1901, the emperor wrote, "Hawerda told me that Felix Weiner is still under observation in the hospital, because his mother would not undertake the responsibility of supervision, and that he still behaves very impudently. If only he would enter a mental institution upon a doctor's decision, for otherwise you will never be safe from his annoyances. . . ."

It is a fact, distressing as it may be to recall, that under Francis Joseph, people who were not downright criminals but who habitually irritated the emperor frequently found themselves spending curative vacations in private sanatoria for the insane. This was not wickedness on the emperor's part. He had been brought up to think that persons who got on his nerves could hardly be in their right senses. The threat to Felix Weiner was therefore grave, and Kathi became as angry as it is possible to be with one's sovereign. It is altogether likely that she had been overwriting the attentions of Weiner and she was now learning how dangerous it is to tease an autocrat who is accustomed to erasing his difficulties simply. When she returned to Vienna, almost immediately, for a short visit, she refused to have anything whatsoever to do with Francis Joseph. His letters at this time, from which the name of Weiner is absent, bespeak a man at the nadir of hopelessness: "Your lines yesterday grieved me very much. I shall annoy you neither with letters nor with inquiries and shall await in patience whether or not your temper is calmed enough for you to allow me to see you. . . . Perhaps you will even be so compassionate as to notify me of your desti-

nation before your departure from Vienna and to let me know
if I may still write you or if my letters are displeasing to you."

But by May, thunder and sarcasm were issuing from his
pen: "I was so naïve as to hope that you would give an indica-
tion of sympathy upon the death of my poor little great-
granddaughter, in remembrance of fifteen years of faithful
friendship. Even in that I was disappointed, and it hurt me
very much. More or less sorrow now alters nothing about the
matter. . . ."

He was wrong, and he must have known it, otherwise he
would not have dared to adopt such masterful tones. In the same
letter he rapped her severely: "Your closing remark: 'Why did
everything have to turn out so?' seems to me to intimate . . .
that you are sorry that it has turned out so. . . . You yourself
certainly chose for it to turn out so."

Not long after, she consented to receive him. They quarreled,
but not badly. Before the summer was over they had met again,
and by August he dared to spell out in a letter a name which,
with relief, we recognize as that of a young man who had not
been locked up in an insane asylum and was still running free
as his fancy listed: "I think of you, dearest friend, and I worry
about your mountain tours . . . and most of all about Felix
Weiner . . . I would like so much to hear something about it. . . ."

That winter, after a separation of a year and a half, Kathi
came back to him, and he knew that she would always come
back to him. A short time later she accepted the title role in
Maria Theresa, a charity performance held at the Deutsches
Volkstheater, and by favor of the emperor she wore for her part
the original garments of his great ancestress and her jewels. A
grumbling set up in court circles about profanity and sacrilege,
but it was all to the good. The world was left in no doubt as
to the value Francis Joseph placed on Kathi Schratt. The sacred
robes anointed her, placed her above criticism, even of archduchesses. This was her last appearance on the stage.

There was more than a decade left of the charming period
called *la belle époque* for them to grow old together, and during
this time, after the death of her husband, Kathi was sometimes
called the "Merry Widow," but more often, "the uncrowned
empress." She acquired a palace on the Kärntnerring, opposite

the opera, and so diverse were the people who flooded her rooms that her concièrge had a bell code: he rang once for ordinary visitors, twice for the nobility, and three times for crowned heads. Every monarch in Europe who visited Vienna and all their ambassadors called on Kathi, knowing that she was the best means of laying their opinions before the emperor. She played this role of powerful *entrepreneuse* unpretentiously and was greatly praised as a typically Viennese woman of common sense and kindliness. She was a famous hostess, and among the hostesses of Europe she was if not the first, certainly one of the first, to establish the Sunday buffet at which, on the servants' day off, gentlemen whose bosoms were decked out like heaven's firmament, and diamond-weighted ladies, served themselves.

Francis Joseph achieved in these last years of his reign what he had longed for since he was a young man, the affection of his people, and at every public appearance of his the crowds turned out in such numbers and showered such myriads of flowers on him that he could not see or speak, but only hold himself stiff and hope that he would not disgrace the Habsburg Dynasty by bursting into tears. Not for a day in all those years, except for the most necessary duty or recreation, did he depart from his formidable routine. "A man must work until he drops," he said. "Only then has he done his duty." And so the people of the empire would bring their children to Schönbrunn to squeeze their faces between the bars in the hope of catching sight of this rarity, this man whose single industry kept their world together, the "keystone of the empire."

"In the park of Schönbrunn," they sang in sentimental *drei viertel Takt*, "there sits an old gentleman, and he worries. Dear, good old gentleman! Don't take things so hard!"

It is possible that the first years of Francis Joseph's reign were spoiled because he was too young, and the last ones because he was too old. History was moving out of his grasp, and he no longer had the vigor to reach after it. For some time Edward VII, pestered him to loosen his ties with the German Kaiser, Wilhelm II. Failing, he sent Empress Eugénie, whom Francis Joseph greatly liked, to win him to join France and England in a girdle which would contain the activities of the incendiary Wilhelm; but neither of them could persuade him.

Once while he was riding with Edward the subject came up, and his coachman heard him say with emotion: "I am a German prince, and I keep my word." But he said later of Edward, "He was hard to resist."

The centuries-old struggle in the Balkans was drawing to its climax. Since the murder of King Alexander and Queen Draga, Francis Joseph's policies toward Serbia had become contemptuous, and he regarded King Peter Karageorgevich as little better than an assassin. In 1914 one of the veritable assassins, Dragutin Dmitrievich, the man they called Apis, as leader of the Black Hand secret society placed revolvers in the hands of Bosnian revolutionaries and with one of them Gavrilo Princip shot the Archduke Franz Ferdinand, the heir to the Habsburg throne. There is hardly a more grievous record of history than that which covers the month between this assassination and the declaration of the First World War. Francis Joseph, apart from the fact of his eighty-four years, cannot be exculpated of allowing events to proceed as they did.

It may be pointed out, however, that no elected politician who came after him has known how to avoid war better than he. For almost a full half-century he had preserved peace for his people, and what they were able to accomplish in that time in the way of music, medicine, psychology, and *Torten* is his princely legacy to us.

From the day war was declared the emperor was never seen to smile. He placed himself on war rations and insisted that black bread be served at his table, even for guests. In 1916, when famine struck his country and children were fainting from weakness in the schools, they did not dare to tell him, lest he deny himself entirely.

For years the emperor had suffered from bronchitis, and after 1913 it had become chronic. In 1916 his lungs were found to be affected. For several days in November he suffered a high fever, and after Frau Schratt had visited him on the nineteenth, Elizabeth's name day, he forbade her to come again, wishing to spare her the sight of death on him. He fought his illness, but he refused the care of nursing nuns. He said that his three servants who had cared for him for years should care for him now.

On November 21, 1916, at half past three in the morning, his valet awakened him with the news that he was at his feet, and the emperor said, "I thank you." He rose, bathed, dressed, and went to his prie-dieu. Then he sat at his desk and applied himself to his documents. During the morning he had a long interview with his prime minister, von Koerber, who at last let him know the full details of the famine raging through the land, the rampant wretchedness, and the rebellious people. His valet heard him say: "If this is the case, then we must make peace—without taking my ally into consideration at all."

He returned to his work. It was like any other day, except that he kept leaving his desk to spend a while at his prie-dieu. Between prayers he returned to his documents, but his pen fell from his fingers, and sadly he bowed his head to rest it on his right hand. He was growing weaker by the hour. A bishop called on him, bringing to him the blessing of the pope, and seeing how weak he was, he deftly turned the conversation into a confession.

At last the emperor was persuaded to go to bed. He said to his valet, "I have not finished my work, so please call me tomorrow at half past three." The bishop then returned with some holy oil and anointed him. His valet brought some tea and raised his head so that he could sip it. He said, "Why must it be just now?"

Then he slept and presently began to cough. The cough became a rattle and he died.

The royal family had gathered in the anteroom: his heir, Emperor Charles "the Sudden," so-called because people had imagined that Francis Joseph was immortal, wore his full field-marshal's uniform with all of his orders and decorations; his handsome wife, Zita of Bourbon-Parma; and the Archduchesses Valerie and Gisela. The archduchesses entered the deathroom first, and seeing on his finger his signet ring fell into an altercation about it, both wanting it. They snatched it off and then, feeling ashamed, they returned it to him.

Kathi Schratt arrived. At the sight of her the Archduchess Valerie fell into her arms. The Empress Zita greeted her with cool courtesy. Emperor Charles proferred her his arm, and with him she entered the room of the dead emperor. She had brought two white roses and she placed them in the clasp of his hands.

A crisis next arose in the imperial family over the coffin. The

Franciscan monk who had been put in charge of the funeral thought that the emperor should have a metal coffin, but the family insisted that it should be a wooden one such as every Habsburg had occupied since the beginning of time. For the last time Frau Schratt stepped energetically into an imperial fracas. She said that he should have a metal coffin. He lies in it to this day in the Capucine crypt.

Katherina Schratt lived until 1940. In the postwar years she became almost a legendary figure in Vienna, very rarely seen. The fortune—the equivalent of a million dollars—the emperor had ordered to be paid to her from his private funds did not survive the inflation after the war, but she was able to support herself by selling her villas and her palace. An American newspaper offered her a great number of solid dollars for her reminiscences, but she said, "One does not change lost happiness into money." Instead she sold little by little the many jewels and valuables he had given her, without revealing their origin, lest the price be increased for that reason.

One day when she was old, she joined a group of tourists being shown around Schönbrunn, which had become a national monument, and as she was listening with the others to the guide's patter, a former lackey of the emperor's, who had been permitted to remain at Schönbrunn as a caretaker, recognized her and bore her off with him. Together they wandered through the well-known rooms and out into the garden, winding up near the door that led towards the Gloriettegasse. She took a key out of her purse and tried it in the door. The key was bright, but the lock was jammed with rust, and she couldn't open it.

NOTES

· I ·

THE HOLY ALLIANCE

Julie de Krüdener has been treated harshly by most of Alexander's biographers, who apparently take it for granted that the opinion of Grand Duke Alexander Mikhailovich* is the correct one. In 1893, however, she found an admirer in Ford, who collected her letters, and again, in 1939, in Knapton, whose scholarly biography contains also a detailed discussion of the background of the Holy Alliance. Both of these recognize her sincerity and exculpate her of charlatanism. They also tend to the belief that Madame de Krüdener was not the tsar's mistress. But in view of the mores of the time, it does not seem reasonable that the pair were not lovers, and certainly their contemporaries who kept a close eye on the affair asked themselves no questions of this nature.

My observation that the personality of Alexander I was affected by eunuchoidism is based on some study of constitutional psychology. I have been struck also by the fact that historical descriptions of Alexander are full of words and expressions similar to those that psychologists are apt to use in describing the eunuchoid pattern of mind: slippery, fluid, sinuous, meretricious, incalculable; tergiversations; core of deep dissimulation; and so forth. The kindness and soft-heartedness of such people may be varied by sudden acts of brutal insensitivity, as was Alexander's; particularly if he was behind the plot to murder his father.

Prince Serge Obolensky, who became the son-in-law of Princess Yuryevsky, formerly the mistress of Tsar Alexander II, questioned this lady as to what she knew about Feodor Kuzmich. She told him that the holy man who was thought to be Alexander I was someone who looked like the emperor. However, she seemed reticent and reluctant to discuss the subject further.

---

* All source citations are to be found in the Bibliography following this section.

· II ·
THE LADY WITH THE WHIP

D'Auvergne is the major source of traditional Lola Montez material. Much new and fascinating information about her life is offered by Holdredge. It was Princess Ekaterina Radziwill who discovered the record of Lola's marriage to Ludwig, and Holdredge who tracked down through living persons the reasons for its failure.

Lola's modern biographers tend to present her, exactly as she would have desired, as an innocent person, much misunderstood, and if I have returned to her old-fashioned image as a villainess, it is because I do not think her qualities outweigh the fact that she went about slashing her unfortunate contemporaries with a whip. I believe that she was an overaggressive woman with a dangerous mental disturbance.

Some of Lola's admirers believe that she won Ludwig by dancing for him in his private office rather than by undressing; perhaps so. Others go so far as to say that she captured him with a passionate harangue about justice to the working girl; this does not ring true, because Ludwig was quite deaf. The scandalous stories about Lola's "male harem" and other unsavory activities of hers in Bavaria rest on the authority of Auguste Papon, a house steward who served her. But he was himself an impostor and liar, and his tales are therefore not considered reliable.

· III ·
THE GAUDY EMPIRE

Almost no reliable information about Harriet Howard was available until recently when Simone André Maurois, noting that the Château of Beauregard was going to be torn down, embarked upon an adventure in historical research and disclosed her findings in *Miss Howard and the Emperor* (Alfred A. Knopf, 1957), to which I am indebted for the principal part of my account. The letter quoted on pages 92–93 is from a private collection unearthed by Mme. Maurois.

The anecdotes about the *horizontales* were the common gossip of the time, collected by Loliée in his *Gilded Beauties*.

The day after Countess Castiglione died the Italian Consul broke into her apartments and removed all her papers, so that we do not know to what extent she was involved in such important diplomacies as Victor Emmanuel's agreement with the pope. The numerous letters she wrote to Estancelin were however discovered by his widow, and Loliée was permitted to examine them for his *Le Roman d'une Favorite*.

I have not been able to find confirmation for the countess' account of the wedding of the Duke of Aosta. Some sources have it that Count Castiglione died at a different wedding, that of Crown Prince Humbert.

· IV ·

ROMANCE AND COUNTER-ROMANCE

Of two descriptions of Katherine Dolgoruky by persons who knew her, one, by Laferté (which may be a pseudonym for Katherine herself) is sycophantic and the other, by Countess Tolstoy, is utterly hostile. Both are therefore useless. The main source of information for the love affair is Paléologue's *Roman Tragique*, which he chose to write in such a tone of high romance that some biographers question its truthfulness. I have decided that Paléologue's facts can be accepted for the following reasons: (1) His other historical and biographical works are reliable; (2) Paléologue, a French diplomat, was a *charmeur* of old ladies. It is obvious that most of his information could only have been gained from Mademoiselle Schebeco, who would have been a truthful and knowledgable informant. Dialogue in the text is almost certainly from Schebeco via Paléologue.

Bibesco's novel *Katia* also provides credible information, though abstracting factual material from a novel is uneasy work. I have accepted certain small incidents that seem uncontrived and which could have been told to Bibesco by an eyewitness, Katherine's cousin, while rejecting others that appear too charming, though in keeping with Alexander's character: for example, that when Katherine was young and lonely at the Smolny Institute, the tsar combed Russia to find her beloved lost governess, and on Christmas day, as an imperial gift to Katherine, placed Mademoiselle Schebeco under the Christmas tree.

An admirable recent biography of Alexander is Almedingen, which presents information about the tsar's romance from family tradition of people who knew Katherine. I am nevertheless unable to accept the conclusion that Katherine provided for the tsar an area of peacefulness in his troubled life. Too many traditions exist to suggest that she was a highly excitable person, mischievous and provocative. Not available to Almedingen were the nine letters published in the *Oxford Slavonic Papers*, Vol. XI (1964), which demonstrate Katherine's distracted and distracting nature.

Several thousand additional letters are said to exist which may one day illuminate the tsar's life, but at present their whereabouts are unknown.

My source for the Zhelyabov-Perovsky story is Footman.

Katherine Dolgoruky is to be distinguished from Princess Alexandra Dolgoruky, an earlier mistress of Alexander's, who is said to have had great influence on his "liberal" turn of mind and was the model for the heroine of Turgenev's *Smoke*. She became the wife of Albedinsky, Governor of Poland.

· V ·

TRÈS BELLE AND TRÈS VIEUX

Every scoundrel has his day before the tribunal of history. A recent biography has spoken kindly of the Marquis de Sade; the Soviets have set up Ivan the Terrible as a national hero; Josephine Tey has proved that Richard III did *not* kill the little princes in the Tower. It is therefore fitting that something be said on behalf of Leopold II, King of the Belgians. His side of the Congo story can be read in the works I have cited by Lichtervelde and Wack.

The British government have not yet permitted historians to examine all of the Casement documents; they are said to be of a nature that if they were released, war with Ireland might easily be a consequence. However, sufficient material is available to suggest that Casement's Congo atrocities were wildly exaggerated, and this is assessed in an objective biography by an Irishman, McColl.

My view of Baroness de Vaughan is opposed to that of Leopold's best-known (unsympathetic) biographer, Bauer. Bauer appears to have gotten his information by word of mouth from Belgians who remembered the baroness with bitterness as a crude harridan. However, those of her contemporaries who dared to set her name down in their memoirs do not remember her badly, and the French *agent de Sûreté* Xavier Paoli, who knew her well, liked her.

Unavailable to Bauer was Caroline's autobiography, from which, though it was ghost written for her by a journalist, she emerges as an uncultivated, naïve, intelligent, humorous woman with a genuine affection for her aged lover.

We have only Caroline's word that Leopold's threat to abdicate in 1902 was on her account rather than because of the Congo scandals, as the history books have it.

· VI ·

THE SERBIAN NIGHTMARE

My main sources for the scandalous happenings in Serbia are the various works cited by Chedomille Mijatovich, Milan's foreign minister. All conversations quoted are derived from him; he was present at some of them.

The story of Natalie's spoiled marriage and her disorderly behavior is described in Gerard. Foolish stories about Milan's love affairs are from Orlow's pamphlet.

After the assassination of Alexander and Queen Draga, Mijatovich made a private investigation, recorded in his *A Royal Tragedy*, taking his information from eyewitnesses, even from the assassins themselves, who for some time were willing to brag about their deed. His description of the actual murder is borne out in *Black Lamb and Grey Falcon* by Rebecca West, who appears to have spoken to one of the assassins present. Their reports contradict stories that Alexander begged abjectly for their lives or that the royal couple were slain while hiding behind Draga's dresses in the closet, the swords piercing the glamorous stuffs.

Readers of Rebecca West's splendid book about Yugoslavia will find that she is much harder on King Milan than I; this is partly because she sympathized with the "Serbian Dream," which I do not, disliking its fanaticism. I heartily wish that Serbs had allowed Milan to lead them into the Habsburg Confederation and refrained from engineering the assassination of Archduke Franz Ferdinand at Sarajevo in 1914.

Unavailable to Miss West were Francis Joseph's recently published letters to his mistress, revealing his good will toward Milan and absolving him from callous disrespect to Milan's remains. On the contrary, the emperor took extraordinary measures to honor his minion in death, and to keep his body out of the hands of Alexander, whom he considered an unfilial son.

I have been interested to note that Rebecca West's conclusions about Draga Mashin's character are, in essence, similar to my own, and that they are partly based on an examination of Draga's photograph. One can *see* that she was not a villainess, and what one sees is borne out by every word of hers and every reliably reported deed. But these opinions contradict Serbian historic studies to this day (*viz. Review*, The Yugoslav Monthly Magazine, November, 1964).

It is not known for certain that Alexander's French tutor was involved in the conspiracy for the dinnertime *coup d'état*. But it was believed that Alexander's several tutors were behind the plot and that they conspired with Milan and Natalie in France; the French tutor was a logical go-between. He was probably the same Albert Malet to whom we are indebted for various stories of Alexander's childhood.

A full description of the séance held at the offices of the *Review of Reviews*, with names and affidavits of the witnesses, is to be found in Wilson.

· VII ·
DIE FREUNDIN

While the many legends concerning Katherina Schratt's beneficial interference in the tangled affairs of the Habsburg imperial family cannot be relied upon in their details, a number of true stories survive in memoirs showing how her amiable tact frequently helped the emperor settle his differences with various army officers and misbehaving noblemen. It is noteworthy also that because of her many friends among Jewish theatrical folk, she acted as a syphon for Jewish petitions and perhaps furthered in her time the traditional amicability of the Habsburg emperors toward the Jewish people.

I have neglected these stories in favor of bringing to the reader excerpts from the emperor's own letters to Kathi, and have used the translations into English kindly furnished me by Evabeth Miller Kienast and Robert Rie of *Briefe Kaiser Franz Josefs an Frau Katherina Schratt*, to be published in 1966 by the State University of New York.

I do not know if the Felix Weiner incidents were a prime cause of the famous separation. But it is obvious that his name appears frequently in the letters written during the quarrel and disappears after the quarrel was settled.

Letters to the Empress Elizabeth are from the works cited by Corti, who delved deep into the Habsburg Archives.

The best source for the life of the Crown Prince Rudolf is the cited biography by Mitis, the former curator of the archives, who is sympathetic to Rudolf. For purposes of the *chronique scandaleuse*, however, I have relied in great part on Count Lonyay's unfriendly but well-documented account of Rudolf's mental deterioration and suicide. Lonyay is in a position to know authoritative details of the tragedy, because Crown Princess Stephanie, after she became a widow, married a member of the Lonyay family. His cited work reproduces a facsimile of Rudolf's suicide note. It would seem to refute the opinions, still widely held, that Rudolf was murdered by a gamekeeper, or by his father, or by the *Schlamperei* of soldiers sent to arrest him.

Lonyay's source for the story of the cantor's daughter are the recollections of General von Gradl and of Bertha Szeps Zuckerkandl.

All conversations recorded in my text are from the works cited by Corti, a reliable recorder who would have gotten them from memoirs of participants or from some other trustworthy source.

The remarks of the kaiserin's hairdresser were recorded by the court lady, Countess von Eppinghoven, in her diary, and this was later published by Fischer.

One of Francis Joseph's major biographers, Tschuppik, believes it to be nonsense that Empress Elizabeth actually chose Katherina Schratt to be the emperor's mistress. He believes the love affair began years before the time quoted in the text. It is true that the emperor, in the course of his official duties, met Katherina Schratt years before; but I have preferred to rely on the word of Countess Larisch, Elizabeth's niece and confidant, who says positively that the empress was the prime mover in this affair. Besides, Tschuppik's *Francis-Joseph et Madame Schratt* is altogether fanciful.

Bibliography

Alexander Mikhailovich, Grand Duke of Russia, *Once a Grand Duke* (New York: Farrar & Rinehart, 1932).

Alexander, King of Serbia, *Aus dem Tagebuch König Alexanders v. Serbien* (1905).

M. E. Almedingen, *The Emperor Alexander II* (London: The Bodley Head, 1962).

(Anonymous), "Assassinat d'Alexandre II," *La Revue de Paris*, January–February 1922.

Ludwig Bauer, *Leopold the Unloved* (Boston, Mass.: Little, Brown & Co., 1935).

Baron Beyens, "Souvenirs sur Léopold II," *La Revue Générale*, May 15, 1932.

Princess Marthe Bibesco, *Katia* (New York: Doubleday, Doran & Co., 1939).

————, *Royal Portraits* (New York: D. Appleton & Co., 1928).

William Bolitho, *Twelve Against the Gods* (New York: The Viking Press, 1957).

Gamaliel Bradford, *Saints and Sinners* (Cambridge, Mass.: The Riverside Press, 1932).

Jean de Bourgoing, ed., *Briefe Kaiser Franz Josephs an Frau Katherina Schratt* (Vienna: Ullstein Verlag, 1949).

Charles Chauncey Burr, *Lectures of Lola Montez (Countess of Landsfeld) including her autobiography* (New York: Rudd & Carlton, 1858).

E. Thornton Cook, *Kings in the Making* (New York: E. P. Dutton & Co., 1931).

Conte Egon Caesar Corti and Hans Sokol, *Kaiser Franz Joseph I* (Vienna: Verlag Styria, 1960).

————, *Elizabeth, Empress of Austria* (New Haven: Yale University Press, 1936).

Virginia Cowles, *Edward VII and His Circle* (London: Hamish Hamilton, 1956).

Edward Crankshaw, *The Fall of the House of Habsburg* (New York: The Viking Press, 1963).

Edmund B. D'Auvergne, *The Coburgs* (New York: James Pott & Co., 1911).

———, *Lola Montez* (New York: Brentano's, 1924).

Pierre Daye, *Léopold II* (Paris: A. Fayard et Cie, 1934).

Eulalia, Infanta of Spain, *Court Life from Within* (New York: Dodd, Mead & Co., 1915).

Frank Eyck, *The Prince Consort, A Political Biography* (Cambridge, Mass.: The Riverside Press, 1959).

Henry W. Fischer, *Private Lives of Kaiser William II and His Consort* (New York: Fred de Fau & Co., Limited Edition).

David Footman, *Red Prelude, The Life of the Russian Terrorist Zhelyabov* (New Haven: Yale University Press, 1945).

Clarence Ford, *The Life and Letters of Madame de Krüdener* (London: A. & C. Black, 1893).

Frances A. Gerard, *A King's Romance* (New York: Dodd, Mead & Co., ca. 1909).

Stephen Graham, *Tsar of Freedom, The Life and Reign of Alexander II* (New Haven: Yale University Press, 1935).

Jean Grand-Carteret, *Popold II, Roi des Belges et des Belles* (Paris: Louis-Michaud, 1908).

Albert Guerard, *Napoleon III* (Cambridge, Mass.: Harvard University Press, 1943).

Lord Frederic Hamilton, *The Days Before Yesterday* (London: George H. Doran Co., 1920).

Abel Hermant, *Madame de Krüdener* (Paris: Hachette, 1943).

Helen Holdredge, *The Woman in Black, Lola Montez* (New York: G. P. Putnam's Sons, 1955).

Eugen Ketterl, *The Emperor Francis Joseph I* (London: Skeffington & Son, ca. 1929).

Ernest John Knapton, *The Lady of the Holy Alliance* (New York: Columbia University Press, 1939).

S. Konovalev, *The Emperor Alexander II and Princess Ekaterina Dolgorukaya*, Nine Letters, Oxford Slavonic Papers, Vol. XI, 1964.

Joachim von Kürenberg, *Katherina Schratt, Der Roman Einer Wienerin* (Bern und Stuttgart: Hallwag, 1953).

Victor Laferté (pseud.), *Alexander II Unbekannte Einzelnheiten über sin Familienleben und seinen Tod* (Basel: H. Georg, 1882).

Comte de La Garde-Chambonas, *Souvenirs du Congrès de Vienne* (Paris: Librairie Historique et Militaire, 1901).

Comte Louis de Lichtervelde, *Leopold of the Belgians*, trans. by Thomas H. and H. Russell Reed (New York: The Century Co., 1929).

Frédéric Auguste Loliée, *The Gilded Beauties of the Second Empire* (London: J. Long, 1909).

——, *Le Roman d'une Favorite (La Comtesse de Castiglione)* (Paris: Emil-Paul frères, 1925).

——, *Women of the Second Empire*, trans. by Alice M. Ivimy (London: The Bodley Head Ltd., 1907).

Count Carl Lonyay, *Rudolph, The Tragedy of Mayerling* (New York: Charles Scribner's Sons, 1949).

Louise, Princess of Belgium, *My Own Affairs* (London: Cassell & Co., 1921).

Albert Malet, "Alexander 1er de Serbie," *La Revue de Paris*, Vol. 4, 1903, pp. 162–172.

John de Courcy MacDonell, *Belgium, Her Kings, Kingdom and People* (Boston: Little, Brown & Co., 1914).

Marie Louise, Countess Larisch von Wallersee-Wittelsbach, *Her Majesty Elizabeth* (New York: Doubleday, Doran & Co., 1934).

——, *My Past* (New York: G. P. Putnam's Sons, 1913).

Simone André Maurois, *Miss Howard and the Emperor* (New York: Alfred A. Knopf, 1957).

René McColl, *Roger Casement, A New Judgment* (London: Hamish Hamilton, 1956).

Cléo de Mérode, *Le Ballet de ma Vie* (Paris: Editions P. Horay, 1955).

Chedomille Mijatovich, *A Royal Tragedy* (New York: Dodd, Mead & Co., 1907).

——, *Memoirs of a Balkan Diplomatist* (London: Cassell & Co. 1917).

——, *Servia of the Servians* (New York: Charles Scribner's Sons, 1911).

William Miller, *The Balkans* (New York: G. P. Putnam's Sons, 1896).

Oskar von Mitis, *Das Leben des Kronprinzen Rudolf* (Leipzig, 1928).

Natalie, Queen Consort of Milan Obrenovic, *Mémoires de Nathalie* (1891).

Edward W. Ney, *Additional Light on Madame de Krüdener's Life & Writings* (Abstract of a thesis, published by New York University, 1956).

Nicolas Mikhailovich, Grand Duke of Russia, *L'Empereur Alexandre 1er* (St. Petersburg, 1912).

Harold Nicolson, *The Congress of Vienna, 1810–1822* (New York: Harcourt, Brace & Co., 1946).

Serge Obolensky, *One Man in his Time* (New York: McDowell, Obolensky, 1958).

Ivan Orlow, "Indiskretionem über König Milan und seinen Hof" (1889).

George Maurice Paléologue, *An Ambassador's Memoirs* (New York: George H. Doran Co., 1929).

———, *Le Roman Tragique de l'Empereur Alexandre II* (Paris: Plon, 1923).

———, *The Enigmatic Tsar* (New York: Harper & Row, Publishers, Inc., 1938).

———, *The Tragic Empress* (New York: Harper & Row, Publishers, Inc., 1928).

Xavier Paoli, *Their Majesties as I Knew Them* (New York: Sturgis & Walton Co., 1911).

Woislav M. Petrovich, *Serbia, Her People, History and Aspirations* (New York: Frederick A. Stokes Co., 1915).

Sir Frederick Ponsonby, *Recollections of Three Reigns* (New York: E. P. Dutton, 1952).

Private Life of King Edward VII, by a member of the Royal Household (New York: D. Appleton & Co., 1891).

Angelo S. Rappoport, *Leopold the Second, King of the Belgians* (New York: Sturgis & Walton Co., 1910).

———, *The Curse of the Romanovs* (London: Chatto & Windus, 1907).

Joseph Redlich, *Emperor Francis Joseph of Austria* (New York: The Macmillan Co., 1929).

Review, Yugoslav Monthly Magazine, November, 1964.

Cameron Rogers, *Gallant Ladies* (New York: Harcourt, Brace & Co., 1928).

Robert Sencourt, *The Life of the Empress Eugénie* (New York: Charles Scribner's Sons, 1931).

Comte de Soissons, *The True Story of the Empress Eugénie* (New York: J. Lane, 1921).

Henry Wickham Steed, *The Habsburg Monarchy* (London: Constable & Co., 1919).

Leonid I. Strakhovsky, *Alexander I of Russia* (New York: W. W. Norton, 1947).

Hans Tabarelli, *Kaiser Franz Josef und die gnädige Frau* (Vienna: Ring Verlag, 1949).

Harold W. V. Temperley, *History of Servia* (London: G. Bell & Sons, 1917).

T. F. Thiselton-Dyer, *Royalty in All Ages* (London: John C. Nimmo, 1893).

Countess Alexandra Andreyevna Tolstoy, *l'Empereur Alexandre II, Détails Inédits* (Paris: Auguste Ghio, 1882).

W. R. H. Trowbridge, *Queen Alexandra* (New York: D. Appleton & Co., 1921).

———, *Seven Splendid Sinners* (New York: Brentano's, 1908).

Clara Tschudi, *Eugénie, Empress of the French* (New York: The Macmillan Co., 1899).

Karl Tschuppik, *Empress Elizabeth of Austria* (New York: Brentano's, 1930).

———, *François-Joseph et Madame Schratt* (Paris: Payot, 1933).

———, *The Reign of Emperor Francis Joseph* (London: G. Bell & Sons, 1930).

Mark Twain, *King Leopold's Soliloquy* (Boston: P. R. Warren Co., 1905).

A. R. Tyrner-Tyrnauer, *Lincoln and the Emperors* (New York: Harcourt, Brace & World, 1962).

Caroline Delacroix, Baroness de Vaughan, as told to Paul Faure, *A Commoner Married a King* (New York: Ives Washburn, 1937).

Vicomte Eugene Melchior de Vogüé, *Social Life in Russia* (New York: Harper & Row, Publishers, Inc., 1891).

Henry Wellington Wack, F.R.G.S., *The Story of the Congo Free State* (New York: G. P. Putnam's Sons, The Knickerbocker Press, 1905).

Sir Spencer Walpole, *Studies in Biography* (New York: E. P. Dutton, 1907).

Rebecca West, *Black Lamb and Grey Falcon* (New York: The Viking Press, 1941).

Baron Carton de Wiart, *Léopold II, Souvenirs des dernières années* (Brussels: 1944).

Henri de Weindel, *Behind the Scenes at the Court of Vienna* (London: John Long, 1914).

Mrs. Northesk Wilson, *Belgrade, the White City of Death* (London: R. A. Everett & Co., 1903).

Horace Wyndham, *The Magnificent Montez* (New York: Hillman-Curl, n.d.).

Princess Catherine Yuryevskaya, *My Book* (London: Eveleigh Nash & Grayson, 1924).

Karoline, Countess Zanardi-Landi, *The Secret of an Empress* (Cambridge, Mass.: The Riverside Press, 1915).